The Ethical Function of Architecture

The MIT Press | Cambridge, Massachusetts | London, England

The Ethical Function of Architecture

Karsten Harries

First MIT Press paperback edition, 1998

©1997 Massachusetts Institute of Technology

This book was set in Bembo by Graphic Composition, Inc.

Printed and bound in the United States of America.

Library of Congress Cataloging-in-Publication Data

Harries, Karsten.
    The ethical function of architecture / Karsten Harries.
      p. cm.
    Includes bibliographical references and index.
    ISBN 0-262-08252-7 (hb), 0-262-58171-x (pb)
     1. Architecture—Philosophy.   2. Architecture—Moral and ethical aspects. I. Title.
NA2500.H375   1996
  723'.1'04—dc20   96-8639
                                          CIP

For Elizabeth

Contents

List of Illustrations

Preface

This book has its origin in some conversations I had, now over twenty years ago, with Kent Bloomer. We spoke of architecture, Yale's undergraduate architecture major, architectural education. In the course of these conversations he invited me to contribute to an issue of the *Journal of Architectural Education* he was guest editing. The result was a brief programmatic essay, which already bore the title "The Ethical Function of Architecture" (*Journal of Architectural Education,* vol. 29, no. 1 [1975], p. 14). Ten years later I developed it into a longer, still far too brief article bearing the same title (in *Descriptions,* ed. Don Ihde and Hugh J. Silverman [Albany: SUNY Press, 1985], pp. 129–140). That I choose this title, now for a third time, for this book shows that the issue it raises continues to challenge me, where "ethical," as I here understand it, has more to do with the Greek *ēthos* than with what we usually mean by "ethics," for example, when we speak of "business ethics" or "medical ethics": this is not at all a book in what might be called "architectural ethics."

These early discussions led me to develop a course in the philosophy of architecture. Although initially aimed at undergraduates, the course also filled a gap in the course offerings of Yale's Architecture School: many, perhaps even the majority of its students were drawn to it, much to my benefit.

As my *Meaning of Modern Art* shows (*The Meaning of Modern Art: A Philosophical Interpretation* [Evanston, Ill.: Northwestern University Press, 1968]), I had long been interested in modern art, especially painting. A certain unease with modern art led me to examine some of its central presuppositions: already with that book and its call for a new realism I wanted to call into question the aesthetic approach that had for so long presided over the progress of art. Architecture interested me precisely because, while on the aesthetic approach an essentially impure, compromised art, compromised by its need to take its place in a world ruled by other concerns, it calls that approach into question, demanding a different approach—and finally not just to architecture but to all the arts. My book on the Bavarian Rococo church (*The Bavarian Rococo Church: Between Faith and Aestheticism* [New Haven: Yale University Press, 1983]) gave me a first chance to develop some of my thoughts with greater precision and close attention to works of architecture. But it was the course that allowed me to really work out my ideas, to test them in conversations with uncounted students, and soon also in public lectures in this country and in Europe. A number of these lectures were subsequently published and for a while I thought I should just gather them, by now some twenty, and publish them as a book. But there were too many repetitions, too many lacunae. Much from these lectures has made its way into this book, but it has been reconsidered, rethought, and, while I did not hesitate to cannibalize my earlier efforts, become part of what is new work.

Some readers may wish I had made more of an attempt to overcome the limitations of a perspective all too obviously bound to my own path to architecture, which led from war-torn Germany to the United States, from a childhood love of architecture to philosophy and back to architecture. A certain one-sidedness is evident simply from the illustrations. Had I been Latin American or Chinese they would no doubt have been very different. But rendering such one-sidedness conspicuous seemed to me preferable to pretending to an inevitably unconvincing universality: the book invites the reader to substitute for the illustrations I have chosen others more in keeping with his or her own very different path. Not only in this case is such translation part of getting closer to what is essential.

This book has also been shaped by my path through philosophy, which has centered on Kant, Hegel, Schopenhauer, Nietzsche, and especially Heidegger. I don't consider these necessarily irreplaceable, but their work has furnished me with what I consider useful models or lenses—and I should be pleased if for some readers this book will prove such a model or lens.

I find it difficult even to remember, let alone to thank, all those who over the years have helped me. Kent Bloomer deserves first mention, for it was his invitation that first led me to spend much of my time thinking about architecture. I would also like to thank the Deans of Yale's School of Architecture, Cesar Pelli, Thomas Beebe, and Fred Koetter, for their support and hospitality, and Yale University for appointing me to a Mellon Professorship, which encouraged me to trespass across academic boundaries that are often much too firm. My thanks go to the many colleagues and architects who have helped me to advance my ideas, especially to Michael Benedikt, William Butler, Günther Dittmar, Barbara Endres, Steuart Grey, Steven Holl, David Kolb, David Leatherbarrow, Bert Olivier, Alberto Pérez-Gómez, Juhani Pallasmaa, Giorgio Ranalli, Joseph Rykwert, Dalibor Vesely, and Heinrich Wirth; equally to those former architecture students who worked closely with me over the years, including Ken Abbott (who deserves special thanks for his photographs, which succeed in capturing something I had been struggling to put into words), Carey Bernstein, I Fei Chang, Enrique Larrañaga, Stuart Lathers, Jeff Montroy, Randy Ott, Eeva Pelkonen, Kelly Carlson-Reddig, Gerald Walker, and Hwa-Fong Wang.

I am grateful to Roger Conover for the care with which he watched over the metamorphosis of a still-unfinished manuscript into a book, to Alice Falk for her ever-thoughtful editing, to Ori Kometani for her design work, and to Matthew Abbate for making sure that what has been such a long process would come to a good end.

My deepest thanks go to my wife Elizabeth Langhorne, who taught me more about dwelling than Heidegger ever could.

Karsten Harries
Hamden, Connecticut

The Ethical Function of Architecture

Introduction: Postmodern Prelude

1

1

For some time now architecture has been uncertain of its way. With Alberto Pérez-Gómez, one might link such uncertainty to "the changing world view ushered in by Galilean science and Newton's natural philosophy," which led to a rationalization and functionalization of architecture that had to turn its back on that "poetical content of reality" that once provided "any truly meaningful architecture" with an "ultimate frame of reference."[1] One might also point to Charles Perrault's distinction between positive and arbitrary beauty, the latter a matter of taste, dependent on ornament and changing fashion and "the architect's special province," a distinction that invites us to understand the architect as "the artist who applies an ornamental dress of various kinds to the immutable substance of architecture," invites the "love affair with alternate visual conventions" that has made post-Enlightenment architecture both more interesting and more arbitrary.[2] The eclectic historicism of the nineteenth century is one consequence; another is its more playful and ironic postmodern counterpart (fig. 1).

To be sure, only a few decades ago modernist orthodoxy could claim to have put an end to the stylistic chaos of the nineteenth century and to have provided architects once more with a sure sense of direction. By the sixties such conviction had yielded to uncertainty. Responding to the changed climate, Sigfried Giedion observed in the 1967 edition of *Space, Time and Architecture,* a book that, more than any other, had given voice to the ethos of modernist architecture: "a certain confusion exists in contemporary architecture, as in painting; a kind of pause, even a kind of exhaustion. Everyone is aware of it."[3] Giedion remained convinced that such uncertainty would soon pass. "We are still in the formation period of a new tradition, still at its beginning," he insisted. Unshaken in his modernist convictions, he reaffirmed what he took to be the main task facing contemporary architecture, "the interpretation of a way of life valid for our period."[4] After three decades of postmodern, poststructuralist, and deconstructive experimentation, the confusion Giedion noted shows no signs of yielding to a new consensus. But is this something to be regretted? We have been taught to be on guard before modernist nostalgia. And yet I find myself unwilling to let go of Giedion's statement of architecture's task. It raises, however, two questions:

Michael Graves, The Portland Building, Portland, Oregon (1980). View from Fifth Avenue. Photo Credit: Paschall Taylor. Courtesy Michael Graves.

1

1. What does it mean to say that the task of architecture is that of interpretation? When we think of works of interpretation, we think first of texts. Are works of architecture then like texts?[5] Do they have a hermeneutic function? What tools of interpretation are available to the architect? Should we not rather consider works of architecture aesthetically dressed-up functional buildings? I have to return to this question.

2. And what way of life is valid for our period? Is not our world, our society with its differences of class and race, gender and religion, too heterogeneous, too filled with confusion and contradiction, to allow us to answer this question with any confidence? Have postmodern suspicions made it impossible to demand that architecture meet what Giedion calls it main task? Is there a way of life valid for all?

Despite such questions, I find it difficult to surrender Giedion's modernist hope. Should architecture not continue to help us find our place and way in an ever more disorienting world? In this sense I shall speak of the *ethical function* of architecture. "Ethical" derives from "ethos." By a person's ethos we mean his or her character, nature, or disposition. Similarly we speak of a community's ethos, referring to the spirit that presides over its activities. "Ethos" here names the way human beings exist in the world: their way of dwelling.[6] By the ethical function of architecture I mean its task to help articulate a common ethos.

2

Usually the task of architecture is understood in a very different way. Consider, for example, the understanding of architecture presupposed by Nikolaus Pevsner, when he begins his *Outline of European Architecture* with the often-cited and seemingly self-evident observation: "A bicycle shed is a building; Lincoln Cathedral is a piece of architecture"[7] (fig. 2). To be sure, like a bicycle shed, Lincoln Cathedral is also a building. The architect builds but also does something more. How is this "more" to be understood? Pevsner's answer to this question is quite expected: what distinguishes works of architecture from mere buildings is that they are "designed with a view to aesthetic appeal."[8] This of course remains quite empty as long as more is not said about the nature of this aesthetic appeal. I shall do so in chapter 2.

Pevsner's understanding of architecture is representative of what, in opposition to the *ethical approach,* I shall call the *aesthetic approach.* On this approach, the point of architecture, as opposed to mere building, is to have aesthetic appeal, however that is going to be understood. Thus the work of architecture is essentially a functional building with an added aesthetic component. An obvious way of creating such a work would be to decorate some utilitarian structure: *work of architecture = building + decoration.* Not that we have to think of the addition of the aesthetic component as a matter of adding decoration as it is usually understood. Imagine someone who in building his bicycle shed is concerned to observe the golden section in every possible way: he, too, would be adding an aesthetic component to a functional shed;[9] so would someone concerned to give her bicycle shed the look of a ruin; or someone who would have us appreciate his shed as a subversive act; or as a riddle filled with markers that reveal their secret only to the initiated; or as an ironic commentary on

2

what architecture has come to mean. In each case the result would no longer be just a bicycle shed, a mere building, but would claim the dignity of a work of architecture. Stretching the term a bit, I want to call such buildings, too, decorated sheds—a term that of course belongs to the authors of *Learning from Las Vegas*.[10]

3

The understanding of works of architecture expressed by the term "decorated shed" follows from the aesthetic approach. Given the widespread acceptance of that approach, it is hardly surprising that it should capture so well the prevailing understanding of architecture. It certainly fits much of what has come to be called postmodern architecture. But it would appear to describe equally well most historical architecture, from which postmodern architecture is distinguished especially by its more playful approach to decoration. As Giedion observed rather tendentiously, modern architecture has given way to "a kind of playboy-architecture . . . : an architecture treated as playboys treat life, jumping from one sensation to another and quickly bored with everything."[11] His formulation suggests that it is not just the aesthetic approach that governs postmodern architecture but a particular version of that approach, ruled by a desire to avoid boredom, that is, to pursue the interesting.

If Giedion had hoped that this turn to "playboy-architecture" would prove a passing fad, such hope went disappointed. Today, as we approach the end of both the century and the millennium, the "romantic orgy" he deplored shows no sign of abating. We only have to walk through one of our cities or just flip through one of our architectural journals to get a sense that architecture still has not found its way. Some will suggest that this is no cause for gloom, that the problem lies precisely with insisting on finding the right way: has not modernism demonstrated the bankruptcy of this project, and are the outlines of a far more open and therefore less coercive consensus not already emerging? That this is wishful thinking was suggested by a discussion published some ten years ago by the American Institute of Architects under the title "Postmodernism: Definition and Debate," with the description, "A Group of Practitioners Looks at a Controversial Phenomenon."[12] The title promised too much: Charles Jencks's catchy label eluded definition that would more than gesture toward an uncertain refusal of modernism, and there was no debate. Voices critical of postmodernism predominated, tempered by others that welcomed the freedom it had brought architects or that praised its emphasis on the architectural tradition. Few of these practitioners still considered postmodernism a burning issue. Helmut Jahn was not alone with his suggestion that what started as "one of the most important esthetic events in the last fifty years" has today become "a loose characterization for many fragmented efforts, primarily concerned with historic style, contextualism, symbolism, and ornament," "an umbrella for all efforts to leave the mainstream of modernism."[13] Today postmodern posturing is beginning to seem a bit dated even as it has become an integral part of today's architectural vernacular.

Jahn's claim that postmodernism began as an important aesthetic event, even if it soon strayed from the greatness of this beginning, raises once more the question: should architecture be concerned with creating important aesthetic events? Could it be that post-modernism went astray precisely because, right from the beginning, it was overly concerned with the creation of such events? But before I attempt to address this question, the term "postmodernism" deserves a closer look. It invites us to think of its meaning as a function of "modernism." Postmodernism would seem to follow modernism somewhat in the way in which Mannerism followed Renaissance or Rococo followed Baroque. This analogy suggests that modernism and postmodernism can both be considered styles to rival the great styles of the past. Something like that had indeed been claimed for modernism by those convinced that Frank Lloyd Wright and Le Corbusier, Gropius and Mies van der Rohe had finally put an end to the stylistic chaos of the nineteenth century. Subsequent developments have shaken such conviction. The important aesthetic event that has given today's architectural landscape its contours would seem to be postmodernism.

Such linear accounts of the history of architecture as a succession of important aesthetic events are of course much too simple. We are still not done with modernism. And how could we be? For what do we mean by "modern" and "modernism"? Does "modern" not refer to a period extending to and including the very present? "Modernism" names an ideology that affirms what is thought to be in tune with the spirit or essence of our own period, in tune with science and technology, with modernity; it defines itself in opposition to what went before, to traditions that retained their hold even as they had become anachronisms. When Giedion demands that contemporary architecture interpret a way of life valid for our period, he speaks as a convinced modernist. By contrast, when we call something "postmodern" we seem to imply that it does not really belong to the present age, just as we do when we call something "positively medieval," although "postmodern" gestures not backward but forward, beyond the present to what we hope is some brighter future that may already have announced its coming but has not yet arrived. "Postmodernism" suggests "futurism," although the future it envisions is defined by its break with at least some of the forces that have shaped modernity and that modernism joyfully embraced, forces today all too naively dismissed as Eurocentric, logocentric, phallocentric.

So understood, modernism and postmodernism would seem to be much more than just important aesthetic events. At issue is "the legitimacy of the modern age." [14] Both movements are born of concern with the shape of the modern world, as postmodernism represents a phenomenon of modernity's bad conscience, of its self-doubt. Such self-doubt has long centered on the hegemony that we have allowed scientific rationality and technological thinking—over our lives, our thinking, and our practices, including the practice of architecture—even as this hegemony has rendered itself ever more problematic. Architectural postmodernism thus represents, in Jahn's words, "a realization and a response to the failures of modernism. Architecture, along the principles of functionalism, programmatic determinism, and technological expressionism, produced buildings without connection to site, place, the human being, and history." [15] As Charles Moore insists, "it has surely become evident to almost everybody (except maybe for a few architects) that when the earlier 20th century's Buck Rogers dream of a future altogether disconnected from the past started, after the 40's and 50's, to come true, helped along by a big war and the devastation of holocaust-style urban planning, it became a nightmare." [16] "Postmodernism" would then name not so much a unified style or system of thought as an attitude born of a humanistic critique of modernism. Vincent Scully could thus celebrate Robert Venturi's *Complexity and Contradiction in Architecture* as a profoundly humanistic work that invites comparison with Geoffrey Scott's *Architecture of Humanism*.[17] So understood, postmodernism, too, can claim to serve what I have called architecture's ethical function.

But does not such rhetoric take postmodernism more seriously than it deserves? Like other postmodern architects, Venturi has enjoyed appearing in humanist dress, but did he not give us a more helpful pointer when he opposed to Mies van der Rohe's "less is more" his own equally quotable "less is a bore"?[18] This suggests that postmodernism has its origin not so much in a humanistic (that is to say, in an ethical) as in a merely aesthetic response to modernism—more precisely, in the already mentioned response that, born of boredom, seeks relief in a cultivation of the interesting.[19] Such cultivation presupposes an understanding of what has come to be established and accepted: to remain interesting one must stay just one step ahead of current expectations, though little thought needs to be given to where one should be going. There is thus a close connection between the pursuit of the interesting and fashion design—and consider how often critics of postmodernism have condemned its practitioners for being mere fashion designers, implying an equation of architectural ornament with feminine dress that demands further discussion.[20]

Since it depends for its effects on expectations that are likely to change, the interesting is essentially short-lived. To give a once notorious example: when Marcel Duchamp presented a quite ordinary urinal as a work of art, calling it *Fontaine,* such confusion of the categories "work of art" and "piece of plumbing" was an important aesthetic event. But this paradigmatic act should not tempt us to drag all sorts of plumbing fixtures into galleries. Similarly, the dislocated temple fragments that now appear in so much postmodern architecture, were, when first seen, interesting. But here, too, the temptation to make such dislocation into a recipe should be resisted. Repeated, what once was interesting will soon become boring. There is, to be sure, a more basic question: should architecture strive to be interesting?

Not that postmodern architecture is adequately understood as a phenomenon of the interesting. I do think, however, that such an understanding provides at least an illuminating caricature that receives support from Lyotard's understanding of the postmodern sublime, which, with its emphasis on negation and innovation, turns out to be just another version of the interesting.[21] Consider what separates neoclassicism from its postmodern counterpart, or look at Michael Graves's Portland building: it certainly is not beautiful in any traditional sense. And yet John Pastier was not obviously right when he called it "on the whole . . . an aesthetic failure."[22] All depends on what is meant by "aesthetic." Given an aesthetics of the interesting, the building has to be considered a success, as the publicity it has generated demonstrates. It can indeed lay good claim to being the "First Monument of a Loosely Defined Style," and as this monument it testifies to the extent to which this style is ruled by pursuit of the interesting.

Have I made too much of Venturi's "less is a bore" and of the aesthetic category of the interesting? After all, Venturi himself preceded that statement with the equally quotable "more is not less," which invites us to look at the movement from Miesian sparseness to postmodern complexity and contradiction as just another example of the periodic swing of the aesthetic pendulum away from "less" toward "more," inviting comparison with the shift from the "classicism" of the early Gothic to the "Baroque" of late Gothic hall churches with their flowing net vaults, or with the turn away from the purity of Brunelleschi's Ospedale degli Innocenti to the complexity of Palladio's Palazzo Chiericati. One might thus consider postmodernism as modernism's Mannerism or perhaps modernism's Rococo. There are of course striking differences: the swings of the aesthetic pendulum have become much more rapid, swings of fashion rather than style. Still, if the evolution of postmodernism invites us to understand it in terms of the interesting, it also invites interpretation in terms of Wölfflin's *Principles of Art History:* do we not discover once again "that the notion of clarity had first to be developed before an interest could be found in a partially troubled clarity," that "to play with the hidden adherence to rule . . . presupposes a stage of obvious adherence to rule," that "a tactile apprehension of things in space" yields to a "type of contemplation which has learned to surrender itself to the mere visual impression."[23]

This, however, returns us to the question, can any merely aesthetic approach do justice to architecture? Do we do justice even to postmodern architecture when we understand it as an essentially aesthetic response to modernism? Without doubt, much recent architecture supports Ada Louise Huxtable's claim, "Scratch a postmodernist and you will find an apostle of art for art's sake."[24] Still, we have to take seriously, more seriously perhaps than they took themselves, those postmodernists who proclaimed themselves humanists and charged modernism not so much with aesthetic as with moral failure. Not only do they invite us to confront the presuppositions of modernism, but they force us to question the limits of the aesthetic approach and thus the maps that have long guided thinking about architecture.

But why charge modernism with moral failure? Were the founders of the modern movement not very much aware of the way architecture helps shape the world we live in and conscious of the architect's moral responsibility? Is this not shown by their strident condemnation of the decorated sheds created in such profusion in the closing decades of the nineteenth century? In these attempts to cover functional shells with borrowed ornament they saw not just a lack of artistic creativity but an irresponsible, vain flight from a rationalism that those fleeing from it had in fact already embraced, along with science and technology. Today such flight may masquerade as postmodern guerilla warfare against an oppressive establishment, while it nevertheless remains a flight: we are still not done with modernist hope. Condemnation of the nineteenth century's split attitude to objectifying reason and thus to modernity was the other side of the confidence that led to the rise of the modern movement: finally this modern world was to find its own proper style, a style that would allow human beings to feel at home in a world shaped by science. Evangelical modernists promised to heal the rift between beauty and reason, form and function: once more, architecture was to be all of a piece. Such hopes are difficult to dismiss.

Today these modernist dreams, too, belong to the history of architecture. We still have not been able to make our peace with a rationality that, even as it promises to make us the masters and possessors of nature, threatens nature's and our own destruction. We have learned to look with different and more loving eyes at an architecture that to convinced modernists demonstrated only cynicism and decadence. But were they wrong? Do we today know better? Or have we only grown more tired, more uncertain, more cynical?

Today, at any rate, architects are returning to the eclectic architecture of the nineteenth century somewhat as nineteenth-century architects turned to the stronger styles of preceding centuries. Eclecticism has been raised to a higher power. The renewed appreciation of neo-classicism has thus given birth to a postmodern neo-neo-classicism, although given the current fascination with the neo-neo-classicism of architects like Troost (see fig. 116) and Speer, we should perhaps speak of a neo-neo-neo-classicism. Just as eclecticism has been raised to a higher power, so has arbitrariness. While the nineteenth century could still take seriously the historical paradigms it adopted, today similar reverence for the past is likely to seem naive. Not that we side with the harsh criticism directed against nineteenth-century eclecticism and historicism by the founders of the modern movement: we lack the faith such fervor requires. If once again we attempt to relieve the dreariness of functional architecture by borrowing from the past, there is less conviction in our borrowing. This may be put positively: today's eclecticism takes itself less seriously than did its nineteenth-century precursor. It is freer, more playful, less intimidated by the past. By the same token it is also less certain of its way.

4

Uncertainty has spilled over into our schools of architecture. Thirty years ago Christian Norberg-Schulz charged that "the schools have shown themselves incapable of bringing forth architects able to solve the actual tasks."[25] Things are no different today although we are more likely to meet with challenges to the very notion of "the actual tasks." Do we know what these tasks are? Is the prevailing uncertainty not at bottom uncertainty about how this question is to be answered? To be sure, we can appeal to what seem to be obvious needs generated by our way of life and can look to scientists, especially to social scientists, to state these needs with a precision that would allow engineers to offer the solutions that would best meet them. But are these needs so obvious? Do we know how to circumscribe the field of our needs? Such circumscription demands a sound understanding of the requirements of human dwelling; without it, there is only stuttering dissatisfaction with all purely functional building. Like our nineteenth-century precursors, we demand "more" without knowing how this "more" is to be understood. Does aesthetics hold the key to what distinguishes works of architecture from mere buildings, as Pevsner suggests? Should works of architecture be works of art, or rather, machines and works of art? As Arthur Drexler remarked in *Transformations in Modern Architecture,* "We are still dealing with the conflict between art and technology that beset the nineteenth century."[26]

Uncertainty is presupposed by the willingness of architects and architectural educators to look beyond their discipline, not just to the natural and social sciences but increasingly also to philosophy. Thus Frampton and Dal Co have looked to Heidegger, Eisenman and Gehry to Derrida. The very word "deconstruction" has helped to build a bridge between architecture and philosophy by reminding us of the way architectural metaphors have figured decisively in the discourse of both religion and philosophy, inviting us to think of God, the philosopher, and the architect all as builders, each in the image of the other two, where figure and figured intertwine in ways that in the end call into question the very idea of a well-founded building that grants possibilities of genuine dwelling. The word "edify" hints at what is at issue: as the *OED* reminds us, originally "to edify"—from the Latin *aedificare* (*aedes,* "dwelling," + *ficare,* "to make")—meant simply to build, to construct. Long ago this meaning fell into disuse, but the word found a new home especially in religious discourse: "to edify" came to mean to build up the church or the soul, to provide something like spiritual shelter—Kierkegaard thus wrote *Edifying Discourses.* Today "edify" and "edifying" are most often used ironically, with a negative connotation. Growing suspicion of philosophy's power to edify can be traced in the changing role of the metaphors of architecture in philosophical reflection: from Descartes and Kant to Nietzsche, Heidegger, and Derrida. But deconstruction has called into question not only philosophical construction but also the architect's efforts to build so that human beings might not just be provided with physical shelter, but be allowed to dwell, a word heavy with nostalgia.

What then do we philosophers have to offer architects? What does philosophy have to do with what concerns the architect? Such questions inevitably lead to another: what is philosophy? In the *Philosophical Investigations* Wittgenstein claims that philosophical problems have the form, "I do not know my way about."[27] Of course, not all problems having this form are therefore already philosophical: to lose one's way in a strange city is not sufficient to make one a philosopher, nor is failure to understand a new piece of equipment. Say my computer misbehaves and I don't know what to do; I don't know my way about. But why does such a loss of way not present us with a philosophical problem? I would suggest that it fails to do so because in such cases our disorientation is only superficial. Thus in the first case I might study a map; in the second, I might ask an expert for help. The problem poses itself against a background of established and accepted ways of doing things to which we can turn to help us decide what is to be done. Genuinely philosophical problems have no such background. They emerge whenever human beings have begun to question the place assigned them by nature, society, and history and to search for firmer ground. In that sense I want to say of philosophy, too—fully aware that this places me at some distance from much that today is called philosophy—what Giedion says of architecture: its main task is the interpretation of a way of life valid for our period. The fundamental question of philosophy remains: where should we be going? In this broad sense all philosophy fundamentally is "ethical reflection," reflection concerning the ethos. At bottom the discourse of philosophy is an edifying discourse.

To claim that architecture today faces a philosophical problem and to suggest that philosophical reflection should be part of any well-constructed program of architectural education is to claim not just that architects have become uncertain of their way and of the maps on which they have been relying, but that such uncertainty reflects a deeper uncertainty about how we ought to live, where our place should be, and how architects are to help shape that place, to "edify," to build in that sense.[28] This, to be sure, is not how philosophers have tended to think about architecture. For some time now philosophy has placed architecture among the arts, so the philosophy of architecture has developed as part of the philosophy of art. The philosophy of art again has come to be all but identified with aesthetics, which has resulted in the widespread tendency to consider the "philosophy of architecture" a branch of aesthetics—Roger Scruton's *Aesthetics of Architecture* is a good example. According to Scruton, the aesthetics of architecture "aims to capture the essence, not the accidents, of architectural beauty,"[29] where beauty is understood as the object of a distinctive kind of pleasure. It is just this approach that I want to question. This book is not a contribution to the aesthetics of architecture. What is needed is something quite different: a rigorous rethinking of the often taken for granted understanding of works of architecture as functional sheds to which an aesthetic component has been added; an understanding of architecture that allows us to take seriously Giedion's imperative that architecture interpret a way of life valid for our period.

5

This leads us back to the two questions I raised earlier concerning this imperative: *In just what sense can architecture be understood as interpretation?* Equally important is the second question: *If the task of architecture continues to be the interpretation of a way of life valid for our period, where do we find the measure of such validity?* Are we not still in search of this measure? Do we know what constitutes genuine dwelling? Indeed, is not the very term "dwelling" too laden with nostalgia, too bound up with a past we must leave behind if we are to be open to the promise of an uncertain future?

But suppose we grant, at least for the time being, that we must know how to dwell if we are to build successfully: what kind of dwelling is appropriate to this technological age? Inseparable from the question, What way of life is valid for our period? is the question of technology. Today our attitude to technology cannot but be ambivalent. On the one hand we know perfectly well that in countless ways technology has improved the quality of human life. One could cite the striking rise in life expectancy; or the revolution in communications; or the impact technology has had on food production. Who could deny that technology has helped lighten many of the burdens of life? Thus even the most passionate critic of technology is likely to accept its blessings gratefully when she goes to the dentist or travels to a conference to discuss the evils of technology. And yet on the other hand there is the dread we feel at landscape being transformed into technoscape, at houses being perverted into machines for living, at love giving way to cybersex, at a world ever more subject to the anonymous dictatorship of technological planning. Technology threatens to transform us into increasingly lonely, rootless, displaced persons. This loss of place invites perhaps dangerous dreams of an architecture strong enough to return us to what has been lost, strong enough to allow us to understand ourselves once more as members of a genuine community. The problem of architecture and the problem of community cannot finally be divorced.

What then does philosophy have to contribute to architecture and to architectural education? In one sense very little: no clear direction; perhaps a few pointers; mostly questions, putting into question presuppositions of our approach to architecture that are often taken for granted and thereby opening up new possibilities. But by putting into question maps on which architects and architectural theorists have long relied and which have been the source of continuing confusion, philosophy can contribute to the drawing up—inevitably tentative—of new maps.

If architecture today is to address what Giedion is right to call its main task, it first has to free itself from the aesthetic approach, which also means freeing itself from an understanding of the work of architecture as fundamentally just a decorated shed. The first part of this book therefore develops a critique of the aesthetic approach and examines some of the consequences of this critique for architecture.

If the main task of architecture is indeed, as Giedion claims, interpretation, architecture must possess the power of speech. But it is not at all obvious that—and, if so, in what sense—architecture can be said to speak. The second part of this book addresses the problem of the language of architecture.

According to Giedion architecture should speak to us of how we are to live in the contemporary world. Developing some suggestions made by Martin Heidegger, the third part examines building in its relationship to the essence and requirements of dwelling.

Our dwelling is always a dwelling with others. The problem of architecture is therefore inevitably also the problem of community, which is only the other side of the problem of the individual. The ethical function of architecture cannot finally be divorced from the political. The fourth and final part will take a few steps toward unfolding this twofold function.

Part One

The Decorated Shed

The Aesthetic Approach

2

1

Pevsner, as we saw, would have us understand works of architecture as buildings "designed with a view to aesthetic appeal." On this "aesthetic approach," works of architecture are buildings intended to appeal also as aesthetic objects. But what is an "aesthetic object"? What constitutes "aesthetic appeal"? Once these questions have been answered, the inadequacy of the aesthetic approach to architecture will become obvious.

Objects with aesthetic appeal are often called beautiful. We call flowers beautiful, or landscapes, or persons. But we could not say that they are "designed with a view to aesthetic appeal"—they are not works of art. For examples of work intended to have aesthetic appeal we can turn to sculpture or painting.

Consider, for example, *Newburyport* by Frank Stella, dating from 1964 (fig. 3), and his description of his aesthetic goal:

I always get into arguments with people who want to retain the old values in painting, the humanistic values that they always find on the canvas. If you pin them down, they always end up asserting that there is something there besides the paint on the canvas. My painting is based on the fact that only what can be seen is there. It really is an object. Any painting is an object and anyone who gets involved enough in this finally has to face up to the objectness of whatever he's doing. He is making a thing. All that should be taken for granted. If the painting were lean enough, accurate enough, or right enough, you would just be able to look at it. All I want anyone to get out of my paintings, and all that I ever get out of them, is the fact that you can see the whole idea without confusion. . . . What you see is what you see.[1]

I would like to underscore a number of points:

1. Stella would have his painting so absorb our attention that we feel no need to look beyond it for meaning. It thus should not present itself to us as a representation that has its measure in the absent represented, nor as a sign that receives its meaning from the absent signified, nor as a symbol gesturing toward absent significance, nor as an allegory figuring absent meaning. Its presence should not be haunted by absence. What Archibald MacLeish said of the poem holds of it, too: it should *not mean, but be.*

2. The painting should be such that it allows us to "see the whole idea without confusion." It should not leave us wondering whether we may be missing something. Noth-

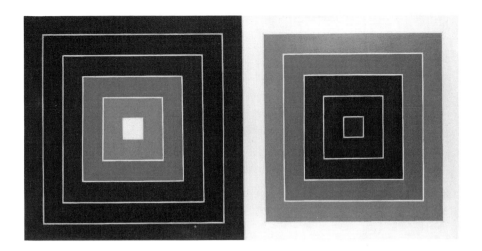

Frank Stella, *Newburyport* (1962). Gift of the Woodward Foundation. Credit: Yale University Art Gallery.

3

ing in it should strike us as superfluous, nor should we experience it as just a fragment of an absent whole. The painting should present itself as *a self-sufficient whole*.

3. Such completeness demands of observers that they leave the painting alone, that they keep their distance from it. This distanced beholding is different from the way we usually relate to things: think of care that seeks to help, of desire that wants to possess, of aversion that would avoid, of hate that calls for destruction. Above all we are interested in what we encounter and interest does not leave things or persons alone. Aesthetic beholding *lets the beheld be* what it is.

4. To the painting's self-justifying presence corresponds the self-sufficiency of our experience of it. Paintings are not useful in any obvious sense; they are not good for anything. But just their uselessness endows them with an appeal denied to anything that answers to our interest. This uselessness allows us to exist in the present, for all interest is directed toward the future. Thus it lets us be present to ourselves in a way denied by our usual engagement in the world. To the plenitude of the aesthetic object corresponds *the plenitude of aesthetic experience*.

What Stella says of his art can thus be generalized and read as a first description of the aesthetic object. In doing so, we obtain the following fourfold characterization—and the fact that a modernist painting here provides the paradigm invites questioning, even as it reminds us of the extent to which what I have called the aesthetic approach has presided over the progress of modern art.

1. The aesthetic object should not mean but be.
2. The aesthetic object should present itself as a whole.
3. The aesthetic object demands aesthetic distance.
4. The aesthetic object promises to put us at one with ourselves.

It should be evident that even this first characterization forces us to question any attempt to understand works of architecture as aesthetic objects in this sense. Buildings and their elements have to carry meanings if they are to function: houses should look like houses, doors like doors; works of architecture should mean, not just be. Nor do buildings readily present themselves in their totality—we always experience them from a particular point of view, from in front or from behind, from inside or outside; thus we never see more than a partial appearance of an absent whole. Nor is aesthetic distance easily reconciled with the way we use buildings: we do not leave buildings alone but enter and leave them, change and transform them depending on our needs. Such use is difficult to reconcile with the plenitude that was said to characterize aesthetic experience. How illuminating is it then to compare works of architecture to paintings or sculptures understood as self-sufficient aesthetic objects.

But is the characterization of the aesthetic object I have offered adequate, or is it an overly simplistic caricature? We can bracket for the time being the question of the adequacy of this first model; it should at least be clear. Also clear should be the tension between what this model of the aesthetic approach demands and the requirements of dwelling and building. Works of architecture resist consideration as aesthetic objects in the sense described here. But this model, notwithstanding its hold on theorists from Lessing and Kant to Greenberg and Fried, also raises the question of the extent to which works of art such as paintings or sculptures are themselves adequately understood as aesthetic objects. Can the aesthetic function be considered *the* function of art? To claim this is to say also that art remains true to its essence only when it presents itself as *art for art's sake*. And if, as I have claimed, the aesthetic approach is presupposed by aesthetics, must not a self-critical philosophy of art question this presupposition?

2

Let me reiterate: "aesthetics," as I here use the term, should not be understood as just a synonym for "philosophy of art." To be sure, that is how these terms are often used, but such synonymy is of rather recent origin. When we call and understand the philosophy of art first of all as aesthetics, we are the heirs of a quite specific approach to art, one that, even though its long prehistory goes back to the Renaissance and indeed to antiquity, triumphed only in the eighteenth century over an older approach that would not grant autonomy to art, instead assigning it a religious, a social, or an ethical function.[2] Think of a medieval altarpiece.

Granted, however, that the best medieval art was art for God's and not for art's sake: can't we distinguish the religious aspect of this art from what gives it aesthetic appeal? Is the latter not the proper concern for someone interested in such a piece, say a church or a cult object, as a work of art? But what here defines propriety—an understanding of works of art as aesthetic objects?

Pulpit, St. Johann Baptist, Oppolding, Bavaria.

4 | Credit: Hirmer Fotoarchiv.

To be sure, all things can have aesthetic significance. As Panofsky points out,

It is possible to experience every object, natural or man-made, aesthetically. We do this, when we just look at it (or listen to it) without relating it, intellectually or emotionally, to anything outside of itself. When a man looks at a tree from the point of view of a carpenter, he will associate it with the various uses to which he might put the wood; and when he looks at it from the point of view of an ornithologist, he will associate it with the birds that might nest in it. When a man at a horse race watches the animal on which he has put his money, he will associate its performance with his desire that it may win. Only he who simply and wholly abandons himself to the object of his perception will experience it aesthetically.[3]

Aesthetic beholding may be defined in terms of such absorption in what it beholds. No longer do our usual cares and concerns dominate our sight; we are free to attend to what lies before our eyes. Some patterns of shapes and colors invite such surrender more than others. The form of a vase, the geometric ornament circling a plate, the upward surging rocaille of an eighteenth-century pulpit (fig. 4) may capture our attention. That I find myself especially moved by the last has no doubt something to do with my particular background and experiences. But what arouses aesthetic interest is not adequately explained in terms of the inevitably different prejudices and interests that different individuals bring to what they perceive. Often strength of pattern or form will assert itself regardless of cultural or individual differences. Certain proportions thus possess a perennial appeal, like the special place belonging to the golden section, favored by both art and nature: asked to pick out the most pleasing rectangle, most people will choose the golden rectangle.[4] Psychologists have thus been able to show that there is considerable cross-cultural agreement about aesthetic preferences of this sort.

The Röttgen Pietà, 14th century. Bonn, Rhein-
isches Landesmuseum. Credit: Foto Marburg/
5 | Art Resource, N.Y.

Textiles and pottery produced by different cultures can teach us that craftsmen have always looked beyond what utility demanded to configurations of shape and color possessing such strength. So understood, a concern for beauty, for what is aesthetically pleasing, is part of all human experience: aesthetic considerations will enter into something as commonplace as setting a table, weaving some fabric, or building even a simple house. But generally this would seem to be only a secondary concern, hardly sufficient to lead to the creation of art for art's or for beauty's sake. The primary concern is to make a house, an urn, a festive garment, a sacred image. Thus the primary concern of the sculptor who carved the Röttgen Pietà (fig. 5) was not to create an aesthetic object. Serving religion, art here attempts to address humanity's deepest concerns. The beauty of the image serves this attempt. Later I shall have more to say about the nature of this service, which, it will turn out, has much to tell us about the beauty of architecture.

Here I only want to suggest that the aesthetic approach to art, which insists that art be for art's or for beauty's sake and makes self-sufficient presence constitutive of both, can hardly be considered the norm by which the production of what we generally call art has been or should be judged. As Panofsky points out, Poussin's assertion that "la fin de l'art est la delectation" was revolutionary in its time.[5] The key to this revolution is provided by what I have called the aesthetic approach to art, by the insistence that the end of art is aesthetic delight.

But have I not placed undue weight on Stella's self-interpretation? To be sure, Panofsky's description of aesthetic experience fits in very well with the fourfold characterization of the aesthetic object I drew from it. Still, more discussion is needed, if this characterization is to support a critique of what I have claimed to be the ruling approach to art and architecture.

20

I have already pointed out that the aesthetic approach belongs to the eighteenth century. We owe both the term "aesthetics" and the establishment of aesthetics as one of the main branches of philosophy to Alexander Gottlieb Baumgarten's dissertation of 1735—a rather short, unusually lucid text, despite its forbidding Latin title, *Meditationes philosophicae de nonnullis ad poema pertinentibus.*[6] Baumgarten hoped to show how room could be made within the framework that had been established by the philosophy of Descartes for the study of art, more especially of poetry. Philosophical aesthetics is thus an offspring of rationalism, part of the somewhat questionable legacy left us by the Enlightenment. In chapter 7 I shall examine this legacy in greater detail. Here I would like to take a closer look at the approach to art Baumgarten's institution of aesthetics both presupposes and interprets.

Baumgarten coined the term *aesthetica* as an analogue to *logica.* While logic seeks to establish the principles that should govern the exercise of reason, aesthetics seeks to establish the principles that should govern judgments of taste. The analogy implies a repudiation of the claim that the pleasure we take in a poem or a painting is not so very different from our enjoyment of the smell of a rose or the taste of a good glass of wine. As Plato had already observed, aesthetic delight is not just a matter of having pleasant sensations. Taste, Baumgarten insists, resembles reason. Both are species of judgment and governed by its law. "The law of the faculty of judgment is as follows: if a given manifold is recognized either as fitting or as not fitting together, then its perfection or imperfection is recognized. This happens either sensually or distinctly. The faculty of judging by means of sense is taste in its widest sense."[7]

Instead of rehearsing Baumgarten's rather involved discussion of beauty and taste, I shall examine only a simile he offers the reader; it sums up much of his understanding of the work of art. A successful poem, and we can generalize and say a successful work of art, Baumgarten tells us, is like a world.[8] "World" here does not name the totality of facts; Baumgarten is thinking rather of the world as described by rationalist philosophers, especially by Leibniz, who took the world to be a perfectly ordered cosmos. In this best of all possible worlds nothing is missing and nothing superfluous, everything is as it should be; perfection means precisely such completeness. The work of art, Baumgarten asserts, should be a similarly perfect whole. Its integrity should be such that to add or subtract anything would be to do violence to its aesthetic perfection.

Quite traditional in its suggestion that, godlike, the artist builds another world, Baumgarten's simile seems innocent enough: after all, ever since Aristotle, unity has been demanded of the work of art.[9] To be sure, we must allow for complexity, tension, and incongruity, but order should triumph in the end, so what at first may appear not to belong, striking us as discordant, finally is recognized to have been absolutely necessary. Baumgarten, too, cites the definition so familiar in the eighteenth century of beauty as *sensible perfection.*[10] To call beauty *sensible* is to insist that our experience of it involves the senses; beauty depends on perception. To speak of it as *perfection* is to insist on the self-sufficiency of the beautiful. The artwork is autonomous: its point is not to refer beyond itself, to express some edifying thought or to represent some cherished object or person. To praise it for being true or to condemn it for being false is to have missed what matters: that it present itself to us as an all-absorbing presence. Presenting itself to us as being just as it should be, a beautiful work of art delivers us from the sense of arbitrariness and contingency that is so much part of our everyday life, that again and again lets us wonder: why this and not that? Absorbed in a work of art, we no longer confront different possibilities. But this is to say also that we no longer face the future. The artwork's perfection lifts the burden of time, allowing us to exist, if only for a time, in a seemingly timeless present.

Compare this understanding of the artwork with Stella's description of his artistic ideal. From Baumgarten's simile we can derive essentially the same four points:

1. Perfection, as Baumgarten, following Leibniz, understands it, entails self-sufficiency.[11] Ideally the work of art should not point beyond itself. Its point is not to describe a reality external to it. Nor is it to make statements about the world. If it succeeds, it does so not as a representation but as a presentation. The step from Baumgarten's understanding of the poem as a perfect whole to MacLeish's dictum—the poem should not mean, but be—is small.

2. The perfection of the artwork demands once more that it be experienced as a whole.

3. The perfection of the artwork demands of spectators that they leave it as it presents itself to them. All they could do to it would only destroy its perfection. The proper response to art is rapt surrender, absorption in its presence. Such absorption satisfies because it grants us a sense of being at one with ourselves denied by our engagement in the world. Aesthetic experience thus quiets care, fear, and hope.

4. To the artwork's perfection corresponds the self-sufficiency of aesthetic experience, which needs no justification but is sought for its own sake.

What matters here is not Baumgarten but an attitude that, as Frank Stella's self-understanding as a painter demonstrates, has continued to shape the way both artists and theoreticians approach art. Although the fact that he gave "aesthetics" its name may tempt us to seek the origin of the aesthetic approach with Baumgarten, doing so would attribute to his thought a significance that does not belong to it. Not only do the thoughts of other thinkers of the period lead in the same direction—Diderot deserves to be singled out—but philosophical reflection only followed a change in attitude that long before gaining dominance in the eighteenth century had begun to shape the development of the different arts.[12]

While Baumgarten offers an obvious point of departure for discussions of the aesthetic approach, I could equally well have turned to Kant, who criticizes Baumgarten on a number of points, questioning especially his understanding of the beautiful as a perfect whole, accusing him of having made aesthetic judgments too much like judgments of reason.[13] But Kant, too, understands beauty as self-justifying presence. The point of his famous determination of the beautiful as the object of an entirely disinterested satisfaction becomes clear once we keep in mind that interest always looks beyond the present to the future. Governed as they are by care and concern, our usual ways of encountering things are essentially interested. Aesthetic experience demands that we leave behind such involvement, that we bracket our ordinary concerns. Such bracketing is a presupposition of the establishment of what came to be called psychical or aesthetic distance. As Paul Weiss points out,

To obtain an aesthetic object we must enter into the common-sense world, with its robust and vital activities, and there, through an act of concentration, detach a portion of it from the rest. The act of bounding is produced by a change in attitude. Instead of being concerned with the world of common sense, as spread out over a large area of space and time and organized by convention, tradition, and social demands, we must so attend to a portion of it that it is torn out of its context, freed from its social role, and infused with our emotions, interests, and values.[14]

There is a sense in which all aesthetic objects have been framed or frame themselves.

Not that Weiss finds himself here in complete agreement with Kant. While Kant speaks of the aesthetic object as object of an entirely disinterested satisfaction, Weiss insists that it is infused with our emotions, interests, and values. This suggests an aesthetic experience less removed from life and richer than it is on Kant's interpretation. But Weiss, too, insists that the aesthetic object is essentially dislocated, framed; such framing may be the result of a conscious effort on our part, but it may also be a gift of the beautiful, which puts us in a different state of mind, absorbing our usual interests as blotting paper absorbs ink. To develop my model of the aesthetic approach, I could also have turned to Schopenhauer, who, appropriating Kant, writes that in aesthetic experience "we relinquish the ordinary way of considering things," "let our whole consciousness be filled by the calm contemplation" of the object present and "*lose* ourselves entirely in this object."[15]

A recent, unusually articulate representative of the aesthetic approach is Michael Fried. His essay "Art and Objecthood" deserves to be singled out as an eloquent defense of aesthetic modernism, a defense that makes the pursuit of presentness constitutive of what Fried considers "the authentic art of our time." Our experience of such art "*has no* duration—not because one *in fact* experiences a picture by Noland or Olitski or a sculpture by David Smith or Caro in no time at all, but because *at every moment the work itself is wholly manifest.*"[16] I could go on. But perhaps I have said enough to show that my "caricature" of the aesthetic approach does capture concerns that at least since the early eighteenth century have given direction to both the theory and the practice of art.[17]

4

Architecture has difficulty rising to the purity found in the other arts, for, as Kant observes, "the suitability of a product for a certain use is the essential thing in an *architectural work.*"[18]

To be sure, it is quite possible to consider and even to build works of architecture as aesthetic objects, as is demonstrated by Alexander Tzonis and Liane Lefaivre's discussion of classical architecture. Invoking the authority of Aristotle, they too insist that the work of architecture, like every work of art, "is a world within the world, 'complete,' 'integral,' 'whole,' a world where there is no contradiction."[19] Given this conception of the work of architecture as another world, all "outside conditions" must be considered "significant obstacles." By its very nature, the aesthetic approach to architecture is opposed to every contextualism. "In ancient Greece, temples" thus "turned a cold shoulder to every structure that happened to be next to them, even if this other structure was another temple."[20] I do not want to raise here the question of the adequacy of this characterization. But the basic point must be affirmed and could be illustrated with modern examples: *to the extent* that the aesthetic approach governs building, works of architecture will turn a cold shoulder not only to their neighbors but to the world that would constrain them with its demands and necessities.

Certainly, the world may not be forgotten. It provides the inevitable, pregiven point of departure. But if the status of the art work as a self-sufficient whole is to be preserved, it may do no more than that. Given the aesthetic approach, Valéry's definition of poetry as "*an effort by one man* to create an artificial and ideal order of a material of vulgar origin,"[21] the material in this case being ordinary language, holds of every work of art. Quite in the spirit of Valéry, Tzonis and Lefaivre thus proclaim that "the *poetic* identity of a building depends not on its stability, on its function, or on the efficiency of the means of its production, but on the way in which all the above have been limited, bent, and subordinated by purely formal requirements."[22] The canon, or rules of composition, that governs classical architecture ensures that such transformation results in ordered, self-sufficient wholes. It does so first by "constraining the placing of the architectural elements that populate a building by establishing successions of logically organized divisions of space" (taxis); second, by ensuring that the elements placed in the framework that has thus been established will "always appear in well-determined sets governed by particular fixed relations" (the genera or classical orders); and finally, by constraining "how elements are chosen and placed in relation both to one another and to the overall structure of taxis," such that the constraint relies on rhythmic organization and on the architectural counterparts of not only such "overt" rhetorical figures as parallelism, contrast, alignment, and analogy but also more "subtle" figures, such as oxymoron and ellipsis.[23]

The extreme formalism of such an approach follows from its commitment to aesthetic perfection, which renders talk of the requirements of dwelling or function simply irrelevant. And yet, as Kant insists, architecture cannot turn a cold shoulder to the world: it has to be both beautiful and practical. Indeed, considerations of utility will almost inevitably take precedence over a concern for beauty. But to the extent that this is the case, beauty in architecture can appear only as an addition to what necessity dictates. This is also to say that the architect inevitably has to compromise his or her artistic vision.

That architects are forced to betray their aesthetic ideals more than other artists is also noted by Weiss. Architecture has to exist "within a context defined by unskilled labor and such practical activities as excavation, engineering, and plumbing. It must conform to building codes written with little concern for artistic needs. No other art is so hemmed in by men, tasks, and conditions relating to nonaesthetic matters."[24] And if nonaesthetic considerations inevitably hem in architecture, we should also expect them to limit the way architects are trained. Weiss thus concludes his discussion of architecture with a historical observation and a suggestion concerning how architectural education might be improved:

It would not be amiss, though, to remark that the history of architecture does not seem to have had many great turning points. There seem to be few great adventurers among the architects, perhaps because they are so overwhelmed by judges, critics, clients, and problems relating to engineering, city planning, and scales. What architecture badly needs today are laboratories where students are not only trained and disciplined, as they now are, but also encouraged to experiment with the building of all sorts of space, in all sorts of ways, with all sorts of material. They should have periods in which they do not care that their work may not interest a client or that no one may ever build it or that it may not fit in with prevailing styles. Not until they take seriously the need to explore the possibilities of bounding spaces in multiple ways will they become alert to architecture as an art, as respectable, revelatory, creative, and at least as difficult as any other.[25]

It would be easy to challenge the claim that "the history of architecture does not seem to have had many great turning points." Abbot Suger of St.-Denis, Brunelleschi, Borromini, Ledoux, and Frank Lloyd Wright argue differently. But Weiss's claim is based not on an examination of history but on his understanding of architecture as an art forced to compromise its aesthetic chastity. Like Kant, Weiss raises the question of the aesthetic respectability of architecture. What threatens this respectability is the architect's inevitable subjection of nonaesthetic constraints.

Once this is acknowledged, the hope Weiss holds out in the end, that architecture might become an art as respectable as the others, must be rejected. Given the aesthetic approach, architecture will never manage to become as respectable as painting or sculpture. If beauty demands aesthetic purity, the beauty of architecture would appear inescapably compromised. For buildings have to be more than objects for aesthetic contemplation. The architect has to take into account the uses to which a building will be put, while those using it will not be able to keep their distance from it. Compared to its sister arts architecture will then have to be considered deficient and impure: a not quite respectable art.

All of this would be of little consequence were it only a matter of some philosophers and architectural theorists arguing among themselves about the essence of architecture. But, as this chapter has made clear, the rise of aesthetics and of the aesthetic approach are only aspects of a more deeply rooted change in sensibility that in the name of reason divorced pragmatic and aesthetic considerations and placed the architect uneasily between the two. On the one hand, the uses of architecture are emphasized; on the other, architecture is supposed to be artistic. Unfortunately, the hopes of functionalists notwithstanding, not only is there no assurance that an economic and efficient solution to practical problems will also be aesthetically pleasing, but given the aesthetics of purity, there is no chance that modern architecture's marriage of art and engineering will be free of tension and compromise. As claimed in chapter 1, on the aesthetic approach the beauty of a building has to appear as something added on to what necessity dictates, as decoration in a broad sense.

The tensions that result from this mingling of pragmatic and aesthetic concerns all but rule out aesthetic completeness.

It is thus hardly surprising that with the rise of the aesthetic approach in the eighteenth century, architecture should have entered a period of uncertainty and crisis from which it has still not emerged. To be sure, already then there were attempts to raise architecture to the status of a purer art. The prophetic designs of Claude-Nicolas Ledoux (fig. 6) offer striking examples. Not surprisingly, Ledoux's most daring dreams remained on paper.[26] An architect who understands himself or herself as an artist in the aesthetic sense, will indeed be tempted to say: "Just because I am an architect, I refuse to build." The pursuit of aesthetic purity has to lead the architect to create utopian fantasies, difficult or impossible to realize. Reality demands compromises; aesthetic vision must be tempered with nonaesthetic considerations.

As long as architectural theory remains ruled by the aesthetic approach, it has to understand the work of architecture first of all as Kant did, as a functional building with an added aesthetic component, that is, as a decorated shed. The following three chapters will therefore focus on the problem of decoration.

Claude-Nicolas Ledoux, House of the Agricultural Guards. From Ledoux, *L'Architecture considerée sous le rapport de l'art, des moeurs et de la législation,* vol. 2, ed. Daniel Ramée (London, 1846), pl. 254. Source: Yvon Christ and Ionel Schein, *L'Oeuvre et les rêves de Ledoux* (Paris: Chêne, 1971).

6

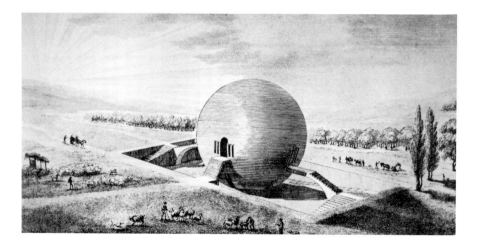

The Problem of Decoration

3

1

The previous chapter explored some of the implications of an understanding of the work of art as aesthetic object. It also showed why architecture has difficulty living up to what such an understanding demands: to the extent that we measure works of architecture by the aesthetic conception of a successful artwork, architecture has to be considered deficient and impure, a not quite respectable art—not quite respectable precisely because never truly autonomous, always bound to the requirements of building. Presupposed is that questionable distinction between building and architecture that Pevsner places at the very beginning of his *Outline of European Architecture.*

In this he had been preceded by, among others, John Ruskin, whose *Seven Lamps of Architecture* offers an unusually clear statement of the aesthetic approach to architecture. Ruskin begins his discussion with a description of building: "To build, literally to confirm, is by common understanding to put together and to adjust the several pieces of any edifice or receptacle of considerable size. Thus we have church building, house building, ship building, and coach building. That one edifice stands, another floats, and another is suspended on iron springs, makes no difference to the nature of this art, if so it may be called, of building or edification."[1] The builder will be concerned about the stability of what he constructs; he will want to make sure that it serves its purpose; but as builder he is not concerned with beauty. Just this distinguishes him from the architect. Had not Vitruvius already demanded that the architect build "with due reference to durability, convenience, and beauty"?[2] While attention to the first two requirements makes every architect also a builder, only attention to the third makes him an artist, that is, an architect.

Ruskin is of course aware that "building" and "architecture" are often used as synonyms, but such "loose nomenclature" is said to run the risk of losing sight of the character of the latter as art. His proposal that we distinguish between the two does indeed seem quite unproblematic: "Let us, therefore, at once confine the name ['architecture'] to that art which, taking up and admitting, as conditions of its working, the necessities and common uses of the building, impresses on its form certain characters venerable and beautiful, but otherwise unnecessary" (p. 16). Works of architecture are never just machines for living. In terms of the necessities of life, what distinguishes architecture from building has to be judged as quite superfluous. The spirit that gives rise to architecture is "therefore most unreasoning and enthusiastic, and perhaps best negatively defined, as the opposite of the prevalent feeling of modern times, which desires to produce the largest results at the least cost" (p. 7). By its very nature architecture is thus opposed to the economic imperative that demands first of all efficiency; architecture, as Ruskin understands it, would perish, were it to attempt to heed what that imperative demands. There is thus a sense in which architecture falls outside modernity: genuine architecture is either pre- or postmodern. On Ruskin's view a truly modern architecture is rather like a square circle.

Ruskin calls architecture unnecessary. Of course, he does not really mean this, for despite or perhaps precisely because of its uselessness, architecture is said to contribute to our "mental health, power and pleasure" (p. 15). This recognizes a need for architecture and implies that modernity, as Ruskin understands it, poses a threat to human well-being. Architecture helps us meet this threat: the quality of life should not be sacrificed to the economic imperative. As Aristotle knew, what makes life worth living is not work but leisure. Our leisure time we should fill with activities that justify themselves. Here there can be no talk of wasting time, for leisure time does not reckon with time in a way that allows it to be wasted; only the economic imperative demands that work be done as efficiently as possible, demands that we make good use of the available time. As we saw in the last chapter, aesthetic experience has long been considered a paradigm of such self-justifying experience. To appreciate art we must leave the work world behind, must be at leisure; that holds also for the creation and appreciation of architecture, at least, if, following Ruskin, we take for granted its art character. The distinction between building and architecture, utility and beauty, thus mirrors the distinction between work and leisure; both distinctions presuppose different ways of experiencing time.

Very much a child of the nineteenth century, Ruskin, despite evident misgivings, affirms the rationalization and organization of work that have shaped the modern world. Yet he also knows about the self-alienation that is the price of efficiency. The more the economic imperative determines our ways of working, the more insistent will be the demand for more free time, for experiences and activities that do not serve some end but rather justify themselves.

Ruskin describes architecture as the art that "adorns the edifices raised by man for whatsoever uses" (p. 15). Architecture is an art of decoration, and the problem of architecture is inevitably also the problem of decoration. That there should be such a problem at all is a function of the quality of modern life: to the extent that this life is ruled by the economic imperative, it will have little use for either architecture or decoration. As well as any modernist, Ruskin already knows that functional building has no need for essentially useless decoration—that is, no need for architecture. And given buildings whose meaning is exhausted by their utility—think of factories, warehouses, shopping centers, silos, bridges, garages, railroad stations, and airports as possible examples—Ruskin, too, would not have us hear of decoration, condemning it with a vehemence that anticipates modernist critiques. He already calls it "a general law, of singular importance in the present day, a law of simple common sense,—not to decorate things belonging to purposes of active and occupied life. Wherever you can rest, there decorate; where rest is forbidden, so is beauty. You must not mix ornament with business, any more than you mix play. Work first, and then rest" (p.

Michael Graves, Hotel Dolphin, Orlando,

7 | Florida. Photo by author.

115). That there is a case to be made for architecture at all presupposes that not all building serves "purposes of active and occupied life." Thus churches and houses invite decoration, for there we rest after the week's or the day's work is done. So do hotels (fig. 7).

But is it desirable, or even possible, to separate work and rest this sharply? It is significant that Ruskin would have us work first, then rest. Despite his celebration of architecture, work is here given the place of honor. And is not time a resource with which we have to reckon? Don't we always have too little time? Heidegger, to be sure, claims that the authentic person always has time.[3] But if so, this only places authenticity as much at odds with modernity as is architecture or decoration. And the reason is the same: the way modernity would have us reckon with time, a way incompatible with authentic dwelling. What Ruskin calls "the prevalent feeling of modern times" would have us subject time, too, to rational planning. If, as Ruskin insists, leisure and rest are necessary for our health, then, even in the interest of greater efficiency, time should be organized in such a way that it allows for both. The entertainment industry serves the organization of leisure time.

This is also to say that rational planning will not stop before the house, which will not remain an oasis in the organized modern world. That there is a need for relaxation and entertainment may be taken for granted. A successful house will serve both needs, just as it will serve our need to shelter and feed ourselves. But does this argue that houses should be more than complex machines? And if not, should we not banish decoration from houses as much as Ruskin would banish them from railroad stations?

But just what Ruskin has to say about railroad stations hints at what is lost when houses are reduced to machines.

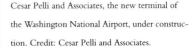

Cesar Pelli and Associates, the new terminal of the Washington National Airport, under construction. Credit: Cesar Pelli and Associates.

8

Another of the strange and evil tendencies of the present day is the decoration of the railroad station. Now, if there be any place in the world in which people are deprived of that portion of temper and discretion which are necessary to the contemplation of beauty, it is there. It is the very temple of discomfort, and the only charity the builder can extend to us is to show us, plainly as may be, how soonest to escape from it. The whole system of railroad travel is addressed to people who, being in a hurry, are therefore, for the time being, miserable. No one would travel in the manner who could help it—who had time to go leisurely over hills and between hedges, instead of through tunnels and between banks: at least those who would, have no sense of beauty so acute as that we need consult it at the station. The railroad is in all its relations a matter of earnest business, to be got through as soon as possible. It transmutes a man from a traveller into a living parcel. For the time being he has parted with the nobler characteristics of his humanity for the sake of a planetary power of locomotion. Do not ask him to admire anything. You might as well ask the wind. Carry him safely, dismiss him soon: he will thank you for nothing else.
(p. 117)

It is easy to criticize Ruskin. His caricature does not begin to do justice to the reality of railroad travel. Most of us like to travel. Just entering a railroad station, or today more likely an airport, has a festive quality: as we are about to leave our everyday behind, life seems to open to the promise of a much larger world, carrying with it the excitement of strange places and unfamiliar pleasures, while to those arriving successful stations or airports should present themselves as a city's foyer (fig. 8). For many of us travel is not just a way of getting from one place to another. Given this special aura, it is easy to understand why the builders of railroad stations should have refused Ruskin's advice, why constructing the railroad station should have developed, in the late nineteenth and early twentieth century, into one of the most significant building tasks.

More important, in this context, is something else: Ruskin is right to insist that, like other modern means of transportation, above all the railroad is meant to save us time. Such reckoning with time Ruskin considers incompatible with what he calls "the nobler characteristics" of humanity. "For the sake of a planetary power of locomotion" we speed things up, allow ourselves to be transformed into "living parcels," into things that are assigned their place by the transportation system. It is easy to see why Ruskin should have insisted that beauty is necessary for our mental health. That reckoning with time, which would speed up not only travel but all work, threatens to empty life of meaning, forcing us to experience ourselves and what we are doing instrumentally as it serves another mode of life in which we are not thus alienated but are at one with ourselves, precisely because not in a hurry. Art allows for such experience. We understand why Ruskin, refusing to sacrifice what he considers genuine humanity to the economic imperative, would have houses be works of architecture and not just plain buildings. We also see why our technological age, just because it invites us to judge all things, including our own activities, in terms of economy and efficiency, demands art and entertainment to complement its distortion of life: the modern metropolis and the entertainment industry, New York and Hollywood, belong together. Ruskin lets us understand the rise of the aesthetic approach, and with it the understanding of works of architecture as decorated buildings, as compensatory. Aesthetic experience—it does not matter here whether we think of high art, decoration, or soap operas—compensates us for that impoverishment of life that is the price of reckoning with time as a valuable resource: *panem et circenses*. Whether such compensation, often bought at the price of covering up our modern reality with beautiful fictions, is at all adequate, is a question that will occupy us in what follows.

2

Suppose we grant the need for such compensation; must we also grant the need for architecture as Ruskin understands it? Were those modernists not right who celebrated art for art's sake but resisted the uneasy compromise between utility and beauty demonstrated by the decorated sheds of the nineteenth century, appealing instead both to the requirements of utility and the requirements of beauty?

That rational consideration of the former leaves no place for decoration, Adolf Loos argues with evangelical fervor in his manifesto, "Ornament and Crime," dating from 1910.[4] The title was already a provocation, doubly so in the Vienna of Otto Wagner, Joseph Maria Olbrich, and Josef Hoffmann, which had embraced decoration with unparalleled passion: ornament a crime? All too often in bad taste perhaps, but a crime, an offense against the public welfare? Loos thought so, and although often self-consciously exaggerated in tone and called into question by his own architectural practice, the argument he advanced is not easily dismissed. Ruskin himself would have had to give it a sympathetic hearing.

It is indeed not altogether original. In many ways Loos's argument parallels one that Enlightenment critics had formulated against the decoration-obsessed culture of the

Rococo:[5] is ornament not frightfully wasteful of time and money that would be better spent on education, food, and medicine? What is ornament good for? Reason demands utility, and utility argues against ornament. Does ornament serve life any better than food prepared to appeal to the eye rather than to satisfy nutritional needs? A rationalist puritanism lets Loos link cookery exhibitions that place the ornate look of a prepared dish ahead of its food value to the decorated sheds of turn-of-the-century Vienna.[6] Loos would have hated our wedding cakes, although he would gladly have granted that here the "art" of the baker comes close to the "art" of architecture. But then, all too many works of architecture do resemble wedding cakes. Why ornament food? We can leave children their animal crackers and Gummi Bears; but we adults of the twentieth century should know better. Both culinary and architectural culture are at odds with modernity as Loos understands it. Haute cuisine and ornament belong together: both are anachronisms that should have disappeared from the modern world. That they hadn't, and especially not in Vienna, home of the Ringstrasse and the Sachertorte, Loos thought a sad commentary on the backwardness of his fellow Austrians, who liked to think that they were still living in the eighteenth century under the rule of Maria Theresia.

Under the rule of a woman: again and again we meet with a tendency to oppose feminine ornament to masculine building.[7] Charles Garnier's remark to the ladies attending the Opéra has symptomatic significance:

Everyone gains from what is stupidly called coquetterie, *which is, in fact, nothing other than art, the most serious art, and the most charming as well, the art of dressing oneself with grace, of walking with distinction, of smiling with finesse. . . . Why is it, Ladies, that you appear at the Opéra, your shoulders bare, diamonds at your neck, flowers on your head, and silk draped about you! You love the sparkle of your eyes and the grace of your smile, you are in a word, beautiful, and you could consent to take your elegance, your charm, your finery into a monument that would not for its part be in gala attire to receive you?*[8] (fig. 9)

Granting the erotic significance of ornament, Loos would no doubt have insisted on the very real price at which such dubious, superficial gain was bought. And he would have found sadder still that today, more than a century later as the twentieth century is drawing to a close, here, in progressive but increasingly self-doubting America, fancy food, dress, and ornament are once again very much in demand: decadence appears to have triumphed over progress.

Loos took it to be his own great discovery, a discovery he was eager to share with the world, that "*the evolution of culture is synonymous with the removal of ornament from utilitarian objects.*"[9] Thus, "the march of civilization systematically liberates object after object from ornamentation."[10] As we have seen, Ruskin had made a similar claim, although he might have questioned Loos's expansion of the realm ruled by considerations of utility. But if, with Loos, we link the evolution of culture to ever more efficient production, we will find it difficult to quarrel with him and will understand his feigned surprise when his "discovery" and his call for building free of ornament met with a rather hostile reception.

9

Jean Louis Charles Garnier, Paris Opéra. General
view. Credit: Giraudon/Art Resource, N.Y.

*I believed that with this discovery I was bringing joy to the world; it has not thanked me. People were
sad and hung their heads. What depressed them was the realization that they could produce no new
ornaments. Are we alone, the people of the nineteenth century, supposed to be unable to do what any
Negro, all the races and periods before us have been able to do? What mankind created without ornament
in earlier millennia was thrown away without a thought and abandoned to destruction. We possess no
joiner's benches from the Carolingian era, but every trifle that displays the least ornament has been
collected and cleaned and palatial buildings have been erected to house it. Then people walked sadly
about the glass cases and felt ashamed of their impotence.*[11]

Why such sadness and hostility? Why this love of ornament? The case against ornament
seemed so obvious; how could reasonable people disagree? Was its love of ornament not
part of that unhappy heritage that kept Austria from truly joining the modern world?

*The stragglers slow down the cultural evolution of the nations and of mankind; not only is ornament
produced by criminals but also a crime is committed through the fact that ornament inflicts serious injury
on people's health, on the national budget and hence on cultural evolution. If two people live side by side
with the same needs, the same demands on life and the same income but belonging to different cultures,
economically speaking the following process can be observed: the twentieth-century man will get richer*

and richer, the eighteenth-century man poorer and poorer. I am assuming that both live according to their inclinations. The twentieth-century man can satisfy his needs with a far lower capital outlay and hence can save money.[12]

The point is difficult to deny. Already in the eighteenth century very similar arguments had been used to compare unenlightened Austria and Bavaria, known for their love of food, drink, sex, and ornament, unfavorably with Germany's more enlightened Protestant north.[13] A caricature of Protestant asceticism is "the Shaker Community," which "forbade sexual intercourse between its married adherents, extinguishing itself in consummate piety and good design. Shaker buildings are undeniably simple and often beautiful, but intelligent appreciation recoils from distortions, wrought in the name of simplicity, which signify death."[14] Loos, to be sure, was not so extreme and later he was to insist, against modernist purists, that he never thought "that ornament should be eliminated systematically and rigorously." Only attempts by architects and applied artists to give ornament an artificial life where the progress of modern culture has already left it behind should be resisted.[15] While eager to preach, Loos had too high an opinion of the individual and his need and right to shape his own life to want to dictate how people should live and build: let the stragglers straggle!

Loos found his shining examples of humanity come of age in progressive England and in the industrious United States, where he had lived from 1893 to 1896.[16] Even their culinary culture, or more precisely their comparative indifference to having such a culture, seemed to Loos exemplary. Just as human beings must dress in order to protect themselves from inclement weather, so they must eat in order to live. But this is a concession we have to make to the animal in us. Reason demands that this concession be kept within proper bounds. To take too great an interest in food betrays a lack of moral fiber. A bowl of oatmeal should suffice for breakfast. Don't praise the hostess for her elaborate dishes: according to Loos, those truly of the twentieth century will not like fancy food; they will prefer their vegetables boiled in water, perhaps with a dab of butter added, and a slab of roast beef to a dish like boeuf en daube on which the cook has been laboring for many hours. How would the Viennese, in so many ways still stuck in the eighteenth century and, what was worse, enjoying thus being stuck, ever join the modern world? How would they ever catch up with the British, let alone with the Americans, as long as so much of their energy went into Sachertorte and decoration? Loos wants food and building to be simple and functional. Truly functional building has no room for ornament. Do we ornament our machines? Builders should think like engineers, not like decorators.

Not that Loos was in love with machines—quite the opposite. The young Loos shared Ruskin's dislike of that modern convenience, the railroad, and applauded the English nobility, which preferred to travel by mail coach—later by car—and left the trains to the servants. "The whole thing is so well suited to the character of the English people, to their profound love of nature. No one abhors machines more than the Englishman. Wherever he can free himself from them he does so. Machines belong to the work world; he tries to keep them far away from his private world."[17] At the center of this private world is an active love of nature, "not just a platonic relationship" but a love that wants to explore the countryside and scale Alpine peaks.[18] "The Englishman does everything himself; he hunts, he climbs mountains, and he saws up trees."[19] And still in the same spirit, although chastened by the experience of World War I and much more aware of the need to address the needs of the common man, Loos later sings the praises of garden work, especially of the *Schreber-garten,*[20] that tiny plot of land leased from the city in which the worker and his family could spend their free time, raising cabbages and tomatoes even while making a significant contribution to the national economy. Here play and work happily join, calling into question a too sharp distinction between work world and private world: "one should not think that the fad of Schreber gardening is a momentary psychosis. For all coming ages the piece of land that the human being works himself, will remain what it is today: the refuge to mother nature, his true happiness and his only bliss."[21] "Bliss" here translates *Seligkeit:* Loos, too, invests "mother nature" with an almost religious significance.[22] The house with a garden, which should be kept small so as not to waste land that should remain available for the enjoyment of all, comes close to what Loos dreamed of: a life that, while taking advantage of all a modern metropolis has to offer, yet stays close to nature; that in order to protect its private pleasures, keeps its distance from the crowd; and, refusing to surrender to the modern love affair with the machine, also keeps its distance from it and remains its master. The refusal to ornament machines, as also the refusal to blur the distinction between utilitarian craft and art,[23] expresses a desire to preserve that distance from the work ethic which is a presupposition of full humanity.

3

"From a thirty years struggle I have emerged as victor: I have liberated humanity from superfluous ornament," proclaimed the old Loos, rather too confidently, in 1930. "'Ornament' was once an epithet for 'beautiful.' Today it is, thanks to my life's work, an epithet for 'inferior.'"[24] The very phrase "superfluous ornament" suggests that not all ornament is here rejected. Loos certainly did not mean to condemn the traditional architecture of his native Vienna, which depends so much on ornament. He was in love with Gothic St. Stephan's cathedral with its deeply moving interior, the "most solemn in the world," with Fischer von Erlach's Karlskirche, with the Palais Liechtenstein, this "most beautiful and monumental example of the Viennese Baroque."[25] Loos admired traditional ways of building, especially the way such building responded to its place and age. But the world has changed and, everything considered, much for the better. We moderns have learned that our deepest enjoyment comes from private pleasures and that we have to defend the border that separates the private and public realms. That goes for sex and that goes for art. Graffiti threaten that boundary by making public what those truly of the modern age would keep private; and so does ornament, which refuses to honor the difference between private art and public building.[26] Not that we should not continue to learn from the great architectural tradition and from its way with ornament: thus Loos likens classical ornament to grammar. Art instruction cannot afford to neglect it. "We owe to Latin grammar and further to every grammar the discipline of the soul, the discipline of our thinking. Classical ornament brings discipline to the forms we give to our utensils, disciplines us and our forms, brings, despite ethnographic and lingusitic differences, a commonality of forms and aesthetic concepts."[27] Loos calls the architect "a mason, who has learned Latin"[28]—Latin, not Greek! "It is no accident that the Romans were unable to invent a new columnar order, a new ornament. For this they were already too far advanced. All that they took from the Greeks and adapted for their purposes. The Greeks were individualists. Every building had to possess its own profile, its own ornamentation. The Roman thought in social terms. The Greeks hardly could administer their cities, the Romans administered the globe. The Greeks spent their power of invention on the columnar orders, the Romans on the floorplan."[29] We should take the Romans for our teachers, as did the architects Loos most admired, Fischer von Erlach and Schlüter in the eighteenth century, Schinkel in the beginning of the nineteenth.[30] Here we can learn the necessary aesthetic discipline. Not that this should lead to timid imitation, nor to buildings covered with ornament drawn from some other age and culture. "The modern human being, the human being with modern nerves, does not need ornament; quite the opposite, he detests it."[31]

But has ornament really become superfluous? That even in the modern world ornament may have a positive function is suggested by Loos's example of a woman who works a loom for eight hours in some noisy factory and is delighted and relieved when from time to time a colored thread appears and a pattern gradually emerges. "The colored thread makes possible the ornament," even as it helps to relieve the monotony of the work routine.[32] Ornament is here given its origin in an opening of the work world to aesthetic pleasure. And must we not, with Ruskin, demand such an opening? Think of the worker who finds bliss working in his *Schrebergarten*. In this sense modernity and ornament are quite compatible: "who of us moderns would consider the different constantly changing textile patterns not modern?"[33] But the designer of such ornament, if indeed it deserves to be called that, should not consider himself or herself an artist. Nor did Loos consider himself an architect, when, functioning as an interior decorator first of all responsive to the client's wishes, he helped to furnish an apartment, an office, or a café. That aesthetic sensibility should guide building is taken for granted, as it should be. What Loos calls into question is ornament that claims to be art: to waste art on objects of use betrays a lack of culture.[34] But he leaves no doubt about the contribution an aesthetically schooled eye can make to the design of better textile patterns, utensils, or buildings. However, the designer should not confuse her contribution with art; and the architect who builds a decent house to suit his client should resist the temptation to call himself an artist, a *Raumkünstler*.

Loos's attack on ornament is therefore quite compatible with his recognition of the fundamental importance of cladding, which, as suggested by Gottfried Semper's paradigm to which Loos is so evidently indebted[35]—the woven mat that from the very beginning invited pleasing patterns—may also have an aesthetic function: "The reasons for cladding things are numerous. At times it is a protection against bad weather—oil-base paint, for example, on wood, iron, or stone; at times there are hygienic reasons for it—as in the case of enameled tiles that cover the wall surfaces in the bathroom; at times it is the means to a specific effect—as in the color painting of statues, the tapestries on walls, the veneer on wood."[36] The order is telling: first the weather, then hygiene, and finally features intended to put us in a certain mood. If what is to be built is a prison, the architect may

want to arouse fear and horror; if a church, a sense of reverence; if an inn, a sense of gaiety;
if a house, a homey feeling.[37] A good architect will know how to provide what is wanted.
Loos's own use of marble might be cited as an example. But all this does not make him
an artist.

Could "cladding for the sake of aesthetic effects" not serve as a definition of ornament? But if so such "ornament," Loos insists, should keep its distance from the ornament
bearer. A tapestry hung on some wall plainly obeys what Loos calls the "law of cladding":
"we must work in such a way that a confusion of the material clad with its cladding is
impossible."[38] Ruled out are the false façades of so much turn-of-the-century architecture
mimicking Renaissance or Baroque palaces.

What matters to Loos here is not some abstract aesthetic principle, but the way
violation of the "law of cladding" so often implies dishonesty. Ornament is condemned by
Loos, because, like kitsch, like padded clothing, it lies, even as it addresses all-too-human
desires: "Whenever I stroll along the Ring, it always seems to me as if a modern Potemkin
had wanted to carry out his orders here, as if he had wanted to persuade someone that in
coming to Vienna he had been transported into a city of nothing but aristocrats"[39] (fig. 10).
Loos is quite aware of the widespread willingness to collude with such deception: "The
simple man, who had rented only one room and a w.c. on the uppermost floor, was overcome with a blissful feeling of feudal splendor and lordly grandeur whenever he looked at

the building he lived in from the outside. Does the owner of an imitation diamond not gaze fondly at the glittering glass? Oh, the tale of the deceiver deceived!"[40] One of those who delighted in such deception was Hitler, newly arrived in the Austrian capital: "From morning to late at night I ran from one object of interest to another, but it was always the buildings that held my primary interest. For hours I could stand in front of the Opera [fig. 11], for hours I could gaze at the Parliament; the whole Ring Boulevard seemed to me like an enchantment out of 'The Thousand-and-One Nights.'"[41] Compare the blissful feeling of Loos's simple man or the enchantment experienced by the young Hitler with the bliss of the worker in his *Schrebergarten*.

4

Loos links the love of ornament to an eroticism that should lie behind us, as incompatible with modern life—should, but never will, just as we will never be done with ornament. Loos admits, even as he deplores this concession to feminine "caprice and ambition," that "ornament in the service of woman will live forever. . . . The ornament of woman, however, resembles fundamentally that of the primitives; it has an erotic significance."[42] In ornament Loos thus locates the erotic origin of painting; here we have the baby talk of art.

The Problem of Decoration

39

Charles Moore, Piazza d'Italia, New Orleans.
12 | Photo by author.

Graffiti comment on the Piazza d'Italia in an adja-
13 | cent street, New Orleans. Photo by author.

The first ornament that was born, the cross, was erotic in origin. The first work of art, the first artistic act which the first artist, in order to rid himself of his surplus energy, smeared on the wall. A horizontal dash: the prone woman. A vertical dash: the man penetrating her. The man who created it felt the same urge as Beethoven, he was in the same heaven in which Beethoven created his Ninth Symphony.

But the man of our own day who, in repose to an inner urge, smears the walls with erotic symbols is a criminal or a degenerate. It goes without saying that this impulse most frequently assails people with such symptoms of degeneracy in the lavatory. A country's culture can be assessed by the extent to which its lavatory walls are smeared.[43] (figs. 12 and 13)

Loos finds modern ornament obscene. He longs for a cleaner, cooler environment. The naked wall becomes a symbol of the victory of logos over eros (fig. 14). The passion with which Loos pleads for that victory—and more than most Loos had been forced to recognize the power of eros—betrays a fear of the erotic: something dirty and irrational here asserts itself. Indeed, human sexuality strikes Loos not just as irrational but as unnatural, perverted,[44] resembling in this our culinary culture: "If man had remained a beast, then the love in his heart would have been aroused once a year. But our sensuality, which we can restrain only with great effort, makes us capable of love at any time. Around the prime of life we are betrayed by it. And our sensuality is not simple, but complicated, not natural, but against nature."[45]

14 | Adolf Loos, Steiner Haus, Vienna (1910). Credit: Foto Marburg/Art Resource, N.Y.

All too often women's dress caters to such base desires, invites us to betray our better selves: "Ladies' fashion! You disgraceful chapter in the history of civilization! You tell of mankind's secret desires. Whenever we peruse your pages, our souls shudder at the frightful aberrations and scandalous depravities. We hear the whimpering of abused children, the shrieks of maltreated wives, the dreadful outcries of tortured men, and the howls of those who have died at the stake. Whips crack, and the air takes on the burnt smell of scorched human flesh."[46] Oh happy England, which had begun to demonstrate that man and woman can be joined by a "platonic love," that "the woman may be no more than a good friend to the man," a possibility that has found its visual expression in unisex clothing, in the "tailor-made costume, clothes made by a man's tailor."[47] The concession that "will be made to the twentieth-century female bicyclist to wear pants and clothing that leave her feet free" is celebrated as the "first step toward the social sanctioning of women's work."[48] Eros should not be permitted to subvert our work-oriented modern culture.

Of special interest is the claim that the first ornament was also the first work of art. Garnier's equation of ornament with both dressing oneself and with high art comes to mind. Garnier gladly embraced that anarchic quality of ornament Loos found so threatening: "Regarding decoration as such, and regarding what ordering and style to adopt, there is no guide other than the inspiration and will of the one who is doing the building; the decorative art has such independence and freedom that it is impossible to submit it to fixed rules."[49] Loos understood such license as a regression to the child's libidinous relation to itself and to the world, in which every empty surface is experienced as an invitation to cover it with spontaneous decoration. But cultural progress demands that the child's polymorphous sexuality be focused, privatized, turned inward. It demands repression: sex belongs in the bedroom. The shape of our culture lets Loos condemn as a crime or a sign of degeneracy what is permitted to the child and to those who have been left behind by the progress of the modern world.

We have already seen that Loos was not insensitive to the positive significance that ornament once had and continued to have for many people. He recognized the public function of conspicuous consumption, so closely tied to the use of ornament to express status or to allow "men from whom others want to withhold a recently acquired right" to assert a threatened sense of self-worth.[50] Loos knew that our enjoyment of ornament is inseparable from our appreciation of it as excess, from its apparent superfluity, although talk of superfluity here is misleading. The creation of ornament, too, responds to a profound need; it answers a dissatisfaction with a reality that all too often denies what we most deeply desire, a dissatisfaction with a world shadowed by disease and poverty, by hunger and death. Ornament helps make the ornamented appear more responsive to our need; the transformation makes it easier for us to bear the burdens of life. Loos's simple man thus loves his apartment house's false façade.

Loos leaves that pleasure to the simple; but nevertheless he looks forward to a world that would no longer need such help. Does it not deflect us from what really needs to be done? Good plumbing is more important than a neo-Baroque façade. Instead of covering up a deficient social reality, we should confront such deficiency and attempt to correct it. Science and technology have rendered us masters of nature in a way that makes it ever less necessary to simply accept what she withholds—not that such mastery can give meaning to life. The need for experiences that justify themselves remains and here, for Loos, the active enjoyment of nature deserves first mention. And has not technological progress freed more and more time for the pursuit of just those activities that make life truly worth living? To be sure, there has been a price: the efficient organization of work has to bring with it a certain self-alienation. But has the gain, so evident in our high standard of living, not justified the cost? Two world wars later and faced with increasing ecological problems, we find it more difficult to answer with an unambiguous "yes."

5

Loos's understanding of cultural evolution as tied to economic progress is certainly not the only nor indeed even the original basis for his case against ornament. His "first battle cry against ornament" was uttered not in the name of utility but in the name of beauty: "To seek beauty only in form and not in ornament is the goal toward which all humanity is striving."[51] We moderns no longer need ornament, because we have something better:

We have art, which has taken the place of ornament. After the toils and troubles of the day we go to Beethoven or to Tristan. This my shoemaker cannot do. I mustn't deprive him of his joy, since I have nothing else to put in its place. But anyone who goes to the Ninth Symphony *and then sits down and designs a wallpaper pattern is either a confidence trickster or a degenerate. Absence of ornament has brought the other arts to unsuspected heights. Beethoven's symphonies would never have been written by a man who had to walk about in silk, satin, and lace. Anyone who goes around in a velvet coat today is not an artist but a buffoon or a house painter. We have grown finer, more subtle. The nomadic herdsmen had to distinguish themselves by various colors; modern man uses his clothes as a mask. So immensely strong is his individuality that it can no longer be expressed in articles of clothing. Freedom from ornament is a sign of spiritual strength.*[52]

The death of ornament is a presupposition of the evolution of an art of an intensity, purity, and often almost hermetic privacy unknown up to this point, an art that has sublimated and thus rendered harmless the extroverted eroticism that disturbed Loos when he looked at graffiti-smeared bathroom walls.

Despite the expected hyperboles, and despite the fact that today a primitive eroticism has reclaimed a good part of art, only to have been embraced in turn by an entertainment industry eager to turn dissatisfaction with the modern world into profit, Loos's main claims deserve to be taken seriously. The shape of the modern world has indeed to a considerable extent been determined by its rationalization of the work sphere. Such rationalization demands the exclusion of everything that does not obey the economic imperative. A consequence is that divorce of utility and beauty, business and art, which insists that "business is business," thus at the same time welcomes those who would pursue "art for art's sake"; what it questions is only the confusion of the two spheres. Ornament is rejected precisely insofar as it represents just such a confusion. In this sense the modern rationalization of the "business" of life demands the death of ornament and accordingly of an architecture of decorated sheds. It does not demand, however, the death of art. Quite the contrary: by insisting on the divorce of utility and beauty it frees art to be truly itself. Ornament gives way to art, an increasingly private art that keeps its distance from ordinary life and becomes truly autonomous. Just such a separation is demanded also by the aesthetic approach, which thus answers to the organization of work demanded by modern life.

The aesthetic approach demands the self-sufficiency of the aesthetic object. From this follows the death of ornament, for by its very nature ornament should serve the ornament bearer. Already in Kant's *Critique of Judgment* we find hints of this death: the same considerations that led Kant to assert the autonomy of the aesthetic sphere force him to question the role of ornament in architecture, especially in church architecture.[53] Kant shares the Enlightenment's inability to accept the profusely ornamented churches of the Rococo, an inability that led to decrees actually forbidding such use of ornament.[54] The Enlightenment's conception of a church had to find this ornament not only inessential but altogether out of place. A purified religion no longer has any use for the aesthetic, just as the pure art demanded by the aesthetic approach refuses to serve religion.

Kant knew that on his aesthetic understanding of beauty, a completely pure art is an impossibility. Demands for a work of art that no longer means, but just captivates us as a beautiful presence, conflict with its art character. For what is art? As Kant insists, the production of art is activity governed by the will, but the will requires reasons. The artist creates having something in mind; his or her creating is governed by an intention. Works of art cannot help but mean. Truly free beauties are encountered only in nature. The dream of an artwork that would not mean, but just be, must remain a dream; even the most abstract work of art presents itself to us as a more or less successful realization of some purpose or intention. Just to look at a work of art as art is to presuppose such an intention. To the extent that the aesthetic approach governs art, its development will tend toward an ideal of presence denied to art by its own art character. Clement Greenberg's claim that what confers presence is "the look of non-art" belongs with Kant's claim that art should look as if it were a product of nature.[55] But what would be examples of such art on the threshold of leaving art behind?

The only examples Kant has to offer are ornament and music: "Delineations *à la grecque,* foliage for borders or wall papers, mean nothing in themselves; they represent nothing—no object under a definite concept—and are free beauties. We can refer to the same class what are called in music phantasies (i.e. pieces without any theme), and in fact all music without words."[56] But are these indeed free beauties? "Delineations *à la grecque*" follow a certain manner, are bound to a certain model; and this model gives our judgment a certain measure that would seem to allow us to call one design more successful than another. But if so, we no longer are dealing with free beauty. Similarly, when judging "foliage for borders or wall papers" we are bound by quite specific expectations. The former makes reference to more or less familiar leaves and borders, and wallpaper has an ornamental—and that means also a serving—function. That music is similarly bound requires no comment.

It is indeed surprising that Kant should have named "delineations *à la grecque,* foliage for borders or wall papers" as his first examples of artificial free beauties. Is not ornament much more clearly a dependent art form than painting or sculpture? But in Kant's day the latter were tied to representation in a way that precluded the pursuit of free beauty. Ornament, on the other hand, while in one sense obviously meant to serve the ornament bearer, did not have to be representational and could be appreciated as an autonomous aesthetic object. Such appreciation is presupposed by Kant's use of it as an example of free beauty. The architectural function of ornament is here bracketed, and ornament is understood as an abstract art *sui generis*. It casts off its servitude and becomes absolute. But thus become absolute, ornament ceases to function as such: it dies as ornament only to be reborn as art for art's sake.

In the refusal of representation and in the transformation of ornament into an independent aesthetic object, we have the twin roots of modern abstract art. A look at the development of art in the years preceding World War I, especially in fin de siècle Vienna, supports this suggestion. Consider, for example, the work of Gustav Klimt. Representation is challenged by the ornamental treatment of the painting: we see colored rectangles, triangles, circles, and spirals; set into these carpetlike surfaces are faces, hands, and bodies modeled with great care, alive and beckoning yet also intimidating and threatening in a way that recalls Loos's remark about the origin of painting in erotic ornament. Related to this are attempts by artists like Kandinsky, Obrist, Behrens, and Endell (figs. 15 and 16). Endell called for an art "with forms that signify nothing, represent nothing, and recall nothing, but will be able to excite our souls as deeply as only music has been able to do with tones."[57]

August Endell, Haus Elvira, Munich (1896).

15 | Credit: Foto Marburg/Art Resource, N.Y.

August Endell, Haus Elvira, staircase, Munich
(1896). Credit: Foto Marburg/Art Resource,

N.Y.

The appeal to the musical paradigm, often supported with the authority of Schopenhauer, is inseparable from that turn to abstraction demanded by the aesthetic approach. Recall that Kant already had placed musical fantasies beside ornament as an example of an artificial free beauty. Endell similarly remarks, "We have now as yet very few works of pure form-art, i.e., formal images that are nothing and mean nothing, that affect us directly without the mediation of the intellect, like the tones, of music," and he calls on other artists to realize these formal images: a nonrepresentational art.[58] The relation between ornament becoming absolute and the turn to abstraction is strikingly documented in the work of the Munich painter Adolf Hoelzel, who before the turn of the century had begun to experiment with abstract forms, which he called, tellingly, "Abstract Ornaments."[59] Just as Loos would banish ornament from architecture, so here it asserts its autonomy and dies as ornament.

The development just sketched raises an obvious question. I referred to Kant to show that the aesthetic approach demands either the death of ornament or its transformation into an autonomous abstract art. But *The Critique of Judgment* dates from the last decade of the eighteenth century, the art I just discussed from the years just preceding World War I. How are we to understand this time lag? Why did the revolution that issued in the birth of modern abstract art, a revolution already implicit in what Kant has to say about "free beauty," have to wait a hundred years to become reality?

But is the assumption behind this question altogether correct? The revolution of modern art and architecture at the beginning of the twentieth century is prefigured by the development of art in the second half of the eighteenth century. If Loos wanted to banish ornament from architecture, he had predecessors among the architects of revolutionary France. Emil Kaufmann can thus discuss Ledoux as the first modern architect.[60] And when Kant discusses ornament as if it were an autonomous aesthetic object, his discussion not only points forward to modern art's turn to abstraction but also mirrors the development of ornament in the eighteenth century.[61]

6

Loos linked the replacement of ornament with "art for art's sake" to the progressive introversion that characterizes modernity. If he is right, then, like clothing, housing today has lost much of its former social function: those truly of the twentieth century no longer dress or build to represent themselves and their place in society to the world. Just as the modern person's inner life is too private and too rich to welcome public representation, so the interior of a modern house constitutes a private realm that protects its privacy behind a simple, unobtrusive exterior. Loos's "twentieth-century man" no longer wants that public representation which was a presupposition of the way past cultures dressed and built.

But has architecture really lost its social function? Loos knew very well that his twentieth-century man is an idealization, that his suggestion that we moderns dress and build less to represent our place in society than to hide ourselves is contradicted by the world we actually live in. Architects and fashion designers would not be flourishing as they are if Loos had been right. Extravagant dress or building, no more than elaborate cooking, have not come to an end. Against Loos we may thus want to insist that his narrow understanding of what constitutes modernity is so much at odds with our much richer humanity that it never could furnish more than an illuminating caricature. Loos might have replied that just as modern attempts to give new life to ornament do not refute his claim that ornament has died, so today's extravagantly decorated sheds do not demonstrate that architecture in its traditional sense remains very much alive. We might counter by pointing to art nouveau: did it not produce a strong ornament? Here is Loos's reply:

Since ornament is no longer organically linked with our culture, it is also no longer an expression of our culture. The ornament that is manufactured today has no connexion with us, has absolutely no human connexions, no connexion with the world order. It is not capable of developing. What happened to Otto Eckmann's ornament, or van de Velde's [fig. 17]? The artist has always stood at the forefront of mankind full of vigour and health. But the modern ornamentalist is a straggler or pathological phenomenon. He himself will repudiate his own products three years later. To cultivated people they are immediately intolerable; others become aware of their intolerable character only years later. Where are Otto Eckmann's works today? Modern ornament has no parents and no progeny, no past and no future. By uncultivated people, to whom the grandeur of the age is a book with seven seals, it is greeted joyfully and shortly afterwards repudiated.[62]

Two kinds of ornament are here distinguished. In one a whole culture finds its expression;[63] the other is the creation of an isolated individual. One is part of an ongoing history, the other has neither past nor future; one has a social function, the other is experienced only as an aesthetic presence; one even today communicates traces of the vigor of its past life, the other arrives stillborn. Loos was by no means the only one to draw such a distinction. And since I, too, want to make use of it in the following discussion, it seems helpful to make a terminological distinction. Up to this point I have used "decoration" and "ornament" more or less as synonyms. From now on I shall call decoration that articulates a communal ethos *ornament* and decoration that we experience primarily as an aesthetic addition to building *decoration*.[64] So understood, *decoration is the aesthetic analogue to ornament.* What is at stake in drawing this distinction should become clearer in the next chapter.

17 | Henry van de Velde, interior of sale room of the Havana Company, Mohrenstrasse 11/12, Berlin (1899). Credit: Foto Marburg/Art Resource, N.Y.

The Promise of Ornament

4

1

We have seen how the aesthetic approach leads quite naturally to an understanding of the work of architecture as essentially a decorated shed. To develop some of the implications of the approach I turned to Ruskin, who understands architecture first of all as an art of decoration. But so understood it is essentially at odds with the "prevalent feeling of modern times, which desires to produce the largest results at the least cost":[1] to the extent that modernity is ruled by this economic imperative, it will have little patience with decoration and therefore with architecture. That Ruskin nonetheless insists on both demonstrates a refusal to let the kind of instrumental thinking that would maximize efficiency and productivity determine the whole of life. His love of architecture presupposes an only half-hearted modernism: unwilling to renounce the high standard of living such thinking has brought and therefore committed to keeping the earnest business of work free of considerations that have nothing to do with its ends, Ruskin yet knows that if we were to allow the economic imperative to embrace the whole of life, human being, too, would be reduced to just another resource, material for the process of production. His "yes" and "no" to instrumental thinking finds expression in the sharply drawn distinction between work time and leisure time, which mirrors itself in the distinction between utility and beauty, between functional shed and added decoration. To the extent that modernity is ruled by the economic imperative, it fails to do justice to the whole human being. And just because of this failure, it needs architecture.

A more resolute modernist, Loos had little patience with the eclectic decoration so well liked by the late nineteenth century. And yet, even in "Ornament and Crime," misgivings resembling Ruskin's announce themselves. It is with these that I would like to begin this chapter.

As we saw in the previous chapter, Loos knows as well as Ruskin that work may not be allowed to take up all of our time, that we need hours when we leave behind the everyday world to which we usually have already lost ourselves and come home to ourselves, that indeed only such hours can give meaning to life. Loos, too, thinks here primarily of the active enjoyment of nature and of aesthetic experience, which is defined by its distance from the work-dominated reality that first of all and most of the time keeps us engaged. He, too, takes the shape of the modern world to be such that genuine humanity has to find satisfaction not by transforming but by taking its leave from it, as by retreating from reality into art: "After the toils and troubles of the day we go to Beethoven or to Tristan."[2] Of art Loos demands more than decorated sheds can offer; their very nature denies them the purity required of genuine art. Given his understanding of art, it is to be expected that Loos, too, should turn to music for his paradigm. By its abstract purity the other arts are judged. Architecture could measure up to what is here demanded only if it were to leave behind the world ruled by our need for creature comforts (and so by economic considerations). Unlike Ruskin, Loos therefore resolutely excludes the house from art: "The work of art is a private concern of the artist. Not so the house. The work of art is placed into the world, although there is no need for it. The house satisfies a need. The work of art is responsible to no one, the house to everyone. The work of art wants to tear human beings out of their comfortable adjustment to the world. The house should serve to make us comfortable. The work of art is revolutionary, the house conservative. The work of art points out to humanity new paths and thinks of the future. The house thinks of the present."[3] This remark from "Architecture," also dating from 1910, forces us to question either our use of Loos as a representative of the aesthetic approach or our understanding of that approach. Notwithstanding his privatization of art, Loos, in a way that anticipates the romantic Marxism of a thinker like Ernst Bloch,[4] most definitely assigns art here an ethical, indeed a political function, even as he insists that the artist is responsible only to himself. Art gains this function as a foil to everyday reality, as the utopian other of the modern metropolis. Pointing to a realm closed to us by the world we have to live in, it makes us uncomfortable with that world, letting us dream of a new world, of radical negation, of revolution.[5] Decoration betrays this revolutionary potential of art by mediating between art and the everyday, by accommodating itself all too readily to the public, to the established and accepted. Unlike genuine art, it means to make us more comfortable, not less so.

Consider once more the presupposition of the aesthetic approach: why so sharp a separation between work and leisure, between times when the business of life fully occupies us and others that leave us free to surrender ourselves to art? Loos may well be right with his suggestion that only the rationalization of work freed art to be truly itself. But do we really work just to have time to listen to Beethoven or to forget the dreary routines of the workday absorbed in the glory of Titian? Loos has indeed a sublime conception of art: if we are to allow what he considers genuine art to take possession of us, we must take our leave not just from work but from the everyday, with all its joys and sorrows, accomplishments and missed opportunities. We sense Schopenhauer's dark shadow. Does this insistence that, for the sake of art, we take our leave from all that is usually considered life, not presuppose a deep and profoundly questionable dissatisfaction—a dissatisfaction not just with a reality distorted by the economic imperative, with the modern metropolis, but with the larger reality, with life? It is hardly surprising that the monument, especially the grave monument, should appear to Loos as the only remaining genuinely architectural task. This conclusion invites a second look at the considerations that led to it.

Just what Loos has to tell us about what ornament once meant and still means to so many people forces us to question the presuppositions of his own condemnation of it. Recall the weaver who delights in a colored thread that breaks the monotony of her work.

Despite his evangelical zeal, Loos recognizes that among his contemporaries remain many who are not yet ready for his stern modernism. Nor does he appear particularly eager to reform them. They should be left their ornament; it would be cruel to deprive them of something in which they find significance.

I am preaching to the aristocrat, I mean the person who stands at the pinnacle of mankind and yet has the deepest understanding of the distress and want of those below. He well understands the Kaffir who weaves ornaments into his fabric according to a particular rhythm that only comes into view when it is unravelled, the Persian who weaves his carpet, the Slovak peasant woman who embroiders her lace, the old lady who crochets wonderful things with glass beads and silk. The aristocrat lets them be; he knows that the hours in which they work are their holy hours. The revolutionary would go to them and say: "It's all nonsense." Just as he would pull down the little old woman from the wayside crucifix and tell her: "There is no God." The atheist among the aristocrats, on the other hand, raises his hat when he passes a church.[6]

Does the gentleness of this aristocratic modernist, his deference to Kaffirs, Persians, and women, betray a certain self-doubt? Nostalgia colors Loos's account of "those below," especially when he says of them that "the hours in which they work are their holy hours."[7] Not yet has work here been split off from the sacred. This suggests that genuine ornament, as opposed to mere decoration, presupposes an understanding of time very different from the one that rules our lives: a premodern understanding. Ornament, here associated with non-Europeans and women, figures an integrated mode of life that had to be sacrificed to the economic imperative now ruling the modern world. This sacrifice may have emancipated a purely aesthetic interest and thus freed art to be truly itself, but such liberation seems inadequate compensation for the self-fragmentation that now comes to be part of life. Together with the *holy* we have lost the *whole:* the modern metropolis presupposes this loss. But while Loos accepts it, without hope or even desire to build a new cathedral, his reference to the holy hints at how much had to be surrendered for humanity to come of age.[8]

2

Today, when modernity and modernism are coming under increasingly critical scrutiny, it is easy to sympathize with those of Loos's contemporaries who, saddened by their culture's inability to produce once more a living ornament, hung their heads and looked back nostalgically to the Middle Ages or perhaps just to the age of Maria Theresia, which, although on the threshold of modernity, found convincing expression in a lavishly ornamental style. Among those was the Viennese novelist Hermann Broch. Writing some twenty years after Loos, Broch was no less critical of the decorated sheds of the turn of the century. Their decadence seemed to him the signature of a decadent age: "It was the age of eclecticism, of the false Baroque, the false Renaissance, the false Gothic. Wherever Western man then determined the style of life, it turned to bourgeois confinement, and, at the same time, to bourgeois pomp, to a solidity that meant stuffiness as well as security. If ever poverty was covered up with wealth, it happened here"[9] (fig. 18).

Perhaps the frightfulness of this age is most palpable in experiences of architecture: when I have walked through the streets I bring home a horrible fatigue. I don't even have to look at the façades of the houses; they make me uneasy, even if I don't raise my eyes to look at them. Sometimes I seek refuge with the new buildings that are being praised so much, but—surely this is unjust—the department store by Messel, who surely was a great architect, seems comical to me in its Gothic dress, and this comedy annoys and tires. It tires me so much that I hardly am able to find rest with classicistic buildings. And yet I love the large-scaled clarity of Schinkel's architecture.[10]

Such scorn for nineteenth-century eclecticism characterizes the cultural situation that allowed architectural modernism to triumph: finally the modern age was to find the architectural style it deserved, instead of slavishly borrowing from the past. Here the lowly craftsman, the tailor, the shoemaker, the plumber, and, even more, the factories and other utilitarian structures could point the way. Did they not demonstrate a living modern style that architects too burdened by the ornamental styles of the past failed to recognize? Was it not here that the creation of a truly modern architectural style, a style defined by its resistance to ornament, had to begin?[11] Thus the Bauhaus promised to heal the breach that had opened up between beauty and reason, art and technology, freedom and necessity.

We have awakened from that dream; it has begun to scare us. Instead of having helped make possible a more humane dwelling, in retrospect it seems to have tended to the opposite direction. The Viennese painter Hundertwasser gave early expression to what today has become an often-repeated charge against functional modern architecture:

*The material uninhabitability of the slums is preferable to the moral uninhabitability of functional, utili-
tarian architecture. In the so-called slums only man's body can perish, but in the architecture ostensibly
built for man his soul perishes. Hence the principle of the slums, i.e. wildly proliferating architecture,
must be improved and taken as our point of departure, not functional architecture. . . .*

*The constructive functional architects' irresponsible mania for destruction is well known. They
wanted to simply tear down the beautiful stucco-fronted houses of the nineties and* Art Nouveau *and
put their own vacuous buildings in their place. I will cite Le Corbusier who wanted to raze Paris to the
ground and replace it with rectilinear monster constructions. To be fair, we ought now to pull down the
buildings of Mies van der Rohe, Neutra, the Bauhaus, Gropius, Johnson, Le Corbusier, and so on,
since in one generation they have become outmoded and morally unendurable.*[12]

Like Hundertwasser, many of us have learned to see with different, more loving eyes an
architecture that our fathers, or perhaps by now our grandfathers, found unbearable, the
same architecture off which Broch read the character of bourgeois decadence. What was
then experienced as a lie speaks to us of a humanity we have lost and would gladly recover.
To many today Loos, who acknowledged the insuperable rift between beauty and utility,
seems to have been closer to the mark than Gropius, who thought that modern architecture
could bridge it; Ruskin, who recognized that rift yet left wide room for an architecture of
decorated sheds, likewise seems closer to the mark than the Loos who would leave an
architecture that took itself seriously as an art only of sepulchre and monument. Few today
have difficulty appreciating the nineteenth century's decorated sheds.

While not sharing such appreciation, Georg Lukács offers us an interpretation of
the failure of modernism's passionate critique of nineteenth-century eclecticism:

*As justified as every critique of architecture since about the middle of the nineteenth century may have
been, it was unable to penetrate to the core, to the decay of its social mission as a result of the distortion
of human existence by capitalism. The fact alone that the point of departure of this casting out of historicizing eclecticism remained a "pure" capitalism that no longer had to look for support in the precapitalist
past made this impossible. To be sure, very different motives helped form the separate strands of the
new architecture. But what remains decisive is that given the dissolution of architecture's social mission,
modernism, just as much as the commercial-ostentatious academicism it so despised—if with other reasons—had to refuse or circumvent architecture's fundamental task: to create a space for human beings by
transforming the constructive possibilities of building into visuality.*[13]

We may not agree with Lukács's Marxist interpretation of the failure of architectural modernism—I shall have to return to it; but few today would dispute the failure to meet architecture's fundamental task. Here I would like to focus on the way Lukács couples his critique
of both nineteenth-century and modern architecture with a suggestion that we look for
support to the architecture produced by precapitalist societies: for example, to the architecture of the Middle Ages. Not that we should attempt to return to what lies irrecoverably
behind us. Yet the contrast between the harmonious appearance of a medieval city and the
fragmented look of its modern counterpart invites critical reflection.

Lukács's response to modernism is quite characteristic of what we can call modernism's bad conscience.[14] From the very beginning, modernism has been shadowed by a nostalgic longing for a kind of integration and organic community denied to it by its own achievements. Broch is an especially articulate exponent of such modernist self-doubt. Like Loos and Lukács, he understands the nineteenth century's decorated sheds as a manifestation of decadence. But much more decisively than either he celebrates traditional architecture and its ornament and hopes for their recovery. This brings us back to the distinction between decoration and ornament.

Once more let me return to Broch's attempt to read off the stuccoed façades of the late nineteenth century the essence of this epoch. Take apartment houses of the time: more likely than not their appearance would be determined by the sharp contrast between a practical architecture and superfluous decoration. This contrast offered itself to Broch as a mirror of the equally sharp contrast, by now already familiar, between a rationalism that demanded "a sober and clear, unvarnished and realistic observation of the world" and an aestheticism that, for the sake of enjoyment, closed its eyes to the cruelty of the world and was able to enjoy even the terrible aesthetically.[15] This determination of the age lets one think once more of Schopenhauer, who, as Lukács remarks, anticipates many tendencies that later were to become general and is the first thinker of note to "proclaim a decidedly bourgeois-reactionary *Weltanschauung*."[16] Already in Schopenhauer's *World as Will and Representation* an often astonishingly sober, almost positivistic attention to the facts meets with an aesthetic-mystical flight from reality. Much more clearly than with Kant, aesthetic enjoyment here means an escape from the world. Nietzsche's epigram, "We possess *art* lest we *perish of the truth*,"[17] captures the spirit of the age of the decorated shed. Rationalism and aestheticism belong together and, if Broch is right, "in all aestheticism, in all decoration, even the most harmless, slumbers cynicism—it, too, a product of rationalist thinking— slumbers skepticism, which knows, or at least suspects, that what is being played here is a "game of transfiguration.'"[18] The decoration of the modern age is said to mirror the decadence that determines its essence.

A number of times I have spoken of "decadence." But what is it? Lukács gives us a helpful hint when he remarks that in matters of decadence Nietzsche, this self-proclaimed decadent, is the unsurpassed expert.[19] What then does Nietzsche have to say?

What is the sign of every literary decadence? That life no longer dwells in the whole. The word becomes sovereign and leaps out of the sentence, the sentence reaches out and obscures the meaning of the page, the page gains life at the expense of the whole. But this is the simile of every style of decadence: every time, the anarchy of atoms, disgregation of the will, "freedom of the individual," to use moral terms—expanded into a political theory, "equal rights for all." Life, equal vitality, the vibration and exuberance of life pushed into the smallest forms; the rest poor in life. Everywhere paralysis, arduousness, torpidity or hostility and chaos: both more and more obvious the higher one ascends in forms of organization. The whole no longer lives at all: it is composite, calculated, artificial, and artifact.[20]

The eclectic decoration of the nineteenth century is decadent in this sense: an aesthetic object added onto a building that could survive quite well without this addition. But so is

Michael Graves, Hotel Swan, Orlando, Florida.

19 | Detail. Photo by author.

much of the decoration produced by today's postmodernism, which too often reminds one of easily peeled-off decals (fig. 19). As an aesthetically pleasing veneer such decoration may draw our attention, without standing in any necessary relationship to the architectonic whole, as if glued to some box. But should we not insist on such a relationship? Is it not just this that distinguishes decoration from genuine ornament? This, at any rate, is how Broch would have us draw the distinction:

> *To consider ornament a mere accessory is not to have understood the inner logic of a building. "Architectural style" is logic, a logic that permeates the entire building, from its ground plan to the outline it traces against the sky, and within that logic ornament is only the last, differential expression for the unified and unifying fundamental thought of the whole. Whether we are dealing here with an inability to create ornament, or an unwillingness, does not matter, but means the same: it means nothing other than that the architectonic form of expression of this age is separated by a gulf from all earlier styles.*[21]

The spirit that animates ornament is said to be the very same spirit that animates the architectural whole.

One architect who out of an understanding of the "inner logic of a building" was able to create what deserves to be called a modern ornament was Louis Kahn (fig. 20). Although he is said to have avoided ornament, in his Yale Art Gallery Kahn teaches us that ornament can still be a concentrated expression or re-presentation of the idea that governs the structure it serves—the triangle ringed by light, which crowns the stairwell's concrete silo, presents itself to us as the abbreviated signature of that building's idea: the penetration of horizontal, tetrahedral slabs by the stairwell's cylindrical shaft. The symbol of the triangle within the circle is of course familiar: in Christian art and architecture it often appears as a

symbol of the Trinity. I do not want to claim that Kahn was drawing on this tradition; however, by re-presenting that symbol in this context, Kahn demonstrates that the symbol's power is not extinguished even when it is no longer supported by the particular textual tradition that once gave it a readily understood public significance.

Some visitors to the Yale Art Gallery may remember that Kahn's development of the tetrahedral slab owed much to Anne Tyng. Ever since I learned that Kahn was the father of her daughter Alexandra, born in 1954, I have found it difficult not to think that, associated as it must have been in his mind with Anne Tyng, the tetrahedral slab carried a very personal significance for Kahn. This would then also hold for the triangle within the circle. But if so, the stairwell succeeds in transforming this personal symbol into an *archē*-symbol that speaks to all of us. Perhaps such metamorphosis provides us with a key to the creation of all great art.

Owen Jones already in 1856 calls ornament "the very soul of an architectural monument": "The very instant that ornament is attempted, we see how far the architect is at the ame time the artist. It is the best measure of the care and refinement bestowed upon the work. To put ornament in the right place is not easy; to render that ornament at the same time a superadded beauty and an expression of the intention of the whole work, is still more difficult."[22] Owen criticizes his age for failing to understand "the grammar of ornament," for substituting for ornament that would give concentrated expression to the soul animating the architectural whole a thoughtless amalgam of decorative motifs drawn from the architecture of the past, without an understanding either of the spirit that gave birth to it or of the spirit of the modern age.[23] The "Exhibition of Works of Industry of All Nations" in 1851 proved to Owen that Europe had lost the ornamental skill still so evident in work produced by other countries, especially in the Mohammedan world.

Whilst in the works contributed by the various nations of Europe there was everywhere to be observed an entire absence of any common principle in the application of Art to manufactures,—whilst from one end to the other of the vast structure there could be found but a fruitless struggle after novelty, irrespective of fitness, that all design was based on a system of copying and misapplying the received forms of beauty of every bygone style of Art, without one single attempt to produce an Art in harmony with our present wants and means of production—the carver in stone, the worker in metal, the weaver and the painter, borrowing from each other and alternately misapplying the forms peculiarly appropriate to each—there were to be found in isolated collections at the four corners of the transepts all the principles, all the unity, all the truth, for which we had looked elsewhere in vain, and this because we were amongst a people practicing an art which had grown up with their civilization, and strengthened with their growth.[24]

Owen Jones's statement of the "grammar" said to rule all genuine ornament is quite in keeping with what Tzonis and Lefaivre claim for the ornament of classical architecture:

It should by now be clear that the moldings—the cymatia, the bead, the fillet, the scotia, and the cavetto—or so-called ornaments of the classical genera, are not in the least "ornamental" or "decorative" in the sense of a frivolous adjunct of an almost superfluous elaboration. They are part of the essential structure of the classical system, vital to its poetics of order. Although the moldings affect small-scale aspects of the composition, their impact is major. They can blur distinctions and clarify them. They make terminations visible and they can sharply demarcate them. The ornament in classical architecture should not be . . . mistaken for the embellishing frills that designers increasingly applied during the nineteenth century for purposes of conspicuous consumption. The ornaments, in the sense referred to here, can make or break the coherence of a classical composition.[25]

This understanding of ornament as an expression of the soul of a work of architecture or as vital to its poetic order fails to do justice, however, to what Broch has in mind, in that it suggests that the whole to which ornament gives expression is adequately understood as a particular building—although Owen Jones, as we have seen, suggests a link between the creation of ornament and the creator's membership in an ongoing community. Broch similarly links ornament to an integrated way of life, which finds expression in a historical style. Think of Gothic or Baroque. The significance of such styles is said by him to extend far beyond architecture: "For style is surely not something whose significance is limited to building or to the fine arts. Style is something that permeates all the different ways in which an epoch expresses itself in the same way. It would make no sense to consider the artist the exception: someone who leads a kind of special existence within the style and produces it, while the others remain excluded.—No, if there is style, then all expressions of life are permeated by it, then the style of an epoch is present just as much in its thinking as in every action."[26] Questionable as Broch's understanding of style is, and I shall have to return to it, it helps us understand why he places such significance on ornament. Somewhat in the way graphologists attempt to read in the seemingly decorative flourishes of a person's handwriting his entire character, Broch attempts to read in the architectural style of a particular period and region an integrated way of being in the world. The unity of the great historical styles makes visible the unity of a shared way of life, of a shared ethos. Style has an ethical function; and so then does ornament, which Broch calls "the formula of a style" (fig. 21). As such it is also "the formula of an epoch and its life."[27] Style thus provides Broch

21 | Zwiefalten, stucco of southern transept. Credit: Hirmer Fotoarchiv.

with the middle term that allows him to understand ornament as the expression of a coherent, communal world.

It is this that gives to ornament what Broch calls its "magical importance."[28] Off an architecture that has substituted decoration for ornament we can read the disintegration of a unified way of life. The death of ornament means not just the falling apart of architecture into aesthetically self-sufficient decoration and functional shed. Such a split figures our world's disintegration, of which the divorce of utility and beauty is just one aspect. By the same token, all genuine ornament carries the promise of an integrated way of life, a promise of full humanity and thus also of genuine community.

Broch was by no means the only one to connect with ornament the promise of a more humane mode of existence. The conservative art historian Hans Sedlmayr offers us a very similar evaluation of ornament in his once influential *Verlust der Mitte* (*Art in Crisis*). Like Loos, Sedlmayr claims that the nineteenth and twentieth centuries were incapable of a new living ornament. The death of rocaille, the defining ornament of the Rococo, means also the death of ornament. And the immediate cause of this death Sedlmayr, too, locates in what I have called the rise of the aesthetic approach: in the striving for aesthetic purity. *"Ornament is the only artistic genre that cannot exist 'autonomously.' "*[29] He continues, "The attempts to give new life to old styles in architecture have given no genuine new life to the ornaments belonging to them. Just in ornament the lifelessness of these renewals shows itself. The age has lost its knowledge of the fact that an ornament can possess *depth,* not in the spatial sense, and can express spiritual relations, a distinctive contact between human beings and things."[30] Broch gestures in the same direction when he calls ornament, in opposition to mere decoration, "the formula of an epoch and its life." Very much like Broch, Sedlmayr laments the inhumanity of an architecture that has banished ornament and interprets its death in the eighteenth century as a symptom of a culture whose center will not hold: Sedlmayr locates that center in the human being who has preserved his or her divine measure.

We meet with essentially the same lament among Marxists. I have already cited Lukács. Here is what Ernst Bloch has to say about the Bauhaus's attempt to rid architecture of ornament:

Every genuine artist loves ornament, even if genuine ornament does not as yet return such love to an epoch stunted by mechanization and kitsch. Architecture's purification of the atrocities of the nineteenth century is being presupposed, this indeed is conditio sine qua non; *but beyond this purification stands a task of world expression that continues rather than destroys the plenitude of what has been relegated to a dead past. A vehement will to color, form, and ornament pervades the world that has been liberated from mechanization, even if as yet that will has by no means been blessed and has not liberated itself from its dependence on and derivation from what was itself dependent and derivative. This will proves that the light that shone throughout history, until the invasion of machine-produced goods, that still fills all our museums, did not go out with the Bauhaus and similarly empty exultation.*[31]

Bloch thus takes the decorated sheds of the turn of the century to have been more filled with light—even if this was only a borrowed light—than the lean architecture once so noisily celebrated by convinced modernists. To be sure, Bloch, too, grants the need to rid architecture of what he himself calls the atrocities of the nineteenth century. He does not deny the legitimacy of the modernist critique of the decorated shed. But this critique loses much of its conviction when coupled with Bloch's indictment of modernism for its more profound failure of not addressing what Sigfried Giedion called the main task facing contemporary architecture: "the interpretation of a way of life valid for our period." Bloch links such interpretation to the creation of living ornament.

Indebted to Bloch, the architect Michael Müller asks similarly:

Looking back, must we understand ornament as the aesthetic objectification of a promise of a truly humane dwelling, as a promise that, once made, was taken back—for reasons that remain to be clarified? Where and how are we to find pointers to the social conditions, which still might bring the promise embodied in ornaments to fulfillment, might render it true? In this connection we may not lose sight of the fact that in its bourgeois employment ornament may indeed have been that aesthetically dressed-up "social lie" as which it was pilloried since the beginning of the twentieth century by the avant-gardists and protagonists of the new functional building.[32]

Has postmodernism provided us with the looked-for pointers? Do we find here ground for optimism? Or does the hope for the creation of a new living ornament remain, as Loos insisted it must, an anachronistic, utopian dream? Do the glories of past architecture offer more than an idle promise for the future?

3

Above the task of purifying architecture of unnecessary decoration Bloch places the task of world expression. The significance of ornament is tied to its ability to place individuals in a shared world, enabling them to experience themselves as members of a genuine community. And on this point there was widespread agreement among those of Bloch's generation, who, following Nietzsche and Spengler, tended to oppose modernity or, to use Spengler's term, "civilization," a word that for others as well carried connotations of decadence, favoring instead that authentic community thought to be a presupposition of genuine ornament: "With the beginning of civilization, finally, genuine ornament dies and with it all *great* art, *'Classicism and Romanticism'* form the transition, and in some manner they do so in *every* culture. The former means enthusiasm for an ornament—rules, laws, types—that has long since become antiquated and lost its soul; the latter an enthusiastic imitation—not of life, but of *earlier imitation*. In architecture taste replaces style. Manners of painting and writing, old and modern, native and exotic forms change with fashion. There is no inner necessity."[33]

Inseparable from the hope (vain, if Spengler is right) for the creation of a truly modern ornament, an ornament of and for today yet worthy of being placed besides the great ornaments of the past—of which rocaille, the ornament of the Rococo, is perhaps the last convincing example—is the hope for the creation of a truly modern architectural style, a style that, more than a mere fashion, would deserve to be placed beside the great styles of the past, beside Romanesque and Gothic, Renaissance and Baroque. That hope lies behind Gropius's call for a new cathedral.

I have suggested that the problem of ornament is inescapably also the problem of style; the death of one means also the death of the other. Talk of the death of ornament can of course be challenged by rejecting the presupposed understanding of ornament as a mystification, by questioning the privileging of ornament over mere decoration and the distinction this presupposes; similarly we may want to question the celebration of the community-shaping power of style. Such questioning, however, must remain uninformed as long as we allow the phenomenon of style, more especially of architectural style, to remain unanalyzed.

According to Nietzsche, "the point of every style is to *communicate* by means of signs, including the tempo of these signs, a state of mind, an inner attunement or pathos." [34] It is primarily by its style that an artwork, more especially a work of architecture, communicates a mood that lets us adopt a definite stance toward whatever we encounter. And in architecture it is primarily ornament that is the vehicle of such communication. Consider the rocaille ornamentation of the bedroom in Munich's Amalienburg (see fig. 28). François Cuvilliés's ornamental play carries us back to the world that gave birth to and now leads a posthumous life in this architecture, the "world" understood not as a whole made up of parts but as a space of intelligibility implying a definite stance toward persons and things. A unified style contributes to our experience of a work of architecture as a whole.

Stronger claims have been made for style. The literary critic Emil Staiger thus understands style as the intangible something that lets "a perfect work of art—or the entire work of an artist or also of a time—agree in all aspects. We recognize Baroque style in an altar and in a palace. Schiller's personal style is as distinct in *Tell* as in *Das Lied von der Glocke*. The style of *Hermann und Dorothea* expresses itself in the structure of the verses as well as in the choice of motives and in the sequence of particular images. In the style the manifold is one. It is the permanent in the changing. It is because of this that everything transitory gains an imperishable meaning through style. Works of art are perfect when they are stylistically of a piece." [35] Staiger is of course thinking of literature. But he himself refers the reader first to architecture, which has indeed furnished theorists of style with the most obvious paradigm.

Staiger's remarks raise a number of questions. Does stylistic integrity assure artistic perfection? Is it not possible to admit that a work is stylistically of a piece and yet does not possess the kind of unity that we demand of a successful work of art? Think of Glastonbury Abbey, a fragment of what once was one of the great achievements of English architecture (fig. 22). Similarly there would seem to be much inferior architecture that is stylistically quite of a piece.

Staiger raises a difficulty of a different sort, as he blurs the differences between the style of a period, of an artist, or of a particular work of art: are they all equally relevant to artistic success? Someone committed to the aesthetic approach would want to insist that what really matters is the particular work of art and what contributes to its unity. If style is indeed important to artistic success, then it must be the style of this unique work of art. To the extent that style leads us beyond the work in its particularity to some supposedly deeper

or more encompassing reality, as personal or period styles tend to do, it leads us away from what constitutes its success as a work of art. Anyone committed to the aesthetic approach will be suspicious of any celebration of the magical significance of style.

The aesthetic approach is indeed put into question by those who long for a return to the strong styles of the past. When Josef Hoffmann or Hugo von Hoffmannsthal,[36] Spengler or Broch, Bloch or Sedlmayr celebrate style, they are not thinking of something that belongs to a particular work of art, nor even to a particular artist, but to a community enduring through time. On this understanding, emphasis on style carries with it the suggestion that what constitutes greatness in a work of art is not its power to let us become absorbed in it, but its ability to illuminate the human situation. Thus great art grants a shared way of seeing, which means also a way of valuing. If architecture is to succeed in interpreting "a way of life valid for our period," it must have style, understood as belonging not to the individual but to an ongoing community, to a particular region and time.[37]

More than the conception of the style of an artwork or a person, the concept of period style has generated heated debate. To be sure, the usefulness of stylistic classifications can scarcely be questioned: the history of art depends on them. But how are we to understand and how do we establish the unity of a particular style? We might begin by pointing to a particular group of works of art that show a certain family resemblance. Guided by a vague sense of what they share, by an intuition of what we experience as their common

The Promise of Ornament   *63*

style, we might then single out specific works that strike us as paradigms of, let us say, Baroque art and try to analyze features that help establish their paradigmatic status. Other works of art would then be considered Baroque to the extent that they resembled these paradigms. Depending on what features we think particularly important, these analyses will proceed in different directions. In my book on the Bavarian Rococo church I attempted something of the sort.

But how are we to understand the unity of what has thus been established? Arnold Hauser has likened the unifying power of a style to a musical theme of which only variations are known.[38] Stylistic analysis would then resemble an attempt to reconstruct this unknown theme. But what is the theme's ontological status? In the case of a personal style one can tie this unity to the way an individual stands in his or her world and point to the person as the bearer of the style. Should we then say that the existence of period styles presupposes some supra-individual reality that we can point to and identify as the bearer of the style? This was suggested by Alois Riegl's conception of a supra-individual *Kunstwollen,* an artistic intention manifesting itself in a common formal language. But it is difficult to make sense of such a *Kunstwollen,* as no one is here doing the willing. The conception invests a collective with qualities that properly speaking would appear to belong only to individuals. It depends on an ideal type by which we might measure the works of particular artists. But such ideal types are fictions, created, to be sure, in response to the phenomena that are to be understood, but reflecting also the prejudices and interests of the particular historian and our incurable tendency to look for meaningful wholes in whatever confronts us. Ernst Gombrich warns against those who insist with Hans Sedlmayr that the phenomenon of style teaches us that groups and spiritual collectives are not mere names but independent realities that manifest themselves in individuals. "By inculcating the habit of talking in terms of collectives, of 'mankind,' 'race,' or 'ages,'" such "mythologial explanations" are said by Gombrich to "weaken resistance to totalitarian habits of mind."[39] There is indeed a connection between the tendency to look to the healing power of a great style and its ornament as an antidote to the fragmentation of modern life—an inclination so widespread in the first decades of this century—and the dissatisfactions and hopes that allowed fascism to capture the imagination of so many and seize power.

But if Gombrich's warning is not easily dismissed, are we today firmly committed to the individualism he presupposes? The emphasis on period style has indeed often carried with it suggestions that what really matters about art is not the contribution of the particular artist but something that transcends him, a suprapersonal force or constellation of forces. Or to put the same point somewhat differently: what communicates itself in a period style is a world that belongs not to a particular work of art, nor to a particular artist, but to a historical community. It is this community that above all speaks to us through the artist and her work. While an uneasiness with aestheticism has been a motive behind the emphasis on style, an uneasiness with individualism has been a motive behind the emphasis on period style, which reflects a longing for an ethos not merely personal but communal and for an art able to establish such an ethos. Having lost faith in God, no longer able to discover our place in that order which, with the death of God, has lost both founder and foundation, we turn to style to recover here the whole that will teach us to understand ourselves as parts of a larger whole in which we can discover our place. The celebration of the great historical styles and their associated ornament is directed against the chaos that threatens when all emphasis is placed on the individual.

How important is it then to recover for our architecture something of the world-shaping power of the great styles of the past? By now it should have become clear why there can be no easy answer to this question, for any answer will presuppose that the question of how the individual should relate to the community has been answered. Different interpretations of that relationship will lead to different assessments of the significance of style and ornament.[40] We may well wonder whether there is still room for style in this sense, whether it is indeed compatible with values that we refuse to surrender, for example, with the value we place on the individual. What feeds the hope for a new style to rival the great period styles of the past is a dream, perhaps a dangerous dream, of an art strong enough to return us individuals once more to a communal whole.

4

I associated decoration with decadence. For an interpretation of the phenomenon of decadence I turned to Nietzsche, who helps us recognize the political significance of the decorated shed, as of the strong styles of the past: to the disintegration of the architectural whole into functional building and applied decoration corresponds the disintegration of the social whole. To quote Nietzsche once more: "every time, the anarchy of atoms, disgregation of the will, 'freedom of the individual,' to use moral terms—expanded into political theory, '*equal* rights for all.'" The turn from ornament to decoration, the rise of the aesthetic approach, and the evolution of liberal democracy belong together and issue from the same root.

A Marxist like Lukács has no doubt about where to locate that root—in capitalism: "Here the moments, the different parts of the economy become autonomous in an altogether new manner. . . . As a result of the objective structure of its economic system, the surface of capitalism appears 'fragmented'; it consists of moments that tend toward autonomy with objective necessity. This of course has to mirror itself in the consciousness of those who live in this society, that is to say also in the consciousness of its poets and thinkers."[41] Ruskin's or Loos's broken response to modernity, their "yes" shadowed by a "no," could be cited as examples of such mirroring, as could the emancipation of aesthetic concern from extraneous interests, as could all manifestations of decadence. According to Lukács the fragmented surface presented by the modern world is supported by the whole of the capitalist mode of production. It is this surface to which Nietzsche responds with his pronouncement that God is dead, Sedlmayr with his lament of the lost center, and, Broch with his thesis of the disintegration of values.

Broch could not have agreed with this interpretation. To be sure, he, too, takes decadence to characterize modernity; we live in the ruins of the old value system, which, having lost its foundation in the sacred, has splintered—each splinter claiming autonomy, each following its own logic, each pursuing its own increasingly narrow ends, each resisting compromise. Like strangers these systems now stand one beside the other.

The economic system of "business in itself" beside a system of l'art pour l'art, a military value system beside the system of technology or that of sport, each autonomous, each "in itself," each "unfettered" in its autonomy, each concerned to draw, with all the radicality of its logic, the last consequences and to break it own records. And woe, if in this struggle of competing value systems, which barely maintain their balance, one should come to dominate, growing above all the other value systems, as the military system has grown in this time of war, as the economic world picture has grown, to which even war is subject—woe! For it embraces the world, embraces all other values, and exterminates them, like a swarm of locusts moving over a field.[42]

Like Lukács, Broch understands the evolution of the modern world as a progressive disintegration of what was once a whole. But while Lukács locates the root of such disintegration in the capitalist mode of production, Broch considers the economic value sphere just one among others and calls for a preservation of their heterogeneity! The ground of decadence he locates not in capitalism but in the absolutism of pure reason, which would subject all life to its hegemony. This absolutism presupposes our all-too-human desire to secure ourselves in the midst of what is by comprehending it.

We can comprehend only what is hard enough to be grasped; similarly, we can comprehend only what endures: we cannot hold on to the magically shifting patterns on a soap bubble, to drifting clouds, or to the wake trailed by a sailboat. To secure ourselves we thus analyze an all-too-evanescent world into enduring elements and reconstruct it as a configuration of such elements. By its very nature reason tends toward a logical, and this means also toward an ever more formal and empty, atomism. As Broch recognized, the still progressing rationalization of modern life has to mean its disintegration, professionalization, and compartmentalization—decadence as Nietzsche understood it: "war is war," "business is business," "art for art's sake." "All this says the same, it all belongs to the same aggressive radicality, that uncanny—I almost would like to say metaphysical—ruthlessness, to that cruel logical spirit that looks to and only to the matter at hand, that does not look right and does not look left."[43] The ruthlessness that must fragment the whole of life is fed by the snake's promise: you will be like God.

Such mastery demands objectivity. To approach objectivity we must attempt to free ourselves of the ways in which mood and interest distort what we experience, transforming ourselves into pure spectators of what is the case. To the purification of the subject corresponds the objectification of reality. Thus objectified, reality has no room for value.

This objectification of reality must be understood in all its ambivalence: on one side we know, as well as Ruskin or Loos did, that in countless ways objectifying reason has improved the quality of life. One could cite advances in medicine, or the revolution in communications, or the impact technology has had on food production. Although countless problems still await a technological solution, who could deny that technology has helped us lift at least some of the burdens of life? There is an obvious sense in which we are less limited by our body and by the accident of its location in space and time than were our predecessors. It would be irresponsible not to affirm the liberating potential of objectifying reason.

But such affirmation may not mean the absolutism of pure reason. For its other side is the often-lamented rootlessness of modern dwelling (fig. 23). No doubt, science and

The Promise of Ornament

technology have brought us greater freedom; both literally and figuratively, we have become more mobile. Such mobility has made us less willing to accept what happens to be the place assigned to us by nature or history, more ready to experiment. Beyond what is, the self-elevation of the spirit has opened up infinite realms of what might be. But this very real increase in freedom has given new urgency to questions about what should be our place and vocation, and for these, Kant's conviction notwithstanding, pure reason has no answers. The same self-liberation presupposed by the objectification of reality lets us live our lives *sub specie possibilitatis,* haunted by a sense of contingency and arbitrariness, of emptiness and futility. Where do we find ground or measure in the infinite realms opened up by reflection? How can we justify the way we live? Reason alone has no answer. And to the extent that objectifying reason has shaped our life world, threatening to debase human beings by reducing them to material to be subjected to planning and organization—just another resource, to be used and used up like any other—that world holds no answer either; it leaves us with dreams of lost meaning, lost plenitude, of a communal existence strongly rooted in both space and time. It is no accident that ornament should have come to figure what is felt to be missing.

I am not pleading here for a romantic renunciation of objectifying reason and of its offspring, science and technology. What we must resist rather is that absolutism which makes reason the measure of reality instead of recognizing the reduction that reality's objectification inevitably entails. Such recognition allows us to understand why objectifying reason should have its complement in the aesthetic approach: should we not add to a reality whose value has been canceled by rationalization an aesthetic component that compensates us for what has been lost? Should we not so beautify objectified reality that we can appreciate it as an aesthetic phenomenon? Does not decoration allow us to cover up the poverty of the world we have created?

So we would have to conclude, were we to equate objectified reality with reality. Then meaning could only be found in a turn to the aesthetic, be it a turn to decoration or to art for art's sake. But objectified reality must be understood as presupposing a more encompassing reality. It is this reality that art, and more especially architecture, should recall and interpret for us. That today remains its main task.

The Decorated Shed

5

1

Developing some of the implications of Pevsner's distinction between architecture and mere building, I have argued that on the aesthetic approach presupposed by that distinction the beauty of architecture has to appear as something added on to what the necessities of building dictate: the work of architecture is essentially a decorated shed. Not surprising then that this approach should fit so well much of the architectural thinking of the nineteenth century.[1] But did Robert Venturi and his associates, Denise Scott Brown and Steven Izenour, from whose *Learning from Las Vegas* I borrowed the term,[2] really call for a return to the half-hearted historicism of the nineteenth century with its borrowed decoration? Their work's subtitle, *The Forgotten Symbolism of Architectural Form,* argues differently: they seem to have deplored not so much the turn away from decoration and ornament, so characteristic of architectural modernism, as the way "modern architects abandoned a tradition of iconology in which painting, sculpture, and graphics were combined with architecture. The delicate hieroglyphics on a bold pylon, the archetypal inscriptions of a Roman architrave, the mosaic processions in Sant'Apollinare, the ubiquitous tattoos over a Giotto Chapel, the enshrined hierarchies around a Gothic portal, even the illusionistic frescoes in a Venetian villa, all contain messages beyond their ornamental contribution to architectural space."[3] We meet here not so much with a demand for decoration as with a refusal of what is experienced as the muteness of modern architecture, with a longing for architecture as text, for buildings carrying messages that can be read in some sense, for a new *architecture parlante*. That, of course, is not a term used by Venturi and his associates. It carries us back to the eighteenth century. Already in 1768 Jean-Charles Delafosse published his *Iconologie Historique,* which Joseph Rykwert calls "the most painstaking attempt to establish an *architecture parlante*."[4] This desire to give buildings a voice, to make them speak, found striking expression in the work of Claude-Nicolas Ledoux.[5] "Many architects have met this requirement by affixing easily understandable symbols to their structures, the caduceus of Aesculapius to medical buildings, the Orphic lyre to theaters. Ledoux, however, wanted to give the structure such a form that it would tell its story by itself. The Surveyors' House is a grandiose symbolization of nature made serviceable to man"[6] (fig. 24).

Ledoux's turn to story is all the more remarkable given his interest in reducing buildings to elementary geometric forms, which allows Kaufmann to celebrate him as the

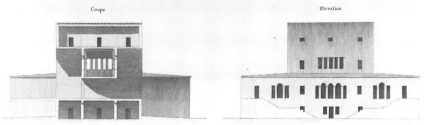

Coupe　　　　　　　　　　　　　Elevation

Claude-Nicolas Ledoux, House of the Surveyors
of the Loüe River. Source: Ledoux, *L'Architecture
considerée sous le rapport de l'art, des moeurs et de la
législation*, vol. 1 (Paris, 1804), pl. 6. Credit:
Beinecke Rare Book and Manuscript Library,
24 ⎪ Yale University.

most striking precursor of modernist architecture: "He was most certainly a seer of future developments when he presented cubic masses, bare walls with frameless apertures, flat roofs, and above all entirely new compositional patterns."[7] How does Ledoux's formalism fit with his concern to create an *architecture parlante*? That the introduction of textuality in architecture clashes with the aesthetic approach as I have analyzed it should be evident: the aesthetic object should not mean but be, should not present itself to us as a sign or a symbol that receives its meaning from some absent signified. Aesthetic presence should not be haunted by absence. Ideally the aesthetic object should be mute. The aesthetic demand for an absorbing mute presence is impossible to reconcile with the call for an architecture of communication. Ledoux's desire to have architecture speak presupposes some misgivings with the turn to the aesthetic, which many of his own designs would seem to illustrate. The title of Ledoux's *L'Architecture considérée sous le rapport de l'art, des moeurs et de la legislation* (1804) speaks for itself: to be true to its ethical and political function, architecture may not be mute.[8]

It is hardly an accident that just when the aesthetic approach became conscious of itself, uneasiness with the divorce of beauty from life with its concerns and duties should have also found a voice. Ledoux's marriage of an aesthetic formalism to *architecture parlante* has an analogue in Kant's refusal to allow his aesthetic formalism to stand in the way of an art that would give visible expression to moral ideals. Despite his analysis of the disinterested character of aesthetic experience, Kant remains suspicious of those who would take such experience too seriously: aesthetes tend to be immoral.[9] Kant thus has little use for art for art's or beauty's sake; his own sympathies lie with Winckelmann's celebration of the art of the ancients for its expressions of "noble simplicity and quiet grandeur," that is, for its moral quality: art should speak to us of ideal humanity and thus provide life with a measure.[10] This desire that art or architecture speak to us of what matters presupposes a refusal of the aesthetic approach.

That also holds for Venturi.[11] We do him an injustice when we understand him as another representative of the aesthetic approach. His turn to textuality implies just the opposite—a critique of that approach. This means also that although I borrowed his term "decorated shed," I did violence to what he meant by it when I claimed that the aesthetic approach demands that works of architecture be understood as decorated sheds.

2

Much in *Learning from Las Vegas* does in fact question the modernist refusal of decoration and call for its restoration to the place it had been assigned by traditional architecture. In this respect the work is representative of a then newly reemerging interest in decoration and ornament: in art nouveau, for example, or in Sullivan's fantastic decorations, or in the ornament of Baroque and Rococo. The same interest finds expression in the decorative treatment of the skin of today's skyscrapers. The rediscovery of the importance of decoration and ornament, ill informed though it often may be, is an important contribution of architectural postmodernism. As much as anyone, Venturi can claim credit for having helped to initiate that development. Here the conclusion of *Learning from Las Vegas:*

When Modern architects righteously abandoned ornament on buildings, they unconsciously designed buildings that were ornament. In promoting Space and Articulation over symbolism and ornament, they distorted the whole building into a duck. They substituted for the innocent and inexpensive practice of applied decoration on a conventional shed the rather cynical and expensive distortion of program and structure to promote a duck; minimegastructures are mostly ducks. . . . It is now time to reevaluate the once-horrifying statement of John Ruskin that architecture is the decoration of construction, but we should append the warning of Pugin: It is all right to decorate construction, but never construct decoration. (p. 163)

Owen Jones called the last "the first principle in architecture,"[12] although he himself calls it into question when he suggests the superiority of the Egyptian capital, where "we feel the whole capital is the ornament,—to remove any portion of it would destroy it," over the

Corinthian, where "the ornament was no part of the construction, as with the Egyptian: it could be removed, and the structure remained unchanged. On the Corinthian capital the ornament is applied, not constructed."[13] Jones's description of the Egyptian capital as constructed decoration does not at all imply criticism. And why should we never construct decoration? Counterexamples come readily to mind. Is not the pulpit in Oppolding (see fig. 4) constructed decoration? Was J. Fergusson not right to place "structural decoration" above decoration added to a structure[14] (see fig. 20)? Venturi, to be sure, is thinking of some of the acclaimed masterpieces of modern architecture: Le Corbusier's Ronchamp (see fig. 95) could be considered constructed decoration; so could Frank Lloyd Wright's Guggenheim Museum; so could Jørn Utzon's Sydney Opera House.

But why should such construction be prohibited? Venturi takes for granted that decoration should serve the supporting structure, should serve construction. As I remarked earlier, by its very nature decoration is first of all a dependent art form. To construct decoration is to make it autonomous, is to create a self-sufficient aesthetic object. With his concluding admonition Venturi thus challenges once more the aesthetic approach: any view of architecture that sees its task primarily as one of creating self-sufficient aesthetic objects will end up constructing decoration. Such an approach is incompatible with the requirements of dwelling. On this point we have to agree with Venturi.

But let me return to Venturi's statement. There is clearly a new or rather renewed appreciation for the tension between construction and decoration, between engineer and artist—the mention of Ruskin hardly comes as a surprise. From the affirmation of this tension follows the rejection of the construction of decoration, which denies it. Such denial is characteristic of those buildings Venturi terms "ducks."

"Ducks" must be thought in opposition to "decorated sheds." That opposition in turn depends on the tension between the "symbolic and representational elements" of a building and its "form, structure, and program" (p. 87). Duck and decorated shed deal with the latter opposition in very different ways: ducks are symbols become buildings, constructed symbols, as opposed to functional sheds to which decorative symbols have already been applied. The American roadside vernacular offers ready examples of the former: not just the "Long Island Duckling" cited by Venturi, which we may consider the flagship of the type, but cheese shops in the form of a wheel of Swiss cheese crowned by a happy mouse, rock shops in the form of a rock, eateries in the form of a hot dog with bun, or of a teapot, or of a lobster trap—the list is endless. But the duck type should not be reduced to such rather trivial and peripheral buildings. There are also architecturally much more significant examples. Ledoux's *architecture parlante* is an architecture of ducks. The pyramids are ducks. So are most medieval churches. Venturi himself makes this point for the nave of Amiens (see fig. 37), which he calls a duck "because its shape is that of a cross," although only after he has already called it "a billboard with a building behind it" and therefore a decorated shed (p. 105). The point can be generalized: all medieval churches were built to symbolize the Church, and that symbolic function determines "space, structure, and program." I shall return to the symbolic dimension of architecture in chapter 7. I cite these examples here only as a warning not to invest "duck" with too negative a connotation.

Robert Venturi, Guild House, Philadelphia.

Photo credit: William Watkins. Credit: Venturi,

25 | Scott Brown and Associates.

Paul Rudolph, Crawford Manor, New Haven.
Photo by author.

Still, the authors of *Learning from Las Vegas* would seem to have a point when they insist that "the duck is seldom relevant today, although it pervades Modern architecture" (p. 87). Were we to allow most of our buildings to speak as loudly as the Long Island Duckling, we would end up with an unbearably noisy environment that would make it all but impossible to hear anything. The decorated shed's greater reticence would appear to make it preferable. But once again we must take care not to let a striking paradigm mislead us. Are not most houses ducks in Venturi's sense, although perhaps also decorated sheds? They not only are but represent houses. In most houses the symbolic form "house" governs "the architectural system of space, structure, and program." Most houses say quite unmistakably "I am a house," although our familiarity with the house type lets us be inattentive to such speech, taking it for granted.

Venturi argues "for the symbolism of the ugly and ordinary in architecture and for the particular significance of the decorated shed with a rhetorical front and conventional behind: for architecture as shelter with symbols on it" (p. 90). He underscores his argument by comparing his own Guild House in Philadelphia (fig. 25) with Paul Rudolph's Crawford Manor in New Haven (fig. 26). The latter presents itself to us above all as an aesthetic object, quite "unequivocally a soaring tower, unique in its Modern, Ville Radieuse world along New Haven's limited access Oak Street Connector" (p. 90). Compared to it, Guild House, built at about the same time, looks and is supposed to look quite ordinary. It does not want to stand out. The choice of structure, materials, and placement was meant to be responsive to its urban context. Not that Guild House is likely to be confused with one of its neighbors: the more time one spends with it, the less ordinary it becomes. First of all, its decorative scheme is unusual: "The continuous stripe of white-glazed brick high on the façade, in combination with the plane of white-glazed brick below, divides the building

[Venturi calls it a "six-story imitation palazzo"] into three uneven stories: basement, principal story, and attic" (pp. 92, 90). At the same time, the invocation of this traditional tripartite organization is contradicted by the building's six stories, especially by the deliberately heedless way in which the white stripe cuts through windows as if indifferent to them. "The central white panel calls attention to the entrance as it extends the ground floor to the top of the balcony of the second floor in the way, and for the same reasons, that the increased scale around the door of a Renaissance palace or Gothic portal does" (p. 92). But once again the invocation of these precursors is taken back by the fat column that blocks our entry somewhat in the way a meaty bouncer at some nightspot might deny entry to unwanted guests.

There is certainly a relationship between this apartment building and nineteenth-century apartment houses with their historicizing facades. But Venturi no longer takes the architecture to which he looks back very seriously. Less than a treasured inheritance, the past has become a reservoir for artistic play, which is not so much light-hearted as self-conscious and ironic, clever in a way that would probably be lost on those meant to live in this house. Yet Venturi's critique of Crawford Manor is not altogether off the mark. We experience Rudolph's tower primarily as the now somewhat pathetic heroic gesture of a leading architect, in which the refusal of ornament and the ornamentalization of the entire building belong together. Both are inevitable consequences of the attempt to build aesthetic objects. But aesthetic objects are uninhabitable. To build apartment houses as primarily aesthetic objects is indeed irresponsible.

That a work like Crawford Manor is not mute, that it, too, has a voice, Venturi would not deny. One thing it tells us is that it was meant to be an original piece of modern architecture. Thus it places itself in the tradition of modern architecture, with its twofold emphasis on space and technology, as well as on the creative imagination of the individual architect. To attribute a voice to a building like Crawford Manor is to suggest also that even as—in keeping with both the aesthetic and a functional approach—modern architecture sought to submerge symbolism, it did not abandon symbolism altogether, though it refused to acknowledge this. In fact it only substituted a vocabulary derived from the industrial vernacular for the historical eclecticism of the nineteenth century. But such substitution is difficult to reconcile with rigorous functionalism. That goes also for "the progressive, technological, vernacular, process-oriented, superficially socially concerned, heroic and original content of Modern architecture" (p. 162).

But if Venturi is right to claim that modernism has only substituted one kind of symbolism for another, must we not question his characterization of buildings like Crawford Manor as ducks rather than as decorated sheds? Must not Mies's symbolic exposure of the steel frame be considered decoration? And is not the same true of Rudolph's use of concrete? To be sure, we are dealing here with a very different kind of decoration, but with decoration nonetheless. Venturi might well agree, but, citing Loos in support, he could add that the difference between shed and decoration is here deliberately blurred, while in a building like Guild House it is deliberately underscored. In this sense the latter structure can claim to be more honest than the former.

3

Venturi would have architects become self-conscious about their use of signs and symbols. With this we return to the longing for an architecture that can be read, for buildings that invite us to understand them in the image of texts. Much architecture of the past invites such reading. Think of a Gothic or a Baroque church: these were much more than just decorated sheds, that is, functional buildings to which an aesthetic component had been added. Beyond or even before an aesthetic function, the added component had a quasi-linguistic function. The decorative elements carried a message, communicated meaning. Like most postmodern architects, Venturi would reclaim for architecture this lost textual dimension. Architecture is to extend an invitation to be read; it is to rediscover its voice. The aesthetic approach, as we have seen, had to muffle this voice; the aesthetic object tends toward muteness, because it had to divorce the aesthetic from the linguistic.

Venturi would have architecture overcome this divorce. Architecture should speak to us; and it should speak to us of our own time. For this reason he calls on us to learn from Levittown and Las Vegas. Here we find symbols and ornament tied to our age: "To find our symbolism we must go to the suburban edges of the existing city that are symbolically rather than formally attractive and represent the aspirations of almost all Americans, including most low-income urban dwellers and most of the silent white majority. Then the archetypal Los Angeles will be our Rome and Las Vegas our Florence; and like the archetypal grain elevators some generations ago, the Flamingo sign will be the model to shock our sensibility towards a new architecture" (p. 161).

"This architecture of styles and signs" is said by Venturi to be "antispatial; it is an architecture of communication over space; communication dominates space as an element in the architecture and in the landscape" (p. 8). While modernist architecture lets space triumph over communication, Venturi would invert that triumph by celebrating "the dominance of signs over space" (p. 9). Meaning is to triumph over what lacks meaning, as spirit triumphs over body.

If architecture is to speak to us, what easier way to ensure this than to decorate buildings with verbal signs? With his turn to the word Venturi is closer to an artist like Duchamp, whom we may indeed consider the prototypical postmodernist, than to a modernist like Stella. Here is how Duchamp understands what distinguishes his work from futurist painting and, by extension, from all modernist art:

Futurism was an impressionism of the mechanical world. It was strictly a continuation of the Impressionist movement. I was not interested in that. I wanted to get away from the physical aspect of painting. I was much more interested in recreating ideas in painting. For me the title was very important. I was interested in making painting serve my purposes, and in getting away from the physicality of painting. For me Courbet had introduced the physical emphasis in the nineteenth century. I was interested in ideas—not merely in visual products. I wanted to put painting once again at the service of the mind. And my painting was, of course, at once regarded as "intellectual," "literary" painting. It was true, I was endeavoring to establish myself as far away as possible from "pleasing" and "attractive" physical paintings. that extreme was seem as literary. My King and Queen was a chess king and queen.[15]

Duchamp went on to assert that "until the last hundred years all painting had been literary or religious," that is to say, had been at the service of words, most often of the Word. I would have dated the change since the rise of the aesthetic approach. From this perspective modern art's turn from the literary to the visual appears as a curious interruption of the mainstream of art.

Similarly *Learning from Las Vegas*, with its call for a literary architecture, may be considered not so much a curious deflection from the triumphant progress of modern architecture as an attempt to return architecture to its mainstream. Duchamp's emphasis on titles has its counterpart in Venturi's emphasis on signs, Duchamp's turn away from the physical side of painting and toward ideas in Venturi's turn away from buildings as primarily articulations of space and toward an architecture of communication.[16]

I sympathize with this call for "an impure architecture of communication" (p. 18), but what language is this architecture to speak and what is it to tell us? To be sure, we are given pointers: we are told to look to the typical American main street with its "false fronts, disengaged and turned perpendicular to the highway as big, high signs" (p. 18); asked to explore the often ugly but symbol-laden suburban edges of our cities, with their magic miles of shopping centers, gas stations, and fast-food restaurants; invited to give Los Angeles and Las Vegas a chance to fire our imagination. But how many of us would care to spend more than a very small part of our lives with an architecture of "signs of persuasion that shout their gorgeous cacophony but hide their constraining order" (p. 77)? Such visually noisy environments make it difficult to listen to oneself and to what really matters. Distraction is of course the point of amusement. We should keep in mind that the architecture of Las Vegas is closely related to that of amusement parks and fairs. Though such architecture has had a long history, it has always been peripheral, and in a much more profound sense than Venturi's talk of the suburban edges of our towns may suggest: peripheral, because it touches only the periphery of our life. It is utopian somewhat in the sense in which earlier I called the aesthetic object utopian. Certainly, there are times when we may want to escape, if only temporarily, from the everyday reality of our lives to some Disney world or other. But as little as Disneyworld's does the architecture of Las Vegas provide a model for building that addresses our needs of working and dwelling as members of a genuine community.

4

This is indeed an important lesson. But with its emphasis on verbal signs, *Learning from Las Vegas* misdirects the needed assessment of the symbolic dimension of architecture.[17] Such signs have their point when we do not know our way about (fig. 27). But human dwelling should be more than an existence on the road, uncertain of where to go and where to stop. In this respect, too, *Learning from Las Vegas* makes central what should be peripheral. Can we really deplore the fact that "The diminutive signs in most Modern buildings contained only the most necessary messages, like LADIES, minor accents begrudgingly applied" (p. 7)? Imagine someone calling attention to the master bedroom with a large neon sign, shouting MASTER BEDROOM. What would our response be? Perhaps the sign would make

The Decorated Shed

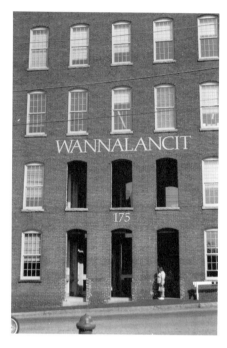

us more thoughtful about this usually taken for granted conjunction of "master" and "bedroom." More likely we would experience it less as a sign than as an aesthetic object. And is this not how Venturi ends up appreciating the signs of Las Vegas? He turns out not to be very interested in these signs as signs, which would mean also a disinterest in what they signify, in the often questionable activities to which they call us. His paramount interest would seem to be their visual appearance, their not at all obvious visual order, "like the shifting configurations of a Victor Vasarely painting. It is the unity that 'maintains, but only just maintains, a control over the clashing elements which compose it.' Chaos is very near; its nearness, but its avoidance, gives . . . force."[18] To the extent that this comparison is just, the symbolic dimension of this architecture has been reduced to material for a purely aesthetic concern. Such a concern lets Venturi compare Fremont Street at night to the Rococo interior of Munich's Amalienburg (fig. 28): both are said to glitter rather than glow. But such superficial similarity only underscores the gap that separates them and the very different ways in which decoration functions in the two cases. The bedroom of the Amalienburg has no need for a sign labeling it BEDROOM; the bed makes this function quite clear enough.

A sign would be not only redundant but an intrusion. And yet there is a sense in which this room speaks to us, both of the room's function and of its intended occupant. The feminine silver ornament, with its evocations of both nature and divine lovers, grants this room a special magic, celebrating at the same time the person for whom it was built—Amalie, the wife of the Bavarian elector—and the power of eros. The glitter here both underscores and transfigures what is an important part of human life. It would be impossible to translate the many-voiced meaning of this ornament into a clear and distinct discourse, although a great deal can of course be said about it.

It is possible to claim something quite similar for the sign architecture of Las Vegas. Does not the gorgeous cacophony of these signs establish the special spirit of this place just as effectively as does the ornament of the Amalienburg? They, too, provide buildings and their functions with an appropriate aura. The quality of this aura is determined by the way signs are allowed to dominate buildings and their articulation of space. Traditionally, works of architecture have granted a sense of place by their articulation of space, enhanced by symbolization and ornamentation. If the sign architecture of Las Vegas grants a sense of place, it does so by pulling us in different directions—each competing for our attention, each beckoning us to lose ourselves, at least for a time. This is a landscape for "crowds of anonymous individuals without explicit connection with each other,"[19] without a place of their own, a landscape for displaced persons, uncertain of where they should be going and for that very reason hungry for signs.

Our response to these signs is likely to be one-dimensional and superficial. Their dominance over space is the dominance of the quickly seen word over a fuller experience of our being in the world, resembling the substitution of a sign LEAF for an actual leaf, which in its insistent presence will inevitably prove richer than all our labels. The sign architecture of Las Vegas belongs with the car and the highway. To catch our attention as we drive by, these signs have to scream; to be understood they must carry a clear message.

To be sure, this is an extreme example. Writing has long played a significant if usually minor part in architecture, often as supplementary text, referring us to a building's function (fig. 29), or to the builders, or to the ethos that governed their building. Writing does not appear here as a screaming sign. There have of course long been signs calling attention to, say, a particular business, but in traditional architecture they are usually not allowed to dominate the building but are made to serve it as ornament. Today such reticence is difficult to reconcile with the pressure to catch a prospective customer's attention. And yet architecture that would take seriously the requirements of dwelling must demand such reticence.

The attempt to cure architecture's loss of voice by substituting signs for merely aesthetic decoration is no answer to the language problem faced by modern architecture. The buildings that often all but disappear beneath or behind these signs are not transformed by them into architecture. For Ruskin's or Pevsner's "work of architecture = functional building + decoration" we may not substitute "work of architecture = functional building + signs." One connotation of the sign culture celebrated in *Learning from Las Vegas* is indeed that architecture in the traditional sense has become quite unimportant and peripheral in the modern world.

Part Two

Representation and Re-Presentation

The Language Problem

6

1

I have spent some time on *Learning from Las Vegas* because, even if we must finally resist its lesson, the book has given particularly striking expression to the linguistic turn that has helped shape recent architectural theory and practice. Heinrich Klotz thus links the principle "at work when the final shape of a building is consciously tied to the recapturing of content that can become the 'narrative substance' of a building's total form and its subsidiary forms" to the goal "to liberate architecture from the muteness of 'pure forms' and from the clamor of ostentatious constructions in order that a building might once again become an occasion for a creative effort, attend not only to facts and utilization programs but also to poetic ideas and the handling of subject matter on an epic scale."[1] The same concern to recover architecture's lost or perhaps just not heard voice shows itself in the vogue enjoyed by talk about semiotic and structuralist approaches to architecture, about architecture's semantics and syntactics. The fact that for more than three decades now architecture and architectural theory have been so fascinated by language and linguistics invites questioning and reflection.[2] As Manfredo Tafuri points out,

The emergence, within architectural criticism, of the language problem *is, then, a precise answer to the language crisis of modern architecture. The proliferation of studies on the semantics and semiology of architecture is due not only to a snobbish keeping up with the current linguistic* vogue: *every snobbism, anyway, derives its reasons from historical events, and the snobbisms of architectural culture do not escape this rule. The attempt to bring the "sciences of man" under the unifying sign of linguistics is rooted also in the current historical situation. One looks for what has been lost, and the need for more and more complex reflex actions in order to discover the meaning of events and things, derives from the discovery that we are among* signs, conventions, myths, that offer us artificial processes as natural, *that manifest themselves as innocent images or rites just where they are least disinterested, and that carefully hide their meanings. From this comes semiology's frantic search for meanings; and it is up to us to make it a* new science *with a formidable capacity for demystification, or to let it become another transient fashion under the flag of evasion.*[3]

Tafuri would have us understand the emergence of the language problem in architectural criticism as a response to the language crisis of modern architecture. But in just what sense can we speak of a *language* crisis in architecture? Such talk presupposes that we can meaningfully attribute a language to architecture, but what do we mean when we claim that architecture possesses a language, or when we speak of architecture as sign? As long as we remain unsure of how these questions are to be answered, all talk about a language crisis in architecture remains too vague to be of use.

Take the word "sign." We call smoke a sign of fire or clouds a sign of rain. By this we mean that one phenomenon gives us a right to expect another. We may want to speak in such cases of natural signs. But does nature give us signs? Does it have something to tell us? Such locutions presuppose an involvement with "nature" that lets us understand it not as a collection of mute facts, but as a context that has already been endowed with meaning by our cares and concerns.[4] We fear the destructive power of fire; depending on what we are up to—say, planting a garden or going on a hike—what we read in a mackerel sky will hold different meanings.

In this connection we should remind ourselves that our first and still most frequent way of experiencing persons and things is not at all detached observation of given objects. Such detachment presupposes prior engagement. Thus, when a philosopher pauses and, groping for an example of what she means by an object, finally comes up with the chalk with which she was writing on some blackboard, she easily forgets that this chalk was present to her in a quite different way when she was actually writing with it than it is now that she has stopped using it and is faced with a mysterious, crumbly object, leaving white dust on her fingers. Before things are thus transformed in reflection, they have their place in a context of meanings that is inseparable from the activities in which we are engaged. Belonging to such a context, they have themselves a meaning. Thus the piece of chalk may be said to signify "chalk," that is, something with which to write on a blackboard. Similarly smoke and cloud are not given to us first as mute objects requiring interpretation; from the very beginning, they carry quite specific meanings that are inseparable from the way we find ourselves engaged in and by the world. But is such engagement and the meanings that it founds sufficient to allow us to say: first of all and most of the time things speak to us? Does it make sense to speak of the natural langauge of clouds? What would "language" mean here? Is there not language only when there is communication?

When we call the cloud a sign of rain, there is no assumption of some person or spirit who by means of this cloud wants to tell us something. Were we to understand the cloud as a sign in this sense, say as a sign from Demeter that it is time to start ploughing, talk of the language of clouds would have an obvious sense. But in the absence of such belief, are not expressions like "the language of clouds" at best crude metaphors, as Roger Scruton insists? "We must distinguish the meaning in 'Clouds mean rain' from that in 'John means that it will rain,' or ' "Il va pleuvoir" means that it will rain.' The first of these provides a case of 'natural' meaning—a case of one phenomenon being a reason to expect another. One is referring to a natural, causal, external relation between events. It is only by the crudest of metaphors that we could, on this basis, speak of a language of clouds; indeed, the metaphor would be so vague as to embrace everything (since there is no phenomenon that does not give some reason to expect another)."[5] For the same reason Scruton rules out talk of body language: "Some have been prepared to say, for example, that there is a *language* of facial expression, simply because expressions are signs of mental states—but this notion of sign has nothing to do with language. The relation of words to their meaning is not natural but *intended*, and this intention is realized through a necessary body of conventions and rules."[6] Scruton would have us speak of language only when there is communication relying on conventional signs. Bracketing for the time being the question of whether talk of a natural language inevitably involves such a gross misunderstanding, whether such metaphorical use of the term must obscure more than it illuminates, let us grant the link between language and communication. If talk of architecture possessing a language is to be at all helpful, works of architecture must not just be meaningful in some sense but must be intended to communicate some meaning. Only if this is the case is there a point to speaking of the semantics of architecture.

Talk about the language of architecture is sometimes justified in a different manner, by pointing out that, like language, architecture is governed by conventional rules. We may thus speak of the syntax of a particular style. The Gothic style, which found paradigmatic expression in the cathedral of Amiens, is governed by such rules, as is the International Style. The classical theory of the orders has given paradigmatic expression to what might be meant by the syntax or the grammar of a style:

The Orders were conceived by Renaissance masters as bodies of mutually dependent constraints; obeying one of these constraints, an architect is forced by its inner logic to obey them all. Thus the use of the Doric order imposes a strict relation between vertical and horizontal dimensions, it necessitates a certain kind of entablature, and certain window openings. It removes all trace of arbitrariness from the ornamentation, for example by giving the architect a compelling reason for inserting triglyphs in the frieze, for simplifying the moulding of the column-base, for cultivating in the walls a certain rugged heaviness. In this way the Orders serve to control the design of an entire façade, to apply grammatical constraints which enable one corner of a building to limit its most distant counterpart: a false move at any point can mar the integrity of the structure, and destroy the thread of meaningfulness that runs through the details of the whole.[7]

Alexander Tzonis and Liane Lefaivre can be said to have analyzed the grammar of the classical style in this sense. But they warn against "a rushed use of words such as 'language,' 'syntax,' 'grammar' " to explain the order of architecture: "Such terms confuse rather than explain classical architecture as a cultural social phenomenon."[8] The same could be said of attempts to describe the "syntax" of, say, the International Style or of a particular architect, say, Mies van der Rohe, perhaps at a particular stage in his career. Not that we do not understand what such an attempt would seek to discover. But is "syntax" the right word here? Is "syntax" not essentially syntax of a language? And can we not speak of language only when there is an intentional act of communication? What do buildings like the Parthenon or Le Corbusier's La Tourette communicate—what do they say?

The linguistic approach to architecture presupposes that there is indeed an illuminating analogy between architecture and language. But what exactly is the analogy? Can we say, for example, that a building is made up of elements just as a sentence is made up of words? This claim was developed in considerable detail by Wolfgang T. Otto in *Der Raumsatz* (*The Spatial Sentence*). He, too, found his paradigm in the Greek temple: he likens the cella, the temple's core, to the subject, the portico or surrounding colonnade to the object, and the manner in which these two elements are related to the verb. The analogy between building and sentence leads Otto to the assertion that "in the well-formed spatial sentence an authoritative space dominates the entire structure. . . . The correctly formed spatial sentence is always characterized by patriarchal order."[9] Otto's use of the adjective "patriarchal" to describe what he considers well-formed buildings should be sufficient to render his central claim questionable, and it is indeed easy to think of counterexamples. Otto knows of course that there is much architecture not so ordered—for example, buildings whose architectural effect depends not on the subordination of the whole to a ruling central space but on the coordination of two or more equally strong elements. Certain designs by Ledoux come to mind, as well as their modern counterparts; Otto himself mentions the corridor house. In the latter, he claims, the patriarchal order that he considers constitutive of good architecture has been "distorted and degraded."[10] Are we to say the same of Ledoux's Prison for Aix (fig. 30) or House for Four Families?

Claude-Nicolas Ledoux, Prison at Aix. From Ledoux, *L'Architecture considerée sous le rapport de l'art, des moeurs et de la législation,* vol. 2, ed. Daniel Ramée (London, 1846), pl. 64. Source: Yvon Christ and Ionel Schein, *L'Oeuvre et les rêves de*

30 | *Ledoux* (Paris: Chêne, 1971).

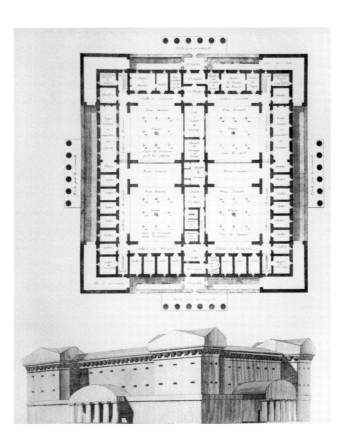

It is clear, at any rate, that such designs, whatever we may think of them, do not fail as an ungrammatical sentence fails. They thus force us to question the asserted analogy between sentence and building; even given Otto's "patriarchal" prejudice favoring hierarchical ordering, as he develops it, the language analogy is too superficial to prove illuminating. In no way does it help to buttress Otto's convictions about architectural order. But does this mean that we should give up on it altogether?

In what sense are buildings like propositions? Roger Scruton notes, "A man who understands language is able to recognize which words can, and which cannot, replace each other in a sentence. He is possessed of certain 'syntactical categories.' Not surprisingly, a similar structure may be noticed in other human activities—for example in architecture, where (depending on the style) an arch may be followed by another of the same kind, or by a concluding pier, but not by an arch of conflicting size and style, nor by a sequence of broken columns."[11] We can thus say "Peter likes Paul" or "Peter hates Paul," but not "Peter if Paul" or "Peter silently Paul." The latter do not constitute complete sentences; they do not succeed in making assertions. As they stand, they are just pieces of linguistic nonsense. We may want to claim that something similar holds of buildings. Take the carved capital of a Romanesque church (fig. 31): it could be replaced with a much simpler cushion capital, but hardly with an Ionic or a Corinthian capital.[12] That would be like introducing a word drawn from another language. It would be stranger still to replace it with, say, a window frame: that would produce architectural nonsense, although we can imagine some postmodern architect attempting to construct just such nonsense, just as a poet may chose to write down what is grammatically nonsensical in order to make a point, so that what at first appears as simply nonsense in the end proves to have a sense after all.

But if buildings and the way their elements are joined are no doubt governed by rules, even if most of these rules can be violated, these elements yet seem to lack something that words possess. Words have meanings that allow them to be joined in propositions that assert something to be the case; with reference to what they assert, propositions can be said to be true or false.[13] Buildings do not make assertions. In that sense they can be neither true nor false. Their unity is therefore not like that of a sentence.

In this connection it is important not to obscure the difference between the kind of unity that belongs to a sentence that makes an assertion and the unity conferred by a style, between *syntactic* and *stylistic unity*.[14] Stylistic unity may communicate itself to us in a writer's preference for certain words, images, or sound patterns. Given an understanding of an author's style, we might say that some word does not fit a certain poem, even though it is quite grammatical and makes good sense; still, it does not fit the tone of the text. We may want to speak here of the musical aspect of language. That "music" does not change the matter that is asserted, but it lets us understand it in a certain way. Style communicates a way of understanding or seeing.

A similar point is easily made about architectural style, be it the style of a period and region, of a particular architect, or just of a particular building. Musical analogies have thus proven quite illuminating in discussions of both poetry and architecture. Tzonis and Lefaivre's analysis of classical architecture provides a good example. While they resist the linguistic analogy, they insist on the analogy with music: architecture is said to be subject to the same fundamental principles of order as music; similarly, the "modulation" within a

building from the Doric to the Ionic order is likened to a change in key; like musical compositions, works of architecture are said to exhibit a certain rhythm; and musical figures such as *Takterstickung,* where "the end of a part or element is fused with the beginning of another," prove just as illuminating in architecture as in music.[15] But such "musical" features do not make a building an assertion. Stylistic unity has nothing to do with syntactic unity.

Similarly, it is important not to confuse syntactic unity with what has long been demanded of a successful work of art, *aesthetic unity.* Nor is syntactic unity like the *functional unity* of an efficient machine. To decide whether a sentence is complete we have to decide whether it succeeds in saying something, in the sense of making an assertion that can be true or false. If buildings could be considered assertions, talk about the language of architecture would have a clear sense. But despite Otto's self-proclaimed discovery of the "spatial sentence," his use of "sentence" proves unilluminating. Stylistic, aesthetic, and functional unity are hardly sufficient to warrant such talk.

Such considerations suggest more generally that we should be on guard before semiotic and structuralist approaches to architecture. As Scruton maintains, they often offer little more than a jargon that obscures more than it reveals. And yet I cannot follow Scruton when, invoking the authority of Frege, he insists that the syntax of language derives from its relation to truth and concludes that for this reason "the whole 'science' of semiology is founded upon a mistake."[16] This presupposes an overly reductive understanding of language even in its literal (perhaps we should say, its proper) sense, an understanding that could not begin to do justice to the language of poetry. If the language analogy has something to offer to architectural theory, it would seem to be the discourse of poetry to which we should look, rather than to the discourse of science with its true or false assertions—to rhetoric rather than to logic.

But often we give the term "language" a wider meaning. We may consider any communication relying on some code language. An expressive sigh, for example, or a style of building may be considered language in this sense: relying on a code, they communicate a particular way of standing in the world, a particular ethos. "Sign" and "signified" here can often be given quite specific meanings. In this sense architecture, too, belongs to language, not because it makes assertions, nor because its "saying" can be translated without significant loss into spoken or written words, but because of its style and particular configurations of elements within that style. Scruton has done us a service by showing that talk about the language of architecture is often careless and misleading. But it need not be: such metaphorical talk can also be illuminating. There is good reason to speak of the language of architecture, to attempt to understand that language, and develop a semiotics of architecture. Such attempts are especially important given the language crisis of modern architecture.

2

It was Charles Morris who defined "semiotics" as "the theory of signs" and distinguished among *syntactics*, which investigates the relationships between signs without regard to how these signs relate to reality, *semantics,* which examines just that relation, and *pragmatics,* which is concerned with the way these signs are actually used.[17] Morris had hoped that this new theory of signs would prove as fundamental for the human sciences as the theory of atoms had proven for the natural sciences.

That language should provide the paradigm of a sign system is to be expected. But this paradigm should not lead us to forget that there are many nonlinguistic sign systems, which can be called "languages" in an extended sense. Think of traffic signs, or of what is often called "body language." Such signs, too, are meant to regulate or at least influence behavior, although their point is not to describe reality. Therefore they do not usually allow us to call their use "true" or "false," at least as long as truth is understood as the correspondence of a thought or assertion and what is the case (though talk of "false signs" and "erroneous traffic signals" has an obvious sense). But even if such signs do not make assertions about what is the case, they nevertheless invite us to look at things in a certain way and thus invite or even demand a certain behavior. In this sense even the most functional architecture may be understood as a sign or rather as a system of signs.

Umberto Eco illustrates this point with an anecdote about some housing units provided for "rural populations in Italy by the 'Development Fund for the South.' "

With modern dwellings complete with bathrooms and toilets at their disposals, the local people, who were accustomed to taking care of their bodily functions in the fields and unprepared for the mysterious sanitary fixtures that arrived, took to using the bowls as cleaning tanks for their olives: they put the olives on some net they had suspended inside, then flushed and proceeded with the washing. So while we can all see that the form of the standard toilet bowl is "made for" the function it normally suggests and permits, and might be tempted to recognize a profound aesthetic and logical tie between that form and that function, in fact the form denotes that function only on the basis of a system of established habits and expectations, and thus on the basis of a code. And when another code (adventitious but not illegitimate) is superimposed on the object, the bowl denotes another function.[18]

We think of toilets as objects that unambiguously declare their function. But, as Eco shows, their form denotes that function only on the basis of long-established habits and expectations. Essentially the same point is made by David Macaulay in his wonderful *Motel of the Mysteries,* in which he imagines some later civilization digging up an American motel.[19] Particularly impressive are the pictures that show the excavation of a bathroom, which these archaeologists misinterpret as a burial chamber. The toilet bowl becomes a sacred urn. Other objects, which to us declare their function quite unambiguously, are similarly misinterpreted. The possibility of such misinterpretation supports Eco's claims that, to function properly, objects must not only be functional but must communicate or denote that function and, second, that they can denote that function only on the basis of a code tied to established habits and expectations. To function effectively as a door, the object in question must look to us like a door. To use Eco's terminology, the door must not only be but denote a door. This is no problem as long as builders and those for whom they build are so embedded in a given practice that the meaning of most architectural elements can simply be taken for granted. Still, Eco is right to insist: no designer can make his or her creations functional without the support of an existing codification. This becomes problematic when new elements are introduced or when familiar elements are given a radically new look.

To return once more to the example of a door: most doors not only are but also look to us like doors, where by "door" we mean a movable barrier made of wood or some other material. But at the same time they carry other significations. They may thus speak to us of the wealth or status of the house's owner; they may be welcoming or discourage entry; they may mark the threshold separating the private from the public, or the sacred from the profane. Eco would say that the door *denotes* its primary function, while it *connotes* a complex of secondary functions (fig. 32). (In certain contexts I find it more natural to speak of secondary meanings.)

32 | Portal, St. Elizabeth, Marburg. Photo by author.

Consider a much more complicated architectural object, a Gothic cathedral (see fig. 37). It, too, can be said to denote its primary function, that is to say a church, a place where people assemble to worship the Christian God. Put more simply: like most churches, a Gothic cathedral looks like a church; it fits the church type. But a Gothic cathedral also signifies the City in Heaven of which the book of Revelation speaks, also the temple Solomon built in Jerusalem, also the ladder of Jacob's dream, also Noah's ark; in addition, it signifies the cosmos—and it would be easy to add other significations. We can show that the secondary meanings associated with the church have changed in the course of history. A Rococo church (see fig. 100) thus has secondary meanings that in many ways overlap yet also differ from those of its Gothic precursor.[20] As these connotations change, architects will search for new means of communication. Without an understanding of these secondary meanings, there can be no adequate understanding of the "language" spoken by, say, a Gothic or a Rococo church, no grasp of its characteristic style. By connoting secondary meanings, a building will inevitably also communicate an ideological perspective, a way of standing in the world, a specific ethos.

If we can speak with Tafuri of the language crisis of modern architecture, this crisis would appear to involve not its denotations or primary meanings—these we can leave to the engineer or builder—but only its secondary meanings. That is, we have become unsure about what works of architecture should connote: should they, for example, gesture toward the machine, toward an autonomous piece of sculpture, or toward a billboard? Each communicates a different ideological perspective. This of course puts the matter much too crudely. Buildings can gesture in countless directions, and such gesturing is likely to vary with different buildings' tasks. But what has been said should be sufficient to suggest that uncertainty about the secondary functions of architecture is inevitably also uncertainty about what our ideological perspective should be; indeed, I would consider distrust of all ideological perspectives itself such a perspective, a perspective that architecture can and today often does communicate.

Should the architect try to fix both primary and secondary functions, denotation and connotations? Let us suppose the building in question is a house. An eighteenth-century farmhouse (fig. 33) strongly determined both its primary and secondary functions and thus in a very strong sense "placed" those dwelling in it. I suspect that most of us would find having to live in such a house spiritually confining, even as we are likely to feel twinges of nostalgia when we now visit it. But we have learned to demand more freedom, more openness.

Very much a postmodernist, Eco suggests that *"the architect should be designing for variable primary functions and open secondary functions."*[21] Yet what does this tell the architect? Does it point him or her in any direction? Consider both parts of Eco's statement: what would it mean to design for variable primary functions? How variable? Consider not a building but an old upright piano that some cabinet maker has transformed into a writing desk or perhaps a bar. Now it has a different primary function. Should the original builder have anticipated such a change? Few would make such a suggestion. But then the primary function of a piano is easily specified. In the case of buildings each specification is more open to question.

Take a church that has been transformed into a museum, or a theater, or a house.
Should the modern church architect design in such a way that the churches will allow or
even invite such appropriation? The result would be an architecture overly concerned about
future contingencies, which would ill serve its present purpose. In this extreme form Eco's
suggestion must be resisted. It becomes much more sensible, but also unproblematic and
therefore uninteresting, when we apply it to a case like the following: when designing a
house, should we design each room in such a way that it denotes a particular primary
function? Think, for example, of what is to be a bedroom. I would tend to answer "yes," but
without much conviction. How does an unfurnished room denote "bedroom"? Consider a
room's location in the house, its relationship to bathrooms and kitchen, the privacy it
affords. When visiting a still unfurnished house, we usually have little difficulty in locating
what are to be the bedrooms; the master bedroom in particular is likely to denote its primary
function quite unambiguously.

Suppose now that our house is built to accommodate a family of five, but that in
the not-too-distant future the children will have left: their leaving is likely to mean that
certain rooms will change their primary functions, so that what was a child's room now
becomes a parent's study. Such transformations of primary function are to be expected. To
be truly functional, the house should not fix these functions so strongly that it discourages
changes that are inseparable from the owner's continuing appropriation of the house. A
house should accommodate and even invite such appropriation. It should therefore be less
like the perfect performance of a symphony than like a score that requires being performed

again and again and always differently. In this sense we should no doubt plan for variable primary functions: how variable will depend on what changes in primary function are anticipated.

More interesting is Eco's claim that the architect should design for open secondary functions. But to say that these functions be left completely open amounts to saying little more than that architecture should be functional in the traditional sense. The architect, on this view, should not try to impose secondary meanings, should not try to impart a particular ideological content to what he or she builds. Yet as Eco also knows, architecture cannot help but communicate some such meanings, some ideological content, even when, like much postmodern architecture, what it communicates may be mainly ideological uncertainty and confusion. Take the problem of building a house in a particular neighborhood, or, to make the matter more manageable, the problem of what roof to give our house. Should it be flat or peaked? If peaked, should it be—to give just a few of the options—a simple saddleback roof, a hipped roof, or a mansard roof? How should our roof relate to those of neighboring houses? And such questions will proliferate. We shall have to consider what those for whom we build, indeed all those who will have to live with our roof, expect a roof to look like. No matter what decision we make, this roof will not leave secondary functions completely open, as Eco demands; it will communicate some ideological meaning, regardless of whether it conforms to the roofs of the neighborhood, or, by being wildly different, denies such solidarity, or, like the roofs of so many neighborhoods today, communicates ideological confusion and uncertainty, testifying to the language crisis of modern architecture.

3

To distinguish between the denotation and connotations of a building, Eco relies on the distinction between primary and secondary functions. Obvious as this distinction may seem at first, it proves increasingly elusive when we attempt to put it to work. Consider the following remark:

A seat tells me first of all that I can sit down on it. But if the seat is a throne, it must do more than seat one: it serves to seat one with a certain dignity, to corroborate the user's "sitting in dignity"—perhaps through various accessory signs connoting "regalness" (eagles on the arms, a high, crowned back, etc.). Indeed the connotation of dignity and regalness can become so functionally important that the basic function, to seat one, may even be slighted, or distorted: a throne, to connote regalness, often demands that the person sitting on it sit rigidly and uncomfortably (along with a scepter in his right hand, a globe in the left, and a crown on his head), and therefore seats one "poorly" with respect to the primary utilitas. Thus to seat one is only one of the functions of the throne—and only one of its meanings, the first, but not the most important.[22]

The same can be said of many buildings, for example, of many houses or churches. Can there indeed be a work of architecture without some such distortion? Is it not just this that distinguishes a work of architecture from a mere building, built only to serve what Eco calls the "primary *utilitas,*" as a house might be built only to provide basic shelter?

But it may not even make sense to distinguish between primary and secondary functions, to understand the former in terms of bodily needs and to privilege it. Consider once more the example of a house. Eco would say it denotes a house, relying on a conventional code (fig. 34). And no doubt, houses tend to look like houses, where the idea of what a house should look like, the house type, will vary with natural and social conditions. Still, the primary function of a house is by no means obvious. To be sure, houses serve the requirements of dwelling. But do we know what it is to dwell and what its requirements are? They certainly cannot be reduced to being protected from a threatening outside: we need to be sheltered not only physically but psychologically. The soul, too, needs a house. With this Eco's distinction between primary and secondary function, between denotation and connotation, begins to blur.

But Eco's semiotic approach raises a more serious problem. As he develops it, it remains so general that instead of illuminating for us what one might call the language of architecture, it leads us away from what is specifically architectural. Take Eco's version of the often-told story of the first human shelter:

34 Houses in Arvada, Colorado. Photo credit: Ken Abbott.

Still "all wonder and ferocity" (to use Vico's phrase), driven by cold and rain and following the example of some animal or obeying an impulse in which instinct and reasoning are mixed in a confused way, this hypothetical Stone Age man takes shelter in a recess, in some hole on the side of a mountain, in a cave.

Sheltered from the wind and rain, he examines the cave that shelters him, by daylight or by the light of a fire (we will assume he has already discovered fire). He notes the amplitude of the vault, and understands this as the limit of an outside space, which is (with its wind and rain) cut off, and as the beginning of an inside space, which is likely to evoke in him some unclear nostalgia for the womb, imbue him with feelings of protection, and appear still imprecise and ambiguous to him, seen under a play of shadow and light. Once the storm is over, he might leave the cave and reconsider it from the outside; there he would note the entryway as a "hole that permits passage to the inside," and the entrance would recall to his mind the image of the inside: entrance hole, covering vault, walls (or continuous wall of rock) surrounding a space within. Thus an "idea of the cave" takes shape, which is useful at least as a mnemonic device, enabling him to think of the cave later on as a possible objective in case of rain; but it also enables him to recognize in another cave the same possibility of shelter found in the first one. At the second cave he tries, the idea of that cave is soon replaced by the idea of cave tout court—a model, a type, something that does not exist concretely but on the basis of which he can recognize a certain context of phenomena as "cave."[23]

Particular caves now have come to denote "cave"—or, more generally, the idea of shelter—and to connote feelings of protection. But the language of denotation and connotation does little work: in this sense anything at all may be said to denote and connote. A particular rose, for example, is seen *as* a rose: it denotes "rose." But "rose" also carries a host of connotations. How then does talk of denotation and connotation help to illuminate the distinctive language of architecture?

Suppose we insist, mindful of the suggestion that to build is necessarily also to communicate, that a building is a human creation that to function must signify how it is to be used. This of course does not distinguish buildings from tools or machines. A hammer, a telephone, or a car, too, not only denotes but inevitably carries connotations. Today the producer is more often concerned with the latter, and its effects on the product's sales, than with the former, which is more easily taken for granted. Buildings, too, can be discussed in this way as complicated tools or machines, but such an approach fails to illuminate the distinctive way in which buildings speak to us. Nor do we make up for this failure when we consider the specific functions buildings serve and inquire into the requirements of human dwelling. Such inquiry threatens to lose sight of the distinctive voice of, say, a house or a factory: buildings speak to us by bounding space.

Works of architecture speak to us as all buildings do, and yet there is the difference insisted on by Ruskin and Pevsner: architecture must be thought both in relation to and also in opposition to all merely functional building. The same goes for its "language"—but how then is that language to be understood? Eco points out that buildings denote the building type they exemplify. Works of architecture, I want to propose—very tentatively, only as a kind of trial balloon and quite aware of how preposterous such a proposal is likely to seem—do not just denote the kind of building they are: they do so by representing buildings. *Architecture is an art of representation.*

Representation and Symbol

7

1

Architecture an art of representation? This hardly seems a promising approach to our problem. There are of course buildings that are representations in the most obvious sense: seafood restaurants that represent lobster traps, cheese stores that represent wheels of Swiss cheese, rock shops that represent rocks. Venturi, as we have seen, considers such buildings "ducks." He also points out that our very inability in such cases to overlook a building's representational character, while often amusing, also prevents us from taking it seriously as a work of architecture. My attempt to saddle architecture with the idea of representation may thus seem much less promising than Venturi's call for an architecture of signs. If the latter invites an architecture of billboards with appended sheds, the turn to representation threatens to elevate the Long Island Duckling into the Parthenon of a new architecture.

Such elevation is hardly my intention. I am fully aware that the lessons the Long Island Duckling holds are for the most part negative: lessons about what to avoid. But if so, what do I mean by "representation"? Consider once more the duck-shaped drive-in. No doubt, we have here a building that represents in a very obvious sense. It does so by resembling a familiar animal: a duck. Venturi calls this architecture as duck a symbol and opposes it to a shed to which symbols are applied: imagine another drive-in as a boxlike structure decorated with painted ducks. In the first case the building itself is a representation; in the second case it is a shed decorated with representations. In both cases "representation" seems to me a better term than "symbol": a painting representing a duck does not symbolize it, nor does a sculpture of a duck, nor does the Long Island Duckling. But I do not want to put too much weight on this distinction: "symbol" and "representation" are used so broadly that there seems little point in insisting that a particular use of the term is the correct one. Often the terms are used interchangeably. However, given the argument of this chapter, I find it useful to distinguish between them.

Both symbol and representation stand for or signify something else. Both may thus be considered signs, but a representation must in some way resemble what it represents; a symbol may but need not resemble what it symbolizes (i.e., some symbols are representations). To say that a representation must in some way resemble what is represents is not to claim that it must look just like it. A map of Washington, D.C., for example, does not look very much like the city, but once you have understood the form of representation, the resemblance becomes quite clear. I should not want to call the map a symbol of Washington, although its form of representation certainly relies on symbols. Some understanding of the way maps represent and should be read is assumed: for example, moving up on the map usually represents going north; if a different orientation is chosen, this will in all probability be indicated on the map. Often maps include a legend, giving the scale and explaining some of the symbols. To understand these symbols is part of understanding the chosen form of representation, of knowing how to read the map. The same goes for reading the floor plan or the section of a building—or for reading a pictorial representation.

"Representation," as I am using the term, means something like "picture." To speak of works of architecture as representations is to ascribe a pictorial function to architecture. To understand the representational character of a particular building, we have to understand just how it pictures, that is, the form of representation employed. As in the case of the map, that form will rely on certain symbols; and as in the case of the map, the representation may not look very much like what is represented.

But must we not agree with Venturi, when he insists that "ducks" are seldom relevant today? And not only today: is there not obvious tension between the demands of building and the demands of representing objects like ducks? This seems to argue against a comfortable joining of architecture and representation. And yet, much traditional architecture is representational in a quite straightforward sense: only what it represents are usually not ducks or cheese wheels, but buildings. Works of architecture represent buildings. Representing buildings, they denote a building type.

2

Once the representational function of architecture has been understood in this way, it is easy to come up with examples. That homes are expected to represent houses is shown by the many attempts to supply what is felt to be lacking, when such expectations are unmet for economic or aesthetic reasons. Take today's mobile homes, designed to provide basic shelter at modest cost. With Eco we may want to say that they denote basic shelter, while at the same time they carry a host of connotations (e.g., "cheap," "mobile," "temporary"), some of which meet with resistance from those who, usually for economic reasons, find it convenient to live in such not very homelike homes. Of particular interest are the different ways in which people have appropriated and transformed such shelter. Seemingly insignificant additions can tell us a great deal about what people expect a home to look like: an added porch, fake shutters, or a lamppost make the mobile home look more like a real house (fig. 35), where the idea of what "a real house" should look like will no doubt differ with different cultural backgrounds, experiences, and individual dreams. Often a pitched roof is a particularly effective way of signifying "home." Such additions cannot be dismissed as a mere frill, as unnecessary decoration. The added ornament, if we can call it that, lets basic shelter represent a house. Ornament here has a doubly representational function: representing a house, it re-presents the shelter in such a way that it connotes "home."

Trailer park, Boulder, Colorado. Photo credit:
35   Ken Abbott.

Such transformation has its analogue in the way some of the masterpieces of modern architecture have been appropriated by those who had to live in and with them. The transformation of Adolf Loos's Steiner House provides a telling example: although it is not only a functional building but an aesthetic object of high rank, the stark purity of the original appears not to have satisfied a later generation, which replaced Loos's quarter circle in the rear with the traditional gable motif and added sgraffito decoration. While no doubt a desecration of a work that has earned its place in the canon of modern architecture, this is also a gesture that forces us to question the presuppositions that governed the formation of that canon. Le Corbusier's Pessac housing project had to suffer a similar desecration.[1] Worse was the fate that befell Minoru Yamasaki's award-winning Pruitt Igoe housing: to Charles Jencks its much-discussed demolition on "July 15, 1972, at 3. 32 P.M. (or thereabouts)" after less than twenty years of occupancy sounded the death knell of modern architecture.[2]

A perhaps more convincing example of representation in architecture is provided by Christ Church in New Haven (fig. 36), which I choose not because it is in any way extraordinary but because it is so typical—any number of nineteenth-century buildings could be used to make the same point. Built in 1895, this church not only is but signifies a church, that is to say, a particular building type, and it does so by representing a church: not just any church, but a Gothic church. And not just any Gothic church: through Victorian glasses (the architect, Henry Vaughn, had studied in England), Christ Church looks back, past centuries and across an ocean, to medieval England. Here, too, representation serves self-representation. Presenting itself to us as it does, the church acquires quite specific connotations, communicates a specific stance. We can almost guess that this would be an Episcopal church, High Church, and upper class.

With the passage of time the church has acquired other, unintended connotations. Isolated now by the rush of traffic, looking a bit lost on its little island, Christ Church testifies to where our priorities lie, regardless of what we hear and statistics tell us about this

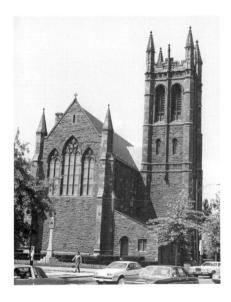

Christ Church, New Haven (1895). Photo credit: Barbara Endres.

36

being a deeply religious society. This church, and many others like it, speak of a religion that for at least two hundred years now has been anxiously looking backward, increasingly pushed to the periphery of life, into a museum. But the point that matters in this context is a different one: presenting itself to us as a representation, not just of a church but of a particular kind of church, the building acquires quite specific connotations that tell us a great deal about those who built it, their values, and their faith. And it does so not incidentally, in the way any useful object connotes countless secondary functions, but by asserting these connotations. Representation is here used self-consciously to endow the church with a specific significance. A different model or a different form of representation would communicate a different understanding of what a church should be.

Any American city is filled with buildings that would serve equally well to make the same point, including courthouses, post offices, museums, and especially banks. We may wonder whether banks were built in the image of temples to show that the glue that holds this society together is not religion but money. In any event, the representation of sacred architecture belonging to another age would appear to have a more modest function: to bathe a building in an aura of significance, to declare that what we are looking at is not just another building but a work of architecture. No longer understood, traditional architecture is plundered by the architect to dress up functional buildings in borrowed finery. As Christian Norberg-Schulz observes, "In the nineteenth century architecture turned away from cultural symbolization. The meaningful forms of the past were devaluated, dome and pediment were used to 'dignify' museums, banks and other institutions, and the stained-glass window was introduced into the private dwelling. Only recently the demand for cultural symbolization has again come to life, because we understand that modern architecture needs this dimension to create a meaningful environment."[3]

I agree that architecture needs this dimension to meet what I have called its ethical function. But did the nineteenth century fail to recognize that need? Consider once more the many buildings that were built to represent temples. Does representation here really have *no* symbolic function? Different building tasks now claim something of the dignity that once belonged only to sacred architecture, giving voice to that claim by representing the sacred architecture of the past and thus usurping its place. Such usurpation reflects the compartmentalization of our life, the splintering of the old value system, each splinter now claiming something of the dignity that once belonged to the whole. Even for those of us who still consider ourselves religious, religion no longer possesses the integrative power that it once had and that may indeed be taken to define genuine religion, which "cannot survive as a particular aspect of life,"[4] a power mirrored in the ability of traditional churches to provide a village or a city with an integrating center (see figs. 2, 68).

3

Even if these examples show that there is representation in architecture, they do not permit the generalization that what raises architecture above mere building is representation. A building like Christ Church suggests that the turn to representation in architecture is born of a nostalgic look at the stronger architecture of past centuries, which was supported by a more integrated way of life and by a faith we now lack.

But need this mean that representation in architecture is necessarily tied to a timid historicism? For an answer let us look at the architecture Christ Church sought to represent: Gothic church architecture. As Hans Sedlmayr and Otto von Simson have demonstrated, the Gothic church, too, can be understood as an architecture of representation.[5] According to Thomas Aquinas's often-invoked definition, "The house in which the sacrament is celebrated signifies the Church and is called 'church'": *Domus in qua sacramentum celebratur, ecclesiam significat et ecclesia nominatur.*[6] A church, according to this definition, is above all a building that has a certain function: it is a house, a public house in which the community gathers to join in celebration of the sacrament. Its size helps to denote this public function (fig. 37). Beyond this, we all have certain expectations of what a church should look like. An inherited code allows the architect to design a building that those for whom he or she builds will recognize as a church, that represent the church type, although today we are unlikely to give much thought to why this type evolved as it did—why, for example, we tend to give towers to our churches. Although we are all familiar with the church type and builders of churches continue to rely on it, we no longer understand it.

But let me return to Thomas's definition. It claims that to really be a church, a building must signify the Church. On this understanding a church should be more than what has been called a prayer barn or a meeting hall, with added decoration or not. When Thomas writes that the church building signifies the Church, "Church" means not a building but the living church, a church underway to the community of the faithful, dwelling with God.[7] To describe this community, St. Paul used an architectural metaphor: "So then you are no longer strangers and sojourners, but you are fellow citizens with the saints and members of the household of God, built upon the foundations of the apostles and prophets, Christ Jesus himself being the chief cornerstone, in whom the whole structure is joined together and grows into a holy temple in the Lord; in whom you also are built into it for a dwelling place of God in the Spirit" (Eph. 2.19–22, RSV). The church building signifies a quite specific ideal of communal dwelling, even as it signifies also the distance that separates our present time-bound existence from this ideal, signifies the journey character of life, speaks of both path and goal. This ideal presided over and informed the evolution of medieval church architecture. It provided something like an invisible theme on which generations of church builders composed countless variations.

How can a building, a material thing in space and time, signify an ideal, invisible community? The Middle Ages found hints of an answer to this question in the traditional conception of the faithful as dwelling with God in an ideal city: the City of God. The church building signifies an ideal dwelling by representing an ideal architecture. This understanding provides the key to any decoding of the language of medieval church architecture, a language that in Catholic countries remained alive well into the eighteenth century.

Such an answer, however, suggests another question: how can the church, a structure very much of this world, represent the invisible City in Heaven, which, it would seem, can be called a city only in a very metaphorical sense? If the thought of that city is to guide builders, the imagination first has to translate it, bring it down to earth, and clothe it in

View of choir, cathedral, Amiens. Credit:
Giraudon/Art Resource, N.Y.

images. But where does such translation find its measure? Medieval Christians had an obvious answer: they could appeal to the authority of Scripture, which, while it does not describe the Heavenly City in detail, yet offers suggestive texts that invite imaginative elaboration. The most important of these is Revelation 21.2–4: "And I saw the holy city, new Jerusalem, coming down out of heaven from God, prepared as a bride adorned for her husband; and I heard a great voice from the throne saying, 'Behold, the dwelling of God is with men. He will dwell with them, and they shall be his people, and God himself will be with them; he will wipe away every tear from their eyes, and death shall be no more, neither shall there be mourning nor crying nor pain any more, for the former things have passed away.'" If this passage gives the builder only the thought of a city "prepared as a bride adorned for her husband,"[8] what follows is somewhat more specific:

And in the Spirit he carried me away to a great, high mountain, and showed me the holy city Jerusalem coming down out of heaven from God, having the glory of God, its radiance like a most rare jewel, like a jasper, clear as crystal. It had a great, high wall, with twelve gates, and at the gates twelve angels, and on the gates the names of the twelve tribes of the sons of Israel were inscribed. . . .

    And he who talked to me had a measuring rod of gold to measure the city and its gates and walls. The city lies foursquare, its length the same as its breadth; and he measured the city with his rod, twelve thousand stadia; its length and breadth and height are equal. He also measured its wall, a hundred and forty-four cubits by a man's measure, that is, an angel's. The wall was built of jasper, while the city was pure gold, clear as glass. (Rev. 21.10–18)

At least since the third century, the church building was understood as a representation of the Heavenly City. "The church is, mystically and liturgically, an image of heaven. Medieval theologians have, on innumerable occasions, dwelt on this correspondence. The authoritative language of the dedication ritual of a church explicitly relates the vision of the Celestial City, as described in the Book of Revelation, to the building that is to be erected.[9] This, of course, still does not tell us how the character of this image is to be understood. The description provided by St. John offers at most a few hints. And even had these been more specific, how could they have been taken literally? Does not the spiritual, ideal character of what is to be represented render all attempts to offer a more or less literal representation of the city described in Revelation hopelessly inadequate? If a church can be said to represent it at all, representation can only be understood as the creation of an analogous image. To understand its form of representation we have to understand its use of analogy.

    It is important to keep in mind that the Heavenly City described by St. John was thought to have been prefigured by other places and structures mentioned in the Bible. To decode a medieval church we have to understand it not only as pointing forward, to the glory to come, but also as pointing backward, to the glory that has been, to paradise; it also points to such divinely inspired structures as Noah's arc, Moses' tabernacle in the desert, and perhaps most significantly to the temple Solomon built in Jerusalem. The church also recalls that place where in a dream Jacob saw heaven open and linked to earth by a ladder: a new Bethel, the church, too, is none other than the gate of heaven. All these anticipations of the Heavenly Jerusalem are by the same token precursors of every church, and to these precursors we can add visionary structures such as the temple described by Ezekiel. Representing these precursors, the church figures the City of God.

Even when expanded in this manner, the description of the church as an analogous representation of the City of God remains too vague to provide clear directives, offering little more than an occasion that invites imaginative elaboration in the light of experience. What then is a city? A place where a multitude dwells together. But in what manner? There are no simple answers to such questions: "city" might connote a sheltered place, whose walls promise security and peace, a refuge from the insecurity reigning outside; or it might connote a festal place, a place of joy welcoming weary travelers with unfamiliar delights, allowing them to forget the toil and pain of the everyday; or it might connote the residence of a ruler. Conceptions of what a city is and should be can be expected to change with time and place.

The early Christian basilica, for example, has been said to imitate a Roman city, complete with entering gate and arcaded streets, a city turned outside in. Its golden or starred ceiling functions as a metaphorical device, designed to show that what is being imitated is not just any city but the City of God, ruled by Christ as king.[10] The turmoil that swept through Europe as the Roman world gave way to a very different order saw the transformation of the city into a walled fortress. This changed understanding of the city is mirrored by the changed appearance of the church, which often is now thought of as a bastion against the forces of darkness. Especially the western part of the church comes to represent a fortress, defended by St. Michael and his angels against the devil's hordes who were thought to dwell in the west and whose darkness daily conquers light, while salvation comes from the east, where every morning light conquers the dark of night. The Gothic cathedral presupposes a still different appropriation of the heavenly paradigm: responding to the qualities of light and order associated with the City in Heaven, it attempts to create an analogous work here on earth.[11]

The fact that one can speak of "the early Christian basilica" or "the Gothic cathedral" shows that in architecture, too, paradigms evolve that determine expectations of what a church should look like: the "normal idea" of a church, which can be expected to vary with history and region. Such paradigms furnish the architect with something like a shared language; paradigms found expression in conventions. Sometimes such paradigms emerge quite suddenly—Abbot Suger's building of St.-Denis provides perhaps the most obvious example. In such cases we may want to speak of revolutions in architecture. To understand this particular revolution we have to look beyond material and liturgical constraints, which remain relatively constant. "What distinguishes the cathedral of this epoch from preceding architecture is not the eschatological theme but the different mode of its evocation. If we seek to understand the birth of Gothic architecture, it is not sufficient to ask *what* the Gothic cathedral represents. The questions on which our attention must focus are *how* the Gothic cathedral represents the vision of heaven and what was the religious and metaphysical experience that demanded this new mode of representation."[12]

To claim that today there exists a language crisis in architecture is to suggest that architects no longer feel bound to a paradigm whose significance compares to Suger's St.-

Denis, a paradigm strong enough to establish a common architectural language, although the establishment of just such a paradigm was one of the goals of the founders of the Bauhaus. Lyonel Feininger's woodcut of a Gothic cathedral in modern cubist forms, which served as the frontispiece of the founding manifesto of the Bauhaus, gives striking expression to Walter Gropius's aspiration: "Together let us desire, conceive, and create the new structure of the future, which will embrace architecture and sculpture and painting in one unity and which will one day rise toward heaven from the hands of a million workers like the crystal symbol of a new faith."[13] Can there be a modern cathedral? Is the idea of one dominant building task, comparable in social significance to the medieval church, compatible with the shape of modernity? Suger's achievement lies behind us. No longer can we take seriously the conception of the church as an image of the Heavenly Jerusalem: we no longer share the worldview it presupposes. Given our very different understanding of reality, talk of the Heavenly City has little more weight than a fairy tale. And yet, the churches of the Middle Ages still speak, though no longer as representations of the Heavenly City; we have to turn to texts by art historians like Hans Sedlmayr and Otto von Simson to learn about the representational character of this architecture. But then in what sense do they still speak to *us*?

4

To understand the medieval church as a representation of the City of God, we have to understand its form of representation. Unfortunately, unlike maps, medieval churches are not accompanied by legends explaining the symbols employed. "Gothic builders have been tight-lipped about the symbolic significance of their projects."[14] Nor did they need to say much: an understanding of the spiritual significance of things was so much part of the medieval worldview that it could be taken for granted.[15]

Consider the medieval use of gold. By its very nature, gold invites connotations of preciousness and immutability. It offers itself to the artist as what I want to call a natural symbol, gesturing beyond this fleeting world toward timeless transcendence. Only this lets us understand why the introduction of the gold background into Western painting, presumably by a monk laboring sometime in the tenth century on the Reichenau in Lake Constance, should have been accepted with such enthusiasm that it has almost come to define our understanding of medieval painting.[16] To make sense of the gold background's enthusiastic reception, we have to understand it as a metaphorical device. Like the "Once upon a time" with which the brothers Grimm begin so many of their fairy tales, like the golden halos that encircle the heads of saints, the gold background of medieval paintings transports us into a realm that knows nothing of linear, historical time. The same holds of the use of gold in medieval churches: especially when illuminated only by flickering candles, altars and paintings, liturgical vessels and furniture glow with an unfamiliar golden light. Again and again Abbot Suger thus dwells on what to a St. Bernard seemed an indefensibly extravagant use of gold—"What does gold have to do in the sanctuary?"[17] Suger's answer invokes the authority of Scripture:

If golden pouring vessels, golden vials, little golden mortars used to serve, by the word of God or the command of the Prophet, to collect the blood of goats or calves or the red heifer: how much more must golden vessels, precious stones, and whatever is most valued among all created things, be laid out, with continual reverence and full devotion, for the reception of the blood of Christ! . . . The detractors also object that a saintly mind, a pure heart, a faithful intention ought to suffice for this sacred function; and we, too, explicitly and especially affirm that that it is these that principally matter. [But] we profess that we must do homage also through the outward ornaments of sacred vessels, and to nothing in the world in an equal degree as to the service of the Holy Sacrifice. For it behooves us most becomingly to serve our Saviour in all things in a universal way—Him Who has not refused to provide things in a universal way and without any exception.[18]

Suger was sufficiently self-conscious on this point, or thought it of sufficient importance, to address it with some verses on the church's gilded main doors:

Whoever thou art, if thou seekest to extol the glory of these doors,
Marvel not at the gold and the expense but at the craftsmanship of the work.
Bright is the noble work; but being nobly bright, the work
Should brighten the minds, so that they may travel, through the true lights,
To the True Light where Christ is the true door.
In what manner it be inherent in this world the golden door defines:
The dull mind rises to truth through what is material
And, in seeing this light, is resurrected from its former submersion.[19]

Gold is understood here as a metaphorical device meant to transport the observer from this world into "the True Light." It is to open up a spiritual perspective. There is thus a sense in which the art of the Middle Ages is more profoundly "perspectival" than the art of the Renaissance: its perspective is "*perspective in the truest sense, in that it looks through the visible to the invisible, through the significans to the significatum.*"[20] The symbolic use of gold stands in the service of the Gothic cathedral's perspectival art of representation.

The stained-glass window, which, just as the gold background has come to be part of our understanding of medieval painting, has come to be part of our understanding of medieval church architecture, is another such metaphorical device: not just decoration but an essential part of this architecture's perspectival form of representation.[21] Suger, by no means the first to use stained glass, leaves no doubt concerning the significance it holds for him:

These translucent panels, "vested," as he put it, with sacred symbols, are to him like veils at once shrouding and revealing the ineffable. What they mean to him, what they were to mean to others, is best shown in Suger's selection of the scene of Moses appearing veiled before the Israelites. St. Paul had used the image to elucidate the distinction between the "veiled" truth of the Old Testament and the "unveiled" truth of the New. In Suger's interpretation it epitomized his very world view, to which, in the footsteps of the Pseudo-Areopagite, the entire cosmos appeared like a veil illuminated by divine light. Such a view was peculiarly that of his century. The image he had found for it in the stained-glass window was so obvious, so irresistible, that it was bound to impress itself on everyone's mind. We cannot be surprised that the image was powerful enough to induce Suger to transform the entire sanctuary into a transparent cosmos.[22]

The spiritual perspective of the Middle Ages made it seem obvious that the light that makes things visible here on earth bears an analogical relationship to the true, divine light. When we today hear the cosmos being described as "a veil illuminated by divine light," we are likely to consider such language "merely metaphorical." For the medieval artist, however, light was more than just another natural phenomenon: it seemed to bridge the gulf separating this world from the sacred beyond. And though the worldview that supported the spiritual perspective of the Middle Ages is no longer our own, we should ask ourselves whether the medieval symbolism of light, or the Platonic for that matter, does not presuppose a natural symbolism of light that still speaks to us, natural because inseparable from the way human beings dwell on earth and beneath the sky. In the next chapter I shall return to the idea of natural symbols and suggest that if architecture is to regain its voice, it must listen to and respond to their language.

As important as the Gothic cathedral's light symbolism is its symbolic use of order. To represent the City in Heaven, the architect had to endow his work with an order analogous to the order that figures so prominently in descriptions of the Heavenly Jerusalem and of its precursors. The works of God, the master architect, were thought to provide the human architect with timeless models. For an expression of the presupposes understanding of reality, von Simson turns to Abelard:

After identifying the Platonic world soul with world harmony, he first interprets the ancient notion of a music of the spheres as referring to the "heavenly habitations" where angels and saints "in the ineffable sweetness of harmonic modulation render eternal praise to God." Then, however, Abelard transposes the musical image into an architectural one: he relates the Celestial Jerusalem to the terrestrial one, more specifically to the Temple built by Solomon as God's "regal palace." No medieval reader could have failed to notice with what emphasis every Biblical description of a sacred edifice, particularly those of Solomon's Temple, of the Heavenly Jerusalem, and of the vision of Ezekiel, dwells on the measurements of these buildings. To these measurements Abelard gives a truly Platonic significance: Solomon's Temple, he remarks, was pervaded by the divine harmony as were the celestial spheres.[23]

The discussion points to the dual significance of the cathedral, which analogously represents both God's creation and the Heavenly City. Given the medieval worldview, such dual reference is to be expected, since the order of the cosmos, especially that of the heavens, was thought to be analogous to that of the Heavenly City, as both had the same divine author.

Although in this case obviously bound to a particular period, the Gothic cathedral's dual reference presupposes a more archaic understanding of human dwelling and building. I use "archaic" here not so much to mean "primitive," suggesting temporal priority; rather by "*archē*" I mean an origin that does not lose its power with the passage of time because it has its foundation in the very nature of human dwelling. To make their home in the world, that is, to build, human beings must gain more than physical control: they must establish spiritual control. To do so they must wrest order from what at first seems contingent, fleeting, and confusing, transforming chaos into cosmos. That is to say, to really build is to accomplish something very much like what God is thought to have done when creating the world. Small wonder that the architect has been so often thought in the image of the Creator, the Creator in the image of the architect.

5

No longer can we take seriously conceptions of the church as representations of the Heavenly City. For us talk of a city in heaven is at best a far-fetched metaphor. And even if for some of us that metaphor has retained a living sense, must what it signifies not be conceived in such spiritual terms that any attempt to imagine it, let alone to represent it here on earth, will be thought to violate its spirituality? Are not all attempts to think of the church as a representation of the City in Heaven illegitimate, because they fail to do justice to the unbridgeable gap that separates God and humanity, Heaven and earth, spirit and body, ear and eye? As we meet with an insistence that divine transcendence inevitably escapes eye and imagination, that it is to be discovered only within by the spirit, the conception of the church as a representation—albeit only an analogous representation—of the Heavenly Jerusalem can no longer be taken seriously. If architecture is to represent anything at all, if it is to be more than a "prayer barn" or an auditorium where people gather to listen to the proclamation and interpretation of God's word, it now will have to find its models on earth, in history. Linked to an ever more radical understanding of divine transcendence,[24] the same spiritual revolution that issued both in the Reformation and the new science led also to a temporalization, and that means also a literalization, of the idea of representation, when that idea was not abandoned altogether, as it increasingly was, especially in Europe's now Protestant north.

But if the Heavenly City was no longer available as a paradigm to be represented, could one not substitute for this ideal architecture historical paradigms? St. Peter's in Rome deserves to be singled out. Moreover, the Bible appeared to offer paradigms built according to a divine plan: Noah's ark, the tabernacle in the desert, and, by far the most important, the temple in Jerusalem. Joseph Rykwert has discussed some of the attempts that were made by Renaissance and Baroque theorists to reconstruct the original appearance of this temple—twice rebuilt, three times destroyed, now forever lost—the most important of these by the Jesuit Juan Bautista Villalpanda.[25]

The broad influence of this reconstruction, extending well into the eighteenth century (fig. 38), is easy enough to understand. If, as the Bible assures us, Solomon built his temple according to a divine plan, it must have been the ideal building, the master paradigm, which, could it only be recovered, would provide all architecture with its measure. The question, What did the temple look like? is thus at the same time the question, What canon should architecture follow? Unfortunately Solomon's temple has left only a faint literary trace: the information the Bible gives us provides no reliable idea of how it might have looked. Once again imaginative reconstruction had to fill in what the Bible had left unsaid.

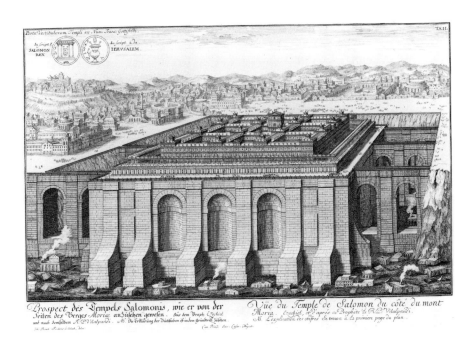

Johann Bernhard Fischer von Erlach, Solomon's temple. Source: Fischer von Erlach, *Entwurff einer historischen Architektur* (Vienna, 1721). Credit: Beinecke Rare Book and Manuscript Library, Yale University.

In the Renaissance renewed interest in the theorizing and architecture of antiquity had suggested that in Vitruvius one could discover

all the elements necessary for architecture that would accord with both reason and nature and therefore be the undisputed, the only true architecture. A further assumption was commonly made: that the Temple in Jerusalem was also built in this manner, with the same magnificence as could be reconstructed from the ruins of classical antiquity. . . . The sixteenth century could not simply make its appeal to nature and reason, or base its procedure on the operations of reason prompted by philosophy; in the sixteenth century rules which had to be invoked constantly, such as that of the orders, had to have the sanction of grace, had to be derived from, guaranteed by divine revelation.[26]

Between revelation and reason, Solomon's temple and Vitruvian principles there could be no contradiction. On this view, all architecture worthy of its name remains indebted to its Solomonic origin, seeks to represent this ideal building.

Representation and Symbol

6

Although still used to justify architectural practice, appeals to God as the master architect soon came to have little more than the rhetorical function of legitimating a practice supposedly in accord with human nature and supported by the authority of what remained of the architecture of the ancients. That the appeal to human nature does not depend on such legitimation is demonstrated by the architectural theory of the Enlightenment.

As the ex-Jesuit Marc-Antoine Laugier's *Essay on Architecture* demonstrates, the attempt to found architectural practice on human nature did not mean that the understanding of architecture as an art of representation was therefore abandoned. According to Laugier, too, it is its power of representation that lifts the genuine work of architecture beyond mere building. What it represents is once more an ideal building, although the authority of this ideal is now based not on the authority of Scripture, nor even on the authority of Vitruvius to whom Laugier is so obviously indebted, but on the authority of nature: "It is the same in architecture as in all the other arts: its principles are founded on simple nature, and nature's process clearly indicates its rules. Let us look at man in his primitive state without any guidance other than his natural instincts."[27]

Laugier begins by asking himself what human beings would build in the state of nature, unburdened by centuries of civilization, without any aid or guidance other than their reason and natural interests. He imagines his "savage" needing a place to rest. By a murmuring brook, he stretches out in the soft grass, but soon the burning sun compels him to look for cooling shade. He finds what he seeks in a delightful forest, but a downpour soaks him; shivering, he looks for a dry shelter. A cave offers protection, but the darkness and the stale, foul air make his stay there unbearable.

He leaves and resolves to make good by his ingenuity the careless neglect of nature. He wants to make himself a dwelling that protects but does not bury him. Some fallen branches in the forest are the right material for his purpose; he chooses four of the strongest, raises them upright and arranges them in a square; across their top he lays four other branches; on these he hoists from two sides yet another row of branches which, inclining towards each other, meet at their highest point. He then covers this kind of roof with leaves so closely packed that neither sun nor rain can penetrate. Thus man is housed. Admittedly, the cold and heat will make him feel uncomfortable in this house which is open on all sides but soon he will fill in the space between two posts and feel secure. (pp. 11–12)

Laugier takes the construction of this primitive hut to be a purely natural process. "Natural," however, cannot mean that buildings rise as plants grow. Is it not precisely nature's indifference to our needs that awakens human ingenuity? If Laugier can claim to have described "the course of simple nature" (p. 12), it is human nature he has in mind (fig. 39).

Architecture is an art precisely to the extent that it imitates the "natural" work of the primitive builder. Like all art, architecture too relies on imitation: "by imitating the natural process art was born. All the splendors of architecture ever conceived have been modelled on the little rustic hut I have just described. It is by approaching the simplicity of this first model that fundamental mistakes are avoided and true perfection is achieved. The

Marc-Antoine Laugier, primitive hut. Source: Laugier, *Essai sur l'architecture* (Paris, 1755), frontispiece. Credit: Beinecke Rare Book and Manuscript Library, Yale University.

39

pieces of wood set upright have given us the idea of the column, the pieces placed horizontally on top of them the idea of the entablature, the inclining pieces forming the roof the idea of the pediment" (p. 12). Given his construction of the primitive hut, it is not surprising that Laugier would admonish architects to learn from the Greeks. We moderns cannot hope to surpass their achievement: "Architecture owes all that is perfect to the Greeks, a nation privileged to have known everything connected with the arts. The Romans, able to admire and capable of copying the excellent models which the Greeks had left them, wished to add something of their own and thereby only taught the world that when the stage of perfection is reached there is no other way than to imitate or decline" (p. 8). Laugier pleads for an architecture that is *doubly representational*: architecture should represent Greek architecture, and by so doing it will most adequately represent the primitive hut that is supported by the authority of human nature. Representing the primitive hut, architecture recalls us to the essence of building, to its *archē*, its timeless origin. Successful architecture recalls this *archē* by representing the "natural" elements of building: post, lintel, and roof. Laugier understands architecture as arche-tecture.

There are at least two things we can still learn from Laugier. First of all we can learn from him the significance of attempts to challenge long-established and therefore easily taken for granted practices by appealing to a more original understanding of building and dwelling, one less subject to the prejudices of a particular time and place, less at the mercy of subjective whim. As Joseph Rykwert points out,

The return of origins is a constant of human development and in this matter architecture conforms to all other human activities. The primitive hut—the home of the first man—is therefore no incidental concern of theorists, no casual ingredient of myth or ritual. The return to origins always implies a rethinking of what you do customarily, an attempt to renew the validity of your everyday actions, or simply a recall of the natural (or even divine) sanction for repeating them for a season. In the present rethinking of why we build and what we build for, the primitive hut will, I suggest, retain its validity as a reminder of the original and therefore essential meaning of building for all people: that is, of architecture. It remains the underlying statement, the irreducible, intentional core.[28]

Appeals to the primitive hut challenge every conventionalism. Conventionalists may seek to escape from arbitrariness by grounding practice in an ongoing tradition; but we moderns have become too reflective, too critical, simply to entrust ourselves to what has been. No longer are we willing to repeat what has long been done, just because it has become part of tradition. At the same time we are not satisfied with departures from tradition motivated only by subjective whim. We have no choice but to attempt to articulate what is essential and natural. Such articulation is the point of speculation about the appearance of the first hut. The primitive hut has played in architectural theory much the same part that the social contract has played in political theory. Whether there ever was such a hut matters as little as whether there ever was such a contract. Both are imaginative constructs informed by reason and meant to legitimate a certain practice. Both are characteristic expressions of the Enlightenment's confidence that the authority of reason and nature could replace divine sanction. And although today we have grown less confident about the power of reason to guide our practices, our confusion leaves us no reasonable alternative to reappropriating the lessons of the Enlightenment. We, too, have to try to recover origins, in a process that is as much a turn back to the past as a turn to what is essential. In this sense Laugier's speculations present an abiding challenge.

The second thing that we can learn from Laugier's *Essay* is to be distrustful of all such constructs.[29] The young Goethe already scolded Laugier for having been too infatuated with the column; an unprejudiced look at the buildings around him should have taught him his error: "The column is not at all an element of our dwellings; rather it contradicts the essence of all our dwellings. Our houses don't originate in four columns in four corners; they originate rather in four walls on four sides, which take the place of all columns, exclude all columns, and where you add them they are an oppressive excess."[30] Important here is Goethe's appeal to "our" houses and dwellings. We need to be wary of appeals to nature: all too often such appeals have been unmasked as historical prejudice claiming an undeserved dignity for what is proposed. Consider once more the way Laugier arrives at his version of the natural language of architecture. Laugier begins with a man in the state of nature. Among his needs is the need for shelter, which forest and cave meet only inadequately. The attempt to remedy that inadequacy leads to the construction of the first house, the paradigmatic building, which is constructed both in the image of the forest and in the image of the cave. In *Intentions in Architecture* Christian Norberg-Schulz was to return to this view: "The cave represents the first spatial element, in contrast to the vertical-horizontal relation which is an ordering principle. The unification of these two factors created what we may call 'the first architectural symbol system.'"[31] As Laugier presents this system, the forest is allowed to triumph over the cave: only columns, entablatures, and pediment are considered essential parts of architecture. Walls, windows, doors, and the like are of course permitted, but they do not have the same importance.[32] They are said to make no essential contribution to beauty.

Supposedly born of the need for shelter and informed by the natural protection provided by forests and caves, the primitive hut turns out to look rather like the then much revered temples of antiquity. Not that Laugier thought the architecture of the ancients beyond criticism: he was too much of a rationalist for that. Only reason can endow past structures with the legitimacy that makes them models worthy of imitation by demonstrating that they are indeed representations of the archetypal building. But it was of course not so much the Greek temple that was constructed in the image of the primitive hut, as that hut that was constructed in the image of the Greek temple (fig. 40).

When Laugier is thinking of exemplary structures, he is not thinking only of the architecture of the ancients. Gothic architecture with its forest of columns is given a similar legitimacy and takes its place beside the architecture of the ancients as a secondary paradigm. Laugier's *Essay* has been shown to have encouraged the early evolution of neo-Gothic architecture.[33] But this only reinforces suspicions that instead of recalling us to the timeless origin of building and dwelling, Laugier's construction of his primitive hut owes far too much to prejudices of his particular time and region. It leads readily to an architecture of sheathed skeletons, appropriate to a heavily forested region where wood is the most obvious building material, rather than to an architecture of continuous surfaces, appropriate to a region where the natural building materials are mud, brick, or stone. Laugier's "nature" speaks with a local voice, and Laugier's interpretation of that voice is very much colored by his particular situation.

But even if Laugier's construction of his primitive hut cannot claim to have recovered the true origin of building, and even if all our ideals of dwelling are precariously constructed by all-too-fallible human beings, inevitably colored by cultural and personal prejudice, this does not mean that the ideals are therefore altogether arbitrary. What gives architecture its direction is the tension between conventional wisdom, inherited paradigms, and what more profoundly and immediately claims us, between what one says and does and what we feel should be said or done. Even if reason can never seize the dream of a building that would do full justice to genuine dwelling, even if all such dreams will prove as elusive as the Heavenly City or the Solomonic temple, as the source of regulative ideals such speculation about the origin of building is indispensable. In this sense Laugier's account, questionable as it is in so many ways, remains exemplary. We are still not done with his primitive hut. And even though, as Wolfgang Herrmann points out, "by the early nineteenth century hardly anyone still upheld the thesis of a direct metamorphosis of the wooden hut into the Doric temple. In Germany Aloys Hirt was probably the last who accepted it without reservation; in England Thomas Hope"[34]—we are still not done with the idea that architecture, too, is an art of representation.

40

Parthenon seen from the Propylaea. Credit:
Alinari/Art Resource, N.Y.

Representation and Re-Presentation

8

1

Earlier I asked: if architecture is to recover its lost voice, what language is it to speak? Quite tentatively, the last chapter suggested an answer, which I would like to repeat now as a question: is the language of architecture, too, a language of representation? Do works of architecture represent other buildings, and, at the same time, an ideal building, a structure that exists only in the imagination as an aesthetic idea? That such an understanding fits at least some architecture is shown by the Gothic cathedral, which represents the Heavenly Jerusalem by representing terrestrial structures, understood as its figures. Laugier's *Essay* demonstrates that this understanding of the doubly representational character of architecture is not limited to medieval church architecture. He too suggests that what lifts architecture beyond mere building is its power of representation. And once again, what Laugier has in mind is a double representation: representing a Greek temple, architecture represents at the same time an ideal building, an imaginative construct, though one supported no longer by the authority of the Bible but, at least so Laugier thought, by reason and nature. Representing the primitive hut, works of architecture recall us to the arche of building. Architecture is building that speaks to us of its essence.

To speak of this essence, architecture has to make conspicuous the usually taken for granted and hardly noticed natural elements of building. The Greek temple architecture that furnishes Laugier with his paradigm is supposed to have accomplished this by translating wooden vertical supports into columns of stone, the supported horizontal members into entablatures, the inclined members that carry the roof into pediments. Such translation represents the translated element; thus translated, it draws our attention. Re-presentation makes visible.

Laugier's account, supposedly based on the authority of reason and nature, clearly owed all too much to the prejudices of the culture to which he belonged, but we should not therefore dismiss the view that building becomes architecture when it re-presents itself, turning to the architecture of the past in order to represent an imagined architecture that answers to dreams of genuine building and dwelling. It would be foolish to look for this ideal building in history or in some timeless Platonic heaven. A necessarily precarious construction of the imagination, it can be expected to change with changing hopes and expectations.

In the eighteenth century Laugier was not alone with his understanding of the representational character of architecture. Such a view seemed an almost inevitable extension of the representational character of all art, which was hardly questioned. For a more explicit statement we can turn to Laugier's contemporary, Francesco Milizia, who took architecture to be "an art of imitation, as are all the other arts. The only distinction is that some of them have a natural model on which the system of imitation may be based. Such a model architecture lacks, but she has an alternative one offered to her by the natural industry of men when they built their first dwellings."[1] Architecture represents building.

That architecture in its highest sense is an art of representation is also the view of Goethe. Goethe distinguishes three stages of the art of building. The first and most basic does not really deserve to be called "art," for here building serves only the human need for comfort. Building is said to become an art only when it is also concerned to create objects that present themselves to the eye as a harmonious whole.[2] So far Goethe simply restates the familiar understanding of the work of architecture as a functional shed transformed by aesthetic considerations. But such a view does not satisfy him. Architecture of the highest rank (and here Goethe is thinking especially of Palladio) requires something else—a turn to poetry, to fiction, and that means also to representation: "Architecture is no art of representation, but an art for itself. But at its highest stage it cannot do without representation. For the sake of illusion, it translates the properties of one material into another, as, for example, wooden construction is imitated by all the columnar orders. It translates the properties of one building into another, as it combines, for example, columns and pilasters with walls. It does this to become varied and rich. And as it is hard for the artist always to feel whether he is doing the right thing, so it is hard for the knowledgeable critic to judge whether he has done the right thing."[3]

Only a few years after Goethe, the philosopher Schelling insisted that representation alone allows us to understand the art character of architecture. For, as Kant observed, by its very nature architecture serves needs that have nothing to do with what beauty requires. If it is to raise itself to the level of art, architecture therefore has to distance itself from functional building, even as it must remain such building. "As long as architecture serves mere need and is only useful, it is *only* this and cannot be beautiful at the same time. This it can become only when it becomes independent of such need. But since it cannot become absolutely independent, since finally, by its nature, it again and again borders on this need, it becomes beautiful only when it becomes at the same time independent of *itself,* becomes, so to speak, the *potentiation* and the free representation *of itself.*"[4]

Hermann Bauer has suggested that this understanding of architecture as an art of representation offers us a key to the architectural sensibility of the late eighteenth and early nineteenth century, to its love of the picturesque and of Palladian architecture.[5] And no doubt it does. But is the significance of such insistence on the representational character of architecture thus limited? Could it be that, as Schelling suggests, it is precisely its self-reference that gives architecture its distinctive voice and raises it above mere building? As I pointed out in the previous chapter, to deserve to be called a work of architecture, a house cannot just be a house; nor does it help to observe, with Eco, that to function successfully as a house, a building must denote the house type. To deserve to be called a work of architecture the house must represent a house, and by so doing, re-present itself as a house: Goethe might say, create the fiction of a house. The same can be said of a church, a museum, a city hall, an airport. Representing other architecture, the work of architecture re-presents itself in the image of an ideal, thus creating a fiction about itself. By its choice of what to represent and of the form of representation, it communicates a particular understanding of what is taken to matter in architecture, signifying a particular ideal of building and thus of dwelling.

The architectural theory of the Enlightenment found in the Greek temple's translation, a supposed original edifice made of wood turned into a structure of stone, the most obvious illustration of the essence of architecture as an art of representation. Consider once more the translation of wooden posts into columns of gleaming marble. Representation here means also translation into a different medium.[6] As a result of such translation a particular building element is rendered conspicuous and that precisely is the point: representing a vertical post, the column re-presents itself in such a way that we attend to its ideal essence. A post, according to Hegel, is simply "stuck into the ground and stops wherever a load has been placed on it. Because of this its actual length, its beginning and end, appear only as a negative determination from without, as an accidental determination that does not belong to it in its essence. But to have a beginning and an end are determinations that are inseparable from the concept of a bearing column, and for this reason they have to be made manifest as features proper to it. This is the reason why a developed beautiful architecture gives the column a basis and a capital."[7] Triglyphs are discussed similarly, following Vitruvius, as representations of the incised heads of wooden beams supported by the architrave, metopes as representations of the spaces between them.[8] Important here is Hegel's insistence that the work of architecture be experienced as a perfect whole,[9] and that means also that its terminations be experienced as intended: the Greek temple thus insists on a gabled roof not because the climate demands this, but because it achieves the re-presentation of a building element meant to be supported, not to support.[10] Architecture perfects building and its elements, where such perfection is understood at the same time as a re-presentation of the essential. From the point of view of function all such re-presentation is of course a frill, as unnecessary as all decoration.

This association of re-presentation and decoration invites a reconsideration of the distinction between decoration and ornament. Can we perhaps understand ornament as decoration that serves to so re-present the decorated that it presents itself to us as a fiction of itself? Ruskin's attempt to locate what distinguishes architecture from mere building in the addition of ornament becomes more plausible when we understand ornament as having a re-presentational function.

Consider a different example. Buildings serve dwelling. It is thus hardly surprising that at least since Carlo Lodoli architectural theorists have appealed to function when they have wanted to challenge inherited paradigms that no longer carried conviction. Taken literally, Lodoli's commandment, "In architecture only that shall show that has a definite function, and derives from the strictest necessity,"[11] appears to leave no room for ornament—nor for representation in architecture, nor indeed for any understanding of architecture as something different from mere building. The architectural manifestoes of the twentieth century demonstrate the continued life of Lodoli's commandment. A rigorous functionalist has to reject all attempts to have a building re-present its functionality. He or she has to be critical of the many buildings designed to have the look of being functional, often at considerable cost: at the price, that is to say, of true functionality. We can thus distinguish *rigorous functionalism* from what we can call *rhetorical functionalism*. The latter aims not so much at functional building as at a building's self-re-presentation as a functional building. Think of the Seagram Building or the Centre Pompidou. Rhetorical functionalism seeks to give buildings the look of being functional; it connotes an embrace of the economic imperative that has helped shape the modern world, acceptance of all the advantages of science and technology. Thus it communicates a modernist ethos and calls us to a particular way of dwelling. We may well want to question this call, wondering whether it does not do violence to the requirements of genuine dwelling, even as it claims to do justice to the shape of modernity. All I want to insist on here, however, is that what makes such buildings works of architecture is the addition of features, of ornament is an extended sense, that let them become representations of an architectural ideal.

An analogous point must be made concerning Lodoli's other commandment: "Architecture must conform to the nature of materials."[12] There is a sense in which the necessities of building enforce such conforming: every craftsworker must understand the nature of his or her materials if the work is to succeed, if knives are to cut or walls to support vaults. But just as regard for function does not mean that an attempt has been made to display that function and to make it conspicuous, so regard for materials does not mean that an attempt has been made to call the nature of the material of which an object has been made to our attention. Quite the opposite is true. When tools work well we often forget what they are made of. We really look at such objects of daily use only when something goes wrong: we lose a heel of a shoe or tear our shirt. Suddenly the familiar and usually overlooked becomes conspicuous and all too visible. The same may be said of buildings: after the unfamiliarity of a newly painted wall has worn off, the broken yellow we have chosen may only call itself to our attention when suddenly made to glow by the late afternoon sun or when it blisters or peels.

But buildings that deserve to be called works of architecture invite us to attend to materials in a very different way.[13] Heidegger thus says of a Greek temple that it "does not cause the material to disappear, but rather causes it to come forth for the very first time and to come into the Open of the work's world. The rock comes to bear and rest and so first becomes rock; metals come to glitter and shimmer, colors to glow."[14] We can distinguish buildings that merely presuppose a regard for the properties of materials from architecture that re-presents these materials and thereby reveals their properties: the heaviness of stone, the glitter of metals, the brightness of colors. Re-presenting its materials, the work of architecture reveals its being. Such revelation requires that materials are worked in a way that invites us to step back from our usual involvement with things. Representation here means quite literally re-presentation: the builders of the Parthenon took up, worked, and re-presented the marble from Mount Pentelicus.

I do not want to plead for what is often called truth to materials, only to insist on the rhetorical function of their re-presentation. Re-presentation lets materials speak. The

41 | Brickwork on houses on Main Street, Northampton. Photo by author.

importance of that function becomes apparent when we consider the variety of materials—for example, materials made available only by modern technology, such as cast iron, steel, concrete, plastics, and tinted glass, as opposed to more traditional materials, such as granite, brick (fig. 41), and wood. Different materials are differently affected by the passage of time, they speak of different attitudes to time and thus of different ideals of building and dwelling. The re-presentation of materials is part of the language of architecture. It helps the architect communicate an often quite specific ideal of building and dwelling.

2

With the suggestion that a building becomes a work of architecture when designed as an idealizing self-representation we seem to have left behind Pevsner's remark that what distinguishes architecture from mere building is that "it is designed with a view to aesthetic appeal." Or could it be that aesthetic appeal and self-representation are more intimately linked than first appears? Such a link is suggested by the familiar conception of aesthetic distance, which may be understood as a corollary of Kant's insistence on the disinterested character of our perception of the beautiful. Consider Edward Bullough's often-repeated claim that aesthetic experience "has a *negative,* inhibitory aspect—the cutting out of the practical side of things and of our practical attitude to them—and a positive side—the elaboration of the experience on the new basis created by the inhibitory action of distance."[15] Such action may issue from both object and subject, in varying degrees; that some particular thing, say a plough, is experienced as an aesthetic object depends both on that thing's appearance and on the observer's circumstances and aesthetic susceptibility. Some persons are no doubt more likely to perceive a particular thing aesthetically than others: a specific configuration of shapes and colors that strangely moves me may leave you quite indifferent. To claim that beauty presupposes "the inhibitory action of distance" is to point out that the beautiful presents itself to us as if in a frame. Thus "framed" it re-presents itself, invites us to have a second look, to look again, now with more open eyes. Recall Hegel's understanding of the column as an aesthetically perfected post.

An obvious way of transforming something familiar and therefore all too readily overlooked into an aesthetic object is quite literally to re-present it by displacing or translating it, as we do when we carry it into a new environment, place it on a pedestal, or put it into a frame. Duchamp demonstrated the revelatory power of such re-presentation with his readymades: for example, when he took a quite ordinary urinal, called it a fountain, and exhibited it as a work of art. While all too easily made into a recipe, such re-presentation of the familiar seizes an essential aspect of all art. Much modern art can be said to have emphasized re-presentation at the expense of representation. What first moves us when we look at a painting by Pollock is less what the painting represents than the way paint and canvas have been re-presented. We can speak here of a realism of materials,[16] which has its counterpart in buildings that do not just use up steel and glass, concrete and stone, brick and wood, but re-present them and thus render them more visible, such that the interest we take in such re-presentation will intertwine with the connotations carried by what is re-presented.

What is usually called representation in art can also be considered a kind of re-presentation, although what is re-presented is here not the material thing itself but only its appearance. Representation in this case does not preserve the material identity of what it represents; it means translation not into a different environment but into a different medium, and such translation may also be a re-presentation that celebrates the material employed. Consider Turner's *Steamer in a Snowstorm* (1842): as a re-presentation of paint, the painting not only represents but reveals its medium's stubborn materiality. The appeal of such works is inseparably bound up with the tension between representation and re-presentation. Not that such tension destroys the unity of the work of art. On the contrary, it gives it life. Think of the Parthenon frieze as both a representation of the Panathenaic Festival procession and a re-presentation of Pentelic marble (fig. 42).

As the last example hints, architecture also lives in such tensions. Consider once more the Enlightenment's understanding of the Greek temple as a representation of a wooden hut: here, too, representation intertwines with re-presentation. The temple's columns represent wooden posts, while at the same time they re-present the marble, let it speak with its own voice, so very different from the voice of dark granite or red brick. Representing posts, the columns also re-present themselves as posts, as vertical building elements whose function is to support the lintel's heavy horizontal, now transformed into an entablature. The column's fluting may seem mere decoration, but it, too, has a re-presentational function: it renders the column more substantial even while re-presenting its verticality (fig. 43).

Parthenon, north frieze. Detail showing young
men with sacrificial cow. Credit: Foto Marburg/
42 | Art Resource, N.Y.

Temple of Hera II, so-called Temple of Poseidon, Paestum, southwest corner. Credit: Foto
43 | Marburg/Art Resource, N.Y.

That this particular configuration of verticals and horizontals moves and speaks to us presupposes what I shall call the natural language of space. This natural language has its foundation in the way human beings exist in the world, embodied and mortal, under the sky and on the earth; it is bound up with experiences of rising and falling, of getting up and lying down, of height and of depth. Buildings speak to us because our experience of space and therefore of particular spatial configurations cannot but be charged with meaning. As a re-presentation of buildings, architecture re-presents and lets us attend to that "speech."

3

In chapter 4 I suggested that ornament must serve the ornament bearer if it is to live as ornament. Returning to this suggestion, I now would like to claim that the nature of such service is above all re-presentation. To be sure, as we have seen, there is much decoration in architecture that possesses something of the self-sufficient presence of a pure aesthetic object. But the more successfully an ornament captures our attention as such an aesthetic presence, the more arbitrary its relationship to the ornament bearer is likely to be; it becomes not so very different from the relationship of a painting to the wall on which it happens to hang or of a drawing to the paper that happens to support it. To become completely self-sufficient, ornament has to die as ornament, perhaps to be reborn as art for art's sake. If it is to live, ornament must serve the ornament bearer, as a bracelet should serve the arm it circles, or as a picture frame should serve the picture framed.[17] There is indeed a profound relationship between ornament and frame.[18] Both serve to re-present, though neither is a necessary condition of aesthetic beholding. As already pointed out, there is a sense in which everything beautiful may be said to re-present, and that is to say also to frame, itself. Beauty re-presents the beautiful. All beauty frames. It is with good reason that we say "pretty as a picture."

The re-presentational power of the frame helps explain Laugier's devaluation of the wall, and thus of windows and doors, his insistence that column, entablature, and pediment are the only "essential parts of architectural Order."[19] Hardly supported by an appeal to nature, this reduction of what is essential in architecture to a mere framework invites us to consider the representational and re-presentational function of these architectural elements: together column, entablature, and pediment not only represent a house, as is suggested by the term "aedicule," but make up a sheltering frame, where an arch may replace the entablature.[20] Taking up a suggestion from John Summerson's *Heavenly Mansions,* Arthur Drexler thus points out that the formal function of the aedicule is that of "a fictive frame around a void"; it is used "to indicate a hierarchy of importance through its intrinsic size, its location, and perhaps through variations in the arrangement of its components."[21] An essential part of modernism's rejection of the kind of architecture represented by the École des Beaux-Arts is the rejection of such frames: "one sure sign by which half-hearted acceptance or rejection or misunderstanding of the modern idiom could be recognized, early in the twentieth century, was a projecting frame around a window or an entrance. The device was correctly associated with the stripped-down classicism with which *Beaux-Arts* architects of an older generation sought to counter the emerging modern style."[22] Failure to understand the function of such framing and failure to understand the re-presentational function of ornament belong together.

One simple way to re-present even a modest building is by careful planting of trees and shrubs (see fig. 88), and another is to paint it: merely by painting a stringcourse a dark magenta red we can re-present it and its horizontality and thereby render a façade more articulate and easier to understand. In countless cities judicious painting has recently given new life to formerly white or grey buildings.

Architects have always known about the re-presentational function of color. According to Owen Jones, it is indeed this function alone that justifies its use in architecture.

The ancients always used colour to assist in the development of form, always employed it as a further means of bringing out the constructive features of a building.

Thus in the Egyptian column, the base of which represented the root—the shaft the stalk— the capital, the buds and flowers of the lotus or papyrus, the several colours were so applied that the appearance of strength in the column was increased, and the contours of the various lines were more fully developed.

In Gothic architecture, also, colour was always employed to assist in developing the panel- work and tracery; and this is effected to an extent of which it is difficult to form an idea in the present colourless condition of the buildings. In the slender shafts of their lofty edifices, the idea of elevation was still further increased by upward-running spiral lines of colour, which, while adding to the apparent height of the column, also helped to define its form.[23]

As Jones here suggests, architectural elements are given a special color primarily to make them stand out, to re-present them. Color directs the eye and helps articulate the organiza- tion of the architectural composition. But different colors inevitably carry different conno- tations: painted blue, ceilings tend to suggest the vaulting sky—think of the many porch ceilings painted a light blue, or of the darker blue we find on the vault of Gothic churches.

Colors do not just serve to re-present buildings and their elements, but they do so in ways that invite a quite specific understanding of their significance. Owen is especially interested in the analogy of building elements to organic forms. Are not "flowers separated by colour from their leaves and stalks, and these again from the earth in which they grow"?[24] He thus discusses the coloring of the Egyptian column as serving to re-present it in the image of the lotus or papyrus, that is to say, of a plant growing toward the light.

Often color helps us to read the figure traced by an ornament on the ground provided by ceiling or wall. Color here functions as the ornament of ornament, serving to re-present what has itself a re-presentational function and rendering it more visible. Some ornament is sufficiently three-dimensional not to require such re-presentation. The lower the profile, the greater the need for color. Good examples are furnished by the transforma- tion of Baroque ornament—with its acanthus leaves, fruit garlands, putti, and vases—into the much more restrained ornament of the Régence period, with its elegant flat bands, which cross and interweave in delicate patterns. While the former does not need color to assert itself, without the aid of color the figures of the latter would drown in the supporting ground. Owen Jones illustrates the same point by pointing to the remains of colored moldings on Greek temples. "High from the ground, and so small in proportion to the distance from which they were seen, . . . they must have been coloured in a manner to render them distinct and bring out the pattern."[25]

I have linked the language crisis of modern architecture to the emancipation first of ornament and, more generally, of beauty from re-presentational function. A pictorial representation of such emancipation is provided by Johann Esaias Nilson's *New Coffee-House* (1756; fig. 44).[26] As rocaille, the ornament of the Rococo, here becomes the object of pictorial representation, the precarious placement of this ornament on the threshold of ornament is revealed, as is the profound relationship of ornament and frame. Rather like ivy, rocaille here aggressively wraps itself around an artless house, although perhaps we are more likely to think of an octopus that has found its prey. Almost enveloping the house, this ornament conceals rather than reveals; instead of re-presenting the house that has to bear it, it presents itself as worthy of our attention in its own right.

Curious as this engraving no doubt is, it was yet very much part of a then thriving tradition of ornamental fantasies that influenced other designers, including architects; it now offers an image of a development that by then had helped shape architectural practice. As I attempt to show in some detail in my book on the Bavarian Rococo church, the architectural ornament of the Rococo is in fact on the verge of emancipating itself from the

Johann Esaias Nilson, New Coffee-House.

Source: Hermann Bauer, *Rocaille: Zur Herkunft und zum Wesen eines Ornament-Motivs* (Berlin: de

44 | Gruyter, 1962).

ornament-bearer, which it often seems to displace rather than re-present (see fig. 4). Such displacement must mean the death of ornament. Rocaille is ornament on the threshold of art for art's sake. There is a sense in which it can be called the last great ornament produced by the West, just as there is a sense in which the Rococo can be called the last of the West's great styles.

Another aspect of the engraving deserves our attention: just as rocaille refuses here to serve the ornament bearer, so the engraving's rocaille frame refuses to respect the normal subordination of the frame to what it frames. Not only ornament but the frame, too, here casts off its re-presentational function. And Nilson's engraving presents this twofold insubordination as at bottom one and the same phenomenon: for as the frame, refusing to function just as a frame, invades the picture, it turns into the ornament that envelops the house. That Nilson should thus link ornament and frame is more than an idiosyncratic invention on his part. As Hermann Bauer has shown, the ornament of the Rococo originated in the cartouche frames of artists like Jacques de Lajoue.[27] Nor is this simply a historical accident: the ornament of the Rococo only makes explicit the essential proximity of ornament and frame. That precisely this ornament should reveal the essential proximity of ornament and frame as perhaps no other ornament could is inseparable from the way ornament here, coming under the sway of the aesthetic approach, begins to shed its servitude and to re-present itself: just as it crosses the boundary that separates it from art for art's sake, ornament reveals the framing function of all ornament, which in turn figures the framing function of all beauty.

4

To insist on the framing function of ornament is to insist also that by itself ornament will not be able to give architecture a voice. Frames should serve the framed. When ornament speaks too loudly with its own voice, as it does when it presents itself to us as a self-sufficient sculptural presence, its voice drowns out that of architecture. Genuine ornament so re-presents buildings that it renders what the buildings have to tell us more explicit. But this is to say also that buildings must have a meaning long before architectural ornament re-presents and thereby let us attend to this meaning. How then is this meaning to be understood? "Semantics" has come to name the study of meaning. Without a semantics my proposal that architecture be understood as an art of re-presentation remains very much incomplete.

"Wherever meaning is present (and where it is not present we cannot properly think or speak) there are always two terms involved: that which means, and that which is meant: or the indicator (in the broadest sense) and the meaning."[28] Often the meaning is readily identified. Representations are meaningful in that sense; so are signs whose meaning habits or conventions have rendered fixed and definite. Take the symbols that help determine a map's form of representation, or traffic lights, or most terms of ordinary language: all these signs may be called "symbols," as I did in the previous chapter. Often, however, especially in the study of art and religion, "symbol" is given a different and more specific sense. Here "symbols" function not "to designate clearly as a means to efficient and assured communication" but "to evoke richness and suggestiveness of meaning, usually at some sacrifice of conventional and utilitarian exactness: e.g. the Cross to a believing Christian, the ominous contrasting connotations of the blood and darkness imagery in *Macbeth,* the mythic Father and Mother archetypes associated respectively with the powers of sky and earth." [29] So understood, symbols have no simple meaning to which we can point. They do not so much denote as carry connotations; they do not so much refer to or describe things as express and communicate a state of mind, a mood, a way of seeing, which endows what is experienced with an aura of significance that finally escapes adequate analysis.

Metaphors can be, but need not be, symbols in that sense. Everyday language is full of metaphors that have no significant symbolic function. A test of this is provided by our ability to translate a metaphor into a less metaphorical discourse without loss. To give just one example, when we today refer to Communists as "reds," we use a term that has lost almost all its former symbolic resonance. Only expressions that resist paraphrase function as symbols. Metaphors are sometimes distinguished from symbols by the suggestion that in metaphorical discourse what is said is different from what is meant, while when symbols are employed what is said and what is meant become entangled in a way that rules out such separation. But is the same not true of every strong metaphor?

I suggested that symbols have an expressive function and that what they express is a state of mind, inseparable from a way of seeing. Let me illustrate this point with a poem by William Carlos Williams, "Queen Anne's Lace":

Her body is not so white as
anemone petals, nor so smooth—nor
so remote a thing. It is a field
of the wild carrot taking
the field by force; the grass
does not rise above it.
Here is no question of whiteness,
white as can be, with a purple mole
At the center of each flower.
Each flower is a hand's span
of her whiteness. Wherever
his hand has lain there is
a tiny purple blemish. Each part
is a blossom under his touch
to which the fibers of her being
stem one by one, each to its end,
until the whole field is a
white desire, empty, a single stem,
a cluster, flower by flower,
a pious wish to whiteness gone over—
or nothing. [30]

What does the poem mean? What is its subject—a woman? a flower? It is easy to call the poem one extended metaphor, but what here is a metaphor of what? The poem's strength is inseparable from the way it rules out a simple answer to that question. This much, however, is certain: having read the poem I shall never be able to look at the flower of the wild carrot in quite the same way, especially not at the purple mole at the center of each tiny bloom. The poem offers no quasi-pictorial representation of Queen Anne's lace, and yet it re-presents that flower in a way that charges it with an aura of significance. It reveals a meaning that cannot finally be put into a univocal discourse. Poetic re-presentation lets the flower speak to us.[31]

Symbols function in architecture much as they do in poetry. The architect, too, lets buildings and the elements of buildings speak by re-presenting them in the image of other things. Consider once more the example—perhaps by now overused—of a column, which could be re-presented in the image of a Greek temple column, a wooden post, a flower, a tree, a person, or perhaps of all of these—the list invites indefinite extension. Such re-presentation is never the end of building. It is only an expressive means. Thus architecture that represents other architecture itself has a symbolic function. It invites us to look at it, and that means inevitably also at its environment, in a certain way—Christ Church (see fig. 36) can serve as an example. The point of symbols in architecture is not to describe but to express. Such expression is essential if we are to experience our environment as a meaningful order.[32]

As we saw in chapter 6, Manfredo Tafuri would have us understand "the emergence, within architectural criticism, of the *language problem*" as an "answer to the *language crisis* of modern architecture."[33] But why should there be such a crisis today? What stands in the way of simply satisfying this need for an architecture that speaks to us? To make the problem facing us a bit clearer, let me draw a distinction between different kinds of architectural symbolization. There is, as Eco can teach us, a sense in which every building cannot help but tell us something about its function and the kind of society that gave rise to it. An atomic power plant speaks to us in this sense; so does a tobacco barn. We can speak here with Norberg-Schulz of indirect symbolization.[34] This indirect symbolization is obviously not at issue when there is talk of a language crisis in architecture or of a loss of the symbolic function. Even the devaluation of traditional symbols, say of column or pediment, stained glass or Gothic arches, speaks to us and says something about the culture that gave rise to it. Thus it speaks to us, although this is hardly intended, of the disintegration of a value system that had its founder and foundation in God. Such speech, however, does not provide the kind of orientation demanded by Norberg-Schulz. What he requires—and what we have in mind when we speak of a disintegration or loss of the symbolic function in architecture—is direct symbolization relying on shared symbols.

Here it is useful to distinguish among different kinds of symbols:

1. First of all we can speak of *natural symbols*. Such symbols have their foundation in those aspects of our human being in the world that have remained more or less constant throughout history. Norberg-Schulz considers cave or shelter and menhir or upright stone (fig. 45) such natural symbols. Similarly the vertical and horizontal, and their intersection, the cross, are natural symbols. As a first step toward what we may want to consider the

| 45 | Menhir from Chamf-Dolent, Brittany. Credit: Giraudon/Art Resource, N.Y. | 46 | Votive column near Banz, Franconia. Photo by author. |

semantics of the natural language of architecture, I shall examine in the next four chapters the natural "language" of space and time, mindful of the metaphorical and therefore problematic character of such talk.

2. This natural language intertwines with *conventional symbols*. Consider once more the cross (fig. 46). Given the Western tradition, reference to that cross on which Christ died is difficult to avoid. Similarly pyramids today inevitably represent their Egyptian precursors, whose function they also recall. The pyramid is thus especially suited to grave monuments. But although now a conventional symbol, I would suggest that there is something about the pyramid form, this time-defying simple crystal,[35] which makes it no accident that the Egyptians seized on it in an attempt to symbolically defeat the terror of time. The conventional symbol presupposes and builds on a natural symbol.

3. Conventional symbols often are supported by the authority of *texts*. As I pointed out in the last chapter, the symbolism of the Gothic cathedral rests on the authority of the Bible. Beyond that, it presupposes a quite specific understanding of the spiritual significance of things. To really understand a Gothic church we have to be familiar with the language in which it is written. Although supported by natural symbols, this is not a natural language. As medieval theologians and poets have not tired of reminding us, this language is founded in the figures found in God's two books, the book of nature and the Bible. In the Middle Ages countless attempts were made to codify these meanings. Herbals and lapidaries furnish us with something like dictionaries to this now no longer living language.[36] Alan of Lille summed up the presupposed worldview in the often-repeated lines:

Omnis mundi creatura,

Quasi liber et pictura

   Nobis est, et speculum

Nostrae vitae, nostrae mortis,

Nostri status, nostrae sortis

   Fidele signaculum.[37]

"All the world's creatures are like a book, a picture, a mirror to us, the truthful sign of our life, death, condition, and destiny." The "to us" is important here. Creation presented itself as such a book to the medieval Christians who read nature, using as their key the word of the Bible, rendered authoritative by faith.

What stands between us and such a view is not just the fact that we no longer find ourselves part of a community united by this faith or, for that matter, by a comparable faith, but the questionable privilege we moderns have granted to univocity, to the simple and literal sense of the text and to an accordingly strict or, rather, narrow conception of meaning and language. We owe this insistence on literalness and univocity to the Reformation and to the new science, to Luther and to Descartes. But with this it becomes difficult, if not impossible, to make sense of anything like the medieval interpretation of the spiritual significance of things. That significance would seem to have collapsed together with the medieval worldview.

But does the collapse of this particular symbol system, based on the authority of a particular text, mean that things no longer speak to us of our life and death, our condition and destiny? Even if this particular symbolic language lies behind us, even if Scripture no longer offers us the key to the decoding of the hidden meaning of things, even if the very idea of a hermeneutics of nature may seem preposterous, nevertheless in some fashion things still "speak" to us.[38] The symbolic art of the Middle Ages may have lost its foundation, but this does not mean that it has altogether lost its voice. Buried in every conventional symbolism lies a natural symbolism, which still speaks to us if we are but willing to listen (fig. 47).

If architecture is to help to re-present and interpret the meaning of our daily life, it first has to open itself to these symbols. Needed today is a recovery of the natural in inherited conventional symbols. Architecture's representations of the architecture of the past should thus have an archaeological function. To repeat: architecture should become arche-tecture.

4. There is yet a fourth form of direct symbolization that deserves mention. A great deal of the symbolism we find in nineteenth- and twentieth-century architecture takes the form of a play with the symbolism of the past, which is no longer or only inadequately understood. Such play has been raised to a higher power by postmodern architecture. Consider the architecture from which Venturi would have us draw our inspiration. All too often, instead of unearthing in inherited conventions a still meaningful core, it mines these conventions to obtain material for aesthetic play. Symbols now become representations of symbols: *metasymbols*. The architecture of Las Vegas is replete with such metasymbols. So are such postmodern creations as Charles Moore's Piazza d'Italia in New Orleans (see fig. 12).

47 | Fence in Alameda County, California. Photo by author.

Enough has been said to allow a first answer to the question raised earlier: how are we to understand the claim that in the nineteenth century architecture lost its symbolic function? What architecture lacks today is what the great styles of the past provided: a developed system of symbols that architects could presuppose and therefore did not have to invent, which is not to say that they could not contribute to its development. We need to ask ourselves whether the possession of such a symbol system is necessarily a good thing. As the medieval example suggests, the authority of that symbol system is inseparably tied to a particular worldview, in this case to an interpretation of visible things as signs of a spiritual reality. That worldview was supported by the authority of Scripture. Today we can no longer appeal to this or any similar authority, nor is it easy for us to understand things as signs of an invisible reality. Talk of the language of things, or of the voices of space and time, is likely to be dismissed as relying on an unilluminating use of metaphor. Human beings speak, we are likely to insist, not things. Things are silent, simply there. Does not all talk of things speaking read our own being into these things?

The understanding of reality presupposed by the shape of the modern world appears to leave no room for natural symbols. On that understanding, must not all symbols be considered human creations? But to hold that there is nothing that transcends human beings and speaks to them, that reality itself is mute and meaningless, means nihilism. If there is to be an alternative to nihilism, it must be possible to make some sense of and learn to listen to the language of things. Our architectural inheritance can teach us both. Once more we have to learn to read in what was once called "the book of nature."

Part Three

Space, Time, and Dwelling

Tales of the Origin of Building

9

1

The previous chapter suggested that we may want to endorse the traditional understanding of the work of architecture as a functional building that art has rendered beautiful, provided that we keep in mind the re-presentational power of beauty. I offered the example of a bracelet, whose point is not so much to be appreciated as a self-sufficient beauty in its own right as to re-present the arm it circles—beauty here as a re-presentational function in a very obvious sense. Similarly the point of architectural ornament is not to be appreciated as a self-sufficient beauty but to re-present the ornament bearer. Denied its re-presentational function, ornament turns into arbitrary decoration.

But to emphasize in this way the re-presentational power of beauty, and more specifically of ornament, is inevitably to raise the question, What should architecture re-present? I sketched a first answer: a work of architecture is a building that re-presents itself in such a way that it renders itself more visible in its essence. But what is this essence?

2

In "Notes Toward a Supreme Fiction," Wallace Stevens has this to say about the origin of poetry:

From this the poem springs: that we live in a place
That is not our own and, much more, not ourselves
And hard it is in spite of blazoned days.[1]

Poetry is said to have its origin in the refusal of our demand for a place that is our own or even ourselves by the indifferent world into which we have been cast. This suggestion, that it is homelessness that provokes human beings to write poetry, applies equally to mythmaking—for what are myths but attempts to so re-present the world that it no longer seems indifferent to our needs, arbitrary and contingent, but is experienced as a place we can call home?[2] Architecture, too, is witness to the fact that we find it hard to live in a place "that is not our own and, much more, not ourselves."

It would therefore seem to be a mistake to suggest, as Joseph Rykwert does, that the Biblical description of paradise is incomplete in that it has nothing to say about a house.[3] What need was there in paradise for a house? Were Adam and Eve not well provided for in that walled garden? Only the Fall, which cast them out of paradise and forced them to toil on cursed ground, brought with it the necessity of building. Now human work had to remedy the deficiency of a world that transgression had rendered inhospitable, wresting from it a place that would allow for a more secure dwelling and in some measure make up for what had been lost.

Stories of the building of the first house tend to begin thus with descriptions of nature as a state of need. According to Vitruvius, for example, "the men of old were born like the wild beasts, in woods, caves, and groves, and lived on savage fare." An accident leads these protohumans to abandon their beastly existence: "As time went on, the thickly crowded trees in a certain place, tossed by storms and winds, and rubbing their branches against one another, caught fire, and so the inhabitants of the place were put to flight, being terrified by the furious flame." But curiosity soon conquered fear, and after the flames had subsided, "they drew near, and observing that they were very comfortable standing before the warm fire, they put on logs and, while thus keeping it alive, brought up other people to it, showing them by signs how much comfort they got from it." In this response to the gift of fire Vitruvius locates the origin of community, language, the art of cooking, and the art of building:

Therefore it was the discovery of fire that originally gave rise to the coming together of men, to the deliberative assembly, and to social intercourse. And so, as they kept coming together in greater numbers into one place, finding themselves naturally gifted beyond the other animals in not being obliged to walk with faces to the ground, but upright and gazing upon the splendour of the starry firmament, and also in being able to do with ease whatever they chose with their hands and fingers, they began in that first assembly to construct shelters. Some made them of green boughs, others dug caves on mountain sides, and some, in imitation of the nests of swallows and of the way they built, made places of refuge out of mud and twigs.[4]

Though they resembled wild beasts, Vitruvius's "men of old" refused to be content with the comforts—only intermittent—that nature provided. Experiencing the fire's warmth, they decided to watch over it, to feed it, thus creating an artificial climate. The construction of the first shelter serves this creation. Vitruvius thus understands the hearth gathering a community around itself as the generative center of the first house, as Gottfried Semper was to do much later: "Before men thought of erecting tents, fences, or huts, they gathered around the open flame, which kept them warm and dry and where they prepared their simple meals. The hearth is the germ, the embryo, of all social institutions. The first sign of gathering, of settlement and rest after long wanderings and the hardship of the chase, is still the set of the fire and the lighting of the crackling flame. From early times on, the hearth became the place of worship. . . . The hearth has kept its age-old significance up to the present. In every room the center of family life is still the fireplace."[5] Frank Lloyd Wright thus celebrated the "*integral* fire place": "To see the fire burning deep in the solid masonry of the house itself" still strengthens our sense of being at home.[6]

While Vitruvius likens his first humans to wild beasts, he also insists on what makes them different: not just their extraordinary ability to use their hands but their capacity to imitate, learn from, and improve on what they observe.

And since they were of an imitative and teachable nature, they would daily point out to each other the results of their building, boasting of the novelties in it; and thus with their natural gifts sharpened by emulation, their standards improved daily. At first they set up forked stakes connected by twigs and covered these walls with mud. Others made walls of lumps of dried mud, covering them with reeds and leaves to keep out the rain and the heat. Finding that such roofs could not stand the rain during the storms of winter they built them with peaks daubed with mud, the roof sloping and projecting so as to carry off the rain water.[7]

It is not surprising that these first buildings should recall the thickets, caves, and nests that shelter animals: such associations are to be expected when the need for shelter is reduced to the need for physical shelter, serving the most basic creature comforts.[8] But while Vitruvius's account of the origin of the house invites such a reductive account of the origin of building, it also calls it into question. For when he describes human beings as "naturally gifted beyond the other animals," he mentions first neither their capacity to use their hands, nor their ability to imitate and improve on what they observe, but their upright posture, which lets them raise their eyes up from the ground and "gaze upon the splendour of the starry firmament."

How are we to understand this remark? What does the sight of a splendor that fingers and hands cannot reach have to do with the construction of the first shelters? Did these early builders associate such splendor with the gift of fire, or did the sublime spectacle of the starry sky lead them to recognize their own precarious existence and glimpse in the unchanging order of the firmament possibilities of a more humane dwelling? At any rate, by linking the origin of the first house to the awe-inspiring sight of the inaccessible timeless order of the stars, Vitruvius gestures toward what distinguishes even the first house from any animal shelter: beyond addressing physical needs inseparable from our bodily existence, it also addressees spiritual needs. Not only the body but the soul too needs a house.[9]

3

It is this latter need that leads Rykwert to his questionable but thought-provoking postulate of a house in paradise. He, too, assumes that in paradise the body's needs were satisfied. Before the Fall Adam did not need to till the ground; nor did he have to worry about rain or cold, nor about fierce animals or unwelcome strangers. If the need for a house can be equated with the need for physical shelter, there was no need for a house in paradise. But, as we learn from Genesis, even in paradise Adam's existence cannot have been altogether untroubled. Not only did he receive the command not to eat of the tree of the knowledge of good and evil, which, like similar commands in fairy tales, presupposes the possibility of transgression and presages disobedience, but also God first created Adam without any companions, and he himself saw that this was not good: "So out of the ground the LORD God formed every beast of the field and every bird of the air, and brought them to the man to see what he would call them; and whatever the man called every living creature, that was its name" (Gen. 2.19, RSV). To feel at home in paradise Adam first had to make what God created his own. Adam's first naming was an act of appropriation. Rykwert invites us to understand building in the image of this first naming as above all an act of appropriation. He thus would have Adam build his house "not as a shelter against the weather, but as a volume which he could interpret in terms of his own body and which yet was an exposition of the paradisal plan, and therefore established him at the center of it."[10] Adam's house mediated between his embodied self and his environment. As this mediation, this house has to be thought of both as a figure of Adam's body and at the same time as a figure of paradise. And must we not require such mediation of all building that would answer to the requirements of dwelling?

That these requirements may not be reduced to the need for physical shelter is shown by Rykwert's discussion of the ceremonial objects used by certain Australian tribes such as the Aranda, tribes so primitive that they do not know even rudimentary buildings: "The only shelter they put up for their own use are windbreaks of bush and scrub which are made by weeding and trimming as much as by piling up. They sleep out in the open, sheltered by these breaks, with small fires to warm them in cold seasons."[11] In the male initiation ceremonies of these tribes curious objects, called *waningas,* play a crucial part: "They consist of one long stick—usually a spear—and one or two cross-sticks, lashed to it at right angles. On this framework string is wound in dense parallel lines, so that the whole object appears as a rectangle with a triangle at each of its short ends." Each such object has multiple references: "the *waninga* represents the totemic animal or object; its different parts and decorative treatment are associated with different aspects of the totem. But its general form also represents some constellations. The Milky Way, the place where the ancestors live forever, is interpreted as a fence made up of *waningas;* and finally the *waninga* represents the coupling of the ancestral pair."[12] But the object does not refer only to sacred history and cosmic order. In the initiation ceremony the initiate embraces the *waninga,* thus identifying with it and the order it represents. This embrace establishes a link between the individual and a transcendent sacred and cosmic order.

I am not concerned here with the details of Rykwert's account. It is important, however, that the *waninga* represents the world as a meaningful order and lets the initiate take his place in that order. The initiate's embrace of the *waninga* lets him belong to the world, as it lets the world belong to him. Rykwert discusses the *waninga* as proto-architecture. Although obviously not buildings in that they do not enclose space, they nevertheless help interpret space as a meaningful order. Crucial to such interpretation is the establishment of a bridge that links human and cosmic order.

Earlier I spoke of the dual significance of the Gothic cathedral, which represents both the Heavenly City, that is to say, the ideal human order, and the cosmos. Worship in such a church is in some ways rather like the initiate's embrace of the *waninga.* To call the *waninga* proto-architecture is to suggest that architecture answers to the human need to experience the social and natural world as a nonarbitrary meaningful order. A mythopoeic intent is part of all architecture worthy of its name. Quite in keeping with Rykwert's understanding of the architectural significance of the *waninga,* Hegel thus locates the origin of architecture, as opposed to merely utilitarian building, in the need for spiritual shelter provided by a sense of the holy, which (with Goethe) he understands as "what binds many souls together."[13] The task of architecture is to build a bridge between humanity and divinity, to provide both individual and community with an integrating center. Works of architecture are primarily symbolic markers, pointing to the divine power dimly felt to preside over both nature and humanity—Hegel is thinking of lingam columns and of obelisks, of sacred paths and gates, of Egyptian temples and pyramids, of self-sufficient structures more like megasculptures than houses; and he is thinking of towers, especially of the Tower of Babel (fig. 48) and also of that Babylonian tower of Zeus Belus described by Herodotus.[14]

Rykwert invites us to understand building in the image of Adam's naming of the animals as above all a spiritual appropriation of the natural environment, that is, as architecture. But the comparison also raises a question. After all, Adam's linguistic achievement proved insufficient to let him feel at home in the world: "The man gave names to all cattle, and to the birds of the air, and to every beast of the field; but for the man there was not found a helper fit for him" (Gen. 2.20). Despite his naming of the animals, Adam remained

48 | Pieter Brueghel, *Tower of Babel* (1563). Kunsthistorisches Museum, Vienna. Credit: Art Resource, N.Y.

alone. The overcoming of this loneliness required a different kind of recognition: outside himself Adam had to recognize another like himself. So God created Eve from one of Adam's ribs and he recognized her as bone of his bones, flesh of his flesh, and, "because she was taken out of Man," called her "woman." This naming is different from the naming of the animals in that it represents a response to a recognition of human community. And must we not demand the same of architecture? The search for its origin intertwines with the search for the origin of community. With good reason Vitruvius thus introduces his account of the construction of the first shelter with a brief description of the establishment of the first community.

4

The dictionary defines "shelter" as a structure offering protection, mainly from the weather but also from animals or unfriendly strangers. To put up a shelter is to establish boundaries that protect us from a threatening outside, to wrest place from space. The last formulation can serve as a first definition of building. Architecture understood as a re-presentation of space would make this function conspicuous.

Consider this definition of architecture, here equated with building, by the philosopher Paul Weiss:

Architecture is the art of creating space through the construction of boundaries in common-sense space. One can bound that space through intent alone, but the result will fall short of what architecture creates. . . . A work of architecture must be made, not merely intended. There is no building without the use of muscle acting on resistant material to produce something palpable and substantial. Whoever accepts the clearing as a possible dwelling bounds it off from the rest of the world. But he who makes a dwelling not only bounds it off but produces roof, walls, windows, door, flooring, each of which itself is a newly created, tensed spatial object, within a larger space.[15]

Architecture is said to establish place by the construction of boundaries, not in the space of geometry or physics but in commonsense space. This raises new questions: How are such boundaries to be drawn? What lets us accept them as convincing or necessary? Where does the architect's bounding of space find its measure?

An obvious answer is to point to what is often taken to be the basic task of building: to control the environment. The kind of control demanded will of course vary with the different purposes buildings serve—the demands made by schools are not those of prisons, the demands made by churches not those of fortresses, the demands of airports not those of shopping malls. Still, certain aspects common to all are easily distinguished: "The most elementary is," as most accounts of the building of the first house suggest, "the creation of an 'artificial climate,' protecting man against rain, wind, cold, heat, moisture, noise, insects, wild animals, enemies, and other evils in the surroundings. We will call this aspect 'physical control.'"[16] To seek the essence of architecture in the provision of *physical control* would be to reduce architecture to mere building and building to the creation of physical shelter. Such an understanding makes it quite possible to speak of "animal architecture"; ant pile and beehive are architecture in this sense. More thought-provoking is the nest-building behavior of chimpanzees, gorillas, and orangutans, which led Nold Egenter to suggest that such "subhuman architecture offers a reliable base on which a scientific architectural anthropology can be founded." [17] Those who, suffering from a surfeit of Eurocentric civilization, follow Bernard Rudofsky and take for their leitmotiv Seneca's saying—"That was a happy age, before the days of architecture, before the days of builders" [18]—may well find in such an "architectural anthropology" pointers for future building.

5

The examples of ant pile, beehive, and nest point to a second aspect of building. Buildings offer a framework for certain activities. Thus they serve and speak to us of a way of life. Buildings furnish what Norberg-Schulz calls a *functional frame*. [19] Obviously this frame will differ with the activities it is expected to serve. Here we have the key to the kind of typology [20] of buildings developed by Nikolaus Pevsner in his *History of Building Types*. While leaving out sacred architecture, because it has received all too much attention in more standard histories of architecture, and domestic architecture, which would have required another volume, Pevsner treats monuments, government buildings, theaters, libraries, museums, hospitals, prisons, hotels, exchanges and banks, warehouses and office buildings, railway stations, market halls, conservatories and exhibition buildings, shops, department and other stores, and factories. [21] And this of course is by no means a complete list: "Schools and university buildings, observatories, concert halls, and barracks, for instance, would have been rewarding, but would have swelled the book to unmanageable proportions." [22] It would be easy to add still other building types.

Despite what such a typology may suggest, nothing in these first two determinations allows us to understand what distinguishes human building from the kind of shelter constructed by animals, let alone functional building from architecture. We learn nothing about what Rudofsky calls rather mockingly "pedigreed architecture," opposing to it primitive and archaic architecture, built by human beings who are made to resemble animals in their apparently quite unproblematic participation in the life of nature.

There is a future-oriented version of this dream of an architecture saved from arbitrariness by its integration into the natural order, in which the paradigm of a human being attuned to nature is now furnished by the engineer. Modernist functionalists thus tolerated architecture only as long as it remained content to be no more than a branch of engineering. In his programmatic statement "Building," Hannes Meyer, who succeeded Gropius as head of the Bauhaus, thus insisted that

architecture as "an emotional act of the artist" has no justification.
architecture as "a continuation of the traditions of building" means being carried along by the history of architecture.

this functional, biological interpretation of architecture as giving shape to the functions of life, logically leads to pure construction; this world of constructive forms knows no native country, it is the expression of an international attitude in architecture. internationality is a privilege of the period.

pure construction is the basis and the characteristic of the new world of forms.

1. sex life

2. sleeping habits

3. pets

4. gardening

5. personal hygiene

6. weather protection

7. hygiene in the home

8. car maintenance

9. cooking

10. heating

11. exposure to the sun

12. service

these are the only motives when building a house. we examine the daily routine of everyone who lives in a house and this gives us the function diagram for the father, the mother, the child, the baby and the other occupants. we explore the relationship of the house and its occupants to the world outside. . . . [23]

Architecture is to receive its measure from an antecedently given way of life. Its careful analysis and translation into function diagrams allows the engineer to design a functional frame that offers what is needed as economically as possible. Such design will bother with ornament as little as Meyer (influenced in this respect, too, by the example set by Loos) bothers with capital letters, presumably part of that Baroque inheritance that, by now pretty much shed by the Anglo-Saxon countries, still held back central Europe—although the reader may wonder whether Meyer's use of boldface does not call into question the manifesto's thesis. Hannes Meyer knows of course that traditionally architecture has been much more than "pure construction" in his sense: for example, "an emotional act of the artist" or "a continuation of the traditions of building." But given Meyer's functionalism, this "more" is as indefensible as Loos considered ornament to be.

Although less extreme, Sigfried Giedion's *Space, Time, and Architecture* points in the same direction:

Architecture has caught up with construction very gradually. Our own period has been slowly finding the ability to express in architecture what construction has for a long while been mutely signifying in its abstract language. This process moved so slowly that around 1900 on the Continent most of the buildings from which the modern development stems lacked all connection with human residence. They were factories, stock exchanges, warehouses, and the like. The building schemes which represent the first solutions in the manner of the present day were set forward in a neutral atmosphere, one far removed from the range of intimate personal feelings. [24]

Three points especially should be noted: (1) The modern architect had to catch up with the engineer, taking as models factories and grain elevators, bridges and bunkers. Modern architecture finds its inspiration in construction. (2) Governed by considerations of economy and efficiency, such architecture is necessarily impersonal, as the building program tends to reduce the architect to little more than an instrument. (3) This new approach to building has first proven itself not in houses but in such utilitarian structures as factories and warehouses.

But if Giedion here seems to state the antithesis of Ruskin's thesis concerning the freedom of architecture from all calculations of utility, we should note that according to Giedion modern architecture "expresses" what functional building mutely signifies. Such expression makes it much more than just an extension of pure construction. In the language of the previous chapter, modern architecture seeks to re-present such construction. Giedion knows that by re-presenting construction, modern architecture failed to express what answers to the complex requirements of human dwelling: the kind of building that is said to have inspired modern architecture "lacked all connection with human residence."[25] As Gropius warned, "Were mechanization an end in itself it would be an unmitigated calamity, robbing life of half its fullness and variety by stunting men and women into sub-human, robotlike automatons. (Here we touch the deeper resistance of the old civilization of handicrafts to the newer order of the machine.)"[26] It is therefore not surprising that, Meyer's hopes notwithstanding, architectural modernists should have found domestic architecture an especially challenging problem: houses are more than complicated machines. Dwelling does not just mean being sheltered.

Consider today's mobile homes (fig. 49). We may deplore the still-continuing proliferation of such homes, but, as a guide to mobile, modular, and prefabricated homes points out, they do indeed offer what is demanded: "Basic shelter at modest cost."[27] As the guide observes, "For many, appearance is secondary to function and the great success of the industry is positive proof that these units are attractively priced and fulfill their purpose. . . . As a result of mounting costs and the overall economic malaise, we anticipate that more and more manufacturers will scale their products down, providing smaller units with fewer frills at lower costs. Housing as an industry may well change its focus from a provider of comfort to a provider of basic shelter" (pp. 30, 3). This suggests that what distinguishes more traditional homes from mobile homes are really just frills, ornament easily dispensed with. What a house provides is basic shelter. But what kind of dwelling do such homes reduced to basic shelter invite?

The very term "mobile home" gives a first answer: even if, as a matter of fact, these units are difficult to move and rarely moved, they are yet mobile. Like a tent, the mobile home stands in no essential relationship to the environment in which it happens to be located: it is a home that does not belong to a particular place or region. What matters here is not the particular example of the mobile home, which only gives particularly vivid expression to the spiritual mobility that is a corollary of the impersonality of construction noted by Giedion. Inseparable from the anonymity of machines is their failure to belong to a particular place. That in fact they may be immobile does not matter: they have the look of mobility (see fig. 34).

But suppose mobile homes do permit only a rootless dwelling—is that a criticism? Are human being like turnips, stuck in the ground? What should be the relation between dwelling and space? I shall take up this question in chapter 11. Here I should point out that our guide does not consider this mobility a defect; quite the opposite—and given an increasingly mobile population, it may well indeed be considered an attractive feature.

More disturbingly, the guide adds another advantage of mobility: the owner of a mobile home has the possibility of becoming a member of an "instant community." "Many

Trailer park, Boulder, Colorado. Photo credit:

49 Ken Abbott.

mobile home parks exist throughout the country. Each park lot has the necessary utilities, and many of these parks offer a variety of recreational and service facilities which can be attractive bonuses. In addition, everyone living in a mobile home park lives in a mobile home, and some might find this reassuring" (p. 27). Not only has the relationship of the home to its environment become accidental, but also the relationship of the individual to the community of which he or she now just happens to be a member. But the instant community of accidental relationships that we can enter and leave at a moment's notice is, in a deeper sense, no community at all. To experience oneself as part of a community one has to experience oneself as belonging to it; this contravenes instant joining and easy leave-taking.

If there is no essential relationship between the mobile home and its social and physical environment, there is similarly no essential relationship between those who live in such a mobile home and the mobile home itself. The impersonality inseparable from the reduction of the home to basic shelter demands this. Their mode of production dictates that "mobile home are similar in appearance and all are constructed in pretty much the same manner. There are no unique mobile homes" (p. 28). The relationship between the individual and his or her home cannot but be accidental; home has become a place where one just happens to live. Perhaps this is what is meant by the reduction of the house to basic shelter. But does a house so reduced allow for genuine dwelling?

The question is made especially troubling by the suggestion that, as a result of the stagnating economy, the housing industry "may well change its focus from a provider of comfort to a provider of basic shelter." This acknowledges that to provide the latter is not necessarily to provide the former. But can the two be dissociated? Is our need to be sheltered not always a need to dwell in some comfort—where what counts as comfort will depend on our own economic situation and that of those in our community, as well as on our ever-changing expectations? Every home reduced to basic shelter is uncomfortable because it so obviously does not meet what we demand of a house. This failure forces its inhabitants to appropriate it, to make it their own by furnishing it with their belongings, by bringing in pictures and plants, pots and pans, curtains and bedspreads. To meet and profit from such demands, manufacturers of mobile home have made an attempt to make them more comfortable by offering the consumer, beyond "basic shelter," "a total living environment." Even bath towels of suitable color and pattern can be made part of the "decor package." There is no longer any need to shape an environment: simply step into one ready-made. To be sure, the customer is offered a selection: "Generally, one has the choice of one of three or more decor packages. Among the most typical are Spanish (wrought iron fixtures, red and black upholstery, perhaps a picture of a bullfight on the wall), early American (colonial-style furniture, flowered upholstery, and an eagle wall-plaque or two), and contemporary (simpler lines). Less common is a Greek decor package and one emulating the life style of the Mediterranean, among others. All of them are designed to suit the tastes of the largest possible public" (p. 39). This is precisely why we should not expect such a home to have much to do with the environment outside. And if the relationship between home and environment has become accidental, so has the relationship between the individual and his or her home.

If the reduction of the home to basic shelter is likely to leave prospective buyers dissatisfied because it is too empty, the difficulty with the "total living environment" promised by the manufacturer is just that totality. The more a home presents itself as such a totality, the more effectively it will prevent those moving into it from really making it their own. Just as an aesthetically complete work of art demands to be left alone, so a total living environment demands of those stepping into it that they fit themselves into the niche it provides. To make it genuinely livable one first would have to destroy the offered totality, throwing out those matching towels, tearing the eagle plaques off the walls, trashing the bullfight picture. A good home needs to be appropriated. In this respect the mobile home that is content to offer no more than basic shelter succeeds better than one that seeks to transform such shelter into a total living environment. Such attempts have an important lesson: they bid the architect resist the temptation to aim at the creation of total environments. This had been the moral of Loos's tale of "The Poor Little Rich Man," whose architect had thought of everything and precisely because he did left his client deeply depressed: "He imagined his future life. . . . For him there were to be no more painters, no more artists, no more craftsmen. He was precluded from all future living and striving, developing and desiring. He thought, this is what it means to go about life with one's own corpse. Yes indeed. He is finished. *He is complete!*"[28]

That mobile homes fail to meet the requirements of dwelling is suggested by the already-mentioned ways in which those who have chosen to buy a mobile home, most often no doubt because it does indeed provide "basic shelter at modest cost," appropriate and transform such a home to make it look like a real house, for example by using "a tip-out, slide-out, or tag unit which will break up the boxlike appearance of the unit while adding additional space. More help would come from adding a porch, patio, deck, trellis, or anything that visually ties the mobile home to its site"[29] (fig. 50). Such additions show that the needs of dwelling are not yet met when adequate shelter has been provided; we also need to feel at home where we dwell. Consider especially the ways in which mobile home are made to lose their look of mobility: porch, patio, or garden may help to bind the home to its environment, giving it something like roots. Trees help to immobilize it, literally and figuratively. Such additions cannot be dismissed as just frills. They answer a need for a sense of place that goes not only beyond the need for shelter but also beyond any merely aesthetic interest. Thus they argue for an approach to architecture that overcomes the simple opposition of art and building.

If mobile homes thus call into question Meyer's "functional, biological interpretation of architecture," it faces another difficulty: any such approach is rendered problematic by the fact that while building may be understood as a function of a given way of life, that way of life is also a function of building. Take some suburban shopping center: here we have a structure built quite obviously in response to certain needs and demands, an example of building as a response to a certain way of life. But it in turn will reinforce and shape that way of life and its subsequent development. Philosophers and literary critics have spoken of the hermeneutic circle in which all interpretation inevitably moves: the meaning of a text is not simply given with that text; different readings are possible; what meaning we discover will depend not only on the text but on how we approach it, on our interests and concerns,

Trailer park, Boulder, Colorado. Photo credit:
50 Ken Abbott.

Walter Gropius, Dammerstock Siedlung,
Danziger Strasse, Gruppe 5, Karlsruhe (1929).
51 | Credit: Foto Marburg/Art Resource, N.Y.

our prejudices and anticipations of meaning—and such prejudices and anticipations will have to be modified or perhaps jettisoned altogether as we struggle with the text. A similar circle joins building and the way of life it serves. Building is inevitably also interpretation. It has a hermeneutic function. There would be no need for interpretation if, with the help of social scientists, we could state the requirements of dwelling so clearly and completely that we could leave building to the engineer. Meyer appears to claim something similar when he asserts that the twelve motives he lists are the only motives possible when building a house. But like a poem, no way of life is given so transparently that it unambiguously declares its meaning. There can be no definitive statement of that meaning; it must be established, ever anew and precariously, in interpretation. All building, and more self-consciously architecture, participates in this work. Building is a response interpreting a way of life (fig. 51).

6

When considering building "as giving shape to the functions of life," we have to keep in mind that our life in the world is essentially a life with others. Whatever we build inevitably has a social significance. Pevsner's different building types cannot be understood without attention to their social purpose. "The social purpose of a building may thus be the expression of a status, a role, a group, a collectivity, or an institution; and a collection of buildings may represent the social system as a whole."[30] Works of architecture not only serve but represent different social roles and institutions. With this we return to what separates architecture from all merely functional building; we see more clearly now why that difference is only inadequately understood in terms of an addition of merely aesthetic decoration to functional sheds. All genuine ornament has a social function, as much in how we clothe ourselves or set a table as in how we decorate our buildings: ornament serves to distinguish the ornament bearer. It thus helps to articulate the built environment, creates hierarchies by establishing figure and ground relationships in a particular building—think of the often profuse ornamentation of portals—or in an urban context.

Such articulation also serves to interpret the social order. "The pediment originally had such a distinguishing function, until it was devaluated in the nineteenth century by being applied to all kinds of buildings. Till the appearance of the 'skyscraper' the tower designated the church and the town-hall. Today the need for 'architectural characterization' of the different institutions is urgent, although we may no longer be content with such 'signs' as colonnades and towers. Instead, we recognize attempts at representing institutions by means of 'showing' their functional structure."[31] To speak of works of architecture as representations of institutions is to point out that they help interpret the social order. There is an obvious link between this social function of architecture and the social function of communal festivals: for example, between the way medieval churches provide representational figures that provide the ground of more ordinary buildings with illuminating foci and the way the great religious festivals, such as Easter, Pentecost, Christmas, and Good Friday, provide temporal figures that illuminate the ground of everyday life. To assert themselves as such figures, both church and festival rely on ornament. Marriage, birth, and death demand public symbolic expression.

In the preceding two chapters I described architecture as an art of representation. I sketched how, looking back to such structures as the Solomonic temple and ahead to the Heavenly Jerusalem, the Gothic cathedral helps shape a particular social milieu by interpreting the place of individuals in a common ongoing history and by inviting them to understand themselves as members of that ideal community, which is the Church. Furnishing individuals with a common ground and measure, it gathers them into a community. The social significance of such an architecture requires no comment. And is the same not true of all architecture worthy of its name? Looking back to precursor structures and ahead to some imagined ideal, it helps gather individuals into a community both by placing them on the ground of a shared history and by gesturing toward an ideal image of communal dwelling.

7

A different challenge to any view that would reduce the function of architecture to that of providing physical control and a functional frame is implicit in Vitruvius's account of the building of the first house. Why does he link the origin of building to the spectacle of the seemingly timeless order of the stars if not to suggest that to build is also to carry something of this promise of a timeless cosmic order into our all too chaotic, arbitrary, and evanescent world? This suggestion is made more explicit by Le Corbusier's version of the Vitruvian tale.

Primitive man has brought his chariot to a stop: he decides that here shall be his native soil. He chooses a glade, he cuts down the trees which are too close, he levels the earth around; he opens up the road which will carry him to the river or to those of his tribe whom he has just left. He surrounds his tent with a palisade in which he arranges a doorway. The road is as straight as he can manage with his implements, his arms and his time. The pegs of his tent describe a square, hexagon, or octagon. The palisade forms a rectangle whose four angles are equal. The door of this hut is on the axis of the enclosure—and the gate of the enclosure faces exactly the door of the hut. . . . You may see, in some archaeological work, the representation of this hut, the representation of this sanctuary: it is the plan of a house, or the plan of a temple. It is the same spirit one finds again in the Pompeian house. It is the spirit indeed of the Temple of Luxor.

There is no such thing as primitive man; there are primitive resources. The idea is constant, in full sway from the beginning.[32]

Le Corbusier's not-so-primitive barbarians recognize what Hegel recognized, what every architect must recognize: that to build is to appropriate and humanize nature. For Corbusier, too, man is the measure of all things. How we are to understand this will depend on our understanding of the essence of human being—and, like Vitruvius, Corbusier recognizes what links us to other animals. But the human being is not just another animal but the *animal rationale.* The *animal* demands physical shelter, the *ratio* spiritual. Both demands must be satisfied if there is to be genuine dwelling. Corbusier understands geometry as the language of the *ratio.* Wherever it meets with geometric order the human spirit feels at home. To be sure, emphasis on the *ratio* may not lead to a denial of the rights of the *animal.* To represent the ideal, a building has to provide for both: shelter and spiritual order[33] (fig. 52).

A narrow functionalist may well want to consider the second unnecessary ornament. And indeed, given a focus on utility there often will seem to be little point to the surplus order on which human beings insist—and not only in architecture. But the point of such surplus is obvious: it is indeed hard "to live in a place that is not our own and, much more, not ourselves."

Le Corbusier, apartment block at Weissenhof-siedlung, Stuttgart. Credit: Foto Marburg/Art Resource, N.Y.

52

Building and Dwelling

10

1

As Joseph Rykwert has shown so convincingly, architectural theory cannot dispense with dreams or stories about an ideal architecture. Thoughts of the Heavenly Jerusalem once gave expression to such an ideal. So did Laugier's reconstruction of the primitive hut. And so do speculations on Adam's house in paradise.[1]

Another such dream finds voice in Heidegger's often-invoked, suggestive, yet questionable description of a Black Forest farmhouse.

The nature of building is letting dwell. Building accomplishes its nature in the raising of places by the joining of their spaces. Only if we are capable of dwelling, only then can we build. *Let us think for a while of a farmhouse in the Black Forest, which was built some two hundred years ago by the dwelling of peasants. Here the self-sufficiency of the power to let earth and sky, divinities and mortals enter* in simple oneness *into things ordered the house. It placed the farm on the wind-sheltered mountainslope looking south, among the meadows close to the spring. It gave it the wide overhanging shingle roof whose proper slope bears up under the burden of snow, and which, reaching deep down, shields the chambers against the storms of the long winter nights. It did not forget the altar corner behind the community table; it made room in its chamber for the hallowed places of childbed and the "tree of the dead"— for that is what they call a coffin there: the* Totenbaum—*and in this way it designed for the different generations under one roof the character of their journey through time. A craft which, itself sprung from dwelling, still uses its tools and frames as things, built the farmhouse.*[2]

Heidegger chooses an example removed from our world. To be sure, many such farmhouses have survived and continue to shape the popular image of landscapes like Germany's Black Forest (fig. 53). These relics invite us to measure our way of life by one not yet shaped by technology. Heidegger himself emphasizes the temporal distance that separates us from the farmhouse, underscoring it with his own archaizing style. This twofold distance may lead us to dismiss Heidegger as a modern day Luddite.

The quoted passage is part of the conclusion of "Building Dwelling Thinking," a lecture first delivered on Sunday morning, August 5, 1951, to an audience composed mostly of architects; it was part of a still war-shadowed *Darmstädter Gespräch*, which that year focused on the theme "Man and Space." The lecture begins by stating what would seem to

53

Black Forest farmhouse. Credit: Foto Marburg/ Art Resource, N.Y.

be obvious: the nature of building is letting dwell. To be sure, Heidegger reminds us, "not every building is a dwelling" (p. 146); in the lecture he mentions a number of such "buildings," including bridges and hangars, stadiums and power stations, highways and dams, factories and market halls. In their different ways they all serve our way of life, but we would not call them dwellings. To work in a factory, to shop in a store is not to dwell; we do not reside there.

Just this equation of "dwelling" and "residing" is called into question by Heidegger's suggestion that even many residential buildings, "well planned, easy to keep, attractively cheap, open to air, light, and sun" though they may be, hold no "guarantee that *dwelling* occurs in them" (p. 146). Of course not, we may want to agree: no more than a hammer can guarantee that it will be used as a hammer can a house guarantee that people will actually reside in it. But such easy agreement would miss Heidegger's point: he is distinguishing genuine dwelling from mere residing, from merely inhabiting a structure or finding shelter. To dwell is to feel at home. Building allows for dwelling by granting a sense of place. The builders of Heidegger's farmhouse did so by placing it on its hillside, orienting the part of the house in which the farmer and his family ate, cooked, rested, and slept toward the valley, leaving the farmhouse's larger back half to cows, horses, and goats.

All this seems obvious enough and hardly worth saying, even as we may wonder in what sense such building and dwelling are compatible with life in a modern metropolis.[3] And yet Heidegger warns us not to settle for what is so readily taken for granted: "As long as this is all we have in mind, we take dwelling and building as two separate activities, an idea that has something correct in it. Yet at the same time by the means-end schema we block our view of the essential relations. For building is not merely a means and a way toward dwelling—to build is in itself already to dwell" (p. 146). Certainly: the farmhouse serves a quite specific kind of dwelling, fitted to a particular landscape. The climate helped dictate that animals and humans share the same roof, while comfort demanded the separation of their quarters, joined only by a narrow walkway. One could thus discuss the farmhouse as a machine for living, although "tool" might seem to fit better. But, Heidegger insists, talk of building serving dwelling fails to consider "the real meaning of the verb *bauen,* namely, to dwell" (p. 146). To support his claim that building and dwelling are inseparably joined, Heidegger appeals to Old English and High German: the now lost, but nevertheless real meaning, of *bauen,* "to build," is said to be "to dwell," and "to dwell" in turn originally meant "to be." Dwelling thus names "the basic character of human being" (p. 148),[4] understood not primarily as a being cast into boundless space but as a being at home in the world. "The relationship between man and space is none other than dwelling, strictly thought and spoken" (p. 157). Such primordial dwelling grounds all building that grants a sense of place.

2

The bridge that spans the Neckar in Heidelberg establishes such a sense of place (fig. 54): "The place is not already there before the bridge is. Before the bridge stands, there are of course many spots along the stream that can be occupied by something. One of them proves

to be a place, and does so *because of the bridge*. Thus the bridge does not first come to a place to stand in it; rather, a place comes into existence only by virtue of the bridge" (p. 154).[5] Establishing a distinctive place, the bridge joins and opens up other places and spaces: the river, the river banks, the city. Place-establishing work first reveals space. Instead of thinking of place in terms of space, Heidegger inverts that order. "What the word for space, *Raum, Rum,* designates is said by its ancient meaning. *Raum* means a place cleared or freed for settlement and lodging. A space is something that has been made room for, something that is cleared and free, namely within a boundary, Greek *peras*" (p. 157). So understood, space is first of all both cleared and bounded. Such clearing and bounding are presupposed by our experience of things, which are inevitably placed in one way or other: the fork on the table, the car on the road, Venus in the evening sky. Inseparable from our encounter with things is the experience of different places and therefore spaces: table, road, evening sky. "That for which room is made is always granted and hence is joined, that is, gathered, by virtue of a place, that is, by such a thing as the bridge. Accordingly, spaces receive their being from places and not from 'space'" (p. 157).

Already in *Being and Time* Heidegger had insisted that our everyday experience of space is intimately linked to the activities we are engaged in. First of all and most of the time the body, especially the moving body, mediates our experience of space: the street is to be walked down, the mountain to be climbed, the bridged to be crossed. To be sure, we can locate the bridge by measuring how far it is from other things: "Thus nearness and remoteness between men and things can become mere distance, mere intervals of intervening space" (p. 155). But just as this is an abstracted understanding of distance, so the understanding of space as the three-dimensional manifold derives from a richer understanding of space—think of the different ways in which we experience rooms, buildings, neighborhoods, cities, landscapes. We have to agree with Heidegger: first of all and most of the time our experience of space is an experience of spaces, mediated by our encounter with things and their places. So experienced, space is regional: this room is a region with boundaries that mark it off from other regions; so is a house, a neighborhood, or a city. Building helps establish regions, and architecture helps re-present them: some dominant structure, a square, perhaps with a fountain, or just a street corner continues to be an effective way of gathering a multiplicity of buildings into a neighborhood, a multiplicity of neighborhoods into a city[6] (fig. 55).

Regions assign to persons and things their proper places; were it not for this, we would be disoriented, could not consider certain things out of place. In the case of a room, the region in question is bounded by floor, ceiling, and walls, but regions need not be bounded in that fashion: a forest clearing is a region, and so is a valley. Regions are nested within regions: the room in the house, the house in its neighborhood, the neighborhood in the city, and so on. The region of all regions is the world, understood now not as the totality of all things but as the context of contexts that assigns everything its place. Aristotelian space, which assigns to the four elements and thus to all things their proper places, is closer to this everyday understanding of space as regional than the space of geometry or the space presupposed by modern science. The space we inhabit is not the homogeneous space of Euclid. We live in a heterogeneous space. Furthermore, that heterogeneity is inevitably

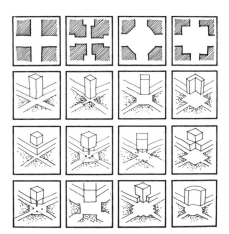

charged with meaning. Take a shopping plaza on a hot summer day, or a meadow used as a soccer field.

It is above all in terms of the activities we are engaged in that we understand proximity and distance. As humanist architecture recognized, the human body furnishes something like a natural measure of space. Bound up with that measure is the qualitative difference of the directions of the space we inhabit. Up and down, front and back, right and left, for example, carry different meanings, as becomes clear as soon as we begin to reflect on the metaphorical use of these terms: "I am down," "he is sinister looking," "she went behind my back." If building is the construction of boundaries in space, this space cannot be understood as a homogeneous given. World space has always already been separated into different regions, of which sky and earth are perhaps the most basic. This allows Heidegger to say that human being is essentially a dwelling on the earth and under the sky. And if dwelling expresses the relationship between humans and world space, that space is always already charged with meanings: space is not mute. Space speaks to us, and only because it speaks do buildings speak to us.

3

"Only if we are capable of dwelling, only then can we build." But if "the nature of building is letting dwell," must we not also hold on to the converse, that dwelling presupposes building? While the particular dwelling made possible by the Black Forest farmhouse can be said to presuppose that more primordial dwelling that is nothing other than the human way of existing, must the latter not presuppose in turn a more primordial building? How are we to understand this "building"? A first answer was suggested in the preceding section: if "dwelling" names "the relationship between man and space," this primordial "building" must mean space, but space understood as placing persons and things. The traditional analogy between human building and divine creation comes to mind: God has often been described as the archetypal architect, who fashioned the world as a perfectly ordered whole, the fit dwelling place for human beings (see fig. 59). I have already touched on the medieval understanding of the church as a representation of the cosmos. This is of course hardly unique: again and again we meet with an understanding of buildings as more or less explicit repetitions of the cosmogonic act. Mircea Eliade thus appeals to construction rites to suggest that in primitive societies the building of every house is

an imitation, hence reactualization of the cosmogony. A "new era" opens up with the building of every house. Every construction is an absolute beginning; that is, tends to restore the initial instant, the pleni-tude of a present that contains no trace of history. Of course, the construction rituals found in our day are in great part survivals, and it is difficult to determine to what extent they are accompanied by an experi-ence in the consciousness of the persons who observe them. But this rationalist objection is negligible. What is important here is that man has felt the need to reproduce the cosmogony in his constructions, whatever be their nature—that this reproduction made him contemporary with the mythical moment of the beginning of the world and that he felt the need of returning to that moment as often as possible in order to regenerate himself . . . even if the experiences aroused . . . are no longer anything but profane— a construction is a new organization of the world and of life. All that is needed is a modern man with a sensibility less closed to the miracle of life; and the experience of renewal would revive for him when he built a house or entered it for the first time.[7]

The primordial building that provides human building with its ground and measure would then be the cosmos. But "cosmos" names precisely the world into which we have been cast, experienced as a meaningful order. Heidegger makes such an experience constitutive of human being: "It is not that there are men, and over and above them space; for when I say a 'man,' and in saying this word think of a being who exists in a human manner—that is, who dwells—then by the name 'man' I already name the stay within the fourfold among things" (p. 156).

With the introduction of "the fourfold" Heidegger takes a step that threatens to leave both the modern world and all phenomenological evidence behind. It is one thing to say that human being is essentially being-in-the-world, in this sense also a being in space; it is quite another to claim that such being-in-the-world is essentially a dwelling, understood now as a "staying within the fourfold" of earth and sky, divinities and mortals, a preserving of "the fourfold in its essential being, its presencing" (p. 150). How can Heidegger claim both: that human being is essentially dwelling and that dwelling is a staying within the fourfold? "How then may we find, among the wayfarers of the metropolis, one who knows how to build because he knows how to dwell? What modern home is able to express the preservation of the *Geviert,* the Fourfold?"[8] Something like the distance that separates us from the Black Forest farmhouse also would seem to separate us from Heidegger's fourfold. If genuine dwelling must indeed be understood as a staying within the fourfold, would this not mean that we moderns are no longer able to dwell in Heidegger's sense? And, if being human should indeed mean "staying within the fourfold among things," then we have lost our humanity. But what justifies such talk? Had Heidegger's *Being and Time* not placed authenticity in opposition to being at home in the world? Why privilege dwelling un-derstood as "staying within the fourfold"? Such questioning returns us to Heidegger's puzzling formulation.

Three of the terms would appear to pose little difficulty, although they do raise questions:

1. By "earth" Heidegger means the ground that supports us, both literally and in the sense that it sustains us with its gifts of food and water: "Earth is the serving bearer, blossoming and fruiting, spreading out in rock and water, rising up into place and animal" (p. 149). Human being is essentially on the earth, and it remains so, despite space flights and dreams of colonizing other planets.

Such a reading, however, fails to capture all that matters here: already in "The Origin of the World of Art" Heidegger had insisted that earth

shows itself only when it remains undisclosed and unexplained. Earth thus shatters every attempt to penetrate into it. It causes every merely calculating importunity upon it to turn into a destruction. This destruction may herald itself under the appearance of mastery and of progress in the form of technical-scientific objectivation of nature, but this mastery remains an impotence of will. The earth appears openly cleared as itself only when it is perceived and preserved as that which is by nature undisclosable, that which shrinks from every disclosure and constantly keeps itself closed up.[9]

"Earth" names here what I would call "material transcendence." What such transcendence transcends is precisely every linguistic or conceptual space in which things must find their place if they are to be disclosed and explained. What invites talk of "material transcendence" is that, even if constituted by our language or concepts and as such appearance, what thus appears is not created by our understanding but given. Inseparable from our experience of things is a sense of this gift, an awareness that our understanding is finite; and that means also that the reach of our words, of all our determinations and calculations, is limited. The rift between thing and word, between earth and world, where "world" names not the to-tality of facts but a space of intelligibility, cannot be closed. Nor can it be eliminated: "The earth cannot dispense with the Open of the world if it is itself to appear as earth in the liberated surge of its self-seclusion. The world again, cannot soar out of the earth's sight if, as the governing breadth and path of all essential destiny, it is to ground itself on a resolute foundation."[10]

What prevents the world from "soaring out of the earth's sight," what opens human beings to material transcendence, this transcendence within the sensible, is above all the body—and here it is important to keep in mind that the embodied self is a caring, desiring self. To be in the presence of the earth is inevitably to be affected, moved, claimed. Earth thus also refers to the elusive affective ground without which all talk of essences, meaning, values, or divinities is ultimately groundless, merely idle talk.

More problematic than this understanding of the earth as the ever elusive, yet indispensable supporting ground of human existence is Heidegger's suggestion, a suggestion that invites appropriation by deep ecologists, that dwelling requires a special respect for our ineliminable dependence on the earth and its gifts, requires "saving" the earth: "To save the earth is more than to exploit it or even wear it out. Saving the earth does not master the earth and does not subjugate it, which is merely one step from spoliation" ("Building Dwelling Thinking," p. 150). That we often fail to save the earth in this sense requires no comment. Genuine dwelling is here opposed to the way we ordinarily deal with persons and things. And if such dwelling is equated with being human, being human here can only name an ideal at a distance from our usual mode of being, calling us perhaps beyond it.

2. By "sky," too, Heidegger means first of all pretty much what we usually mean by the word: "The sky is the vaulting path of the sun, the course of the changing moon, the wandering glitter of the stars, the year's seasons and their changes, the light and dusk of day, the gloom and glow of night, the clemency and inclemency of the weather, the drifting clouds and the blue depth of the ether" (p. 149). Again, such a reading fails to capture what matters: human beings not only look up to the sky, but such looking up has long provided natural metaphors for the way human beings are never imprisoned in the here and now but are always "beyond" themselves, ahead of themselves in expectation, behind themselves in memory, beyond time altogether when contemplating eternity. Such power of self-transcendence is part of the meaning of "spirit." The second term of the fourfold thus not only means the familiar sky but opens that meaning to what may be called the ineliminable spiritual or ecstatic dimension of human being.

But once again Heidegger questions the way we live first of all and most of the time when he insists that dwelling requires an openness to the sky as sky. Those who dwell "leave to the sun and the moon their journey, to the stars their courses, to the seasons their blessings and inclemency; they do not turn night into day nor day into a harassed unrest" (p. 150). The challenge to our modern way of life is evident, inviting us to question not just this way of life but also the assumptions behind Heidegger's words: would he have us live in a pretechnological world? The distance that separates us from Heidegger's farmhouse turns out to be a version of the distance that separates the fourfold from the technological world. What special lesson do this house type and the way of dwelling it presupposes hold for us today? What not choose some more familiar building, say a house in some American suburb, with its television sets, VCRs, telephones, radios, and lightbulbs? Surely we could say of it, too, that it was built by "a craft which, itself sprung from dwelling, still uses tools and frames as things"—although, uncomfortable with such stilted talk, we may just want to say that the suburban home, too, both makes possible and presupposes an established and often taken for granted way of life. What separates such language from Heidegger's invites us to reflect on the distance that separates our modern dwelling from the dwelling that built the farmhouse. Is it also the distance that separates us moderns from genuine building?

3. Heidegger's "mortals" are of course we human beings. To speak of "morals" is to emphasize the precariousness and finitude of our existence. Already in *Being and Time* Heidegger had linked authenticity to a resolute appropriation and affirmation of our essential mortality, and with good reason: as long as we remain unable to make our peace with the fact that we grow older and sooner or later must die, remain unable to make our peace with the passage of time, we also will be unable to make our peace with all that binds us to time—with our bodies, for example, with our sexuality, and with the setting of the sun, with the coming of winter, and with the earth, which so often withholds its gifts. The inability to save the earth and to receive the sky appears linked to the difficulty we have accepting ourselves as the mortals we are.

4. The most problematic of the four terms is the last. How are we to understand Heidegger's "divinities"? What place do they have in our modern world? Heidegger calls

them "the beckoning messengers of the godhead" (p. 150)—this is how angels have traditionally been understood and, following the poet Hölderlin, instead of speaking of "divinities" or "gods" Heidegger will also speak of "angels." But what is such talk to us? How are we to understand Heidegger's "godhead"?

Following Hölderlin, Heidegger understands godhead as the most fundamental measure of human being. Is he then simply returning to the traditional conception of human being as created in the image of God? But that God, for Heidegger as for Nietzsche, is a poetic fiction that, while it once may have assigned human beings their place and thus allowed them to dwell, today has lost its authority. God remains unknown. And yet Heidegger insists, once again citing Hölderlin, that it is precisely this unknown God who grants our dwelling its measure. What sense can we make of this? How can the unknown function as measure? Heidegger answers cryptically: "The measure consists in the way in which the God who remains unknown, is revealed as such by the sky."[11] God is revealed, yet remains hidden; he is revealed in the endless variety of the things that surround us, in "everything that shimmers and blossoms in the sky and thus under the sky and on earth, everything that sounds and is fragrant, rises and comes—but also everything that goes and stumbles, moans and falls silent, pales and darkens. Into this which is intimate to man, but alien to the God, the unknown imparts himself, in order to remain guarded within it as the unknown."[12] Heidegger gestures here toward the many-voiced ground of all meaning and value. To be touched by that ground in a specific way that gives direction to our lives is to receive some divinity's message; depending on the message received, we may name that divinity Aphrodite or Hera, Dionysus or Apollo. But any attempt to name the gods and God—and, in doing so, to take the measure of human being, if only to return that measure to human beings and to let them dwell—is a violation of the unknown essence of divinity, putting the namer in danger of obscuring divinity with some golden calf.

Heidegger knows that the godhead and its messengers are not present to us moderns as is the earth, that we cannot receive them as we can the sky. The divinities, he tells us, we can only await: "Mortals dwell in that they await the divinities as divinities. In hope they hold up to the divinities what is unhoped for. They wait for intimations of their coming and do not mistake the signs of their absence. They do not make their gods for themselves and do not worship idols. In the depth of misfortune they wait for the weal that has been withdrawn" ("Building Dwelling Thinking," p. 150). But if we can only await the divinities and if they are yet part of the fourfold within which genuine dwelling must stay, it seems that such a dwelling must also elude us: hoped for perhaps, but something that cannot be willed. Heidegger asks us to dwell in the knowledge of the absence of the godhead's messengers, to resist the temptation to dance around some golden calf and substitute idols for angels, measures we have created for measures gained by interpreting the messages of the godhead's messengers. But how then is our dwelling to find measure and direction? His suggestion, that we wait for what has been withdrawn, hardly provides the content necessary to give guidance to our dwelling and building, and it threatens to render his essay quite useless to the architects whom he was addressing.

This much, however, has become clear: when he understands essential dwelling as "staying within the fourfold," Heidegger attempts to reappropriate the archaic view that gives human building measure and ground in some more primordial building, in sacred order. And even if Nietzsche is right and the old God is dead, even if with this death the building in which Europeans dwelled for so many centuries lost founder and foundation, Heidegger nevertheless insists that we can learn to dwell only by learning to listen to an all-but-silent call. If we follow Heidegger, the architect's task, too, is to heed that call and to let the building designed be an inevitably precarious response.

4

But the question returns: what can such talk—perhaps suggestive but disturbingly vague, freighted with Christian and in Heidegger's case more specifically Hölderlinian associations—still mean to us?

I pointed out that Heidegger's lecture was delivered in August 1951 to an audience composed largely of architects, when in the wake of World War II Germany was suffering from a severe housing shortage and the *Wohnungsfrage,* the question of dwelling, was thought of above all in terms of the need for shelter.[13] In this context Heidegger's pronouncements must have seemed especially strange. For according to him, the need for shelter was not at all the real problem: "However hard and bitter, however hampering and bitter, however hampering and threatening the lack of houses remains, the *real plight of dwelling* does not lie merely in a lack of houses. The real plight of dwelling is indeed older than the world wars with their destruction, older also than the increase of the world's population and the condition of the industrial workers. The real plight is this, that mortals ever search anew for the nature of dwelling, that they *must ever learn to dwell.* What if man's homelessness consisted in this, that man still does not even think of the *real* plight of dwelling as *the* plight" (p. 161). Heidegger invites his audience to consider the essence of dwelling. Even though generally unrecognized and unthought, that essence confronts us moderns as *the* task.

Did Heidegger's discussion of the fourfold and the concluding example of the Black Forest farmhouse intersect with the problems faced by his listeners, who heard him in respectful silence? Where was he pointing? Heidegger certainly did not mean to suggest that the Germans ought to build as their backward forebears built two hundred years ago. "Our reference to the Black Forest farm in no way means that we should or could go back to building such houses; rather it illustrates by a dwelling that has been how it was able to build" (p. 160). But just what were his listeners and what are we to learn from this illustration? The dwelling that built the farmhouse did not know what Heidegger calls the misfortune of the withdrawal of the godhead's beckoning messengers. It had its measure in a sacred order. Like Heidegger's audience, we no longer know such a measure. Is it then still possible for us to dwell in anything like Heidegger's sense? Are we, on Heidegger's view, condemned to fail to live up to what the essence of dwelling demands? I am too much of a modernist to be able to take such suggestions very seriously. Should we then dismiss his example as hopelessly, perhaps even dangerously, anachronistic? The Black Forest farmhouse belonged to a world not yet touched by the Enlightenment or shaped by technology—to a premodern world. And if the Black Forest farmhouse should indeed lie irrecoverably beyond and behind us, can we deplore this? Who of us would want to change places with Heidegger's Black Forest farmer? Only if we are able to substitute for the kind of dwelling that built this farmhouse one genuinely of this age will we be able to arrive at a notion of building that is not anachronistic. Does Heidegger's understanding of the essence of dwelling even allow us to delineate such a contemporary dwelling? What would it be like?

Recall once more Heidegger's problematic gloss on what is means to "receive the sky as sky": *not* to turn night into day. Is artificial light incompatible with Heideggerian dwelling? Or think of the revolution in communications and the way it has shaped the world we live in, especially our sense of space, and consider the gain in freedom bound up with this revolution. For Heidegger's Black Forest farmer the particular place into which he happened to have been born tended to become a destiny from which he could not escape, limiting the possibilities available to him in a way we would find intolerable. Place severely circumscribed vocation and community. Inseparable from such a strong sense of place is a lack of freedom. The rootedness of his existence was bought at a price few of us would and should be willing to pay. However we might want to reappropriate Heidegger's remarks on dwelling, such reappropriation will have to recognize technology's ability to liberate human beings and thus to allow them to become more truly themselves.

Just this promise of liberation is called into question by Heidegger's juxtaposition of dwelling as a staying within the fourfold and our inhabiting a world ruled by the essence of technology understood as the *Ge-Stell,* the construct.[14] Technology, Heidegger insists, is not just a means to an end, an instrument we use as we might use a hammer. It is rather a way in which whatever is presents itself to modern man. This calls into question Gropius's confident pronouncement that "in the last resort mechanization can have only one object: to abolish the individual's physical toil or providing himself with the necessities of existence in order that hand and brain may be set free for some higher order of activity."[15]

Neither "construct," nor "configuration," nor the now common translation of Heidegger's term, "enframing," begins to preserve the wordplay and the associations of the German *Ge-Stell,* in which we should hear at least these two senses of *stellen:* to put something in a place or set it somewhere and to hunt it down or bring it to bay, as for example a wild animal. So understood, *stellen* means also *herausfordern,* "to challenge." Our science places nature before us by challenging it: its search for truth is a hunt. The mode of uncovering that Heidegger associates with technology thus already governs the science that is a presupposition of what we usually call technology. In its essence technology is therefore a way of understanding the being of what is, a way clearly marked by Descartes's famous promise in the *Discourse on the Method,* which opposes to "that speculative philosophy which is taught in the Schools, . . . a practical philosophy by means of which, knowing the force and the action of fire, water, air, the stars, heavens, and all other bodies that environ us, as distinctly as we know the different crafts of our artisans, we can in the same way employ them in all those uses to which they are adapted, and thus render ourselves the masters and possessors of nature."[16] Nature comes to be understood first of all as available material, to be used and to be disposed of when no longer of use. But such understanding fails to be open to things as they are. In this sense Heidegger can say: "*In the essence of the* Gestell *happens the neglect* (Verwahrlosung) *of the thing as thing.*"[17] We inhabit the world neglecting things.

Like *Gestell, Verwahrlosung* is a quite ordinary German word, meaning precisely "neglect." Yet "neglect" fails to capture all that Heidegger has in mind. He would have us listen more carefully to the word, hearing in it not just *verwahren,* "to guard or keep something," so that *Verwahrlosung* would name the state of being left unkept or unguarded, but in *verwahren, wahren,* "to watch over and protect," and *wahr,* "true." *Verwahren* thus would mean: to watch over the thing so that it can present itself as the thing it is, as it is in truth.

Heidegger thinks the presencing of things in relation to the world, where "world" is understood as the way in which human beings relate to whatever they encounter. In this sense we can speak of the world of the Middle Ages or of the modern world. "World" names here a space of intelligibility in which all things present themselves. So understood, "world" names a necessary condition of all experience and as such cannot be lost. But Heidegger thinks the essence of technology more specifically, against the background not just of his understanding of human being as essentially being-in-the-world but of his understanding of genuine dwelling, and that means also against the background of the world thought of as the fourfold of heaven and earth, mortals and divinities. Only to think the world as the fourfold, he claims, is to think it in its essence. To present itself "in truth," a thing must also present the fourfold, which alone lets it be. But that objectifying reason which has shaped our modern world cannot make sense of the fourfold. What Heidegger calls the *Verwahrlosung* or "neglect" of the thing is therefore necessarily also a refusal (*Verweigerung*) of the world, a "world" that now no longer means just a space of intelligibility but also the fourfold. To *this* world Heidegger would have architecture recall us.

Talk of the modern world now becomes problematic, for, ruled by objectifying reason and subject to technology, the modern world represents a refusal of the fourfold and thus conceals or hides its own essential being as world. The modern world is thus the *verwahrloste Welt,* the "neglected world." As Heidegger understands it, this neglect is not something for which we bear responsibility; rather it is part of our destiny, of a piece with the history of Being thought of as the process of metaphysics from its Greek beginnings to Cartesian rationality, a "progress" that has its other side in the transformation of the work of art from a world-shaping power, from work having an ethical function, into an aesthetic object.[18] But even today art can be more than a production of aesthetic objects. If the world understood as the fourfold refuses to present itself to us moderns, poets and artists yet preserve its traces. Architecture, too, should serve such preservation.

Heidegger's understanding of the threat posed by technology to genuine dwelling is made clearer by a third proposition: "The *Ge-Stell* orders all that presences to be present as the always available items of the available material."[19] Once again the translation is inadequate. *Bestellt* does indeed mean "orders," as one orders a meal; it also means "sends for," as well as "cultivates," as one cultivates a field. Whatever is, is ordered by the *Ge-Stell* in a way that reduces the many dimensions of its being to just one: it is ordered to present itself as "always available material at hand." That includes human beings. "The need for human material is subject to the same regulating ordering that characterized mobilization in time of war, as is the need for books of entertainment and poetry. . . . All material, including the raw material 'human being,' is used up for the technological establishment of the unconditioned possibility to make anything at all. Although hidden, such use is determined by the complete emptiness in which the materials that make up what is real now stand."[20]

Written down at the time of World War II, these last remarks could be said to presuppose a caricature of reality that we have happily left behind. To that caricature corresponded the dehumanizing architecture of Hitler's Germany, including its concentration camps. But we cannot simply shrug off Heidegger's claim that the technological spirit presiding over the modern world threatens to reduce human beings to material subject to calculation and planning as just another resource. Think of traffic engineering, or of modern medicine, or of modern war—Heidegger would add Hitler's Final Solution to such examples.

Heidegger, too, understood the extermination camps as factories of death, buildings built to reduce human beings to human material, built to betray the essence of building because built to betray what is a condition of genuine dwelling: staying within the fourfold, which also means preserving the possibility of really dying. "Do they die?" Heidegger asks of those who perish in the extermination camps. "Hardly noticed," they are *umgelegt,* "cut down," "liquidated." Such perishing is not dying in Heidegger's sense. The death dealt by the Nazis to millions of innocent victims would deny them full humanity by denying them the possibility of a genuine dying. "Only those able to die become mortals in the full sense of this word. A mass of misery, of countless, dreadfully undied deaths everywhere—and all the same, the essence of death remains blocked. Not yet are human beings mortals."[21]

"Not yet are human beings mortals," Heidegger mournfully proclaims, inviting us to understand the concentration camps as an extreme example of what in "Building Dwelling Thinking" is called "the plight of dwelling," to recognize their "architecture" as the horrifying realization of the counterideal buried in the essence of technology: the antitype to Adam's house in paradise.[22] Something of the leveling of distinctions Heidegger ascribes to the essence of technology reverberates in his own words. He does not name the murdered victims. He does not speak of Jews, Gypsies, or homosexuals. An inhuman detachment, according to Heidegger himself bound up with that technological age which revealed its monstrous essence in National Socialism, allowed him to say the following: "Agriculture is now a motorized food industry; in its essence the same thing as the manufacture of corpses in gas chambers, the same thing as blockades and the reduction of a region to hunger, the same as the manufacture of hydrogen bombs."[23] But monstrous as they are, it is not difficult to make sense of Heidegger's equations. They are indeed demanded by his understanding of the essence of technology and the plight of dwelling.

5

Despite the pressing housing shortage, few of those listening to Heidegger could have disputed that "the real plight of dwelling does not lie merely in a lack of houses," that "the real plight" is rather "that mortals ever search anew for the nature of dwelling, that they *must ever learn to dwell.*" Such dwelling, Heidegger had told his audience, is possible only where there is strength to resist the temptation to make gods for ourselves and to worship idols. This must have touched those who heard him: had the Germans not fallen into idolatry when they substituted a house built by Hitler for that primordial building whose outlines haunt and elude us? And had Heidegger himself not participated in their dance around the golden calf? Convinced that with the death of God the edifice of our culture had lost founder and foundation and lay in ruins, Heidegger had hoped to recover the archaic truth of pre-Socratic Greece for the modern age. That hope let him be receptive to the Nazis' promise of a new order raised on blood and soil. Those who seek inspiration and a sense of direction in the much-cited temple passage in "The Origin of the Work of Art" should remember that it was written at a time when Nazi Germany sought to reappropriate the Greek paradigm, which has played such a fateful part in German history, giving it architectural expression in its own brand of neo-classicism. Postmodern architects and theorists have shown increasing appreciation for both Heidegger's reflections and the Nazis' sublime perversion of Athenian architecture. To them especially I would recommend Robert Jan van Pelt's "Apocalyptic Abjection," which begins with a discussion of Heidegger's failed attempt to serve a distinctly German reappropriation of the greatness of our culture's Greek beginning; passes on to a discussion of Nazi architecture as a repetition of the architecture of Athens, of Hitler's attempt to make Berlin "into a mondial acropolis," Nuremberg into a national agora, Munich into a German necropolis; and concludes with an interpretation of Auschwitz as the topsy-turvy city Hitler built.[24] It should be obligatory reading for all who seek to appropriate Heidegger's thought for architectural theory, indeed for all who dream of recovering the greatness of its Greek beginning and also the seductive simplicity of Heidegger's Black Forest farmhouse for our modern culture.

Still, as long as we recognize that such farmhouses lie irrecoverably behind us, they help us understand more clearly what Heidegger calls the plight of our own dwelling, even as the failure of Heidegger's disastrous attempt to reappropriate the archaic in the modern age speaks to the threat of idolatry. We still must learn to dwell. But by saying that as mortals, we "*must ever learn to dwell,*" Heidegger also suggests that it is not given to us to arrive at our true home. What he calls "the *real* plight of dwelling" is not something to be got rid off. We cannot really be at home in the world as long as we fail to accept that we are wayfarers, nowhere fully at home. This is how we must understand Heidegger's question, "What if man's homelessness consisted in this, that man still does not even think of the *real* plight of dwelling as *the* plight?" as well as his answer: "Yet as soon as man *gives thought* to this homelessness, it is a misery no longer."[25]

Space and Place

11

1

Only if we succeed in substituting for the kind of dwelling that built Heidegger's farmhouse one genuinely of this age do we have a chance of arriving at an understanding of building that is not anachronistic. Such substitution calls for a reconsideration of his privileging of place over space. Consider once more the revolution in communications and the way it has shaped the world we live in, especially our sense of space and the gain in freedom it has brought. Place circumscribed the freedom of Heidegger's Black Forest farmer in a way that we would find intolerable. Television, radio, and telephone, satellites, cables, and computers let us experience whatever place we are in increasingly as a place we just happen to occupy and may want to exchange for another, should economic opportunities, love, or perhaps a promise of spiritual growth prompt us. If we are no longer rooted in one place, as farmers were for countless generations, this comparative lack of rootedness is just the other side of a vast increase in freedom.

The lure of freedom that challenges the binding power of place is as old as humanity. The story of the Fall, an ambiguous story of both place and self-assertion, provides a paradigm for stories of human beings refusing to keep their assigned place, stories that are inevitably also stories of liberation. Walls and closed doors have always been experienced as invitations to trespass. Attempts to diminish the importance of distance did not have to wait for modern technology: think of the history of transportation, beginning with the invention of the wheel and the taming of horses. The desire to defeat the tyranny of place is as old as humanity; technology has simply provided us with far more effective means—just consider the automobile and the possibilities of separating home and workplace that it has brought. Like all repetitions of the Fall, this attack on distance has to be understood in all its ambivalence. Certainly, it must bring with it increased rootlessness. Inseparable from such rootlessness is not only a loss of place but a loss of community. The closed community of Heidegger's Black Forest farmer has given way to the far less restricting, multidimensional community, or should we say communities, to which we all belong. Part of this splintering, which threatens to bring about the disintegration of community altogether, is the greater emphasis on the different roles played by the persons we meet with: the employer, the salesperson, the police officer, the teacher, the wife, the husband, all threaten to obscure the person. Along with this goes greater anonymity, the substitutability of individuals.

But once again: we must not lose sight of the gain in freedom this development has brought. If the loss of place can be mourned, must it not also be welcomed as an essential part of the increasing emancipation of the individual from the rule of the accident of place? Place no longer need be destiny, as it undoubtedly was for the Black Forest farmer. The more we want to emphasize freedom, the more likely we are to insist that emphasis on place should yield to a recognition of the value of open space (fig. 56). I remember how disturbed I was, when I first came to the United States, by buildings that did not seem to belong to the landscape. But inseparable from my uneasiness was a sense of openness and excitement. I can well imagine an American who, carrying with him memories of his hometown's magic mile and coming to one of Europe's old cities, city walls still enclosing and sheltering the houses within, the entire city still an organic whole, would find all this order terribly depressing and confining. "Something there is that doesn't love a wall,/That wants it down." Robert Frost was not speaking of city walls, not even of walls of rooms or houses, but of a New England stone wall—and it is hard to want that down. But "Mending Wall" is of course not only or even primarily about such a wall:

"Something there is that doesn't love a wall,
That wants it down." I could say "Elves" to him,
But it's not elves exactly, and I'd rather
He said it for himself. I see him there
Bringing a stone grasped firmly by the top
In each hand, like an old-stone savage armed.
He moves in darkness as it seems to me,
Not of woods only and the shade of trees.[1]

Open spaces have long been linked to freedom. This is not a new point. At roughly the same time Heidegger's farmer is said to have built his farmhouse, the far more enlightened Joseph Addison expressed a very different ethos:

Our Imagination loves to be filled with an Object, or to grasp at any thing that is too big for its Capacity.
We are flung into a pleasing Astonishment at such unbounded Views, and feel a delightful Stillness and
Amazement in the Soul at the Apprehension of them. The Mind of Man naturally hates everything
that looks like a Restraint upon it, and so is apt to fancy it self under a sort of Confinement, when the
Sight is pent up in a narrow Compass, and shortened on every side by the Neighborhood of Walls and
Mountains. On the contrary, a spacious Horison is an Image of Liberty, where the Eye has Room to
range abroad, to expatiate at large on the Immensity of its Views, and to lose itself amidst the Variety
of Objects that offer themselves to its Observations.[2]

"A spacious horizon is an image of Liberty." The open ocean or the view from some mountain top is preferred to the bounded beauty of a Black Forest valley. What announces itself here is not only the developing sensitivity to the sublime but also the connection between the sublime and freedom, which was to play such an important part in Kant's analysis. What so many travelers from Europe found and still find exciting about the American landscape, and not just about unspoiled nature but also about its often chaotic cities, is this openness in which a democratic ethos finds expression. This is true even of the suburban landscape with its jumble of supermarkets, hamburger joints, crisscrossing highways, and cars, which would seem to provide almost the perfect illustration of what is meant by "loss of place." Rootlessness and freedom both find expression in such an environment. This landscape is often striking in its ruthless disregard of physical place (fig. 57). But such disregard reflects the fact that place and with it proximity and distance are less and less determining facts of our lives. The accident of place no longer determines the job we are going to take, who our friends are going to be, where we are going to shop, and so on.

Undoubtedly this has to mean the breakdown of neighborhoods in the traditional sense. But this breakdown need not be deplored: the diminished power of place, a consequence of technological advances that allow the individual to participate in an ever-increasing number of groups and subcultures, may be taken as an index of modern, civilized living. The house or apartment house becomes just another place where one happens to sleep, eat, make love, perhaps raise a family—at any rate not a place that allows for an integration of all the important human functions. It is a place, Heidegger would say, where one merely resides but does not dwell. Life in the metropolis scatters individuals into different activities. What matters are these activities. Such a life demands functional frames in which distance matters less and less, requiring efficient systems of communications that minimize the power of place and distance.

The full consequences of this attack on distance remain uncertain. It seems difficult not to welcome the way it has helped free human beings from what I have called the accident of location: no longer is place destiny. Such liberation, however, is attended by its frightening shadow: the attack on distance also threatens us with a homelessness never before known. Some, to be sure, have suggested that the revolution in communications has allowed us to make the whole world our home, that we are on the verge of the global village, but such metaphors are, I fear, products of wishful thinking. Consider once more television. There is no doubt a way in which it negates distance: the far away and the nearby are equally brought into our living room, but only as pictures from which the observer is excluded. Or think of the telephone company's advertising slogan, inviting us to reach out and touch someone. Anyone in love will know that this call is only a very deficient mode of touching. Genuine intimacy demands a different kind of proximity.

The attack on distance also has to turn against intimacy. Intimacy and a sense of distance go together: eliminate one and you eliminate the other. That goes also for the sense of personal distance, established, for example, by distinctions between formal modes of address or by dress codes. Where everyone is called by his or her first name and sex becomes a matter of casual encounters with increasingly interchangeable partners, genuine intimacy becomes difficult to achieve as we deprive ourselves of the symbolic distances whose breakdown makes such achievement possible.

Instead of genuine proximity we are increasingly offered only its perverted analogue: the equidistance and thus the homogeneity, the indifference, of place—think of television programs and our relationship to their heroines and heroes. This attack on distance brings with it a loss of place of which the mobile home is but an expression: there is a sense in which most of us today live in mobile homes. It is not surprising then that such houses are easily left, exchanged for another. The ease with which we relocate ourselves and replace buildings is witness to a more profound displacement that may be welcomed as an aspect of humanity's coming of age or deplored as a loss of genuine dwelling. When all places count the same, we can no longer place ourselves and become displaced persons. This raises the question: if modern life demands minimizing the importance of distance and that means inevitably also the significance of place, does it also demand the death of an architecture that grants a sense of place?

It would be a mistake to see in this progressive displacement of human beings only the result of technological progress. That progress, a precondition of the modern metropolis with its lonely crowds, only realizes a displacement founded in the commitment to objectivity on which rests our technology and the science on which it depends. This commitment has shaped the world we live in and our sense of reality.

What does "objectivity" mean here? I would like to define it in opposition to our usual way of understanding things. First of all and most of the time we find ourselves caught up in the world. The way we experience the world is inseparably tied to the activities in which we are engaged. Our interests determine what we pay attention to. Our encounter with things is also subject to a point of view that is ours because of whatever place we happen to occupy. Our experience of things is mediated by our body, and therefore dependent on its makeup and subject to the accident of its location in space and time. Thus each person sitting in some room experiences it in a different way, from a different perspective, and yet each experiences the same room. This sameness of the room is not itself something seen; it is rather a presupposition of our seeing, which is inescapably bound to a particular place and point of view. That we nevertheless understand ourselves to be in the same room shows that our location is not a prison. Nor must we change positions to see things differently: in imagination we can put ourselves in other places even without moving. It is thus possible to ask someone to draw a picture of some room as it would look from an unavailable point of view, say at the center of the ceiling. And we can also ask for descriptions of the room less ruled by perspectival distortions, less subject to the accident of location; we call these descriptions more objective. Complete objectivity entails freedom from all perspectival distortion. Science aims at descriptions that are objective in this sense. It thus rests on a self-displacement by which the subject elevates the embodied self into a thinking substance. Such self-elevation is the point of Descartes's turn to the *cogito*. The thinking self that is the ideal subject of science has freed itself from the limits imposed on it by its body and the accident of its location. That liberation, however, is a liberation only in thought. We lack eyes to see things objectively. To make sure that its descriptions of the world are more than fantastic constructs, science therefore returns to the world in the form of experiment and technology. Technology carries the liberation from the accident of location into the world. Such liberation is at the heart of what Heidegger discusses as the rule of the *Ge-Stell*.

The commitment to objectivity that is a precondition of science and technology has to transform our sense of space, which leads to a characteristically modern sense of homelessness. To make this point a bit clearer let me turn to a thought experiment by the fifteenth-century cardinal Nicholas of Cusa, which helped to destroy the geocentric worldview of the medievals.[3] Cusa asks us to imagine someone on a moving ship, drifting in a large body of flowing water: might not such a person, unable to see the shores, think himself the unmoving center of the world; and were not his contemporaries like such a person, when they proclaimed the earth to be the center of the cosmos? But such security is false and rests on perspectival illusion. With equal right a lunarian could claim the moon to be that center, a Martian, Mars. Rest and motion, the cardinal insists, are relative notions. What we take to be fixed depends on our point of view. This reflection was to help give others the courage to reject the geocentric worldview, but Cusa was not a forerunner of Copernicus; he did not place the sun at the center of the cosmos but rather denied that it makes sense to speak of such a center at all. Infinitely extended, space, according to the cardinal, has no center, just as it has no boundaries. Once again it is the freedom of thought that helps us to escape from the accident of location and to break out of the prison of perspective. As that prison is shattered, so is the closed world of the Middle Ages. Unlike that world, a world that assigned to man and to all things their proper places, the boundless space of the moderns leaves us lost in space. Space here conquers place. The Copernican revolution transformed the earth quite literally into a mobile home. Nietzsche is right to speak of "the nihilistic consequences of modern science. . . . Since Copernicus man has been rolling from the center toward X."[4]

There were those who, like Giordano Bruno, welcomed this liberation as a liberation of the spirit that would soon lead to political change. But enthusiasm was to yield to despair. The infinite space thus opened up began to fill humanity with terror. We could turn to Donne or to Pascal, or to Schopenhauer's famous introduction to the second volume of *The World as Will and Representation:* "In endless space countless luminous spheres, round each of which some dozen smaller illuminated ones revolve, hot at the core and covered with a hard cold crust; on this crust a mouldy film has produced living and knowing beings; this is empirical truth, the real, the world."[5] Nietzsche was to appropriate Schopenhauer's dismal vision in the very beginning of his early fragment *On Truth and Lie in an Extra-Moral Sense,* so popular with postmodern critics weary of all centers. It is the same vision Turgenev lets the nihilist Bazarov express in *Fathers and Sons:*

I'm thinking life is a happy thing for my parents. My father at sixty is fussing around, talking about "palliative" measures, doctoring people, playing the bountiful master with the peasants—having a festive time in fact; and my mother's happy, too. Her day is so chockful of duties of all sorts, of sighs, and groans that she does not even have time to think of herself; while I . . . I think. Here I lie under the haystack. The tiny space which I occupy is so infinitely small in comparison with the rest of space, which I am not, and which has nothing to do with me—and the period of time in which it is my lot to live is so petty besides the eternity in which I have not been and shall not be. . . . And in this atom, this mathematical point, the blood is circulating, the brain is working and wanting something. . . . Isn't it loathsome.[6]

Bazarov experiences himself adrift in the infinite, a stranger unable to find a place to call his own. What foundations are left to build on, what centers by which to orient oneself? The more technology carries the attack on place into our everyday life, the more we can expect that life to be tinged by a sense of being on the road, of not belonging, of being denied the possibility of really dwelling somewhere. Hopper's paintings offer illustrations of what I want to call the terror of space (see fig. 77).

Inseparable from this terror of space is the need for boundaries strong enough to establish place. Architecture has one source in the attempt to make what is originally a strange and alien environment more our own, to transform space into place, so that instead of being cast into a strange and alien world we are allowed to dwell. It thus has offered defenses against the terror of space, and such defenses are especially needed in a culture that has attacked distance as effectively as our own. This is one lesson Heidegger's Black Forest house has to teach us. But again the question returns: is it still possible for us to have such an architecture? It may appear that this suggestion demands something that is not only undesirable, but impossible—undesirable because it glorifies the mystery of belonging to a particular place or region at the expense of freedom, impossible because it asks us to step back into a pre-Copernican world, to return to a pre-Copernican understanding of space.

An answer to this question is implicit in the recognition that the human being cannot be reduced to a thinking substance or a disembodied freedom. Human being belongs to both body and spirit, to the earth and to the light. An adequate understanding of dwelling must do justice to this twofold belonging, which is never without tension. Such tension may be found intolerable and may lead to attempts to negate it; two strategies of negation offer themselves:

1. We human beings may try to assert ourselves as essentially free spirit and attempt to reduce nature, including our own bodies, to mere material to be understood and controlled. Such assertion must demand open space as the only environment that can do justice to a genuinely human dwelling. But should spirit triumph altogether over the earth, architecture would lose its point. For if our true home is of the spirit, there is no reason to place much emphasis on our material home. The accident of our location must then not only be accepted but welcomed. It is in such self-assertion that the look of mobility so characteristic of our architectural environment has its deepest foundation.

2. Conversely, aware that such one-sided emphasis on the spirit must lead to nihilism, one may glorify an existence that reduces human beings to no more than part of nature and idealize the person with roots. But roots that are too strongly developed imply a lack of freedom and thus a less than full humanity.

We have to recognize the rights of both body and spirit. Our building must acknowledge both the sheltering power of place and the indefinite promise of open space (fig. 58).

58 | Farm buildings and windmills, Alameda County, California. Photo by author.

3

I have cited Nietzsche's maxim that ever since Copernicus, we have been drifting toward X. But do we in fact live in a post-Copernican world? To some extent that is surely the case. Astronomy has pushed toward the limits, which is also to say toward the origin of the universe. We have sent rockets to and beyond the moon, and dreams of placing human beings on other planets no longer seem altogether utopian. Still, in many ways the space of our everyday experience remains pre-Copernican. We have to grant Heidegger at least this much: first of all and most of the time the space we live in is not the space of astronomers nor the space of Euclidean geometry with its x, y, and z coordinates. These spaces only open up in reflections that presuppose what I have called the pursuit of objectivity and with it a disengagement from the world, a profound self-displacement. But disengagement presupposes a prior engagement. Engagement and place have at least temporal priority.

Once more I would like to return to the problem of distance. We tend to take the objective approach to distance so much for granted that distance tends to be understood as a neutral quantity. That a place three miles away is farther away than a space one mile away seems so obvious that it hardly merits further reflection. Given a certain way of looking at the world it is indeed obvious. What is not obvious, however, is that we should always look at the world in this way. In what sense is it obvious that Greenland is closer to the United States than England? Look at a map, measure the distance! But when is the ruler an adequate guide to what is close and what is distant? In the world we live in, distance cannot be reduced to a quantitative measure. That goes especially for the space of architecture, if not for that of civil engineering.

Let me give an example: imagine a bedroom in which you are lying in a bed placed against the outside wall. As you lie in that bed, you start considering that this wall right next to you is only a few inches thick; you think of the rosebush without, invisible to you yet separated from your head by only a few inches, only a few bricks between you and the red flowers and prickly thorns. Such reflection may strengthen your sense of the room as *your* room. Everything in that room is close to you, as the rose is not. But the more you focus on the objective proximity of the rosebush, the more a sense of the uncanny, perhaps even a sense of dread, is likely to come over you. The normally sheltering wall threatens to give way. A sense of homelessness seizes you that is not without its own excitement and freedom.

Compare the way we experience space first of all and most of the time with the objective world picture presented by a modern mapmaker: to her distance means quantitative measure. Depending on her specialty, the mapmaker may have as good an understanding of the topography of New Guinea as of that of Connecticut, representing it in quite the same way: the form of representation chosen is not bound by the accident of location. Is it obvious that such a modern map is better than a medieval *mappa mundi,* which placed paradise at the top, hell at the bottom, and Jerusalem at the center and perhaps projected the whole on the body of Christ, thus asserting a profound harmony between cosmos and humanity? The modern mapmaker no doubt gives an objectively far more correct account, which does greater justice to the quantitative aspect of space. If you want to use the map to get from one place to another, the modern map will prove much more useful. The medieval world map, in contrast, helped interpret the significance of humanity's place in the world; it articulated an ethos. Mapmaking here had an ethical function. The map represents the world as a meaningful order, a building built by God, who joined spaces so that human beings should be able to dwell. Similarly, medieval cosmology represents the world as a cosmos, as a well-joined order sustained by God in which human beings have their proper place near the center (fig. 59). Is this cosmology less adequate than the modern? In an obvious sense this is no doubt the case. It is less true, less adequate to the way things are, given that the discovery of "the way things are" requires objectivity. But we should keep in mind the measure of adequacy that is here being presupposed. Science's pursuit of truth is indeed inseparably bound up with the commitment to objectivity. But despite journeys to the moon, despite all we have learned about space, the world we live in remains in many ways geocentric. Still the sun rises and goes down again.

59 | Piero di Puccio da Orvieto, *God Holding the Universe*. Camposanto, Pisa. Credit: Alinari/Art Resource, N.Y.

Let me give another, more architectural, example. It has become customary to build churches with towers (see fig. 68). Why? One could reply: the tower has become an established convention, an accepted and expected part of the church type. Eco might have said that it helps the builder to denote "church." But if so, what is the origin of this convention? Was its establishment arbitrary? Traditionally towers were generally placed in the west. In the past few hundred years this tradition gradually eroded, as other considerations came to be more important. One reason towers were once placed in the west, oriented toward the setting sun, was that they were thought of as bastions against the forces of evil, bastions perhaps presided over by St. Michael as general of the heavenly host. Evil was tied to the west, because it is here that light is daily defeated by the forces of darkness. Presupposed by the church type is the natural symbolism of light, which intertwines with that of space, giving different meanings to east and west, and therefore also to north and south.

I have tried to contrast two conceptions of space; one objective, homogeneous, neutral with respect to value, the other regional, heterogeneous, and freighted with values. If we rest content in the conviction that the objective interpretation is simply the correct one, we fail to consider human being in its full range. To reduce space to objective space is to make it impossible for human beings to ever discover their place in the world. As Nietzsche pointed out, such impossibility is the mark of nihilism, which could be understood simply as the inability to understand the world as a dwelling. But such inability rests on a false, because overly reductive, understanding of our own being in space. We must not forget that the objective understanding of space presupposes a much richer experience, is the product of a reflective transformation of space, and that in the course of this transformation gain is balanced by loss. What is gained is greater objectivity and with it truth; what is lost is precisely the dimension of meaning. Space ceases to speak, but only to those who have lost touch with their own being. To be sure, we live in a technological world, a world shaped by science and its pursuit of objectivity, but not all the dimensions of the world we live in are circumscribed by technology. Technology must be affirmed and put in its place. That means to recognize its liberating potential as well as the threat it poses. To recognize the latter is to perceive also how important it is to recover what has been lost: a sense of place. We still need architecture, we moderns especially.

The Voices of Space

12

1

If architecture can be understood as the construction of boundaries in space, this space must be understood as commonsense space, a space that possesses meanings and speaks to us long before the architect goes to work.[1] The architect can, to be sure, build in a way that does not heed these meanings, indeed that self-consciously denies them. He or she can also be open to them, re-presenting and thus revealing them. In this chapter I would like to consider some of these meanings in more detail and thus take a small step toward developing what one might call a semantics of the natural language of space.[2] Not only past architecture but paintings, poems, novels, and fairy tales all offer rich material for such explorations.

The key to this language is provided by the fact that we exist in the world, not as disembodied spirits, nor as beings who just happen to have bodies, but as essentially embodied selves, who by their bodies are inevitably assigned their place in the world—on the earth and beneath the giant hemisphere of the sky (fig. 60). When Heidegger claims in *Being and Time* that first of all and most of the time we experience things as "ready-to-hand," this technical term recognizes the importance of the hand, that is, the mediating function of not just the eye but the body, the moving body: I reach for something—it is too high; I try to pick something up—it is too heavy; I want to walk somewhere—it is too far. The body not only gives us our first understanding of proximity and distance but also provides us with a matrix, a set of coordinates—up and down, right and left, front and back. However, it may be misleading to speak here of coordinates, for the term fails to do justice to the way body-centered space privileges front, which opens the self to the world, over back and up over down (fig. 61). For architecture at least, the human being is indeed the measure of all things, and that means first of all, although by no means exclusively, the human body, especially the arm, the foot, the hand, the finger.[3]

Inseparable from our understanding of the body matrix is the different language spoken by verticals and horizontals. We have no difficulty understanding Frank Lloyd Wright when he deplores the tendency "to tip everything in the way of human occupation or habitation up edgewise instead of letting it lie comfortably flatwise with the ground where spaciousness was a virtue"[4] (fig. 62). I do not want to criticize or support Wright's idea "that the planes parallel to the earth in buildings identify themselves with the ground, do most to make the buildings belong to the ground";[5] here I only want to call attention to the very different meanings of vertical and horizontal that let us understand his assertion,

Rudolf Schwarz, earth and sky. Source: Schwarz, *Vom Bau der Kirche,* 2nd ed. (Heidelberg: Lambert Schneider, 1947).

60

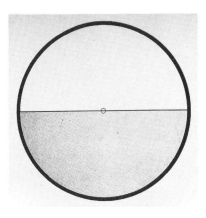

Rudolf Schwarz, the body matrix. Source: Schwarz, *Vom Bau der Kirche,* 2nd ed. (Heidelberg: Lambert Schneider, 1947).

61

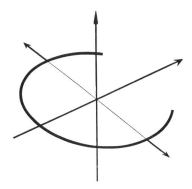

Frank Lloyd Wright, Martin House, Buffalo, New York. Detail. Photo by author.

62

63 | Megalith, Locmariaquer, Brittany. Credit: Giraudon/Art Resource, N.Y.

regardless of whether we agree or disagree: the horizontal, whether line, plane, or slab, ties a building to the earth, just as it ties us humans to the earth when we are asleep or dead (fig. 63).

Wright himself, to be sure, emphasized that his attitude to the horizontal plane—parallel and close to the earth, while yet tending to spread itself out indefinitely—and to the house—not a cave, but a "broad shelter in the open, related to vista"—was that of someone "born an American child of the ground and of space," thus reminding us of the way the language of space is inevitably refracted by history and landscape. But Wright also insisted on its universally human significance, "welcoming spaciousness as a modern human need as well as learning to see it as the natural human opportunity."[6] Once again the sight of a seemingly endless open plain is linked to thoughts of freedom and democracy.

Horizontals not only speak of shelter, even as they carry a promise of freedom; they hold their own terror. The painters of the sublime knew about that terror, and Caspar David Friedrich in particular exploited it again and again. On first seeing Friedrich's *Monk by the Sea* (fig. 64) the poet Heinrich von Kleist wrote: "Nothing can be sadder and more uncomfortable than this position in the world: the only spark of life in the wide realm of death, the lonely center in a lonely circle. With its two or three mysterious objects the painting lies before us like the Apocalypse, as if it had Young's *Night Thoughts,* and since in its uniformity and boundlessness it has no foreground except the frame, when one looks at it, it is as if one's eyelids had been cut away."[7] The sweep of the painting's horizontals, which extend themselves beyond the seemingly arbitrary boundary of the frame, threatens

to annihilate the lonely Franciscan in the picture, hinting at the end and its beyond: the *mysterium tremendum et fascinans* of death and the infinite. The other side of such fascination is a longing for eyelids, for frames, boundaries, centers, for verticals strong enough to challenge the horizontal's centrifugal power, which figures the centrifugal power of infinite space.

While the horizontal not only suggests comfort or an indefinite beyond, full of the promise of as yet unknown opportunities, but also hints at surrender, at sleep and rest, at death and disintegration, the vertical is assertive. Effort is needed to stand, to pile stone on stone, to build a pyramid or a skyscraper. Firmly planted in a landscape, towers establish centers, wrest place from space, reach up to heaven. Consider the way churches with their spires punctuate the flat Dutch landscape in a painting by Jacob van Ruisdael (fig. 65):

The Voices of Space   *183*

"They stand in awe-inspiring immutability where the great tracts of land (from below) and clouds (from above) meet; they provide the main vertical accent—relatively small, but all-important because only they stand out."[8] Countless villages and towns still are gathered together by church towers, whose verticality has remained unchallenged by more recent, even taller, commercial structures; they still allow us to experience the power of the vertical to gather a community by providing it with an axis, connecting earth and sky. The language of domes is related: "Whereas the tower, however, appears as a compact mass, the dome is experienced as a volume which contains an interior. The dome therefore does not only define a center, but also acts as a condensed image of the surrounding world."[9] The Pantheon thus represents the cosmos (fig. 66; see also fig. 83).

There is an obvious connection between the assertiveness of the vertical and human pride. Pride built the towers of the Gothic cathedrals as it built our skyscrapers, as it now lets cities and architects build (fig. 67) and dream of ever taller buildings: the building Donald Trump proposed for lower Manhattan was to have 150 stories; Skidmore, Owings, and Merrill proposed a 165-story office building for Chicago; and there has been talk of buildings 200 or even 500 stories tall. The mythic paradigm of such structures is the Tower of Babel (see fig. 48). With this tower, we are told, its builders hoped to make a name for themselves, hoped to guard against being scattered across the face of the earth and to rescue themselves from the terror of boundless space. A communal work, this piled-up mass of stone was to be the bond that held the community together, its visible center.[10] The gathering power of its vertical, firmly planted on the ground, was to conquer the scattering power of open space as a humanly established *axis mundi*.

In this post-Freudian age it has become fashionable to associate such assertive buildings with masculinity, more narrowly with "the American male," and to interpret their strong verticals as phallic symbols. I suspect rather that in making the phallus into a symbol we have presupposed rather than founded the natural symbolism of verticals and horizontals, although like everything significant, the phallus not only receives its significance from an established world of meanings but from the very beginning is part of and helps constitute that world.

If the Tower of Babel furnishes architecture with a paradigm, this paradigm carries a warning: as we all know, the tower could not be finished—this center would not hold. By confusing the builders' languages and scattering them abroad, across the face of the earth, God inflicted on them just the fate they had sought to avoid. One point of the story is no doubt to suggest that by themselves human beings lack the strength to furnish themselves with a center.

While the story of the Tower of Babel links the vertical to futile self-assertion, the story of Jacob's ladder gives it a very different meaning. Read for many centuries as part of the consecration rite, it served to establish the traditional symbolism of the church as house of God and gate of Heaven:

And he [Jacob] came to a certain place, and stayed there that night, because the sun had set. Taking one of the stones of the place, he put it under his head and lay down in that place to sleep. And he dreamed that there was a ladder set up on the earth, and the top of it reached to heaven: and behold, the angels

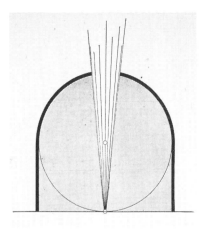

Rudolf Schwarz, diagram of the Pantheon.
Source: Schwarz, *Vom Bau der Kirche,* 2nd ed.
66 (Heidelberg: Lambert Schneider, 1947).

Cesar Pelli and Associates, Kuala Lumpur City
Center, Kuala Lumpur. The world's tallest skyscraper, now under construction. Credit: Cesar
67 Pelli and Associates.

of God were ascending and descending on it! And behold, the LORD *stood above it and said, "I am the* LORD, *the God of Abraham your father and the God of Isaac; the land on which you lie I will give to you and to your descendants; and your descendants shall be like the dust of the earth, and you shall spread abroad to the west and to the east and to the north and to the south; and by you and your descendants shall all the families of the earth bless themselves. Behold, I am with you and will keep you wherever you go, and will bring you back to this land; for I will not leave you until I have done that of which I have spoken to you." Then Jacob awoke from his sleep and said, "Surely the* LORD *is in this place. . . . This is none other than the house of God, and this is the gate of heaven."* (Gen. 28.11–17, RSV)

Here it is not prideful humanity that seeks to pierce the clouds with its towers, but God himself who bridges the gap between heaven and earth. A particular place is experienced as filled with the presence of the divine: it is the house of God. But this place, this Bethel, not only is God's dwelling place but also opens up to a higher reality: it is the gate of Heaven. The ladder of the dream with its angels ascending and descending symbolizes that linkage. Jacob responds to this dream experience by rising—that is, by raising himself from a horizontal into a vertical position—and by raising the stone that had served him for a pillow from a horizontal into a vertical position. This simple altar, a celebratory re-presentation of the supporting stone,[11] as well as a representation of the dream ladder, becomes the archetype of the church and perhaps of sacred architecture: building as a response to the *genius loci,* to the divinity dwelling in that place. Countless churches have reenacted that establishment, especially with their towers, which so happily allowed the desire to serve God and an all-too-human pride to merge (fig. 68).

68 | Tower of St. Martin, Landshut. Photo by author.

Not that the Biblical text establishes the symbolism of vertical and horizontal, up and down. The symbolism is not limited to any particular tradition nor projected into the world. It can be called natural in that it has its foundation in the nature of human being in the world, in experiences of lying down and getting up, of climbing and descending, of lifting, raising, and supporting: experiences of the opposition of earth and sky, darkness and light, matter and spirit. As the traditional definition of man as the *animal rationale* suggests, we are amphibians. Wright recognized this amphibian character of human being when he called himself "an American child of the ground and of space." In a tale by Tibullus, to which Heidegger calls our attention,[12] we find the suggestion that man is called *homo* because care shaped him of *humus*—earth—and because it is to earth that he shall return in death. Jupiter gave man his spirit and he, too, shall receive back what belongs to him. Essentially the same understanding of human being guides the Biblical account, which has God create Adam from the dust of the earth, but in his own image. The verticality implicit in such conceptions becomes explicit when Zwingli understands man as the being who looks up to God, or when Vitruvius suggests that man looks up to and measures himself by the divine order of the sky. Verticals figure our relationship to the spiritual, horizontals our temporal death-shadowed dwelling on earth: the cross figures the intersection of the two. Sacred architecture has thus been traditionally distinguished by its greater verticality: think of Gothic parish churches and the way they tower over their cities, or of Mayan temples, or of death-defying pyramids.

It is not surprising then that Schopenhauer should have located the very essence of architecture in the conflict of verticals and horizontals: "its sole and constant theme is support and load. Its fundamental law is that no load be without sufficient support, and no support without a suitable load; consequently the relation between these two may be the exactly appropriate one. The purest expression of this theme is column and entablature; hence the order of columns has become, so to speak, the thorough-bass of the whole of architecture."[13] Once again the Greek temple is held up as the paradigm of architectural purity, and once again it is easy to criticize this view by showing how very much in keeping it is with the taste and conventions of the day. Schopenhauer was a conservative, and not just in politics. He had little patience with the then-growing vogue in favor of Gothic architecture. To be sure, he was well aware of how Gothic architecture might be justified along the lines he has sketched:

if we try to discover an analogous fundamental idea in Gothic architecture, it will have to be that the entire subjugation of gravity by rigidity is here to be exhibited. For according to this the horizontal line, which is that of the load, is almost entirely vanished, and the action of gravity appears only indirectly, disguised in arches and vaults[,] . . . whereas the vertical line, which is that of the support, alone prevails and renders palpable to the senses the victorious action of rigidity in extremely high buttresses, towers, turrets, and spires, without number, unencumbered. . . . From this arises that often observed analogy with a crystal, whose formation also takes place with the overcoming of gravity.[14]

But, Schopenhauer insists, before admitting Gothic architecture as an equally valid paradigm, we should remind ourselves "that the conflict between rigidity and gravity, so openly

Piet Mondrian, *Tree* (ca. 1911). Private collection.

69 | Credit: Giraudon/Art Resource, N.Y.

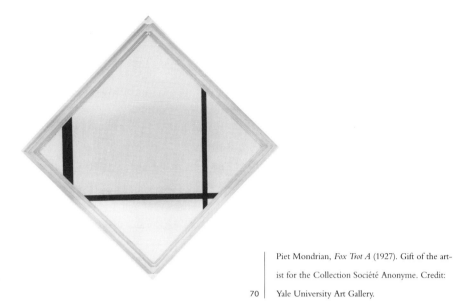

70

and naively displayed by ancient architecture, is an actual and true one established by nature. On the other hand, the entire subjugation of gravity by rigidity remains a mere pretense, a fiction testified by illusion."[15] Schopenhauer knew that such "pretense" was able to communicate to countless believers a sense of eternal security, of safety from the vicissitudes of the temporal and earthbound: "Death, where is thy sting?" Gothic verticality seemed to shout. But Schopenhauer is unable to take seriously this apparent victory of the vertical over the horizontal. Despite all self-assertion, human beings are vulnerable and mortal, and full self-affirmation requires the recognition of our limits. Gothic architecture is governed by what Schopenhauer rejects as a false ethos. He would have architecture be more open to the tragic condition of human being, a condition figured by the contrast between the heaviness of entablatures and the assertiveness of supporting columns, between verticals and horizontals—that is, by the Greek temple.

We may not want to follow Schopenhauer and place classical architecture over Gothic. But whatever our response may be to a Greek temple or a Gothic church, it presupposes our understanding the different meanings of verticals and horizontals, meanings that are inseparable from our being in the world. That Schopenhauer's reflections have a significance beyond the particular period and place that gave rise to them is suggested by Piet Mondrian's insistence that "the first aim in painting should be universal expression. What is needed in a picture to realize this is an equivalence of vertical and horizontal expressions. This I feel today I did not accomplish in such early works as my 1911 'Tree' paintings. In these the vertical predominated. A 'Gothic' expression was the result."[16] No doubt, some may prefer the "Gothic" look of the tree paintings to the cooler "classical" look of a mature Mondrian (figs. 69 and 70). I am less interested here in such disagreement than in what it presupposes: an understanding of the language of verticals and horizontals. Only when this language is understood does it make sense to be concerned about "an equivalence of vertical and horizontal expressions" or about attempts to have one triumph over the other.

2

I have spoken of the vertical dimension of our being in the world: we exist on the earth and beneath the sky, belonging to both. But this is also to say that we belong to darkness and to light, a moving light that changes with the moving clouds, the times of day, the seasons, and localities—not an artificial light we bring into the world but a gift, above all the gift of the sun.

As the place of the rising sun, the east possesses a special significance. The chambered tomb at Newgrange thus privileges the midwinter sunrise (fig. 71), while the axes of many Greek temples came to be fixed by the position of the rising sun on the feast day of the divinity to which the temple was consecrated. There is a sense in which such structures may be considered sun dials: on the feast day the doors of the cella were opened and for a minute the rays of the rising sun were able to penetrate the dark of the cella's interior and light up the image of the deity. At that moment the façade of the temple is almost free of shadows and reveals itself in an unusual purity.[17] The Romans placed less emphasis on such considerations. Practical considerations that had little to do with religion or with the natural symbolism of space and light decided its placement: for example, considerations of how to fit the temple into the urban fabric. But when Emperor Constantine in A.D. 324 erected a large basilica over the grave of St. Peter, its entrance was once again oriented toward the east, as had been the entrance of the Greek temple.[18] Soon there were objections to this orientation. In a sermon dating from 450 we hear Pope Leo the Great objecting to the way such architecture invited a mingling of Christian faith with pagan sun worship: "Such customs lead to that godlessness that has some people, who do not know any better, venerate the sun when it rises at dawn from elevated places; some Christians, indeed, consider it especially pious, when, before entering the basilica of St. Peter, consecrated to the one living and true God, and having ascended the steps, they turn around toward the rising sun and with bent neck bow down before the gleaming disc. . . . Even if some venerate the creator of the beautiful light more than the light itself, such form of worship cannot be permitted."[19] To counter such paganism the church's orientation was reversed. This discouraged worshipers from reversing direction as they approached and entered the church: the church now becomes a path leading east, to the true light, to Christ.[20] In keeping with the natural symbolism of light, this path leads from west to east, from darkness to light. After the Middle Ages this orientation loses much of its former significance. The churches of most modern cities face in every possible direction.

This may suggest that the natural language of light and dark is no longer alive for us, and we should note that this language is one not only of light but of a light that changes with the times of the day and the times of the year. Certainly, our placement of buildings, and not just of churches, tends to give little weight to such considerations; other factors have come to be more important. How much attention is paid by architects, when siting a house, or in planning where bedroom, kitchen, and dining room should be, to this ever-changing light (fig. 72)? We are, of course, in this age of artificial light and central heating and air-conditioning, much less dependent on such considerations; but, as Heidegger would

teach us, such comparative independence also has made it more difficult to build houses in which human beings can dwell rather than reside. Think back to places where you have lived: how much or how little did the natural light illuminating these spaces mean to you? How much does it still mean? I like to wake up in a bedroom facing east, especially so in the spring, at Easter time.[21]

3

Bound up with the language of verticals are the different meanings of up and down. Once again a few suggestions have to suffice. I have already spoken of that verticality of human being which Vitruvius takes to distinguish us from the animals. Our feet tie us to the earth; our head, seat of eyes and mouth, ties us to light and spirit, to the logos. "Up" and "down" thus invite very different associations. In Greek and medieval geocentric cosmology the value of up far outweighs that of the center: the world above the moon—the realm of the sun, the stars, and the planets, unreachable but visible, whose ageless order is a continuing challenge—contrasts with the sublunar world to which our body binds us, a realm ruled by growth and decay, birth and death. The devil dwells at the earth's center. Geocentrism came to mean diabolocentrism.

The different meanings of up and down are revealed to us in experiences of ascending and descending. Think of the step or steps leading up to the front door, or of the way steps are used in sacred architecture—for example, in churches: a few steps may lead to the portal, a few more steps separate the nave from the more sacred space of the choir. In a traditional church the way east is also a way up. Holy stairs and holy mountains figure in religions the world over—Sinai, Olympus, Golgatha; Meru, Haraberazaiti, Garizim.[22] How much of this remains alive in us today when we climb a mountain? When we reach a cross on the top of some Alpine peak, this of course refers back to that mountain on which Christ died (fig. 73). The meaning of cross and mountain are here tied to a particular religious tradition. But the sacredness of neither is limited to the Christian tradition, which could be said to have appropriated the natural symbolism of mountains, inseparable from the symbolism of up and down.

In this connection we should not forget the very different meaning of descent: going down into a cellar, into the underworld, descending into hell. In many medieval churches we often find beneath the light-filled choir a crypt: narrow steps wind down into its musty darkness. If the altar above is given to light and eternal life, beneath is the realm of darkness and death. The crypt is the cellar of the church. Here human pride is shattered.

4

To the language of up and down we have to add that of inside and outside, bound up with the awareness of our own bodies, with their openings so much like the windows and doors of buildings. Just as our experience of verticals and horizontals is profoundly ambivalent, so

Cross on mountaintop. Photo by author.

is our experience of inside and outside. Think of the many poems, mostly romantic, in which some lonely wanderer looks into a house where people have gathered happily around a festively decked table: it may be Christmas, the cold without making the warmth within seem all the more desirable. Closely related to this is Rudolf Schwarz's plan for a simple church: "To celebrate the holy feast of the Lord, one needs a space of good proportions, not too large, in its middle a table, on which is placed a bowl with bread and a chalice with wine."[23] This suggests that a circular space, a space built in the image of the Pantheon perhaps, might furnish a proper setting for such a sacred feast (see fig. 66).

Yet, as Schwarz insists, how hopeless is the unmitigated, perfect closure of ring and hemisphere; "ring and dome are the dreariest of all forms. Forever they remain a self-preoccupied circling, forever only a throw that begins to rise, climbs to a peak only to fall back into heaviness, as natural life returns itself to the earth."[24] We want to break open the ring, open it to some other, less earthbound place, and fill it with light as the builders of the prehistoric tomb at Newgrange allowed the light of the midwinter sun to enter the tomb's darkness, refusing to let the sheltering, dark earth have the last word. When my wife and I built a small pavilion on the island of Vieques, our architect, Edward F. Knowles, persuaded us to open it, Pantheon-like, to the sky, asserting that vertical dimension of human being insisted on already by Vitruvius (fig. 74). It is a good place to sleep. The oculus above quiets and calms—it is magical to wake up at night, just long enough to recognize the head of Scorpio overhead. Spaces thus open to the seemingly eternal firmament are fit for sleeping and burial: the Pantheon thus provides builders of cenotaphs with an obvious

The Voices of Space

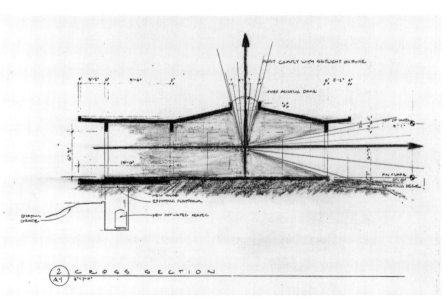

74 | Langhorne Pavilion, Vieques, Puerto Rico. View to the east. Charcoal drawing by author.

75 | Langhorne Pavilion, Vieques, Puerto Rico. Section by architect, Edward F. Knowles; overdrawing by author.

paradigm (see figs. 111, 112). But life demands the horizontal; and so we opened up the space, especially to the east, to allow the moving sun to wake us and draw us out of the house (fig. 75).

"Inside" can promise shelter, but it can also mean a suffocating darkness that our imagination peoples with images that both fascinate and terrify. Think of the sad windows that accompany the traveler as the train is about to plunge into the tunnel leading into Grand Central Station: broken windows, blind eyes that recall those soulless, mirrored eyeglasses that shut us out as they shut their wearers in, glasses for a fellowship of *Symparanekromenoi*,[25] persons who have buried themselves while still alive. Inside—prison and shelter; outside—threatening other and our true home: how we experience one or the other will have much to do with our experience of the world. Those who experience the world as already a fit dwelling place, as paradise, if you will, do not have to build at all. The more we feel at home in the world, the less we will want to shut it out. The need for building is founded in the deficiency of the world, first apparent in the need for physical shelter. That deficiency is readily linked to thoughts of the deficiency of human being, thoughts of an essentially free spirit cast into the body's prison and thus subjected to the accident of its location. Gnosticism holds such a view, and there is a Gnostic side to Platonism and to Christianity. Were one to think that way, one would be likely to associate "shelter" with "prison" and dream of an architecture beyond the distinction of inside and outside, an architecture that would furnish a humanity that had asserted its mastery over its own body and the physical environment and liberated itself from the age-old need to seek refuge in dark interiors.[26] Paul Scheerbart was such a dreamer. The enthusiasm with which he spoke of glass architecture that, fusing inside and outside, would return us to a paradisal state recalls the enthusiasm with which Giordano Bruno three centuries earlier greeted the destruction of the medieval cosmos:

We live for the most part within enclosed spaces. These form the environment from which our culture grows. Our culture is in a sense a product of our architecture. If we wish to raise our culture to a higher level, we are forced for better or worse to transform our architecture. And this will be possible only if we remove the enclosed quality from the space in which we live. This can be done only through the introduction of glass architecture that lets the light of the moon and stars into our rooms not merely through a few windows, but similarly through the greatest possible number of walls that are made entirely of glass, colored glass.[27]

Why mention moon and stars and not the sun? And why colored glass? Medieval stained glass comes to mind. Scheerbart, too, is dreaming of cathedrals for the modern age.

The fascination with transparency cannot be denied: there is something intoxicating about the possibility that glass offers of integrating inside and outside. It offers at least an illusion of dwelling in nature, under the open sky, looking up to the stars and the moon, as Adam and Eve must have done in paradise. But we are not in paradise. Who of us would want to live in a glass house? Soon we would be searching for some corner that was really our own, enclosed, offering protection from the world and from others. The need for enclosed spaces is tied to the need for privacy, the need to be left alone: for example, when we want to dwell, at least for a time, in our own inner space, with our own dreams and thoughts; or when, ashamed of our nakedness, we want to avoid the look of the other, say when we need to use the toilet. There is a side to building that invites us to locate its origin in shame. To do so is to understand it in the image of the traditional origin of clothing, the fig leaf. In this connection it is interesting to observe children who, even in their rooms, sometimes even in their beds, construct other, more intimate spaces. One of my sons called it his "groove corner."[28]

If there is something inhuman about the openness of glass architecture that threatens to deprive us of a private sphere, equally inhuman is an architecture that deprives us of a sense of outside. In the film *Last Year at Marienbad,* a disturbing architectural environment was created simply by showing the insides of the Baroque palaces in which the film was shot, Schleissheim and the Amalienburg near Munich, in such a way that you couldn't see a window. As a result normally airy, light-filled spaces assumed a labyrinthine quality that recalled Piranesi's *Carceri.* Many of the atria currently so popular similarly disturb me: creating an artificial "outside," often complete with trees and flowing water, inside some large structure (say a hotel in Atlanta), they deprive us of a sense of the world we live in as a home, hint at possibilities of a totally artificial environment, invite thoughts of a time when we may have made nature so uninhabitable that only such artificial environments will be found tolerable. In a very different way, Gothic stained glass, too, suppresses our usual experience of the window as an opening to the outside world and thus denies us a sense of that world as our home; instead we are presented with figures of what is taken to be our true home, a home not of this world.

As these observations suggest, a good way to explore the ambivalent meaning of inside and outside would be to listen to what windows and doors have to tell us. Often a poet or painter will place us inside a room, looking out. Dutch genre painters thus liked to establish the interior as a private, intimate realm with the presence of windows, hinting at the public world without. Very different is the voice of the window in Caspar David Friedrich's *Woman by a Window* (fig. 76). Here the luminous outside hints at freedom; the mast of a ship that remains invisible hints at journeys to distant places. How very different is the voice of its tenuous vertical from that of the window's cross. Slight as it is, it effectively separates outside from inside, which in this painting seems strangely cramped, stifling, a prison.

Different again is the voice of the open door in Hopper's *Rooms by the Sea* (fig. 77). It allows the openness of light and ocean to invade the interior so that it can be neither prison nor shelter. Here open space triumphs over the sheltering wall. There is something exciting but also inhuman about an architecture that allows space to triumph over place. Even "cavemen" apparently did not live in the interior of caves but instead found their shelter under overhanging rocks.[29] The depths of caves were holy places, sacred spaces removed from everyday life, spaces given to the *mysterium tremendum et fascinans* that touches us whenever we touch the boundaries of our life. If this is right, there is a sense in which caveman lived between cave and open nature, somewhat like the cliff dwellers of Mesa Verde. And do we not still demand dwellings that allow us to live such a life—sheltering walls *and* doors and windows through which light and air can enter?

76

Caspar David Friedrich, *Woman by a Window* (1818). Nationalgalerie, Berlin. Credit: Foto Marburg/Art Resource, N.Y.

Edward Hopper, *Rooms by the Sea* (1951). Bequest of Stephen Carlton Clark. Credit: Yale University Art Gallery.

77

5

There are other aspects of the language of space we should consider. I have already touched on the symbolism of the center, which has often been thought inseparable from human dwelling. Every enclosed area or volume implies a center, more strongly when compactness and regularity are greater. Circles and squares, spheres and domes are strongly centered. The Pantheon is such a space, although its center remains inaccessible, a divine center from which we are excluded (see fig. 66).

Neighborhoods and cities require such centers if they are to be experienced as coherent regions; they invite us to mark or re-present these centers, be it with some prominent structure or with a square, which may in turn find its center in some monument or fountain.[30] If center and boundary go together, centers are also suggested whenever axes intersect, inviting re-presentation by broadening the intersection into a square. By proliferating such intersections, the grid devalues any particular intersection, posing a threat to the formation of such regions as functioning neighborhoods. To counteract this tendency a particular square may be singled out by being left unoccupied: such squares function as potent negative figures. Squares provide natural centers for the life of the community, proper places for buildings that serve a communal function. But every intersection invites special emphasis, invites re-presentation as center of some neighborhood: street corners are special places and invite special treatment (see fig. 55). Stores here find a natural place.

An obvious paradigm for such centered spaces is paradise, that bounded garden, which has in its midst the tree of life—and also that of the knowledge of good and evil. It would be easy to add other such paradigms: the symbolic significance of the center seems inseparable from the human situation, bound up with the requirement of dwelling. Inseparable from our feeling at home in a certain region, it presides over that region as a force holding it together. For archaic people, Eliade writes, the center is thus "pre-eminently the zone of the sacred, the zone of absolute reality." Thus, "Attaining the center is equivalent to consecration, an initiation: yesterday's profane and illusory existence gives place to a new, to a life that is real, enduring, and effective."[31] Those who built the Tower of Babel as an *axis mundi* sought to furnish themselves with such a center. Every temple or sacred structure re-presents the center, like the ladder of Jacob's dream, a hinge holding together heaven and earth—hence its gathering power. As such a center it is also a sacred mountain, a place where heaven and earth meet.

The center of our individual life-world would seem to be foremost whatever place we find ourselves. But this is only a place where we happen to be, for we can move and think of other places: if some sense of center is thus given by the body matrix, it would be absurd to invoke here the symbolism of an *axis mundi*. Furthermore, we are not alone: our being is inevitably a being-with-others. Whatever sense we can make of the center of our world, that center cannot be just the individual's own but must belong to and be supported by the community of which she or he feels a part. To be experienced as a genuine center a place must be experienced as gathering a multitude into a community. And to have that power it must in some sense still be experienced as a place where the earth opens up, perhaps no longer to heaven but to the divine—or, if no longer to the divine, then to the values that we take to preside over our lives.

How much does this symbolism of the center still mean to us? Can we think of Washington as the center of the United States, opening this land up to its firmament of values, helping to gather it into a genuine community? Think of the Mall with its monuments (fig. 78), of the Capitol and White House; consider the function art and, more especially, architecture have in establishing this vast expanse as a center. Something similar, although inevitably more modest, would seem to give (or perhaps just attempt to give) coherence to just about every community, although everywhere the centrifugal forces that are a corollary of our celebration of the individual at the expense of community continue to diminish the importance of all centers. The grid here symbolizes a mode of organization in keeping with the open democratic society in which we live. Does such openness pose a threat to dwelling and thus also to community? The visible and growing disintegration of our cities does suggest a profound displacement of large parts of this society, a loss of centers that testifies to a growing inability to dwell.

But all invocations of an archaic, centered dwelling demand questioning. If the shape of modernity militates against all centers, should we not welcome this? Suppose I

78 | Mall, Washington, D.C. Photo by author.

were to discover a place that deserved to be called not just a center but the center of my world, were to discover, say, the place where I truly belong, my true home: how could I bear to leave it? Were I to dwell in such a home, I would no longer know where to go; in an important sense there would be no longer be a place to go, since *that* place I would already be occupying. The voyage of my life would have ended. So understood, the plenitude suggested by dwelling at the center means death, and it only seems appropriate that the devil was thought to dwell in the earth's center and God somewhere beyond the periphery, beyond the firmament, everywhere and nowhere.

To be genuinely at home in this world, we have to affirm our essential homelessness, a homelessness illuminated by shifting ideals of genuine dwelling, figures of home, and precarious conjectures about what it might mean to dwell near the center. Temples have functioned as such figures. But every attempt to step into the true center, to come home in this sense, more especially to make the house into such a home, denies the essential ec-centricity of human dwelling—an "ec-centricity" that needs to be thought in relation to a center, but a center that withdraws whenever we seek to seize it.

Learning from Two Invisible Houses

13

1

While it makes sense to speak of a natural language of space, this language is inevitably mediated by particular landscapes, particular histories, particular stories. Thus space will speak differently in a desert climate than in the rainy north; differently on a plain and in the mountains; differently in a peasant and a modern industrial society; differently in a Christian and in an Islamic country. Not least among the factors that mediate our understanding of space are the buildings we have grown up with, especially the house or houses that for the first few years of our lives gave us a sense of security, houses that have inscribed themselves into our consciousness as figures of an ideal building, more dreamed of than remembered. For each of us, Bachelard claims, there exists "an oneiric house, a house of dream-memory, that is lost in the shadow of a beyond of the real past"[1] (fig. 79). Dreams of that house intertwine with dreams of a more integrated way of life, a more authentic dwelling.

Bachelard's oneiric house presupposes a relatively stable environment, not quite as stable perhaps as Heidegger's Black Forest farm, but still an environment in which families tended to stay together, in one house, long enough for the house to inscribe itself into the child. Today the cultures that provided such an environment are rapidly eroding. Many children, to be sure, continue to be raised in similarly stable environments, but the evolution of the modern life-world seems to point in a very different direction: how does a much more unstable lifestyle—in which families move, disintegrate, and reform; in which often there is no family at all, but a single parent struggling to maintain a home—affect our dreams of houses? Of what houses do the inhabitants of our ghettoes dream?

Bachelard's dream house presents itself to the reader as very much an ideal building, of a piece with other such buildings that would call us to a more authentic dwelling. As for Heidegger, so for Bachelard, too, that call is a call away from the dispersal in the world that is inseparable from modern life, from the many roles that we have to play, the changing possibilities that invite us to improve and expand ourselves, to seek out what we have not yet tried, and to experiment with new lifestyles, with new partners, with ourselves. Bachelard's dream house challenges such experimentation. Dreaming of this house, we hold on to ourselves, save ourselves from drowning in an ocean of possibilities.

Without it, man would be a dispersed being. It maintains him through the storms of heaven and those of life. It is body and soul. It is the human being's first world. Before he is "cast into the world," as

Dickelschwaig near Ettal, Bavaria. Photo by author.

claimed by certain hasty metaphysics, man is laid in the cradle of the house. And always, in our day-dreams, the house is a large cradle. A concrete metaphysics cannot neglect this fact, this simple fact, all the more since this fact is a value, an important value, to which we return in our daydreaming. Being is already a value. Life begins well, it begins enclosed, protected, all warm in the bosom of the house. (p. 5)

Bachelard challenges the claim that building has its origin in the fundamental opposition between human beings and the initially strange and indifferent world in which they have to live, an opposition that finds expression in the phrase "cast into the world." When Bachelard speaks of a "certain hasty metaphysics," "a secondary metaphysics" that "passes over the preliminaries, when being is being-well, when the human being is deposited in a being-well, in the well-being originally associated with being" (p. 7), he is no doubt thinking of *Being and Time:* Heidegger's fundamental ontology had indeed made homelessness constitutive of human being.[2] First of all and most of the time we have lost ourselves to the world into which we have been cast. Into this state of lostness breaks the silent call of conscience, which, calling from far away, calls us beyond the world, back to ourselves. But in calling us back to ourselves, conscience does not call us to a specific place. This analytic is strikingly similar to Gnostic thinking. Heidegger's later conception of human being as a dwelling within the fourfold moves closer to Bachelard: the Black Forest farmhouse is his oneiric house. And Heidegger's dream house, too, presupposes that primordial dwelling is a being at home in the world. But for the present age, the age ruled by the *Ge-Stell*, the analysis offered in *Being and Time* retains much of its validity.

Bachelard's assertion that life begins well recalls the traditional account that would have humanity begin sheltered, in paradise. These memories or memory dreams of being at home are then projected into an indefinite future; both past and future contrast with the present, in which we are not really at home. We get thus a four-term matrix: home, the opposition of self and the social and natural environment into which it has been cast, and the projection of a future home. This matrix should seem familiar: we recognize a version of it in the traditional view of man as fallen, having been expelled into an alien world in which he has to struggle to survive, haunted by memories of the paradise he has lost and by dreams of regaining what has been lost. In romantic literature we meet again and again with images of the hero who has left home, who had to leave home in order to become an individual confronting an often hostile world, and yet who now, haunted by dreams of what he has lost, faces the task of homecoming. Jung saw in this matrix an archetypal pattern.[3] Something like it would indeed seem to be inseparable from our development into thinking, self-conscious beings: the self constitutes itself by leaving home and going out into the world, struggling to make its place in that world and guided in that struggle by dreams of home, of a more intimate dwelling that it casts ahead of itself into the future.[4]

Different experiences of different individuals will clothe this archetypal structure in different images. Bachelard suggests that all the different houses in which we have lived make a contribution to our image of our dream house. "And after we are in a new house, when memories of other places we have lived in come back to us, we travel to the land of Motionless Childhood, motionless the way all Immemorial things are. We live fixations, fixations of happiness" (p. 5). Our encounters with houses are illuminated by memories of a past that has been endowed with a mythical significance, as childhood figures the integral life.

How important is the actual house in which we were born and to which we are tied by our first memories? Bachelard gives it great importance: "But over and beyond our memories, the house we were born in is physically inscribed in us. It is a group of organic habits. After twenty years, in spite of all the other anonymous stairways, we would recapture the reflexes of the 'first stairway,' we would not stumble on that rather high step. The house's entire being would open up, faithful to our own being. We would push the door that creaks with the same gesture, we would find our way in the dark to the distant attic. The feel of the latch has remained in our hand" (p. 5; fig. 80). We have to wonder how true this remains in a culture with much greater mobility than Bachelard's France. I, for example, cannot remember the house in Jena in which I was born: we left it when I was two. And yet in some way that house, together with its large garden, does seem to have inscribed itself into me: how else could I explain my love for a certain washed-out red that I associate with the color of the red hawthorn? That color still carries connotations of a special well-being. For a long time I found my liking of this color inexplicable; I thought of myself as the sort of person who should prefer colors like an emerald green hinting at tropical water, or a glowing deep orange. Much later I learned that a good part of the first summer of my life was spent in the garden of that no longer remembered house, beneath a large red hawthorn. The first house I remember is a two-story house in Berlin's Eichkamp, also with a large, magical garden, with red, black, and white currants, an emerald lizard that seemed to come right out of a fairy tale; the white magic of house and garden was darkened

Front door and stair in a house in Tamworth, New Hampshire. Photo by author.

by the black magic of bomb splinters that I collected, tearing the pockets of my pants, darkened also by the spectacle of searchlights before a fiery sky, an incendiary bomb crashing into the attic.

According to Bachelard the house (or houses) of our childhood, together with other houses in which we have lived, only visited, or perhaps just read about or glimpsed in illustrated books, furnishes material for our dreams of houses; it serves to make concrete or to schematize our idea of the archetypal home, to which Bachelard attributes a healing power, healing in the sense of making us whole, rescuing us from the dispersal of life. And no doubt, the way buildings and spaces speak to us is tied to quite specific personal memories, memories inevitably tied to a particular place, a particular landscape. The more similar our experiences, the more likely it is that themes I stress when speaking of my dream house will resonate with your dreams. But while we should not lose sight of the dependence of Bachelard's oneiric house on personal experiences, many aspects of our dream house are less tied to specific regions and places. This is borne out by what Bachelard calls his topoanalysis, his analysis of the different places of his dream house.

2

Bachelard, too, emphasizes the special poetry of up and down. "Verticality is ensured by the polarity of cellar and attic, the marks of which are so deep that, in a way, they open up very different perspectives for a phenomenology of the imagination" (p. 17). Thoughts of attics invite thoughts of roofs with which the house relates itself to the sky. This relation gives the roof a special significance. "A roof tells its raison d'être right away: it gives mankind shelter from the rain and the sun he fears. Geographers are constantly reminding us that, in every country, the slope of the roof is one of the surest indications of the climate. We 'understand' the slant of a roof" (p. 18). It is difficult to be objective here. How much understanding is there of roof angles when there is no dominant roof angle, when roofs are flat or come with all sorts of angles and coverings? But we do understand the slant of the roof of Heidegger's Black Forest farmhouse or its Alpine counterpart—flatter, its shingles weighed down with stones. Compare its look to that of farmhouses in the Pyrenees or the Himalayas. All these roofs speak of mountains and the weather. One could draw maps of traditional roof angles: such maps would show boundaries almost as sharp as those that separate dialects or languages. To be sure, we are thinking here first of all of premodern societies and their buildings. What I earlier called modernity's liberation from the tyranny of place mirrors itself in the way we build. Today versions of the Alpine roof can appear just about anywhere, for example, in California or Massachusetts.

Still, for traditional architecture Bachelard is right: often the roof does offer us something like a key to the soul of a building. To give just one example: we associate the Gothic cathedral with a complicated exterior, with its flying buttresses, a peaked roof over the raised central aisle, and lean-to roofs over the side aisles. When you compare this with the large Gothic churches that were built in Germany in the fifteenth century we notice a considerable simplification: now one large roof spanning the nave in its entirety dominates; the buttresses are greatly simplified and have become simple step buttresses, if they have not disappeared altogether on the outside to reappear inside as wall-pillars. This not only leads to very different, plainer exteriors but also transforms the interior spaces, as the basilica gives way to the hall church with all the aisles of roughly equal height. With this, the view down the central aisle to the high altar loses some of its importance, as diagonal vistas become more significant. Changed also is the experience of windows and walls, now often obscured by pillars and wall-pillars. The forest metaphor become irresistible. That such different spaces also invite a different spirituality is to be expected and can be demonstrated. In explaining these differences the most important variable is the weather, although we also have to keep in mind the geographically conditioned difference in building materials, say the use of brick rather than limestone. The creation of very different spaces intertwines with different expectations of what buildings should look like. These buildings in turn help shape the way space generally is experienced.

To what extent do we today still understand the language of roofs? I have already noted that our urban environments exhibit a much greater variety of roof types than more traditional communities. But our expectations of what a house should look like are shaped not only by houses we have seen but also by illustrations of houses, found in all sorts of books and journals. The illustrations of houses found in children's books seem to be quite conservative; this impression would have to be tested by systematic study.

3

Bachelard develops the topoanalysis of his oneiric house by exploring the language of attic and cellar. "The cellar is first and foremost the dark entity of the house, the one that partakes of subterranean forces. When we dream there, we are in harmony with the irrationality of

Frank Lloyd Wright, Martin House, Buffalo,
New York. Photo by author.

81

House in Haslach near Traunstein. Photo by
author.

82

the depths" (p. 18). When I was eight I lived in a house in the Franconian Königshofen that had a marvelous old cellar, hewn into the local limestone. For a long time the house had served as a grocery store and the cellar especially was filled with mysterious smells—I remember especially vinegar and apple. Do houses need cellars, or at least dark spaces that fill its function? Frank Lloyd Wright would have answered with a vehement "no." His dreams of houses on the open prairie excluded the cellar: "I had the idea that every house in that low region should begin on the ground, not in it, as they then began, with damp cellars."[5] The house was to begin at ground level—belong to the earth, yes, but not dig into it, enter its darkness—and this relationship to the earth was to communicate itself to anyone looking at such a house. Similarly, indeed even more insistently, Wright called for the elimination of the attic: "First thing in building the new house, get rid of the attic, therefore the dormer. Get rid of the useless false heights below it" (p. 32; fig. 81).

Bachelard's dream house, on the other hand, has both cellar and attic (fig. 82). To the latter one can escape from the family, perhaps from reality. Attics are thus good places to think, dream, play, write poetry. Poets belong in garrets and I write these words in an attic. Once again the question returns: to what extent is Bachelard speaking from his own French, European, bourgeois perspective, and to what extent is he describing phenomena that remain alive for us? Should a house have an attic and a cellar, corners and nooks where one can hide things and oneself? Wright wanted the house to offer a broad, unified shelter, a simple space that was easily surveyed and gathered around a central hearth. Bachelard's dream house, in comparison, would seem to be a rather messy affair with many nooks and crannies. That regional and political differences help to account for these different ideals requires no comment.

Still, perhaps we need houses in which doors can be slammed shut and things shoved out of the way, into some cellar, attic, or closet, to be forgotten for many years, only to be rediscovered much later, perhaps only by children or grandchildren. From his ideal house Wright sought to banish all such spaces: closets, too, "disappeared as unsanitary boxes, wasteful of room, and airy wardrobes in the room served instead" (p. 17). We should ask ourselves what kind of dwelling goes along with such open, unified spaces, and Wright was of course quite aware of their ethical implications. "Yes, architectural forms by this interior means might now grow up to express a deeper sense of human life values than any existing before. Architecture might extend the bounds of human individuality indefinitely by way of safe interior discipline" (p. 20). Discipline within and a new freedom: these are shelters open to the land whose vanishing walls have been replaced by glass, this "super-material qualified to qualify us; qualify us not only to escape from the prettified cavern of our present domestic life as also from the cave of our past, but competent actually to awaken in us the desire of such far-reaching simplicities of life as we may see in the clear countenance of nature" (p. 46). Here, too, the dream of a simpler, more natural life, a life not weighed down by the burdens of the past (both historical and personal), burdens we keep dragging with us, often without knowing what weighs on us.

But, when we shed these burdens, are we not also in danger of shedding what gives depth and continuity to our lives? Think of throwing out some old photographs, letters, report cards. All of these have the power to raise memories of persons and events that have made us who we are. Both the historical and our personal pasts have shaped our likes and dislikes, our dreams and fears. Neither past is spread out before us like an open book. We are all prejudiced, and usually that prejudice is so much with us that it is not recognized as such. Just for that reason it is important to be confronted with traces of the person we once were and in some measure still are. To free oneself of a deep prejudice requires much work and may be impossible if it is deeply enough ingrained. Yet to confront one's prejudices, to expose them to other horizons, is part of autonomy.

As Gadamer has insisted, the prejudice against prejudice must also be questioned and can indeed be shown to be itself a prejudice, of a piece with the prejudice against perspective. Just as our sight is always governed by some point of view or other, so our values and ideals are always governed by some personal and social prejudice or other, whose roots reach back far into history and down deep into our subconscious. An adequate understanding of human being must recognize the importance of what usually remains below the level of consciousness. Our psyche, too, has its attics, cellars, and closets. But if so, theories of dwelling should not attempt to elide them. In our buildings, too, we need spaces that play the part of the subconscious, spaces where we store what we do not seem to need, spaces where the relics of our lives are allowed to accumulate, spaces where we may rummage some day to be confronted with some long-forgotten aspect of our past, spaces that provide our dwelling with a usually obscured continuity. Attics, cellars, and closets are such spaces.

4

The above discussion also is governed by its prejudice and invites challenge. Does Frank Lloyd Wright's dream house not have as much to teach us as Bachelard's? Wright's call for houses that invite us to "escape from the prettified cavern of our present domestic life as also from the cave of our past" will not be dismissed. The promise of open space, which figures the promise of an open future, must not be sacrificed to the stifling comfort of place, which figures the way we have been bound by our past. Wright's reference to cavern and cave brings to mind Giedion's remark that the so-called caveman in fact lived between cave and open nature. Should we not think of genuine dwelling also as such a being in between caves and open space, a dwelling in between past and future, in between memories and hopeful and still unformed expectations? This would suggest that we should build our house somewhere between Bachelard's oneiric house and Wright's ideal prairie house. We can agree with Bachelard on this: we all dream of houses. But not always of the same house; sometimes our dreams are of huts, sometimes of palaces, sometimes of intimate shelters that shut out the outside, sometimes of tents open to the forest and its animals; sometimes they lead back into the past, sometimes forward into the future. We must navigate among a multitude of such dreams when we attempt to imagine our ideal house.

It is not only our personal history that gives content to that house. Again and again the past has yielded images that gave direction to building. The historical past becomes especially important when confidence erodes in the tradition in which we stand, when measures and values long taken for granted have become questionable, when personal dreams have proliferated in such a way or speak with so many voices that they no longer can offer a clear direction. We may turn to reason for the needed authority. But reason alone has proven unable to rescue our decisions from arbitrariness.

When the specter of arbitrariness thus threatens our confidence in our own decisions, we tend to appeal to history to supply the needed authority. Heidegger's *Being and Time* offers an example. After developing a view of authenticity that appears to rule out all appeals to God or to pure practical reason, to essences or norms, and recognizing that there can be no responsible choice without criteria to guide it, Heidegger comes to claim that "the sole authority which a free existing can have" is that "of revering the repeatable possibilities of existence."[6] Heidegger was by no means the only one to invest the past, in his case pre-Socratic Greece, with such authority. Historicism in architecture can be similarly defended. William Hubbard, for example, offers just such a defense in *Complicity and Conviction*:[7] the indispensability of appeals to the past is acknowledged. Relating his or her structure to precursor buildings, while yet attempting to make an original contribution, the architect

adds a link to what is a continuing chain. Hubbard invites us to take Harold Bloom's interpretation of poetic achievement, which focuses on a creative reading or rather misreading
of precursor texts, as a model for understanding achievement in architecture.[8]

A difficulty with this and similar views is that history does not speak with one but
with many voices. Some past event becomes authoritative only when recognized as worthy
of repetition. Heidegger himself does not speak of "recognizing" but of "choosing": to live
a meaningful life the individual must choose his hero.[9] Following Bloom we may want to
say, must choose his precursor. But how can I choose some historical or perhaps fictional
character as my precursor unless I recognize in that precursor a paradigm worth reappropriating? Can such recognition be willed? Must there not be something about my situation,
about what now moves and claims me, that lets me recognize in this particular individual
my precursor and to make that earlier stance the measure of my own? We fall back into
arbitrariness unless choice is tied to recognition. Essentially the same considerations apply
to the architect who turns to the past to find there a hero or a paradigm to appropriate.
Where should he or she look? to the Greek temple? the Gothic cathedral? to Palladio? or
perhaps to Corbusier? Where do we find a binding, nonarbitrary reading of history?
If history is to provide authoritative guidance, it may be experienced not as a reservoir of
more or less interesting motifs, which we can pick up or discard as we see fit, but as a tradition that determines our place and destiny, in which we stand and to which we belong. So
understood history could provide orientation similar and supplementary to the orientation
furnished by Bachelard's oneiric house. But do we today still stand in history in this way?
There is a sense in which we moderns have fallen out of history. We may indeed know
more about history today than ever before, but precisely in making the past an object of
scholarly investigation we have lost the sense of belonging to history. The very successes of
our historians betray a profound historical rootlessness: for many historians time has become
a coordinate on which they move back and forth with equal facility. The expert on Roman
history of the first century B.C. is as close to her subject matter as the historian of Elizabethan
England. But with this historical displacement, the past has to lose its authority, as it becomes
no more than a reservoir of materials that we may incorporate in our constructions as we
see fit. The problem of arbitrariness returns.

To defeat such arbitrariness Hubbard appeals to an evolving ideal image of human
being: "The architect has in mind an ideal about how people ought to live, and he has
chosen those particular conventions because he sees a way in which he can use them to
express that ideal."[10] There is good reason to take seriously Hubbard's Bloomian account of
works of architecture as offering creative misreadings of heroic precursor structures. Consider the Pantheon (fig. 83) and its countless successors, including Vaudoyer's House of the
Cosmopolite, Jefferson's University of Virginia (fig. 84), and the Jefferson Memorial. What
gave direction to these departures? And what gave authority to the original paradigm in the
first place? Why the Pantheon and not some other structure? If choice and departure are
not to seem arbitrary there must be something about the paradigm that speaks to us; it must
answer to some perhaps still ill-formed and inarticulate, but nevertheless potent preunder-
standing of genuine dwelling. And the same goes for the deviation. Hubbard appeals to an
ideal of how people are to live. If that ideal were rejected, the architecture that serves it,

Pantheon, Rome. Exterior. Credit: Alinari/Art

83 | Resource, N.Y.

Learning from Two Invisible Houses

too, would meet with little sympathy. But Hubbard, a committed conventionalist, also suggests that all ideals are human creations and as such finally groundless and arbitrary: "We in society want to be able to believe in ideals about the places we inhabit, but we know that such ideals are indefensible."[11] On Hubbard's view the architect can count on this will to believe. Architecture helps to replace meaningless reality with an architecturally or rather theatrically transformed reality, which draws us in and, as we surrender to it, gives us an illusion of meaning. The architecture of Hitler's Third Reich comes to mind, or that of Stalin's Russia. But examples need not be so distant or so unsavory. Take some late-nineteenth-century neo-Gothic church or collegiate Gothic building. Hubbard has faith in the human ability to create values from nothing, to found meanings in a meaningless world. This faith "says that of course the world, as given, doesn't make sense, but that we can make sense of it and we are the only ones who can."[12]

This, I am afraid, is a vain hope. Values or meanings cannot finally be made or invented. They must be discovered. That goes also for the meanings of architecture. All meaning that presents itself to us as freely created must seem arbitrary, and whatever is experienced as arbitrary to that extent fails to convince. If the ideals that guide our appropriation of the past are indeed, as Hubbard suggests, human creations, they need not be therefore arbitrary. To carry authority they must be experienced as creative responses to a more primordial and still inarticulate understanding of what it is to dwell. Without such a ground to guide the architect's choice of a precursor structure and his departure from it, both must be experienced as arbitrary by him. And if we do not share the same ground, they will seem arbitrary to us.

Thomas Jefferson, Rotunda, University of

84 Virginia. Photo by author.

Building seeks to transform space into place. Such transformation depends on a prior sense of place. This conviction is at the core of the persistent view that architecture should be a re-presentation, a reestablishment of an archetypal building, thus making our dwelling a repetition of an archetypal dwelling. Talk of a dream house or of the architecture of some golden age—whether sought in ancient Greece, medieval Europe, Renaissance Florence, or Jefferson's Virginia does not matter in this context—is born of the attempt to recall human beings to this more genuine dwelling. Such talk should not mislead us into thinking that there should ever be a realization of the house of our dreams. Bachelard is right to insist, "Maybe it is good for us to keep a few dreams of a house, that we shall not have time to achieve it. For a house that was final, one that stood in a symmetrical relation to the house we were born in, would lead to thoughts—serious, sad thoughts—and not to dreams. It is better to live in a state of impermanence than in one of finality."[13] Genuine dwelling means not so much a being at home but at most a continuous journeying home, a continuous homecoming, haunted by changing dreams of home. If architecture really were to realize the house of our dreams it would put an end to this journey. We would have arrived and our dreams would cease. But with these dreams would cease our humanity. In this sense Bachelard could agree with Wright: for the sake of freedom, openness must be preserved in the houses we actually build. But Wright could in turn agree with Bachelard: a genuine house must provide shelter and it cannot do so except by wresting place from open space.

Building, Dwelling, and Time

14

1

Architecture has been understood as the art of bounding space.[1] If not particularly illuminating, such an understanding seems at least unproblematic, in keeping with the traditional division of the arts, which goes back to Lessing's *Laocoon,* between arts of space and arts of time, formative and expressive arts.[2] The distinction has a certain obviousness, even inevitability. Lessing drew this distinction in order to reject the Horatian dictum that a poem ought to be like a picture: *ut pictura poesis.* In this rejected view both poet and painter paint, one with colors and the other with words; both poetry and painting are arts of representation, distinguished only by their medium. Challenging this understanding, Lessing insists on their profound difference: "I argue thus. If it be true that painting employs wholly different signs or means of imitation from poetry—the one using forms and colors in space, the other articulate sounds in time—and if signs must unquestionably stand in convenient relation to the thing signified, then signs arranged side by side can represent only objects existing side by side, or whose parts succeed each other, in time."[3]

Lessing broadens this questionable argument to distinguish between arts of space and arts of time, between formative and expressive arts, and therefore also between arts of presence and arts of absence. Painting, sculpture, and architecture are included among the former, poetry and music among the latter. Because they are concerned with space, the formative arts are limited to stable forms: visual art "should express nothing essentially transitory. . . . All phenomena, whose nature it is suddenly to break out and as suddenly to disappear, which can remain as they are but for a moment; all such phenomena, whether agreeable or otherwise, acquire through the perpetuity conferred upon them by art such an unnatural appearance, that the impression they produce becomes weaker with every fresh observation till the whole subject at last wearies and disgusts us."[4] So understood the visual arts confer perpetuity, as they come to preserve at least a semblance of eternity. That is part of their appeal: they help banish the terror of time.

Obvious as such a distinction may seem, it is easy to think of examples that call it into question. The very fact that we speak of expressionist art, and even of expressionist architecture, makes one wonder. Is expressionism in some sense deficient because it engages time? Take abstract expressionism: here the painting preserves traces of an action and gestures beyond itself to its absent origin. Something of the temporal quality of that action is preserved by what appears on the canvas.

Lessing was of course quite aware that his distinction between arts of space and time makes it difficult to do justice to certain types of visual art. Were this not so, the distinction would indeed lose its polemical point, for with his distinction Lessing sought not so much to describe as prescribe. Not that he could have been concerned about modern expressionism. In the *Laocoon* Lessing sides with neo-classicism against the visual culture of the Baroque and Rococo. For example, consider a sculpture by Bernini, says his *Daphne,* in which the artist attempts to represent in marble Daphne's transformation into a laurel, as described in Ovid's *Metamorphoses.* Lessing would have found it difficult to defend such art: as the *Laocoon*'s subtitle makes clear, he wanted to write *An Essay upon the Limits of Painting and Poetry.* Invoking these limits, he sought to refute Horace. The divorce of painting from poetry was to allow each to become more truly itself. Lessing sought to establish the proper boundaries of the different arts. The art of Bernini pushes beyond these boundaries.

So does the expressive architecture of a Borromini. But it is not just the architecture of this architect or of this particular period that refuses to accommodate itself to Lessing's aesthetic legislation. There is a sense in which all architecture demands to be considered as also an art of time. This is suggested by the way we almost inevitably resort to temporal metaphors and to metaphors suggesting motion or its absence when we describe works of architecture. Geoffrey Scott has called attention to the way we speak of "springing arches," "swelling domes," "soaring spires."[5] Are such metaphors mere metaphors? What allows them to be understood? Appealing to Theodor Lipps's theory of empathy, Scott suggests: "*We transcribe architecture into terms of ourselves.*"[6] Such self-projection is said to be the foundation of humanism in architecture. It is important to keep in mind that the self in question here is the embodied self, which is essentially an active self: sometimes busy, sometimes at rest, sometimes tense, sometimes relaxed. We should thus expect architecture, too, to strike us sometimes as busy or tense, sometimes as restful or relaxed. To speak here of self-projection, however, does not recognize that just as we read ourselves into architecture, so we read ourselves in the image of architecture. Our experience of buildings is inseparably tied to the experience we have of ourselves, of our bodies, just as our experience of our bodies is affected by the spaces we inhabit. Scott indeed precedes the just-cited principle with its complement: "*We have transcribed ourselves into terms of architecture.*"[7] Such reciprocity is to be expected if human being is, as Heidegger insists, a being-in-the-world.

But being-in-the-world cannot be divorced from temporality, from care and activity, from expectation and memory. That dwelling has a temporal dimension requires no comment, and the same holds of buildings. Consider once more a metaphor such as "soaring spires": it ascribes an activity to a tower (see fig. 68). Literally, of course, the adjective is misplaced: towers are not like kites; they rest firmly on the ground. But we do not experience architecture as a pair of disembodied eyes, frozen in a single moment. The experience of the soaring spire is inseparable from our experience of our own body. Not only does the tower draw our eyes upward, but part of our experience of its height is also a self-projection that places us up there. An understanding of the effort it would take to get up there, of the way the world would look from up there—such and similar expectations provide our experience of height with often quite specific connotations. Inseparable from our experience of the tower's height are anticipations of future possibilities.

2

When considering the temporality of architecture it is helpful to keep in mind how the different ways in which we experience a painting, a sculpture, or a work of architecture place us in different relationships to time. We generally stand before a picture; most sculptures invite us to change our position, perhaps even to walk around them; works of architecture invite us not only to change our position but to enter and move around within them. Generalizing we can say that body and body awareness become more important as we turn from painting to sculpture to architecture. Take the example of a painting that obeys all the rules of one-point perspective. Such a work presupposes a specific point of view. Ideally, it should be seen only with one eye, through a peephole, as Brunelleschi showed when he demonstrated his new system of perspective.[8] As a matter of fact, when we look at such a painting we never quite meet these conditions: we use two eyes, our eyes move, and we move as we observe the painting. Yet all this matters little to our experience of the painting, which remains focused on the self-sufficient aesthetic object, not on our relationship to it. That remains true when representational perspectival painting gives way to modern abstract and aperspectival art. Recall the discussion of the aesthetic approach in chapter 2 and my use of Frank Stella's characterization of his artistic intention as a paradigm: it is no accident that I turned to a painter rather than a sculptor or architect. By its very nature painting accommodates itself more readily to the demands of the aesthetic approach. Absorbed in such a painting, we forget time. Not the mortal, embodied self, but the disembodied eye is the measure of this art.

Painting, and more especially perspectival painting, can of course be put to very different use. Michael Fried thus calls attention to a class of works that far from letting us forget time, invite us to meditate on it: "The connection between spatial recession and some such experience of temporality—almost as if the first were a kind of natural metaphor for the second—is present in much Surrealist painting (e.g., de Chirico, Dalí, Tanguy, Magritte). Moreover, temporality—manifested, for example as expectation, dread, anxiety, presentiment, memory, nostalgia, stasis—is often the explicit subject of their painting."[9] Fried calls art that would thus communicate some experience of temporality, bound up with an awareness of a subjective state of mind, "theatrical" and opposes to it another type that strives to transcend time and the individual subject in order to pursue *presentness*. As I pointed out earlier, the pursuit of presentness and, bound up with it, of the ideal of the artwork's timeless self-sufficiency has come to dominate both the theory and the practice of art to such an extent that I am tempted to call it the standard view. Lessing's *Laocoon* helped to inaugurate that tradition, a tradition Clement Greenberg sought to reclaim for the modern context with his "Toward a Newer Laocoon," which located "purity in art" in "the acceptance, willing acceptance, of the limitations of the medium of the specific art."[10] Now these limitations were drawn from a much more specific understanding of the art's medium, which was recognized to resist not only narrative and poetic expression but also three-dimensionality. "The history of avant-garde painting is that of a progressive resistance of its medium; which resistance consists chiefly in the flat picture plane's denial of efforts to 'hole through' it for realistic perspectival space."[11] Committed to this tradition, Michael Fried considers an art of presentness the only legitimate art of modernity. Theatrical art is condemned in a way strictly analogous to the way in which so many neo-classicists of the eighteenth century condemned Rococo and Baroque art. Peter Eisenman is right to associate the classical with presentness and timelessness: beauty against time. And so understood, classicism includes aesthetic modernism.[12]

Sculpture accommodates itself to the pursuit of presentness not quite as readily, as it involves the body more completely than does painting. Sculpture, we may say, is more intimately tied to time than is painting. Following Fried, we may want to say that, by the very nature of his or her art, the sculptor is more drawn to theatricality, has to struggle harder to defeat it. Egid Quirin Asam's high altar at Rohr (fig. 85) may be taken as an illustration of the theatricality of sculpture. But perhaps we should say rather: an illustration of the way Asam embraced and exploited a possibility implicit in his chosen medium.

85 | Egid Quirin Asam, high altar, abbey church, Rohr. Credit: Hirmer Fotoarchiv.

That modernist sculpture, too, can embrace theatricality is shown by the work of Robert Morris. Morris celebrates the observer's relationship to sculpture; as Michael Fried remarks, his best work lets observers recognize that they themselves are establishing relationships as they "apprehend the object from various positions and under varying conditions of light and spatial context."[13] But a sculptor need not welcome such theatricality. He or she may choose to resist it. Fried thus cites works by David Smith and Anthony Caro as examples of successfully modernist sculpture: by the strength of its configuration of forms, such sculpture renders what happens to be our point of view unimportant.

In a more obvious way architecture is experienced with the moving body: we approach a building, walk by or around it, perhaps enter it, walk down a corridor or an aisle, up some steps, open the door to a low-ceilinged chamber, open a window to look at distant mountains. Recall Fried's remark that spatial recession offers "a kind of natural metaphor" for the experience of temporality—I would delete the qualification. Our experience of recession, and more generally of distance, is inseparable from anticipations: the walk down a church aisle thus offers itself as a natural metaphor for the journey of life from birth to death, as the Christian church also holds out the promise that death will not be allowed to triumph.

When characterizing painting, sculpture, and architecture in terms of their different relationships to time, we must not make such characterizations too rigid. We have to keep in mind not only the many different kinds of painting, sculpture, and architecture but also that just as there is no constant relationship of architecture to time, so there is no constant relationship of architecture to painting and sculpture. There is architecture that, like some Renaissance paintings, invites or even prescribes a specific point of view. Renaissance perspective shaped visual imagination so powerfully that it helped shape the progress of all the visual arts. Baroque and Rococo architecture and city planning provide ready examples.

While the architect may work with one dominant point of view, he or she may also invite us to explore a sequence of shifting points of view. Eero Saarinen thus shaped the passage between Morse and Stiles colleges at Yale as a shifting frame for the neo-Gothic tower of Payne Whitney Gymnasium, inviting us to stop and look, but not for too long (fig. 86). Part of our pleasure lies in how, as we walk, changing points of view yield new pictures. We have here a modern version of a picturesque architecture, which is inevitably also a theatrical architecture. The theory of the "picturesque" belongs to the late eighteenth century, and as so often theory intertwined with practice: in countless English parks we find follies—an artificial ruin, a classicizing temple, or perhaps some monument—designed not so much to be entered as to be experienced in a pictorial way by someone walking through the park, encountered as motif giving rise to edifying reflections. Significantly, the experienced "pictures" are themselves not of fully present aesthetic objects but of structures haunted by narratives, also by past plenitude now denied.

The same concern for the "picture" or "pictures" can also govern interior design. Baroque or Rococo architects may thus be said to have moved architecture into the vicinity of painting, a painting still intimately tied to narrative and allegory. In the Augustinian priory church at Diessen, for example, frescoes spanning the nave play a crucial part in pictorializing interior space. The privileged point of view near the entrance allows us to experience

Payne Whitney Gymnasium framed by Stiles and Morse colleges, Yale University, New Haven.

86 Photo by author.

Kevin Roche and John Dinkeloo, Knights of Columbus building and Coliseum, New Haven.

87 Photo by author.

not just the frescoes but the whole interior as a pictorial composition having its center at the high altar[14] (see fig. 100). The strength of this picture arrests us and invites contemplation. But this invitation is counteracted by the pull of other points of view that beckon to be explored, beckon us forward. A contemporary example of the picturesque is Louis Kahn's British Art Center at Yale. The task of building a gallery to house mostly framed pictures provided Kahn with an occasion to explore and play with the ideas of frame and framing: framed pictures are in turn framed by the architecture; spectators are framed; Kahn's windows frame the Old Art Gallery across the street, now visible as never before.

As there is pictorial architecture, so there is also architecture that we experience as a self-sufficient piece of sculpture. Think of the pyramids. Or of the Parthenon. Or of Santa Maria della Consolazione in Todi. Kevin Roche's Knights of Columbus building in New Haven has a sculptural strength that almost allows us to forget its interior. Roche conceived the building and its basic geometry in relation to the moving traffic on the Connecticut Turnpike as a stable beacon in a restless world, seeking with this building both monumentality and presentness (fig. 87). Together with the adjoining Coliseum's strong horizontals, the Knights of Columbus building recalls medieval cathedrals with their strong towers and sheltering roofs—note how difficult it remains to build monumental architecture that does not evoke either churches or temples. Despite the strength of their seemingly timeless forms, time enters such buildings after all, as the present is haunted by the absent plenitude of an idealized past.

3

I have suggested that architecture, too, is an art of time. Whether it does so deliberately or not, architecture cannot but help shape our experience of time. To develop this point let me turn to Wölfflin's *Principles of Art History* as they apply to architecture.

1. First of all Wölfflin distinguished between the *linear* and the *painterly*. "The elementary phenomenon is this—that two totally different architectural effects are produced according to whether we are obliged to perceive the architectural form as something definite, solid, enduring, or as something over which, for all its stability, there plays an apparent, constant movement, that is change." [15]

Whenever architecture is experienced as a picture there is a certain "de-realization," as what is three-dimensional is challenged in its solid three-dimensionality. In

House framed by trees. Photo credit: Ken 88 | Abbott.

this sense the Rococo interior of a church like Diessen seems not quite solid, where fresco and ornament, as well as the use of indirect light (enhanced by the interior's fundamental whiteness), contribute to the dematerialization of this architecture. In this connection we should keep in mind the importance of natural light, which is inevitably a changing light. While direct sunlight gives definition and solidity to what it strikes—disembodied spirits were thought to cast no shadows—indirect light spiritualizes and renders what it illuminates weightless.

The painterly character of a building is underscored by plants, whether trees, shrubs, or some climbing vine. A pair of trees standing firmly before a house bathe it in an aura of continuity and thus help banish the terror of time (fig. 88). Aged brick evokes the passage of time. Or think of rust stains on concrete: the stains on Kevin Roche's Coliseum endow a rather stark architecture with a mysterious life (fig. 89).

The linear and painterly, as analyzed by Wölfflin, stand in a different relationship to time: in the case of the painterly he speaks of the play of an apparent constant movement, while linear architecture is said to be experienced as definite, solid, and enduring. Painterly architecture appears to embrace time, while linear architecture reaches beyond time to the plenitude of a timeless present.

2. Essentially the same relationship holds for Wölfflin's other paired principles. Take the second pair: *plane* and *recession*. Wölfflin himself raises an obvious objection: does

89 | Coliseum, New Haven. Photo by author.

not architecture always depend on recession? "Planimetric architecture" sounds dangerously like nonsense (p. 115). And yet the point of the distinction is clear enough:

What else is it but a deviation from frontality when the posts of the porch of a villa no longer look forwards but turn towards each other? With what other words can we describe the process which the altar passes through in which a purely frontal construction becomes more and more interspersed with recessional elements until, in the end, in rich baroque churches, there stand enclosures which draw the essence of their interest from the recession of the forms? And if we analyze the plan of the baroque staircase and terrace, such as the Spanish Steps in Rome, not to speak of any other detail, the spatial recession is brought out merely by the multiple orientation of the steps in such a way that the classically strict layout with straight flights looks flat beside it. (p. 115)

3. Wölfflin's next pair opposes *closed* or *tectonic* to *open* or *atectonic* form:

The tectonic style is the style of strict arrangement and clear adherence to rule: the a-tectonic, on the other hand, is the style of more or less concealed adherence to rule and of free arrangement. In the former case, the vital nerve in every effect is the inevitability of the organization, absolute immutability. In the latter, art plays with the semblance of the lawless. It plays, for in the aesthetic sense, of course, form is bound by necessity in all art, but the baroque tends to conceal the rule, loosens the frame and joints, introduces dissonance, and, in decoration, verges on the impression of the casual. (p. 149)

We should question whether play in art is indeed always bound by necessity. It is clear, however, that the open or atectonic form, as Wölfflin understands it, means freedom, openness, mutability. The turn from modern to postmodern architecture may be characterized as a turn from closed to open form. Ambiguity, complexity, and contradiction in architecture belong with open form. It would thus be easy to draw parallels between Baroque or Rococo architecture and postmodern architecture, as Venturi himself has done.[16]

4. Wölfflin's fourth pair, *multiplicity* and *unity,* does not quite name what he has in mind. He opposes an architecture of multiplicity, which constructs an architectural whole out of parts that retain their separate identities and an independent value not swallowed up in the larger whole, to another architecture, which strives to create wholes that are more integrated, organic, and difficult to grasp. "No longer do beautiful elements combine in a unity in which they continue to breathe independently, but the parts have submitted to a dominating total motive, and only the cooperation with the whole gives them sense and beauty" (p. 185). The cruciform church plan as used by Brunelleschi offers a good example of the former; its Rococo transformation by Balthasar Neumann illustrates the latter, yielding a mysterious space, haunted by absence.

5. Finally, Wölfflin opposes *clearness* to *unclearness* or *absolute* to *relative clearness.* Once again he develops his pair by contrasting classical with Baroque:

In the one case, form which is completely apparent; in the other, a creation which is, it is true, clear enough not to trouble the eye, but still not so clear that the spectator could ever reach the end. In this type late Gothic proceeded beyond high Gothic, the baroque beyond the classic Renaissance. It is not true that man can only take delight in the absolutely clear: he at once desires to get away from the clear to what can never be exhausted by visual perception. However manifold the post-renaissance transformations of style may be, they all have this remarkable quality, that the picture in some way eludes perfect comprehensibility. (p. 221)

The transformations Wölfflin has in mind all tend toward an architecture that refuses the ideal of readily comprehended form, insisting on absence rather than presence. Of course there have always been reactions to such developments: one is neo-classicism, which in turn provoked a romantic counterreaction, and there is a good deal of romanticism in nineteenth-century eclecticism. Modernism reasserted the classical ideal, postmodernism the Baroque reaction—although these are generalizations, in need of qualifications: how, for example, would Frank Lloyd Wright's open house plan fit into Wölfflin's categories?

It should have become apparent that it is almost impossible to isolate any one of these pairs from all the others. It is thus possible to combine them and to contrast an *atectonic, organic* approach with a *tectonic, inorganic* approach. Using the terms broadly, we can call one Baroque, the other "classical." The former invites metaphors that suggest absence, change, life, time; the latter invokes metaphors that suggest presence, stasis, death, eternity. In this sense we may want to call postmodernism modernism's Baroque. Wölfflin's principles show that architectural style communicates a particular relationship to time. That relationship in turn helps communicate a particular ethos (as I tried to show in some detail in my book on the Bavarian Rococo church) or, to use Heidegger's term, a particular mode of dwelling. But then we will have to supplement Heidegger's assertion that "the relationship between man and space is none other than dwelling, strictly thought and spoken,"[17] with another: "the relationship between man and time is none other than dwelling." Architecture helps shape that relationship, regardless of whether it sets itself up against time, defying it, or instead affirms the inevitability of time's passage.

4

These remarks should suffice to suggest that time is as intimately involved in our experience of architecture as space, that the two cannot finally be separated. Any view that understands architecture as the art of establishing place by the construction of boundaries in space is inevitably one-sided. While dwelling requires the establishment of place, place must also be understood temporally. In chapter 10, I discussed Heidegger's heterogeneous and regional understanding of lived space. An analogous point must be made with respect to time. The time of our experience is primarily not the homogeneous linear time so readily represented by an infinite straight line; our experiences sort themselves out into events and episodes that give a specific meaning to the associated times. Thus what in *Being and Time* is called "region" must have its temporal counterpart—the young Heidegger spoke of "situation."[18] "Region" and temporal "situation" belong together. An afternoon of gardening, a restless night, a week spent in the hospital, this past winter semester, a summer spent traveling, childhood, our life, the war years—all these name such temporal situations. This brief list suggests that just as regions do not exclude one another but instead overlap and permit the nesting of regions within more comprehensive regions, so our temporal situations overlap and possess varying scopes. What gathers experiences into situations are particular activities and their associated projects and motivations. Each situation has its specific tendency and duration. Although usually not attended to in this way, whatever situation we are caught up in colors the experiences that belong to it, gives them a specific, unified character and significance. Sooner or later, to be sure, the unity of the situation will disintegrate. Such disintegration will inevitably change the quality of our experiences and may open our eyes. Heidegger gives the example of climbing a mountain in order to witness the sunrise: "One has arrived at the top and each person experiences in silence. Entirely given to the experience, one sees a sun disc, the clouds, the masses of stone, having this definite form, but not as a definite mass that I have just climbed. The 'I' still persists. But a theoretical objectivity is no longer possible. The objects are no longer held together by the situation; they are isolated. But a new, different context is constituted by the meaning of our orientation toward objects."[19] As the situation collapses our vision is freed. We allow ourselves to become absorbed in the spectacle opening up before us. At the same time the "I" is displaced, loses its historical place, becomes homeless. Such sublime beholding is incompatible with dwelling.

Dwelling, as Heidegger understands it, requires the establishment not just of places but of temporal situations: just as the establishment of place must respond to a prior sense of place, must be founded in a more primordial dwelling, so the establishment of temporal situations must respond to a more fundamental temporal situatedness. In his description of a Black Forest farmhouse Heidegger therefore insists not only on the spatial but on the temporal dimensions of dwelling and building. Heidegger describes the farmhouse as situated not simply in a particular region but in a particular temporal situation—it is said to have been "built some two hundred years ago by the dwelling of peasants"—but more importantly in the rhythm of the seasons, of the passing generations, of birth and death. The farmhouse responds to this situation and its different strands by making "room in its chamber for the hallowed places of childbed and the 'tree of the dead'—for that is what they call a coffin there, the *Totenbaum*—and in this way it designed for the different generations under one roof the character of their journey through time."[20] Building is here understood as an establishment interpreting the temporal situation of human existence. I would like to underscore the emphasis placed by Heidegger on the way the farmhouse gives room to death. If building is to let us dwell in Heidegger's sense, that is, as the mortals we are, it must grant death its place. Dwelling in this view presupposes authentic being-unto-death, as Heidegger had analyzed it in *Being and Time*. But Heidegger also knows the difficulty human beings, and especially we moderns, have accepting death, which also means inevitably we have difficulty in dwelling. The whole classical tradition with its celebration of plenitude and presentness testifies to this difficulty. That Fried should have made the pursuit of presentness constitutive of what he took to be the only authentic art of our time could not have surprised Heidegger, although he would have added that, so understood, "authentic art" is a manifestation of inauthenticity.

There are places where Heidegger suggests that we moderns not only find it difficult but have become altogether unable to dwell, because we have become incapable of really dying. For this to make sense we have to distinguish what Heidegger calls "dying" from what we usually mean by the term. "Dying" cannot mean here simply the ending of life: "to die," according to Heidegger, "means to carry out death in its essence. To be able to die means to be capable of this carrying out."[21] World War II, especially the horror of the extermination camps, taught Heidegger that circumstances can make such an authentic dying impossible. But Heidegger refuses to understand the inhumanity of the camps as a uniquely monstrous aberration. As I pointed out in chapter 10, he would have us understand their inhumanity as bound up with the technological essence of modernity, which leaves no room for what Heidegger calls dying: therefore no room either for dwelling or for the kind of building exemplified by the Black Forest farmhouse. This invites a repetition of Ruskin's opposition of modernity and architecture in a Heideggerian key.

5

I have already questioned Heidegger's tendency to see the modern world as so completely ruled by technology that any attempt to recognize both its legitimacy and its limits is ruled out in principle, just as I have questioned his idealizing description of an eighteenth-century farmhouse. Those who find themselves moved by that description should remember that the aristocracy of the eighteenth century similarly idealized a past rural life. To the artificiality and corruption of the present it opposed the natural goodness of happy shepherds and shepherdesses. Both visions may be understood as reoccupations of the place once held by paradise. But attempts at such a reoccupation threaten to sacrifice the future to an idealized past and thus do violence to the requirements of dwelling.

The human condition precludes the attainment of states of plenitude and perfection. Nor need we mourn the Fall as the loss of something so important that, while it can never be recovered, its loss must be made bearable by turning to such metaphorical substitutes as the happy suburban life complete with colonial residence and large garden. Thus burdened, any such substitute is bound to prove disappointing. If Heideggerian dwelling demands plenitude, we must resist its idealization as incompatible not just with our modern world but with our humanity; then our inability to dwell would be no cause for lament. We must renounce the pursuit of presence and plenitude, renounce also whatever traditions participate in that pursuit. Only such renunciation allows for full self-affirmation.

But just such renunciation is made difficult by our mortality. In Genesis we read that Adam and Eve ate of the tree of knowledge but not of the tree of life: the human condition is shadowed by death. Not only are we humans vulnerable and mortal, but we know of our mortality, know that all that now is and all that still awaits us will some day be past. And so will everything that we can hope to leave behind: children, friends, works. The past will overtake every present. In related images Goya and Bosch have given unforgettable expression to such knowledge: Saturn devouring his children; the devil, hawk headed, seated on a throne that is also a potty chair, stuffing bodies into his beak, farting them into a dark circular void (figs. 90 and 91). Where is there a power strong enough to challenge the triumph of death? Schopenhauer never tired of repeating such sad wisdom: "Man consciously draws every hour nearer to his death; and at times this makes life a precarious business, even to the man who has not already recognized this character of constant annihilation in the whole of life itself. Mainly on this account, man has philosophies and religions."[22]

Heidegger's Black Forest peasants found in their faith the strength to die. Where are we today to find such strength without self-deception? And that is also to ask: how are we to dwell in Heidegger's sense? The more reflective the individual, the more heavily the terror of time is likely to lie on him or her. Our historical situation gives special weight to the call for some meaning that escapes destructive time. The more developed our sense of history, the more pronounced this terror is likely to be, now not just a terror of time but a terror of history. "In our day, when historical pressure no longer allows any escape, how can man tolerate the catastrophes and horrors of history—from collective deportations and massacres to atomic bombings—if beyond them he can glimpse no sign, no transhistorical meaning—if they are only the blind play of economic, social, or political forces, or worse, only the result of 'liberties' that a minority takes and exercises directly on the stage of universal history?"[23] Just as the modern, post-Copernican conception of space threatens a loss of place, so does the modern conception of history. Just as human beings need to locate themselves in space, so they need to locate themselves in time, find their place in time. If there is to be genuine dwelling we must be able to defeat the terror of time, to genuinely situate ourselves in time: that is, we must discover our home, not just in space but in time. Earlier I spoke of architecture as a defense against the terror of space and I suggested that such a defense is especially necessary in a culture in danger of losing its sense of place. I now want to add: we are in even greater need of architecture to defend ourselves against the terror of time.

Francisco de Goya y Lucientes, *Saturn Devouring His Children* (ca. 1819–1823). Museo del Prado, Madrid. Credit: Giraudon/Art Resource, N.Y.

90

Hieronymus Bosch, *Garden of Earthly Delights* (ca. 1510). Detail from right panel: Satan. Museo del Prado, Madrid. Credit: Giraudon/Art Resource, N.Y.

Building, Dwelling, and Time

The Terror of Time and the Love of Geometry

15

1

As long as humans are terrified by time, genuine dying and thus genuine dwelling, as Heidegger understands these, are precluded. But can architecture help us deal with this terror? A possible first answer is hinted at already by Vitruvius, when in his discussion of what elevates his primitive builders above the other animals he mentions first of all the upright posture, which allows them to lift up their eyes and to "gaze upon the splendor of the starry firmament."[1] The very word "firmament" promises a timeless order not subject to the ravages of time. To build in the image of that order is to endow our work with at least a semblance of eternity.

Architecture deals with the terror of time first of all by wresting from an unstable, uncertain environment a more stable order, transforming chaos into cosmos. Le Corbusier thus has his primitive builder insist on simple geometric forms, straight lines, right angles, regular polygons. What power do such forms possess? Take two lines: one a circle, clean and hard, drawn with a compass; the other an expressive squiggle, a swirling line resembling handwriting. The two lines stand in a very different relationship to time: the first comes as close as a visual statement can to the timeless realm of the spirit, while the other has an organic look and seems to embrace time. Or compare one of Kandinsky's *Improvisations* to a mature Mondrian. The applicability of Wölfflin's principles is apparent: if we can call the Kandinsky Baroque, the Mondrian is classical.

Classical architecture—"classical" in that broad sense discussed in the previous chapter—copes with the terror of time by spiritualizing the environment, by remaking what is sensible and changeable in the image of a higher, timeless reality. We can speak of a perennial Platonism that surfaces again and again in the course of the history of art and architecture. Beauty is here understood in opposition to time. In the *Symposium* Plato grounds that understanding in a particular understanding of human being. Beauty is there defined as the object of eros. Human beings, according to Plato, are fundamentally erotic beings because they exist in time, are born only to grow older and die, and yet belong to and desire being, eternity. Or, we can say, human beings are possessed by eros because they have fallen from their eternal true home into time and now dream of homecoming. Eros is nothing other than this desire for being, the desire to transcend becoming and thus to return home. On its lower levels eros tries to achieve this by making sure that something of the individual will survive him in time: children, for example, in whose memory we may continue to live, or fame, or works of art, especially works of architecture. The higher mysteries of eros lead beyond time, to the eternal forms.

Whenever we see something beautiful, according to Plato, we are reminded of the fact that we belong to being rather than to becoming, and we touch a realm that knows nothing of death. Time has no power over what is most essentially human, over the spirit. Given this Platonic aesthetics, the language of beauty is essentially a language of the spirit, and for Plato this means above all the language of geometry. Particularly revealing is this passage from the *Philebus*:

I do not mean by beauty of form such beauty as that of animals or pictures, which the many would suppose to be my meaning; but, says the argument, understand me to mean straight lines and circles, and the plane or solid figures, which are formed by turning lathes and rulers and measures of angles— for these I affirm to be not only relatively beautiful, like other things, but they are eternally or absolutely beautiful, and they have peculiar pleasures, quite unlike the pleasures of scratching. And there are colors, which are of the same character, and have similar pleasures; now do you understand my meaning?[2]

The passage deserves careful attention. First Plato draws our attention to a kind of beauty he considers deficient: (1) the beauty of animals and (2) the beauty of pictures, that is, of representations of what is perceived. This is a beauty too much involved with the world to promise deliverance from the terror of time. Such beauty is contrasted with the beauty of simple inorganic forms, beauty that is created not by the body but by the spirit. Indeed, in creating such forms the body will prove a hindrance: try to draw a straight line or a perfect circle. Soon you will look for aids, for ruler and compass, and the making of cylinders and spheres will call for more complicated machines—Plato speaks of turning lathes. We get here a hint why this perennial Platonism should so easily have allied itself with a machine aesthetic. The machine technology of the twentieth century has indeed allowed us to envision beauties Plato could not have dreamed of. But the main point remains the same: the Platonic idealization of the beauty of geometric forms leads easily to a machine aesthetic. The machine-made object, the machine-made look, is given the nod precisely because it bears the imprint of the human spirit. As Theo van Doesburg explains: "Every machine is a spiritualization of an organism. . . . The machine is, par excellence, a phenomenon of spiritual discipline. . . . The new artistic sensibility of the twentieth century has not only felt the beauty of the machine, but has also taken cognizance of its unlimited expressive possibilities for the arts."[3] Craft and the hand have no place in the art that is being envisioned.

The pursuit of the plenitude of being expresses itself not just in a choice of particular forms but also, as Plato points out, in a choice of particular colors. Primary colors have a timeless quality compared with broken greens and browns, which hint at the changing earth. Similarly, certain building materials, such as wood or brick, stand in a different relationship to time than vinyl siding or formica. There is a sense in which the machine-made environment, created by human beings, looks human as the natural environment does not. Someone will no doubt counter by insisting that such a machine-made environment is just the opposite, inhuman rather than human, precisely because by one-sidedly answering to the spirit, it excludes or reduces traces of the hand, the body. Both claims are easily defended; each presupposes a different conception of human existence. If, on the one hand, the machine-made environment is experienced as more human than the natural environment, then human being has been identified primarily with the "spirit." If, on the other hand, such an environment is dismissed as inhuman, then the human being has been understood more concretely as an embodied self, which cannot hope to find refuge from the terror of time in abstract realms of the spirit without losing itself.

2

Especially in the twentieth century this perennial Platonism has surfaced again and again. It indeed came close to evolving into the aesthetic of the modern movement. Le Corbusier and Ozenfant's programmatic essay "Purism" has a symptomatic significance: "Nothing is worthwhile which is not general, nothing is worthwhile which is not transmittable. We have attempted to establish an aesthetic that is rational and therefore human."[4] What is worthwhile in art here is equated with what is general and can be understood by everyone. This presupposes that there is a universal language of art, for which the language of geometry provides a ready model. What is human is equated with what is rational. But let me continue with the essay:

It is true that plastic art has to address itself more directly to the senses than pure mathematics which acts only by symbols, these symbols sufficing to trigger in the mind consequences of a superior order; in plastic art, the senses should be strongly moved in order to predispose the mind to the release into play of subjective reactions without which there is no art. But there is no art worth having without this excitement of an intellectual order—architecture is the art which up to now has most strongly induced the states of this category. The reason for this is that everything in architecture is expressed by order and economy.[5]

Not that technological considerations offer a solution to the problem of arbitrariness; they merely limit creativity in a way that joins "subjective reactions" to a higher, transpersonal and transtemporal realm. In this sense technology may be considered the salutary discipline of the artist, which prevents creativity from degenerating into capricious play. But creativity is indispensable.

Corbusier calls what is art in architecture a pure creation of the mind.[6] His choice of the adjective "pure" links up with a widespread striving for purity in modern art—we meet with talk of purity in music, poetry, and painting. Generally "purity" in the arts has been associated with form: Kant understands a pure or free beauty as one that pleases by virtue of its form alone. Such formal pleasures open the individual to a realm that transcends the rule of time. Essentially the same conviction governs Hans Hollein's demands for an absolute architecture.

Architecture is a spiritual order, realized through building.
Architecture—an idea built into infinite space, manifesting man's spiritual energy and power, the material form and expression of his destiny, of his life. From its origins until today the essence and

meaning of architecture have not changed. To build is a basic human need. It is first manifested not in the setting up of protective roofs, but in the creation of sacred structures, in the indication of focal points of human activity—the beginning of the city.

All building is religious.[7]

Religion here need mean no more than the commitment to the human spirit and to its ability to defeat the terror of time. Significantly, Hollein takes the space relevant to architecture to be not the regional space of lived experience but the infinite space of geometry. Into that space architecture casts its geometric figures.

For Hollein, too, the need that leads to architecture is not the need for physical shelter, but the need human beings feel to recognize their own spirit in the world in order to thus feel at home in it. Building is an act of spiritual self-assertion. "Architecture dominates space. Dominates it by shooting up into the heights; it hollows out the earth, projects and soars far above the ground, spreads in all directions. Dominates it through mass and through emptiness. Dominates space through space. This architecture is not a matter of beauty. If we desire beauty at all, it is not so much the beauty of form, of proportion, as a sensual beauty of elemental force."[8] The beauty of architecture—if indeed we are allowed to speak here of beauty at all—lies, according to Hollein, in the way it forcefully asserts itself against infinite space and time. Architecture is an act of self-assertion in the face of the terror of the infinite.

Architecture is purposeless.

What we build will find its utilization.

Form does not follow function. Form does not arise out of its own accord. It is the great decision of man to make a building as a cube, a pyramid, or a sphere.[9]

Precisely because architecture here strives to become a pure expression of the human spirit, ideally unconstrained by gravity or matter, it needs to enter into an alliance with technology. As Hollein understands absolute architecture, it needs to deny or defy the natural difference of up and down, of earth and sky. Consider once more his claim that "architecture dominates space. Dominates it by shooting up into the heights; it hollows out the earth, projects and soars far above the ground, spreads in all directions." Given this ideal of architectural purity we can understand the fascination that the sphere exerted on an architect like Ledoux (see fig. 6). What fascinated him above all must have been the force of this simple geometric form. In the same spirit Boullée refused to follow Vitruvius in defining architecture as the art of building, claiming instead "that the first principles of architecture are to be discerned in symmetrical solids, such as cubes, pyramids, and, most of all spheres, which are, in his view, the only perfect architectural shapes which can be devised"[10] (see figs. 111, 112).

Why single out the sphere? Why does just this form become the emblem of a new architecture? Ledoux's projected spherical house is decisive not simply in its simple geometry but in the resolute way in which it defies gravity. The vision of the architect is allowed to outstrip the capabilities of the builder. But this did not prevent the paradigm from becoming influential: born of modernist self-assertion, the ideal of a gravity-defying architecture was to inspire much modernist architecture. The following three characteristics help circumscribe the new ideal:

1. The difference between up and down is minimized.
2. The building looks as if it could be stood on its head.
3. The building does not appear tied to a particular landscape or history. It is mobile in its very essence, regardless of whether mobile in fact.

How pervasive such ideas were to become in modern architecture is suggested by Van Doesburg's "Towards a Plastic Architecture," which demands of architecture "a floating aspect (in so far as this is possible from a constructional standpoint—this is the problem for the engineer!) which operates, as it were, in opposition to natural gravity."[11] What is demanded here is an unnatural, spiritual look. Consider one of Malevich's *Suprematist Compositions* (fig. 92), which float geometric shapes on a white background that figures the infinite void. Such ideas found their architectural realization in structures like Rietveld's villa in Utrecht (fig. 93). At first blush such designs may seem to have little to do with the spheres of Ledoux or Boullée. The sphere is a simple geometric solid, and Theo van Doesburg will have nothing to do with such solidity: "The new architecture is *anti-cubic;* that is to say, it does not attempt to fit all the functional space cells together in a closed cube, but projects

Kasimir Malevich, *Suprematist Composition*

(1915). Stedelijk Museum, Amsterdam. Credit:

92 | Foto Marburg/Art Resource, N.Y.

functional space cells (as well as overhanging surfaces, balconies, etc.) centrifugally from the center of the cube outwards. Thus height, breadth, and depth plus time gain an entirely new plastic expression."[12] Van Doesburg does not want firmly enclosing walls. Inside and outside are to interpenetrate, as in the open flowing interiors that had been first pioneered by Frank Lloyd Wright. And yet, in spite of such difference, I would like to maintain that the architecture that emerges from these principles shares the elements that I outlined above: it, too, emphasizes simple geometric forms, defies gravity, invites an inversion of up and down. That such a spiritual architecture should want to liberate itself from the need for enclosure is to be expected. The general approach is readily illustrated in the work of Mies van der Rohe. Take the Farnsworth House: the way the living space seems suspended between two floating planes is striking. Visually the house possesses a mobility not altogether unlike that of a trailer. It has no basement—is not rooted in the ground; nor does it sit comfortably on the ground as Frank Lloyd Wright demanded. Rather it looks as if some giant had placed it there, seeming just to wait for someone to lift it up and cart it off into some museum devoted to the masterpieces of modern architecture: "more nearly a temple than a dwelling."[13]

Such separation of building and ground is indeed a key characteristic of modern architecture. In his "Five Points towards a New Architecture," Le Corbusier insists on just such a separation:

Gerrit Rietveld, Schroeder House, Utrecht. East façade. Credit: Foto Marburg/Art Resource, 93 | N.Y.

The earlier foundations, on which the building rested without a mathematical check, are replaced by individual foundations and the walls by individual supports. Both supports and support foundations are precisely calculated according to the burdens they are called upon to carry. These supports are spaced out at specific, equal intervals, with no thought for the interior arrangement of the building. They rise directly from the floor to 3, 4, 6, etc. meters and elevate the ground floor. The rooms are thereby removed from the dampness of the soil; they have light and air; the building plot is left to the garden, which consequently passes under the house. The same area is also gained on the flat roof.[14]

Take the Villa Savoie (1928–1930), or the design for the League of Nations Palace (1927); the separation reappears in the Unité d'Habitation in Marseilles (1947–1952; fig. 94). Despite attempts to defend the separation of the building from the ground in terms of functional considerations, for instance by appealing to the way it allows the garden to pass right beneath the building—imagine trying to raise tomatoes in such a place!—the design would seem to convey above all an expression of the spirit's power to defy gravity and the earth. The engineer allows the modern architect to triumph over the earthbound character of traditional architecture, a character underscored by Bachelard's dream house. In the floating look of so much modern architecture a modern, post-Copernican ideal of dwelling finds striking expression. Closely related to this is the rejection of the gabled roof. Although Le Corbusier insisted on what separates the artist in the architect from the engineer, there is supposed to be no tension between artistic vision and the new technology—quite the opposite. Both are expressions of the same spirituality, of the same will to power: a will to power that in Hegelian fashion looks to the constructive spirit for answers to the terror of both space and time. The spirit is thought to provide a timelessly valid vocabulary on which the artist can draw to generate an art that will have not only a personal, or regional, but a truly universal and timeless significance. So understood, perennial Platonism demands a downgrading of the individual, and it is not surprising that it should have hailed the machine as a force that will break down national and class boundaries and destroy the cult of the

Le Corbusier, Unité d'Habitation, Marseilles.

94 Credit: Giraudon/Art Resource, N.Y.

individual. The alliance between Platonism and Marxism is characteristic of the architectural thinking of the twenties. Does such an aesthetic do justice to human reality? Does it offer more than alienating metaphors of an impossible perfection? Must not this turn against time, and therefore inevitably also against the body—note the problem of scale one encounters so often with this architecture—do violence to the whole human being?

3

I called attention to how readily perennial Platonism allies itself with technology, an alliance that to an architect like Le Corbusier seemed a prerequisite of a truly modern architecture. Technology appears indeed as such a Platonism's necessary supplement, for as the cited *Philebus* passage hints, spiritual form by itself lacks the reality to offer an embodied self more than a dream of security. Perennial Platonism therefore wants to carry its spirit into the world, transform the world in its own image, assert itself as master of the world. Technology promises to transform a nature that initially presents itself as a hostile and alien other into a genuinely humane environment. Governed as it is by reason, it also promises an escape from the problem of arbitrariness. The beauty of bridges and silos that so impressed modernists appears to confirm this promise. But how adequate is such confirmation? Does technology lead to a nonarbitrary architecture?

One could approach that question by examining the work of Jean-Nicolas-Louis Durand, whose publications, reprinted again and again, were characteristic of the generation of architects that followed Boullée and Ledoux—Durand had been a draftsman for the former.[15] According to Durand, architecture has nothing to do with the proportions of the human body, nor with the forms of the primitive hut. The same might have been said by a formalist like Ledoux, but Durand is no formalist either. He is closer to Lodoli when he insists that what matters are first of all "convenience" and "economy."[16] Economy, according to Vitruvius, is "the proper management of materials and of site, as well as a thrifty balancing of cost and common sense in the construction of works."[17] Economy also demands careful consideration of the purpose a building is to serve. In these terms the preference for straight lines is easily defended because it is the shortest line between two points. A concern for economy is thus likely to lead to geometric forms, even if geometry is not allowed to become autonomous. Architecture is said to please when it is practical and economical. But Durand knows that the appeal to economy still leaves options requiring decisions that must be based on more than functional considerations. It is in this reduced role that the old formalism retains some of its significance.

Durand's position has a certain similarity with that outlined by Le Corbusier in *Towards a New Architecture*. Corbusier begins by drawing a distinction between the engineer's aesthetic and architecture. The two should march together, but Corbusier finds them unhappily apart: while the engineer's aesthetic is at its peak, architecture is caught up in an unfortunate state of retrogression. Like Loos, Corbusier takes the engineer, inspired by the law of economy and governed by mathematical calculations, to be working in accord with universal law.

There is a difficulty with this view, as Le Corbusier himself recognizes. When it is a matter of designing an airplane the task is reasonably clear. It should be clear when designing a car as well, but cars of course also serve the self-representation of the owner, which complicates matters enormously. The matter of defining the task becomes much more complicated when the problem is to build a house. Thus while Le Corbusier calls the house "a machine for living in," he also points out that the problem of the house has not yet been stated, and as long as it has not been stated, the engineering approach will necessarily lack direction.[18] It works best when functions are easily defined. Once more silos and bridges furnish obvious examples. Factories and office buildings already pose a more complicated task; with the house the task itself becomes an issue.

Le Corbusier recognizes this. As emphatically as Ruskin, he denies that architecture can ever be reduced to the level of the machine. Architecture, he insists, goes beyond "utilitarian needs."[19] Functional considerations only provide certain constraints. It is with these that the architect must begin, but the genuine architect will not stop there: "Contour and profile are the touchstone of the architect. Here he reveals himself as artist or as mere engineer. Contour is free of all constraint. There is no longer any question of custom, nor of tradition, nor of construction, nor of adaptation to utilitarian need. Contour and profile are a pure creation of the mind; they call for the plastic artist"[20] (fig. 95). Le Corbusier's distinction between the engineer and the architect is characteristic of the tension between form and function that is a necessary result of a thinking that insists on the purity of art. A more rigorous functionalist, such as Hannes Meyer, Gropius's successor at the Bauhaus, would see in Le Corbusier's insistence that the architect take account of but go beyond the engineer an unfortunate throwback to the nineteenth century and its insistence on dressing up functional sheds in a historicizing skin.

95 | Le Corbusier, Chapelle de Notre-Dame du Haut, Ronchamp. Credit: Art Resource, N.Y.

I have called the connection between technology and perennial Platonism a natural alliance, natural because both are born of the same ill will against time. To support this claim, let me begin by positing—with Nietzsche, from whom I took the expression "ill will against time"[21]—a will to power in human beings, coupled with a recognition that we never have enough power to secure our existence, that we are subject to time, vulnerable and mortal. It is this will to security that finds expression in a Platonism that opposes to temporal reality a realm of timeless forms, opposes being to becoming. Christianity finds such security in God, who is believed to have delivered human beings from the tyranny of time and to have robbed death of its sting. But the death of God has to raise once more the problem of insecurity. How are we moderns, at least those of us who do not find in God deliverance from the tyranny of time, to find such deliverance? If we cannot expect security from some power beyond us, must we not assume responsibility for our security ourselves and transform the world in our own image? In the end all such attempts at self-assertion must fall short of their goal. Hobbes offers a good description of what is at least the situation of modern humanity: "I put for a general inclination of all mankind, a perpetual and restless desire for power after power, that ceaseth only in death. And the cause of this, is not always that a man hopes for a more intensive delight, than he has already attained to—or that he cannot be content with moderate power, but because he cannot assure the power and means to live well, which he hath at present, without the acquisition of more."[22]

We never have enough power, never enough security. This leads to endless organizing, calculating, manipulating. Technology and organization try to fill a void that cannot be filled. As Heidegger puts this point: "Everywhere, where there is too little of what is—and increasingly there is too little of everything—technology must leap into the breach and create *Ersatz* and use up raw materials. But in truth *Ersatz* is not a passing stopgap."[23] For a humanity unable to accept its fundamental insecurity, out of touch with the earth and with itself, everything must become *Ersatz*. Instead of entrusting themselves to what is, human beings encounter what is only as material for their plans and calculations. This progressive organization of everything comes to no end. On this point Heidegger finds himself in considerable agreement with the authors of the ABC manifesto, although while Heidegger speaks in resigned tones, they would have us embrace the machine and all it entails: no longer is the machine an instrument we can use for this or that end. Today the machine has become a dictator who, whether we like it or not, determines ever more the possibilities open to us, the way we live and the way we build. "*The machine* is neither the coming paradise in which technology will fulfil all our wishes—nor the approaching hell in which all human development is destroyed—*The machine* is nothing more than the inexorable dictator of the possibilities and tasks common to all our lives."[24]

The manifesto goes on to suggest that we find ourselves in a transitional age. Our still-ambivalent attitude to the machine, our simultaneous "yes" and "no"—a "yes" and a "no" that find expression in our decorated functional sheds, which take advantage of all that technology has to offer yet resent the way it tends to mechanize our life—may be understood as representative of that transitional status. We live in a technological society and want to enjoy its benefits, yet at the same time we want to keep our distance from it.

Especially in the houses we build we like to invoke the aura of some preindustrial age. Or think of the widespread fondness for handcrafted things: we participate in the technological age, yet by living in a half-timbered house or just by buying a hand-woven rug we pretend to ourselves that we can keep our distance from it. This is precisely what the manifesto denies. The machine, it insists, is not our servant but a dictator:

It dictates how we are to think and what we have to understand. As leader of the masses, who are inescapably bound up with it, it demands more insistently every year the transformation of our economy, our culture. It permits no pause for breath in the armchair of philosophy, no compromise with pacifist phrases. It grants no prospect of an agreed peace, no aesthetic distance from the demands of life. Reality shows us how far we have already gone today in obeying the dictates of the machine: we have sacrificed our handicrafts to it. We are in the process of sacrificing our peasantry to it. We have had to allow it to provide our most important means of travel and the basis of our great industries. Under its pressure we have evolved the new method of mass production. Because of it we have had to place greater and greater organizational power in the hands of the State and even to internationalize our most sacred national goals.[25]

The intervening years have not robbed the manifesto of its relevance. The machine is indeed a force that compels homogeneity, uniformity. And if the authors of the manifesto are right, there can be no effective opposition to this dictatorship. As Ruskin would have agreed, this would have to mean also an end to architecture in its traditional sense. To the extent that our culture has indeed fallen under the dictatorship of the machine, architecture lies behind us.

But if there is no effective opposition to the dictatorship of the machine, why does the manifesto call for this dictatorship? With this call the authors betray their partisanship, showing that they do not so much describe an inexorable process as take sides and welcome it. Their pleading suggests that the dictatorship of the machine remains either a longed-for or a feared ideal, that the world we live in, although shaped by technology, still knows other dimensions. Consider in this connection the widespread reassertion of intolerant regionalisms in our world—to the technological rationalist, and not only to him or her, a deeply disturbing phenomenon.

Heidegger sees much of what the authors of the manifesto see. He too insists that technology—although he prefers to speak of its essence, the *Ge-Stell*—increasingly determines the shape of our life, circumscribing our possibilities. Inevitably this process envelops human beings themselves, who increasingly are considered no more than material to be organized and subjected to planning and calculation. Growing uniformity and homogeneity go along with this. The one-dimensionality inseparable from the dictatorship of technology will reflect itself in our urban environment. More and more, the world's larger cities look alike. Heidegger would not have us understand this dictatorship as a fate that must be accepted, but as a force that threatens to rob human beings of their essence. In the face of that threatening dictatorship he reasserts the essence of dwelling. But his response to technology remains profoundly ambiguous: on one hand, he insists that living as we do in a modern world we cannot and should not do much about the hegemony of technology and the developments that go along with it; on the other, he wants us to keep our distance from it. I have already invoked his simultaneous "yes" and "no" to technology: the "no" born of the recognition that technology, were it to gain total dominion, would have to destroy the essence of humanity, the "yes" of the conviction that we belong to this modern world and that we would not want it any other way. It would be irresponsible to renounce the benefits technology has given us, the ways it has helped us lift at least some of the burdens of life. Think of the ways it has transformed medicine, agriculture, transportation. Heidegger's "yes" and "no" betray a split attitude to technology, a kind of aesthetic leave-taking from the world in a manner similar to that of so many who hope to escape from the problems of modern life—if not to a hut in the Black Forest, perhaps to some remote corner of New England. In the end all such half-hearted responses seem unsatisfactory.

And yet, if we admit with Heidegger that the dictatorship of the machine does not admit genuine dwelling, and if we further refuse to surrender our claim to such a dwelling, we have no choice but to put technology in its place: to affirm it, even to welcome it, but only as a servant. Architecture on this view must accept technology, even as it cannot grant it autonomy. In this sense Ruskin appears right when he insists that we need architecture for our mental health. Ruskin of course linked architecture to ornament, which he understood in fundamentally aesthetic terms as mere decoration. I have argued that ornament be understood instead as possessing a re-presentational function. Re-presenting natural symbols, it should recall us to a more genuine dwelling. This returns us to the question: what constitutes genuine dwelling? What I have said so far has provided no more than a few pointers.

Mold and Ruins

16

1

No one has inveighed more passionately against what I have called perennial Platonism than the Viennese painter Hundertwasser. In his "Mould Manifesto against Rationalism in Architecture," read in 1958 at the abbey of Seckau, Hundertwasser speaks as an artist claiming for architecture, too, the freedom that painting—whose great turning point is said to have been "tachist automatism," a remark that indicates his aesthetic preferences—had come to take for granted. But the plea for artistic freedom in architecture quickly becomes an ethical plea for buildings that should answer much more immediately to the desires and whims of people than what actually gets built: "No inhibitions should be placed upon the individual desire to build! Everyone ought to be able and compelled to build, so that he bears real responsibility for the four walls within which he lives. We must face the risk that a crazy structure of this kind may later collapse, we should not and must not shrink from the loss of life which this new way of building will, or at least may exact."[1] We may question such a call to force people to build for themselves, unhampered by codes, not just as hopelessly utopian—after all, isn't it precisely the exaggerated, utopian tone of manifestoes that has often introduced a salutary note into the ongoing discussion concerning the future shape of architecture?—nor because the word "compel" smacks too much of an authoritarianism that, inspired by what it takes to be its higher wisdom, feels justified in forcing people to become free, but because of the assumption that freedom can and indeed must be divorced from the reason that finds expression in perennial Platonism. It is the underlying understanding of how we should dwell, with its implication that to really live we must be willing to risk life, that needs to be confronted.

Hundertwasser is convinced that modernist architecture with its right angles and straight lines is "morally unendurable." He prefers "the material uninhabitability of the slums" to "the moral uninhabitability of functional, utilitarian architecture. In the so-called slums only man's body can perish, but in the architecture ostensibly planned for man his soul perishes. Hence the principle of the slums, i.e., wildly proliferating architecture, must be improved and taken as our point of departure, not functional architecture" (p. 157). The Hundertwasser-Haus in Vienna, by now one of that city's tourist attractions, points to where such a change in direction might take us.

Hundertwasser deplores the way we tend to live in buildings that for the most part we have found pretty much ready-made, simply moving into them. "The occupant has no relationship to the building. Because he hasn't built it but has merely moved in. His human needs, his human space are certain to be quite different. And this remains a fact even if the architect and bricklayer try to build exactly according to the instructions of the occupant and employer" (p. 158). Only where architect, builder, and occupant become one and the same person would Hundertwasser have us speak of architecture, which thus names an ideal that has found its most convincing realizations in primitive societies and, in the modern world, in slums.

More significant, given my concerns in this section, is the war waged against straight lines. If Loos called ornament a crime, fifty years later his fellow Viennese calls the use of the ruler, this "symbol of the new illiteracy," criminal. The "jungle of straight lines, which increasingly hems us in like prisoners in a goal, must be uprooted. . . . The straight line is not a creative, but a reproductive line. In it dwells not so much God and the human spirit as rather the comfort-loving, brainless mass ant" (p. 159). Given such remarks it is to be expected that Hundertwasser should celebrate mold and rust. To claim that the human spirit does not dwell in straight lines is surely hyperbole, refuted by the history of building. But this hyperbole does force us to ask: does what I have called perennial Platonism do justice to human beings and allow for a genuine dwelling? This is of course a question that can have no single correct answer, for at issue is precisely where humanity should go and that issue remains open. That makes it a question with which each one of us has to wrestle. Certainly, the beauty of geometric forms is not the only kind of beauty, as Plato recognizes when he opposes to the higher beauty of straight lines and circles the beauty of animals and representations, or Wölfflin when he opposes an atectonic to a tectonic approach. A distinction between two kinds of beauty, standing in different relationships to time, is indeed easy to draw, regardless of which one prefers; besides the beauty of timeless forms there is beauty inseparably linked to time. Think of shifting cloud patterns, or of the wake of a boat, or of a soap bubble that grows ever more beautiful as it comes closer to bursting: as we attempt to hold on to some particular form floating on its surface, it dissolves, gives way to another. How different is the beauty of these elusive colors and patterns from the beauty of a cut diamond. Their very elusiveness is part of our appreciation of their beauty. The beauty of rust and mold celebrated by Hundertwasser is of the same kind. Something in us human beings is fascinated by impermanence, demands change, and finds Platonic order stifling and bloodless; we prefer the organic over the inorganic, for though the former lacks the permanence of geometric forms, it lives.

We must grant that from the very beginning architecture, as opposed to that ephemeral building Hundertwasser would have us consider genuine architecture, has embraced geometric forms. Given that tradition, the "architecture" Hundertwasser calls for is indeed an antiarchitecture. That this is so becomes disturbingly clear when in a pamphlet of 1957 Hundertwasser claims that "the air raids of 1943 were a perfect automatic lesson in form; straight lines and their vacuous structures ought to have been blown to pieces, and so they were" (p. 157). Ruins on his view are spiritually more inhabitable than so-called functional architecture. "When rust settles on a razor blade, when mould forms on a wall, when moss grows in the corner of the room and rounds off the geometric angle, we ought to be pleased that with the microbes and fungi life is moving into the house, and more consciously than ever before we become witnesses of architectonic changes from which we have a great

deal to learn" (pp. 159–160). In keeping with his understanding of the spiritual uninhabitability of modern architecture, Hundertwasser's manifesto calls for what amounts to an architecture of ruins: "we must strive as rapidly as possible for total uninhabitability and
creative mouldering in architecture" (p. 158).[2]

2

The built ruin is the most obvious example of architecture built against architecture. Here
we have the counterimage to structures that seek to defeat the terror of time with images
of permanence. To use a term that has become fashionable, we can say that in the artificial
ruin architecture deconstructs itself; and something of the appeal of ruins has indeed resur-
faced, transformed, in contemporary architecture's deconstructive impulse. The artificial
ruin betrays a crisis in the confidence that architecture is able, or should even attempt, to
provide for anything like Heideggerian dwelling. This suspicion of architecture figures a
deeper distrust of the Cartesian dream that reason will render us the masters and possessors
of nature.

Franz Kafka's never-completed story "Der Bau" ("The Building") challenges that
dream in a way that lets us understand the antiarchitectonic passion of a Hundertwasser.[3]
The protagonist of Kafka's story is an animal—we are not told what kind. "The Den" or
"The Burrow" might therefore be a better translation. What strikes the reader first is a
pervasive mood, a sense of helplessness and hopelessness, bound up with this animal's desire
for total security that drives its tireless building. Feared, suspected, but unseen enemies lead
it to think of ever more elaborate defenses. But whatever defenses this animal constructs,
the security they promise is outstripped by thoughts of other, still-unmastered threats. Dedi-
cated to the pursuit of security, its life is shadowed by what will not be mastered. Unable to
possess the world, the animal attempts to withdraw into the artificial environment it has
constructed. But a threatening outside and a death-shadowed future will not be eliminated.
How much there is that it cannot grasp and control! All this weighs on the animal, as every
noise comes to be experienced as a threat and absolute quiet is sought as an assurance of
security. But certain noises will not be eliminated, especially a barely audible, curious hissing
that seems to indicate the hidden proximity of some death-dealing enemy.

Who is this creature? Obviously not an ordinary animal. This is an anxious animal,
an animal that, fleeing its anxiety, calculates and builds; it is an animal that reasons. *Animal
rationale* is one of the traditional definitions of the human being. But the animal of Kafka's
story is a figure not just of the human animal but of the human animal demanding absolute
security: if he were only able to become truly "the master and possessor of nature." The
animal recognizes, with Descartes, that such mastery requires all-embracing technological
control. Presupposed here is a will to power that cannot forgive itself its lack of power or
its own embodied, temporal being and, precisely because of this, experiences so keenly the
terror of time, has such difficulty facing up to the reality of death, is unable to die in Heidegger's sense. The animal of Kafka's story is the human being whose inability to accept his
own temporality shuts out reality, imprisons him in his own creation. Frantic building and
planning cannot grant the so desperately sought sense of security; the turn to technology

increases rather than diminishes the terror of time. Genuine dwelling demands the shattering of such prisons, demands the destruction of an architecture that is their figure; it welcomes ruins.

Such distrust of architecture finds expression in the way the development of ruin architecture intertwines with that of the landscape garden. The two belong together; both express a desire to rediscover in organic nature lost divinity and humanity's true home. Artificial ruins speak of a desire to return to nature, to become part of it, not to master it. Perennial Platonism's demand for permanence here is deliberately given up. I don't know when the first artificial ruin was built in Europe, but by the middle of the eighteenth century, just when the Cartesian dream of a world-building based on reason promised to become reality, the artificial ruin had become an established architectural type in France, England, and Germany; this fact hints at what we can call modernity's bad conscience.

The building of artificial ruins was preceded by a general fascination with ruins that can be traced especially in paintings. Take Jacob van Ruisdael's *Jewish Cemetery,* a painting Goethe praised in his "Ruisdael as Poet" (fig. 96). As Goethe points out, time here appears to triumph over all human labor can establish. In their ruined condition, the grave

Jacob van Ruisdael, *Jewish Cemetery* (ca. 1660). Gemäldegalerie, Staatliche Kunstsammlungen, 96 | Dresden. Credit: Alinari/Art Resource, N.Y.

monuments point to something "more than past": they have become monuments of monuments, monuments raised to the second power. Precariously the ruin in the background—the painting joins a Jewish cemetery near Amsterdam to a Christian monastery ruin and a brook—asserts the vertical, but it, too, seems near collapse; a freestanding wall appears especially ready to fall. In the back we see mourners, busying themselves with less splendid monuments—"as if the past," Goethe writes, "could leave us nothing but mortality."[4] Goethe concludes his discussion by turning to the brook, which, no longer kept by human labor, is now seeking its own way through what was once presumably a tidy cemetery, through the graves, into a desolate wilderness; and he turns to the light, breaking through the clouds and illuminating a dead tree, symbol of the infinite life of nature, which joins life and death, indifferent to human self-assertion. The transcendent power of nature is revealed by the vanity of human attempts to establish their own lasting order and thereby to rescue themselves from the terror of time. Even memory cannot conquer time: the once-splendid graves now lie neglected, those buried in them forgotten.

Such fascination with ruins presupposes the Biblical suspicion of architecture, linked to the conviction that our true home is not to be found in this fallen, death-burdened world. In keeping with this conviction painters liked to place the Nativity in a ruin, a structure declaring the insufficiency of human building and thus the need for the Redeemer. Is not the dream of the builder as a second god, able to deliver us from the terror of time, a dream born of pride, a false dream that covers up the condition of fallen humanity and blocks out visions of our true home? From the very beginning the Bible places building in an ambiguous light. Cain, condemned to be "a fugitive and a wanderer on the earth" (Gen. 4.14, RSV), is said to have built the first city. To be sure, the Heavenly Jerusalem, too, is a city, although its architect is of course God and it is not of the fallen world in which we have to make our way.

The decision to build a ruin or to give buildings a ruinous look betrays a crisis of confidence in the architect's ability to provide shelter. To be sure, we are more likely to think of ruins as picturesque and rightly so: the artificial ruins of the English landscape park were indeed intimately linked to the emergence of the picturesque as an aesthetic category. But there is a profound connection: Hans Sedlmayr is right to suggest that "the picturesque appears as the mortal enemy of the architectonic." The appeal of picturesque ruins hints at something in us that desires the death of architecture.[5] Sedlmayr calls attention to the remarkable decision by painters like Hubert Robert and Caspar David Friedrich to paint not just ruins but buildings that were still intact, such as the Louvre or churches in Meissen and Greifswald, as ruins.[6] Hitler is said to have had artists draw the architecture of his Thousand Year Empire in a ruined state, presumably unaware that history would so quickly catch up with his dreams.

Earlier I discussed architecture as an art of representation. That the artificial ruin is very much architecture that represents architecture hardly needs comment; what is represented is usually an architecture associated with a particularly strong period in history, say a Greek temple or a medieval church. The effect of the ruin is heightened by the viewer's reflections on how even the best that the past was able to build had to succumb to time: in countless English parks we find such structures, which look as if they had collapsed under the onslaught of nature and time. But the chosen paradigm is deliberately devalued and reduced to no more than a picturesque motif, its authority undermined by the passage of time. And yet, instead of despairing over the impotence of human beings revealed here, we rejoice in it, for we sense that architecture is unable to satisfy our deepest desires.

3

Sedlmayr's claim that "the picturesque appears as the mortal enemy of the architectonic" invites interpretation in light of the different relationship in which architecture and painting stand to time. It was hardly an accident that painting much more than architecture should have furnished aestheticians with ready examples of aesthetic objects: in aesthetic contemplation linear time and its before and after are supposed to lose their power over us. This, at any rate, is the implication of Kant's determination of the beautiful as the object of an entirely disinterested satisfaction. Interest is necessarily directed toward the future and, as such shadowed by the terror of time. Only the disinterested person will experience what presents itself to him or her as a plenitude. As Kant points out, part of such an experience is indifference to the existence—the reality—of a particular object. An aura of unreality is inseparable from beauty so understood. Schopenhauer suggests that to aesthetic perception it does not matter whether it is this tree that is seen or some precursor, which bloomed a thousand years ago. In the moment of aesthetic appreciation linear time is abolished as past and present appear to fuse.

Michael Fried aligns himself and modernity with what is essentially the same view when he suggests that the authentic art of our times strives for presentness, understood as requiring that that the artist create objects strong enough to defeat their own objecthood through the strength of their shape. Once again what is sought is redemption from the terror of time. In Fried's words: "Presentness is grace."[7] We owe such grace to art. While Fried's discussion focuses on what he terms "modernist" painting and sculpture, he insists that it be extended to all the other arts. But what would it mean for architecture to defeat or suspend "its own objecthood though the medium of shape"?[8] Would not a modernist architecture so understood have to be an architecture that through the strength of its pictorial or sculptural form suspends itself as a structure to be entered and explored, an architecture that for the sake of presentness renders itself uninhabitable and in this respect comes to resemble a ruin—in other words, an antiarchitectural architecture? To the extent that we understand aesthetic experience not as a recollection of timeless reality but as an experience that is as if it had no duration, beauty will have to be at odds with the requirements of dwelling. On this modernist view, the beautiful lifts us out of the life world, out of reality, carries us to a paradise that, like every paradise, has no room for a house. Human beings now turn to beauty not to illuminate temporal reality, so that they might feel more at home in it, but to be relieved of it, to abolish time within time, if only for a time.

That such a modernist conception of beauty must lead to dreams of an uninhabitable architecture is readily apparent. With Schopenhauer a look of uninhabitability thus becomes a mark of the beauty of a building: "But above all else, the beautiful in architecture is enhanced by the favor of light, and through it even the most insignificant thing becomes a beautiful object. Now if in the depth of winter, when the whole of nature is frozen and stiff, we see the rays of the setting sun, reflected by masses of stone, when they illuminate without warming and are thus favorable only to the purest kind of knowledge, not to the will, the contemplation of the beautiful effect of light on these masses moves us into a state of pure knowing, as all beauty does."[9] Giorgio de Chirico was to make of such descriptions a recipe—a recipe, however, not for building but for painting. Beauty as it is understood here invites the transformation of architecture into painting or sculpture, demands its de-realization, demands the picturesque.

Just as de Chirico repainted what is fundamentally the same picture over and over, so he liked to retell what is essentially the same experience:

I remember one vivid winter's day at Versailles. Silence and calm reigned supreme. Everything gazed at me with mysterious, questioning eyes. And then I realized that every corner of the palace, every column, every window possessed a spirit, an impenetrable soul. I looked at the marble heroes, motionless in the lucid air, beneath the frozen rays of the winter sun which pours down on us without love, like perfect song. A bird was warbling in a window cage. At that moment I grew aware of the mystery which urges man to create certain strange forms. And the creation seemed more extraordinary than the creators.[10]

I am interested here not in de Chirico but in what by now has become a quite common kind of revelation. Its occasion may be three American flags strangely visible and forlorn in the evening sky over the New Haven Green, or the back of Sterling Memorial Library transfigured by a late sun into a mysterious presence. Especially significant in the cited texts is the celebration of isolation and, associated with it, the dissociation of light and love, of light and life. The rays of the winter sun are frozen, as is the land they illuminate. Schopenhauer adds the claim that architecture, illuminated by loveless light, moves us as all beauty does. If we accept this, we have more here than just examples of a particular and strange kind of aesthetic experience. Rather we are led to the very heart of the aesthetic approach as I discussed it in chapter 2. More clearly than any other thinker, Schopenhauer lets us recognize behind that approach a deep morbidity, a *taedium vitae* born of an inability—or is it an unwillingness?—to love, which welcomes the cool clarity of a loveless light.[11] Or is Schopenhauer interpreting the essence of beauty in terms of his own personal or perhaps cultural perspective, a perspective governed by the terror of time? Only this terror makes it necessary to think beauty in opposition to time.

Michael Fried would no doubt object to this association of what he terms modernist art with de Chirico, whom, as we saw in chapter 14, he mentions among those artists whose preoccupations with time lets them become theatrical and whom he thus places in opposition to modernist sensibility. I wonder, however, whether an artist or critic who seeks grace in presentness is not also preoccupied with time. In this connection it is interesting to compare Fried's use of presentness with that of the sculptor Robert Morris, whom Fried criticizes for his theatrical literalism. Unlike Fried, Morris emphasizes the temporality of the aesthetic experience and of the art work. "What I want to bring together for my model of 'presentness' is the intimate inseparability of the experience of physical space and that of an ongoing immediate present. Real space is not experienced except in real time. The body is in motion, the eyes make endless movements at various focal distances, fixing on innumerable static or moving images. Location and point of view are constantly shifting at the apex of time's flow."[12] Like Fried, Morris wants to suspend or defeat the objecthood of the object, but this move beyond the object would appear to lead him in a very different direction. While Fried would let the strength of an object's shape defeat its objecthood, Morris wants to return the object to space and time: "Any time the object becomes specific, dense, articulated, and self-contained, it has already succeeded in removing itself from space. It has only various visual aspects: from this side or that, close up or farther away."[13]

Since real space, as Morris points out, is not experienced except in real time, this also means that the more a work-of-art-become-object has removed itself from real space, the better it succeeds in defeating the terror of time. One could point out that as long as an object is experienced in a particular situation, as one object among others, including the observer, this defeat must remain incomplete. If this is right, Fried's celebration of presentness may be understood as a call for a more rigorous attack on the terror of time, in which one must be willing to pay the price of reality to gain victory. When Morris speaks of presentness, in contrast, he envisions an art that challenges the denseness of objects in order to open us up the mystery of space and time. The connection between this mystery and the enigmas that fascinated de Chirico is apparent and Fried is right to link the two. I would like to suggest the following analogy: the presentness sought by Fried is to that sought by Morris as the beautiful is to the sublime. And just as Fried can appeal to Kant to support his understanding of modernism, so can Morris, although a different section of the *Critique of Judgment* becomes appropriate: "The Analytic of the Sublime."

Kant's understanding of the sublime leads no closer to an inhabitable architecture than does his understanding of the beautiful. Morris wants not the comforts of enclosed and domesticated space but masses that appear on the verge of "sliding out into space," returning us to the mysterious presencing of things, in which the experiencing self is always copresent. Domestication of space implies a domestication of self. The presencing of things, which is at the same time their continual "sliding out into space," lets the self return home: not to a home in space, in the world, but home to its true, essentially free and homeless self. That self is not subject to time and calmly contemplates its terror. Here lies the key to the power of the sublime.

Given his attempt to open objects to space, Morris's fascination with ruins comes as no surprise:

Approached with no reverence or historical awe, ruins are frequently exceptional spaces of unusual complexity, which offer unique relations between access and barrier, the open and the closed, the diagonal and the horizontal, ground plane and wall. Such are not to be found in structures that have escaped the twin entropic assaults of nature and the vandal. It is unfortunate that all great ruins have been so desecrated by the photograph, so reduced to banal image, and thereby so fraught with sentimentalizing historical awe. But whether the gigantic voids of the Baths of Caracalla or the tight chambers and varying levels of Mesa Verde, such places occupy a zone which is neither strictly a collection of objects nor an architectural space.[14]

The return of once-firm buildings to space and time calls into question any view of architecture as the domestication of space. Intended her is not so much a domestication as a liberation of space, which means also of time. The terror, or rather the *mysterium tremendum et fascinans* of time, is awakened rather than banished.

4

The Bible places building in an ambiguous light; and how can we avoid understanding the replacement of God's creation with an artificial, human-made environment as anything but an act of prideful self-assertion? Already the agrarian Cain, I pointed out, unlike his herdsman brother Abel, is a builder of cities. Joseph Rykwert calls attention to a passage from *The Living City* that shows Wright's proximity to the Biblical vision. "Go back far enough in time, mankind was divided into cave-dwelling agrarians and wandering tribes of hunter warriors. . . . The cave dweller became the cliff dweller. He began to build cities. . . . His God was a malicious murderer. . . . He erected his God into a mysterious covenant. When he could he made his God of gold. He still does."[15] Note the associations: the necessarily sedentary life that attends agriculture permits or even demands the establishment of cities; with it comes the introduction of money as represented by the value placed on gold, a metal that resists change and comes to figure the association of value with permanence. This is the realm of Cain, who thus invites comparison to Kafka's animal as another symbol of the ill will against time, which is inevitably also an ill will against reality. But let me return to Frank Lloyd Wright: "But his swifter, more mobile brother, devised a more adaptable and elusive dwelling place—the folding tent. . . . He was the adventurer. His God is a spirit: devastating and beneficent as he was himself."[16]

A rooted mode of life appears here as base: Wright links true humanity to mobility. The modern city dweller in contemporary America is seen as in many ways closer to the tent-dwelling Abel than to the agrarian Cain: "So a human type is emerging capable of rapidly changing environment to fit desires, one amply able to offset the big city of today: remnant of the great ancient 'Wall.' In the capability to change we have a new type of citizen. We call him democratic."[17] And does human nature not demand mobility, demand mobile homes? If this is granted, the city of today seems still too burdened by the city of the past, the city of Cain. Is Hundertwasser not right to oppose perennial Platonism and the cities it has built? Do we not need to oppose, in architecture, too, to the Platonic aesthetics of permanence an "aesthetics of change"?[18] But does it even make sense to imagine the city of Abel? How would it look—like a trailer park? like Las Vegas?

Presupposed by this ideal of a city responsive to ever-changing desires is a refusal to grant that human beings are adequately understood as beings with fixed needs, to be satisfied in fixed ways. Is it not only to a small extent that human needs are fixed by nature? And if this is granted, should not changing needs also reflect themselves in an architectural environment that not only changes but welcomes change? To a large extent, human needs would appear to be socially induced. One might even argue that human beings need their needs to change, for suppose that there were a fixed set of natural needs: for example, hunger, sexual desire, the need for shelter. Suppose further that all these needs have been more or less satisfied. Schopenhauer suggests that at this point boredom would overcome us. How then do we escape from boredom? Precisely by raising our needs beyond the natural level, by developing, if you will, unnatural needs. Artificially induced needs would seem to take over to the extent that natural needs are satisfied. It is precisely the need to have needs that makes us so vulnerable to advertising and to changing fashions. The aesthetic of change appears here as an aesthetics of the interesting.

Popular art and fashion provide ready illustrations. Charles Jencks gives us a good example of an aesthetics of change when in his discussion of British postwar architecture he traces the development from the pop artists belonging to the Independent Group to the attempts of *Archigram* to lead architecture beyond architecture. Once more we have an effort to have architecture deconstruct itself, although now this needs to be understood in a quite different sense: architecture is opened not so much to time and space, but much more specifically to the promise of the immediate future: "The new aesthetic will be an aesthetic which will be 'used up' as fast as the product and quickly forgotten: an aesthetic which is based on popular images of power, sex, and other forms of social emulation, and an aesthetic which is above all popular, which will sell, which is always just one step ahead of the common dream—'on the frontier of the dream that money can only just buy'." [19] So understood, the aesthetics of change will try to retain contact with what is established and accepted but will refuse to settle for that, for what everyone expects is boring. We should therefore try to be just a bit outrageous, move just a bit beyond what is understood to be in good taste—not far enough to turn off the consumer, but far enough to titillate.

The interesting now becomes an important value—in life, and in architecture. This is the meaning of staying "just one step ahead of the common dream." And it is important that this dream not be altogether beyond our reach, that it be "the dream that money can only just buy": the slightly too expensive CD player, car, house. Hardly a dream of Bachelard's oneiric house, it does not have its foundation in memories of childhood nor in recollections of some archetype. Whatever natural needs there may be have been absorbed and restructured by the needs of the market. The short life of the commodity follows, for the needs that it satisfies are themselves short-lived and give way to others. The objects that filled them can then be discarded. The aesthetics of change here becomes the "Throwaway Aesthetic." [20] In keeping with such an aesthetic, Peter and Alison Smithson suggested that the Detroit-produced automobile should serve as model for the house of the future. [21] No longer a dwelling place, the house has become a machine designed to fill rapidly changing and easily manipulated needs. The modern market, this child of Heidegger's *Ge-Stell*, threatens to embrace all of life, as "dwelling" gains its significance and is defined by advertising. On this view the human being has no stable essence but is indefinitely malleable and plastic.

And why insist on the permanence of human relations? Think of the community created by a successful outdoor music festival, or by an artistic event such as Christo's wrapping of the Reichstag, or by a football game, or by a night spent together in some motel room. Here we have instant communities, often intense in their own way, yet of only short duration. And are not all communities increasingly of that sort—not very long lasting, created by shared but inevitably changing interests, communities that we can join and leave with ease? The disintegration of marriage as an institution is a symptom. Does it still make sense today to insist on stable environments, be they homes or cities? Do we not need more flexible solutions, solutions that will accommodate an inevitably open future with its new desires and associations? That such solutions would leave architecture in its traditional sense behind is evident (fig. 97).

But instead of mourning the erosion of traditional communities, perhaps we should celebrate a new kind of community and environments that can be quickly put together, which share some of the character of the tent. Inflatable architecture might help meet this need. Or we might take mobile homes and the instant communities they make possible as pointers in the right direction. In the issues of *Archigram* we find much more provocative and utopian solutions, utopian in the sense that the imagination has outstripped what can now be realized. But what is here suggested does challenge us not to sacrifice the promise of the future to the past. A dynamic counterimage to the traditional city emerges: a city held together by a relatively stable support structure that would take care of plumbing, electricity, communications, and the like, but would allow for maximum flexibility with respect to the location and nature of our dwelling.

Giedion and Doxiadis feared in such experiments a new inhumanity,[22] and yet the main idea behind *Archigram* can, it would seem, be defended with quite traditional arguments. We can return to the tent-dwelling Abel, who, Wright supposed, shifted his home as his spirit moved him. Why be stuck in one place? Why not dream of radically mobile homes? The new technology has made utopia seem less distant: paradise regained on the basis of the new technology! Should an old-fashioned emphasis on place and dwelling, on the values of traditional architecture, be allowed to stand in the way of such hopes? Wasn't it the Nazi Schulze-Naumburg who wanted German architects to build houses that sunk their roots into the ground and drew strength from the soil? And did not Heidegger, too, compromise his thinking when he placed it at the service of Hitler? But even if such associations force us to question the promoted ideals of dwelling and building, questioning here should not mean dismissal. That the visions of *Archigram,* too, point in the wrong direction is shown when we push the idea of a technology-based artificial environment responsive to our every need to its limit—a machine that will fulfill every need as it arises: "It's all the same. The joint between God-nodes and you, eat-nodes and you is the same. Theoretically, one node could service the lot. There's no need to move. Cool it baby! Be comfortable. Godburgers, sexburgers, hamburgers. The node just plugged into a giant needery. You sit there and need—we do the rest! Green stamps given."[23] What has happened to Abel, to the tent dweller who was supposed to be closer to paradise than his agrarian brother? But perhaps such utopian visions do bring us toward paradise. If we think of paradise as a place where no want needs to be repressed or go unfulfilled, where Adam and Eve were hungry only to see the fruit that would still their hunger, where they felt desire only to reach for what would quiet their desire, are we not very close to paradise with Greene's vision?

At this point the link between the aesthetic of change embraced in the issues of *Archigram* and perennial Platonism begins to manifest itself. Consider the imperatives: Don't worry about what is far off! Don't plan too far ahead! Live in the moment! Enjoy and forget

"Western Landscaping," Boulder County, Colorado. Photo credit: Ken Abbott.

97

yourself! These are old recipes against the terror of time. What links *Archigram*'s utopian projections to perennial Platonism is what Nietzsche called the spirit of revenge, that ill will against time and its "it was," which is inevitably also an ill will against ourselves as mortals. As Heidegger has shown, it is our sense of death that gives us our sense of being this particular self. Architecture, if it is to serve dwelling, must speak to us of our mortality. The utopian visions of Pop Art and *Archigram* tend to dissolve persons into collections of changing needs, which are easily manipulated and induced by advertising. Just as we can forget ourselves in the moment, absorbed in, say, a great work of art or a television program, so David Greene's "giant needery" would have us forget ourselves. Lost would be the individual and, with him or her, community. Returning to the analogy with paradise: in paradise Adam and Eve were not yet persons in the full sense of the word; they became such persons only when they insisted on knowing for themselves, when they refused the place they had been assigned by God. But inseparable from such an awakening is the recognition of human vulnerability and mortality, is the terror of time, the loss of paradise. To be sure, dreams of paradise will haunt us, but if we are to save our humanity they must remain dreams. Any attempt to realize paradise here on earth must lead to a destruction of full humanity. A genuinely human dwelling requires the renunciation of paradise and an affirmation of ourselves as essentially fallen.

Death, Love, and Building

17

1

No doubt we have much to learn from recurrent attacks on perennial Platonism and its insistence on the timeless and universal. Such insistence leaves important needs simply unanswered; both body and individual are shortchanged. We have to challenge the one-sided emphasis on geometry, on the spirit, on the universal and eternal, that is so much part of modernist architecture. This challenge can take two quite different forms:

1. Its more radical form is a denial that there is anything like a universal language of art and architecture, a language that transcends particular cultures and ideologies. We meet with an insistence on the merely conventional character of all architectural languages: are not the codes of architecture, too, governed by what is accepted in a particular society, at a particular time? Reyner Banham thus attacked the very idea of a "universal" style as misconceived. Is that style not itself just another convention?[1] Conventions change, often rapidly. Architecture, too, has its fashions, and phenomenologists must take care not to embalm past conventions by elevating them into supposedly universal conditions or essences.[2] And am I not guilty of just such a backward-looking, false essentialism? But if I have argued that the language of architecture has its ground in human being in the world, I have also insisted that this world is historical: inevitably the language of architecture has been mediated by particular histories and landscapes. This, however, does not mean that we are so immersed in our particular historical situation that we cannot criticize aspects of it by appealing to the human condition, including deep-rooted needs and desires that have changed little since *Homo sapiens* first appeared on the earth.

An examination of human being in the world provides the key to what we can call "natural symbols" or "the voices of space." The language of "straight lines and circles, and the plane or solid figures, which are formed by turning lathes and rulers and measures of angles" extolled by Plato's Socrates is part of that understanding,[3] which is not to say that human beings must seek refuge from the terror of time in such forms: many have experienced such refuge as a prison. But, as the previous chapter showed, even the refusal of an architecture of right angles and straight lines presupposes an understanding of its message and appeal. The very fact that Plato and Mondrian share an understanding of the beauty of geometric forms suggests that there is good reason to speak of a perennial Platonism, that we are dealing here with aesthetic preferences that cannot be dismissed as just another fashion. The appeal of the language of geometry transcends particularities of time and of place. Radical conventionalism is untenable, and untenable also is its challenge to perennial Platonism. The very temporality of our existence endows geometric forms with their special aura.

2. But the challenge to perennial Platonism must be reraised in a less extreme form: does the universal language on which it insists do justice to the entire person? Here the answer has to be negative. Inseparable from this turn to the universal is a downgrading of time, the body, the senses, the concrete person inevitably embedded in particular communities. An environment made up only of such forms must leave most human beings dissatisfied, which is not to deny that this spiritual dimension is indeed essential and that an architecture that neglects it altogether also loses something essential. But its significance should not be exaggerated. Hundertwasser is right to meet such exaggeration with his equally exaggerated praise of mold and rust. One-sided emphasis on the seemingly timeless and universal has to lead to an abstract architecture that cannot do justice to the requirements of dwelling. The individual is rendered accidental. In the demand for an aesthetics of change the legitimate claims of the body and of the person make themselves heard.

And yet, when in the last chapter we turned to the utopian quasi-architecture celebrated in the issues of *Archigram,* we encountered there, too, inhumanity. Instead of a joyful acceptance of human temporality, we once again met with an escape from the terror of time. Only instead of escaping from becoming to being, to an abstract realm of the spirit, here an attempt is made to lose oneself in the present: don't worry about what is far off! The terror of time is to be covered up by short-lived enjoyment, the pleasure of the present moment. Here, too, we meet with an ill will against time. But this ill will means also an ill will against ourselves as inevitably concrete embodied individuals, for our sense of being a self is inseparable from the awareness that we must die. As Freud knew and as Heidegger demonstrates, it is the awareness of our always possible death that gives us our sense of being a particular self. "But if death is the aspect of life which confers on life individuality, independence and separateness, then a priori the repression of death should produce symptoms which exhibit on the one hand a flight from independence and separateness and on the other hand the compulsive return of the repressed instinct. But such an ambivalent attitude toward independence and separateness is at the heart of all neurosis, according to Freud's later clinical writings."[4] If this is anywhere near the mark, our dwelling should confront death; and this in turn suggests that the built environment, too, should speak to us of mortality. Heidegger's Black Forest farmhouse is therefore exemplary when it gives room to death by giving the coffin its proper place. Another house might have a special door reserved for funerals and similarly momentous occasions. Cemeteries similarly give room to the dead and form therefore a not-to-be-neglected part of the urban fabric. And sacred architecture has always had as perhaps its main task the illumination of life in the face of death: in the churches of the West, bells, clocks, grave monuments, and crypts thus sound their *memento mori,* while crosses and the bones of martyrs testify that the right death leads to genuine life.[5]

But are not God and the promise of eternal life in the City of God fictions born of the terror of time, veiling that terror only by veiling our own essential temporality and consequently our mortality? That promise, however, at least recognizes that any ideal building has to promise shelter to the embodied self, not to a disembodied spirit. The embodied self is unable to recognize in Plato's realm of forms its true home.

2

Brueghel's *Tower of Babel* not only presents us with the paradigm of an architecture born of prideful self-assertion, of what Augustine called the *libido dominandi,* but also calls it into question by contrasting that tower with the far less pretentious buildings of the surrounding city and with the sheds that nestle against the tower's walls. It is essentially the same contrast we find in Piranesi's *Vedute di Roma* (fig. 98), where the overscale remains of proud antiquity contrast with more recent and much more modest buildings; or in Caspar David Friedrich's *Ruins of Eldena Abbey* (fig. 99): not just architecture here returns to nature, a nature that as in Ruisdael's *Jewish Cemetery* includes life and death, but a church, the representation of the old faith. In the ruin of the old faith modern humanity establishes their much more modest building—a figure for us disinherited heirs of the Jewish-Christian tradition?

Vulnerable and mortal the embodied self demands both physical and psychological shelter. But if such shelter is to provide more than a false escape, if it is to provide genuine shelter, then building must confront and acknowledge the essential precariousness of human dwelling and building. But how can buildings do both—promise security and at the same time acknowledge the precariousness of our dwelling and building? Bachelard addresses this apparent paradox when he speaks of nests: "A nest—and this we understand right away—is a precarious thing, and yet it sets us to *daydreaming of security.*"[6] Nests are not built by the *libido dominandi* but by a very different love. In this connection it would be interesting to examine how talk about nests and related metaphors function in our everyday talk about dwelling—think of the expression "nest egg." What do we have in mind when we think of nests? The word "nest" connotes shelter but, at the same time, fragility. Yet the latter is unable to undermine the former: "And so when we examine a nest, we place ourselves at the origin of confidence in the world, we receive a beginning of confidence, an urge toward cosmic confidence. Would a bird build its nest if it did not have its instinct for confidence in the world?" (p. 102). The metaphor of the nest suggests a love supported by confidence in what the future holds: to consider one's home a nest is to trust in the world without sufficient reason for this trust. And it is precisely such trust, Bachelard suggests, that is a condition of genuine dwelling. "Human life starts with refreshing sleep, and all the eggs in the nest are kept nicely warm. The experience of the hostility of the world—and consequently, our dreams of defense and aggressiveness—come much later. In its germinal form, therefore, all of life is well-being" (pp. 103–104). Bachelard contrasts an original sense of well-being, tied to a sense of being part of a larger order, with a more strongly developed self-assertion that places the self into an antagonistic relationship to the world.

That the former deserves to be given ontological priority had already been asserted by Bachelard in his discussion of the oneiric house, where he suggests that we comfort ourselves by reliving memories of protection, memories that carry us back to "the land of

Giambattista Piranesi, view of the Forum of
Nerva (*Vedute di Roma*). Credit: Beinecke Rare
98 | Book and Manuscript Library, Yale University.

Motionless Childhood" (p. 6) and play here somewhat the same part as Platonic recollection, although these memories carry us not to a timeless realm of forms, which by its very nature has no place for the body, but to a home for the embodied self. They are therefore closer to imaginative journeys to paradise. Yet do such memories really have the power to defeat the terror of time? Our reason stumbles over suggestions of a reconciliation of time and eternity, of a dwelling that is both in time and yet unburdened by time, timeless, eternal. Does "the land of Motionless Childhood" not belong with the "once upon a time" of myth and fairy tale? Are the "fixations of happiness" (p. 6) that are to illuminate life not sources of a false light, this turn to an imaginatively transformed past not in fact an escape into fiction?

Bachelard would not have us build the oneiric house any more than he would have us build nests. Our houses should only recall them, in this sense repeat them, and thereby grant our dwelling something of that world confidence that the already-discussed story of Jacob's ladder, with its divine promise of an ever-growing community stretching indefinitely into the future, places at the origin of sacred architecture.[7] Bachelard, to be sure, does not cast his point in religious language, but his invocation of a return to "the origin of confidence in the world," of "an urge toward cosmic confidence," recalls Eliade's suggestion that "primitive" cultures were able to banish the terror of time by interpreting human buildings as repetitions of the cosmos. Cosmos implies here the changeless order that assigns to human beings, too, their proper places. Interpreting what is as constituting a cosmos allows human beings to feel at home in the world. Building can help to establish or reinforce such interpretations. A building that is experienced as a repetition of divine building can claim to give our dwelling its proper measure and foundation. Construction rites invite such readings, helping to endow the builder's work with the aura of reliability, whose ground is sought in a reality untouched by the ravages of time in which the consecrated building participates. "A 'new era' opens with the building of every house. Every construction is an absolute beginning; that is to say, tends to restore the instant, the plenitude of a present that contains no trace of history" (p. 76). Linear time and its before and after are abolished. A higher reality becomes present in the building in a way that lifts the burden of time. "In the last analysis, what we discover in all these rites and all these attitudes is the will to devaluate time. . . . Like the mystic, like the religious man in general, the primitive lives in a continuous present. (And in this sense the religious man may be said to be a 'primitive'; he repeats the gestures of another, and through his repetition, lives always in an atemporal present.)" (pp. 85–86) Once again dwelling is understood as repetition, which has as its goal the abolition of history and thus of death. Primitive building invites such repetition by presenting itself as a repetition. The traditional symbolism of temple, church, or house, which establishes a particular building as a repetition of some divine archetype, lets those worshiping or dwelling in it participate in a timeless archetypal pattern.

Repetition implies a certain affirmation of time. It thus is not subject to quite the same critique as what I called perennial Platonism. Repetition recognizes time even as it refuses to recognize death.

Caspar David Friedrich, *Ruins of Eldena Abbey*
(1824–1825). Gemäldegalerie, Staatliche Museen,
Berlin. Credit: Foto Marburg/Art Resource,
99 | N.Y.

Still, the question returns: can we grant Bachelard's nests and oneiric houses the kind of priority on which he insists? And what sense can we make of Eliade's claim that the primitive lives through repetition of a timeless archetype in an atemporal present? The claim attributes to primitive life something of the quality that theorists of the beautiful have attributed to aesthetic experience, with the difference that Eliade's primitive life denies the distance between life and aesthetic experience on which the modern aesthetic approach insists. Like Platonic recollection, repetition stamps the character of being on becoming, indeed fuses the two, as they appear paradoxically fused in the eternal life promised to the Christian. What sense can we make of such fusion? Are not such consoling thoughts, like thoughts of eternal life in the City of God, also born of the terror of time—alienating, repressive thoughts that fail to take death and thus also the individual seriously enough? Is Augustine not right when he insists on the healing power of the confrontation with death, remaining right even when we deny personal immortality?

That confronting death possesses such healing power is suggested by Aristotle's account of tragedy, which invites us to consider the essentially tragic character of genuine dwelling. According to Aristotle's famous definition, a tragedy is "the imitation of an action that is serious and also, as having magnitude, complete in itself; in language with pleasurable accessories, each kind brought in separately in parts of the work; in a dramatic, not in a narrative form; with incidents arousing pity and fear, wherewith to accomplish the catharsis of such emotions."[8] What is meant here by pity and fear? What pleasure do we take in their representation? The answer to this question is tied to what Aristotle means by "the catharsis of such emotions."

In the *Poetics* Aristotle has rather little to say about pity and fear, devoting more discussion to what kind of plot is likely to arouse them. This deficiency is made up to some extent by a number of passages in the *Rhetoric,* where fear is defined "as a pain or disturbance due to a mental picture of some destructive or painful evil in the future." First of all and most of the time we do not fear death, for although "we all know we shall die," "we are not troubled thereby, because death is not close at hand."[9] Absorbed in the everyday and its activities, we give little thought to death. Tragedy shakes us out of such absorption, confronting us with death in such a way that we recognize our inability to make certain that our death is indeed a long way off. It thus lets us fear for ourselves. To say that tragedy should arouse fear is to say also that it should rob us of the sense of security that is part of our everyday existence: what is happening to those on stage could be happening to me; a destiny may overtake me that I do not understand and of which I am not the master. Consider Oedipus, or Pentheus in Euripides' *Bacchae.* Both show the inability of reason and calculation to finally secure human existence.

But what is edifying about their failure, about the pity we feel? Aristotle defines pity "as a feeling of pain caused by the sight of some evil, destructive or painful, which befalls one who does not deserve it, and which we might expect to befall ourselves or some friend of ours, and moreover to befall us soon."[10] Tragedy, on Aristotle's view, reveals to the human being who he is: noble in his desire to give order and structure to his life and world, pitiful in his inability to secure himself. But again: what is edifying about such recognition? What is the meaning of catharsis? Unfortunately the definitive explanation that Aristotle is supposed to have given in the *Poetics* has been lost, but a few hints in the *Politics* permit us at least to sketch an answer. Tragedy, according to Aristotle, has a purgative and a healing effect: our souls are lightened and delighted. This is to suggest that most of the time we bear a burden, weighed down by the usually repressed fate of mortals to be at the mercy of powers greater than they are, the powers being fate and the gods. What weighs on us is not so much that we are powerless, but that we repress that powerlessness and the associated emotions. It is a burden imposed on us not by time as such but by a self-assertion that makes it hard to fully accept our temporality. This inability is what prevents us from affirming ourselves in our entirety. First of all and most of the time we live in flight from ourselves. Tragedy returns us to who we really are. This is its healing power.

We should not lose sight here of the way the emotions are controlled by tragedy. First of all they are distanced: the events we see on stage are not real and it is precisely their unreality that allows us to confront them and through them ourselves. Second, the represented events have been rescued from arbitrariness: the tragedy's beautiful form, its closure, serves to establish an ordered, controlled aesthetic space, in which everything appears to hold significance. Happenings otherwise terrifying and opaque are transformed by the poet's art into significant, bounded, and timeless "situations."[11] Tragedy, too, relies on repetition. Aristotle thus admonishes the tragedian to keep to the traditional stories, centered on a few tragically fated families, with each tragedy repeating such a story in its own way, but so that it is experienced as a repetition of the same. It is important, however, that what is repeated is not some version of paradise but the interplay of life and death, which the poet's art so embraces and bounds that we are able not only to confront but to affirm it. Here is the key to its healing power: tragedy calls us back to ourselves, to the tensions within ourselves, tensions that are constitutive of our dwelling.

But if so, should we not attempt to think of buiding, too, in the image of tragedy, as not a poetic but now an architectural repetition of the interplay of life and death, as an establishing of meaningful situations, open to the tension that finds expression in the opposition of Dionysus and Apollo? That opposition, as Nietzsche understands it, is also the opposition between reality—joyful but also death shadowed—and poetic illusion. Does our dwelling then require the healing illusion of art? And if tragedy, too, depends on the power of illusion, does it really allow us to affirm ourselves as the mortals we know ourselves to be? Is not the problem with this turn to tragedy that it, too, is finally just another version of the flight from the terror of time into aesthetic illusion?

Aristotle's account of the healing power of tragedy invites comparison with Heidegger's account of the healing power of the anxious anticipation of death. First of all and most of the time, Heidegger insists in *Being and Time,* human beings cover up their essential mortality and with it their own essence, losing themselves to the world, to different roles and activities. The resolute anticipation of death rescues us from such dispersal, making us whole and healing us in that sense. As the possibility that means the end of all my possibilities, death circumscribes my life and gathers it together, giving weight to every one of my actions. To be open to this possibility is to acknowledge how inescapably my life is my own.

All self-assertion is thus shadowed by nothingness. Just because of this human beings tend to flee from death into the world, finding refuge in work routines or pleasure and seeking solace in the seemingly timeless spheres of science and art. Most often we will turn for comfort to other human beings.

But do we have to speak here of flight? Can we turn the matter around and interpret the link that Heidegger establishes between authenticity and the resolute anticipation of death as a running away from life? We have to grant Heidegger that death is constitutive of individuality. But human beings do not only exist as solitary selves; we also belong to larger wholes, stand in the tension between both, experience the claims of both. This twofold stance is presupposed by the recurring distinction between two kinds of love, true love and love of self. Better than *Being and Time,* Plato's *Phaedo* teaches the art of dying. As long as I remain convinced that my own death will put an end to all my possibilities, to all I am and to all that could and should matter to me, why should I worry about what will happen after my death, to those I love, to others, to the world? Does not the finality of death lead to the recognition that I have only this one life to live and should do whatever is in my power to make this life as pleasant as possible, as long as I can—and put an end to it when pain has come to outweigh pleasure? After me the deluge! Fear of death teaches selfishness, as it is born of a selfishness that would make the death-bound self the measure of all value. It is of course possible to develop something like a morality on that basis, but, as Plato's Socrates shows us with his teaching and his example, such selfishness must render life hollow: life becomes truly worth living only when there is a recognition that there are matters weightier than my death. Of such recognition is born the courage to face death as Socrates was able to face it.

But the question returns, a question raised already in the *Phaedo:* where are those convinced that death will have the last word to find such courage? Socratic courage is linked to a conviction that we belong not to ourselves but to the gods; that is to say, we are neither the authors nor the masters of ourselves, but stand under demands and commands that issue from a transcendent domain that assigns us our place. Heidegger later was to gesture toward this dimension when he replaced the earlier analysis of authentic being-unto-death with his analysis of genuine dwelling as a staying within the fourfold, an analysis that requires us to make sense of his talk of gods, divinities, or angels—messengers of the godhead, at any rate—that is, make sense of a logos that claims human beings and of which they are not the author. The realm of forms is Plato's interpretation of this realm. Condemned to die, Socrates does not console his grieving friends with a promise of personal immortality. That is the childish view, born of a natural selfishness, which in the *Phaedo* finds expression in the anxious questioning of Socrates' interlocutors, who have not understood the true significance of the soul. "Soul" names not something like an immortal person, wearing a mortal body as one wears a coat, but that which lets the individual belong to and "hear" a transcendent logos that provides him or her with a measure. To take care of or to neglect the soul means to cultivate or to neglect the claims issuing from that timeless realm. These claims have to be experienced, have to be "recollected." Reason cannot substitute for such recollection; and when our fear of death prevents us from responding to or even from hearing these claims, we have to be charmed with stories like the dialogue's final myth, which, despite its surface appearance, is not so much about what will happen to us after death as it is about this life and its timeless measure.

What makes our lives worth living is love. *Phaedo* and *Symposium*, *ars moriendi* and *ars amandi*, the art of dying and the art of loving, belong together. The prospect of his own death cannot crush the lover precisely because he cares more about what he loves than about himself, whether that be a person, a country, humanity, the gods, or justice. Love lets us take ourselves less seriously, teaches us to be less self-centered. That time and death hold less terror to the lover is suggested in the *Symposium* by the story of Alcestis, whose courageous willingness to sacrifice her life so that her husband might live is so admired by the gods that they release her soul from Hades: only when we learn to transcend our death-bound selves in love, learn to take ourselves not too seriously, do we begin to truly live.

The paradigmatic lover in the *Symposium* is of course Socrates, who, himself taught by Diotima, teaches that the aim of love is perpetual possession of the good. Eros demands eternity. On its lower levels it tries to achieve this by making sure that something of the individual will survive him—children, for example, or fame, or works. Isn't it love that builds all nests? This then is how most human beings attempt to make their peace with time. But eros refuses to be satisfied with such temporal counterparts of true eternity. The higher mysteries of love lead beyond time, which is to say, on Plato's view the soul's true home is not of this world, not in time, but in eternity.

Plato's distinction between the lower and the higher mysteries of love thus helps support what I have called perennial Platonism. But as already pointed out, the problem with this Platonism is that, while it perhaps answers to the demands of the spirit, it short-changes the whole human being. We are after all not angels, and we don't need ethereal homes fit only for angels. We need to build our homes on the earth, in this time-ruled reality. Any approach to building that shortchanges time and the body will prove inadequate. This is also to say that we must challenge Socrates' privileging of the "higher" mysteries of eros and give greater weight instead to its "lower" mysteries, which are said to seek a semblance of eternity in time. Such a semblance is provided first of all by children, then by fame or great works. In each case the individual is asked not to take herself, her own life, that life that must end with her death, too seriously. The lower mysteries of eros invite us to understand ourselves as part of an ongoing temporal context. Building responsive to these mysteries would interpret our place in that context. Schools could become such buildings.

What justifies such a revision of the Platonic account is the same relatively constant human nature that justifies talk of natural symbols. Schopenhauer is one thinker who can help us to correct the one-sidedness, different in each case, of the Heideggerian and the Socratic account, when he insists that as an essentially embodied self, the human being is not only a mortal but also a sexual being. Rather than understanding sex as the lowest manifestation of eros, Schopenhauer, preparing the way for Freud, invites us to acknowledge the fundamental significance of sex, which, he insists—and something like this is recognized already by Socrates—is misunderstood when it is reduced to an instrument that we use to amuse ourselves and others. It would be more correct to call the individual an instrument of the species, which through sex strives for immortality. As this instrument the human being belongs to a larger ongoing order. Given such an interpretation, the individual who, as Heidegger's authentic person does, takes his or her own death to be the end that circumscribes all others, would exist inauthentically precisely because of that refusal to acknowledge the tragic tension between individual and species in human being.

The human species should not be understood here in a too narrowly biological fashion. The human being is after all the *animal rationale, zōon logon echōn*. Species therefore means also an ongoing community, community in turn depends on communication, and to understand the possibility of communication we have to open our understanding of species to the logos presiding over it. This understanding of the primacy of Diotima's lower mysteries makes Alcestis an exemplary heroine. A love strong enough to confront and accept death defeats the terror of time: love of another, love of community, love of humanity.

4

This revision of Heidegger's understanding of dwelling calls for building responsive not just to our individuality and mortality but to that love which lets us experience ourselves as essentially incomplete, in need of others, in need of community. Such building has to provide interpretations of our place in an ongoing historical context. Heidegger recognizes the need for such interpretation when he says of the Black Forest farmhouse that "it designed for the different generations under one roof the character of their journey through time."[12] This then is a house built not for an individual but for successive generations. Temporal reality is interpreted here as a historical order in which we stand, an order that assigns us our place and charges us with responsibility. This is to say that just as buildings establish regions, wresting place from space, so they establish temporal situations, placing the individual in time—and not just in time, but in a communally shared time, in history. History stands in somewhat the same relationship to time as cosmos to space: without some understanding of our place in history we lose our sense of belonging to an ongoing community, a sense that is still our most effective weapon against the terror of time.

How can a building place us in time? In the final part of this book I shall have more to say about such placement. For a first answer I could turn to an Egyptian temple, which presents itself to us first as a path to the final chamber with its sacred ship. Or to a medieval cathedral: "From west to east leads the path: steeply the space rises and from above light falls upon the path—intimated more than present, a long space, a clearing in God, holy path through holy darkness, deep on the bottom of a gorge, accompanied by light, and protected high up under light vaults. Path space through an uncertain world, not more, but very festal and noble in its proportions"[13] (see fig. 37). But let me turn instead to a church roughly contemporary with Heidegger's farmhouse: the Augustinian priory church in Diessen (1732–1739).[14] As in so many churches, our progress toward the high altar, to the cross, figures our own progress toward death (fig. 100). Of death speak the altar paintings, while time presides quite literally over our progress in the now broken clock above the choir arch. Of death, too, speaks a stone in the pavement under our feet that calls attention to the vault beneath the choir in which the founders of the church lie buried. We

100

are not allowed to forget that this church is a grave of saints, and just as we approach the balustrade that separates us from the more sacred space of the choir, which finds its culmination in the high altar with its promise of victory over time, this sepulchral character asserts itself forcefully: we see in glass shrines the bones of two of the founders, whose names and relics speak of the triumph of time, but also of a saintliness that triumphs over time. Although dead, they live in this church, living, even for us who no longer believe, in the same sense in which Socrates still lives in the *Phaedo* and the *Symposium*.

If the nave's horizontal encourages movement, the choir discourages it. Steps and balustrade stop us; the architect's shift in vocabulary, from the nave's pilasters to full columns, from the semi-ellipses of the arcs spanning the nave to more festive semicircles, helps mark the choir's more sacred character. Particularly significant is the shift from the scalloped frames of the nave frescoes to the ringlike frame of the choir fresco, which suggests a hole cut into the vault through which we are allowed to see the church's founders, buried in the crypt below, assembled in Heaven. Visually and symbolically the choir thus establishes a vertical axis that links heaven and earth, transforms death into triumph. But only the high altar, place of the divine sacrifice, really unites heaven and earth: only in the representation of the Assumption of the Virgin to which this church is consecrated are the two visual zones into which the nave spearates really brought together.

No longer does our world allow for such building. The dwelling that built it lies just as decisively behind us as the dwelling that built Heidegger's farmhouse. To be sure, Christians still worship in this church. Candles are still lit for the Virgin. Still, like so many of the great churches of the West, for most of its visitors this church, too, has become an aesthetic object, a musuem of sorts. As Heidegger says of the temple at Paestum or of Bamberg cathedral, "the world of the work that stands there has perished"[15] (see figs. 120, 121). The perishing of a world means inevitably also the perishing of a history, and when such a history perishes, so does a community. The church at Diessen preserves traces of this history, traces of a world that has vanished. Preserving these traces the church speaks to us moderns of our history, helping us place ourselves.

As the recent successful renovation of this church demonstrates, the preservation of such structures is considered important. But is it important only in the sense in which preservation of any aesthetic object of similar significance is important? Suppose we were dealing with buildings whose only virtue was their age: should they be protected? The problem of how to deal with the architectural inheritance became particularly acute in Europe following the end of World War II. What was one to do with often half-ruined cities? Especially in the beginning there were many voices who, in the spirit of Le Corbusier's suggestion that Paris be razed, called for radical reconstruction: narrow medieval streets should finally give way to the demands of the traffic engineer; building should free itself from the burden of the past. Much was accomplished to transform medieval towns into modern cities, but it is interesting to observe how in different countries those who insisted on expensive, painstaking rebuilding and restoration increasingly had their way. And soon they not only restored the damage of the war but went further, restoring the appearance of a bygone era. The reconstructed tower of the Diessen church offers an example. The original tower had been hit by lightning in the nineteenth century and was rebuilt in a then-fashionable medievalizing style; only very recently was the decision made to tear that tower down and to go back to Johann Michael Fischer's original design.

Should we be upset if someone were to tear down some venerable, but really quite ugly, city hall to make room for an up-to-date facility (see fig. 101)? What difference does it make whether we live or work in a building that not only has a history but represents and perhaps interprets this history? I knew a couple in Andernach on the Rhine who lived in what was once a monastery's town house, a house that spanned all the styles of Western architecture. Its cellar was still Roman; subsequent centuries built on these foundations, often without much success. Given considerations of economy and efficiency that house should probably have been torn down: with its enormous roof and landmark status, which meant that no substantial changes could be made, it proved impossibly expensive to keep up. The owners tried to give it to the city for a museum or the like, but for a long time no one was interested.

What does history matter? Genuine community requires both a shared past and a hoped-for future. Once that future found binding expression in the ideal architecture of the Heavenly Jerusalem. But we face our future very much as an open possibility, no longer able to look forward and up to the Heavenly Jerusalem or to any similar ideal. We might fear that as long as such an ideal is missing, genuine community is also missing. Still, some sense of community is granted by a shared past, which remains also a promise and a ground from which to start building a stronger community. The now often almost desperate concern with the past betrays an anxiousness that community might be lost altogether, to be replaced with more or less accidental associations of individuals who find such associations to their mutual advantage. Preservation of the architectural past is an inseparable part of any attempt to establish and preserve a genuinely public space that allows individuals to find their separate places in an ongoing order. The historical dimension of our environment must be preserved and represented if we are to keep open the possibility of genuine dwelling. And we do not preserve or re-present history by just playing with its fragments.

Part Four

Architecture and Community

Architecture and Building

18

That from the very beginning modern life should have been shadowed by the promise of a simple, more authentic life invites examination. As Bernard Rudofsky observes: "There is a good deal of irony in the fact that to stave off physical and mental deterioration the urban dweller periodically escapes his splendidly appointed lair to seek bliss in what he thinks are primitive surroundings: a cabin, a tent, or, if he is less hidebound, a fishing village or hill town abroad. Despite his mania for mechanical comfort, his chances for finding relaxation hinge on its very absence. By dint of logic, life in old-world communities is singularly privileged."[1]

Many of us have experienced the lure of the unfamiliar, be it the Alaskan wilderness, an Italian hill town, or a Zambian village. But what lessons can be drawn from the modern urbanite's nostalgia and usually quite temporary escapes to more primitive modes of dwelling, from her willingness to put up with diarrhea, mosquitoes, and cramped quarters just to take a brief step out of her civilized world into a different mode of life? Do such escapes allow us to infer that, as Rudofsky suggests, life in old-world communities is singularly privileged? Would we exchange our own way of life for theirs?[2]

Just like Heidegger's dream of a Black Forest farmhouse, Rudofsky's images and descriptions of what he calls "nonpedigreed architecture" carry the utopian promise of human beings living in harmony with each other and with the earth. Burdened neither by technology nor by what is usually thought of as "architecture," this architecture belongs to a specific region, just as do its rocks and caves, trees and animals. "The untutored builders in space and time—the protagonists of this show—demonstrate an admirable talent for fitting their buildings into the natural surroundings. Instead of trying to 'conquer' nature, as we do, they welcome the vagaries of climate and the challenge of topography." Ephemeral as some of these structures may be, "the shapes of these houses, sometimes transmitted through a hundred generations, seem eternally valid, like those of their tools."[3] Contextualism, regionalism, and apparent timelessness here go hand in hand.

Ecology-minded postmodernists will listen sympathetically to Rudofsky when he suggests that

Vernacular architecture owes its spectacular longevity to a constant redistribution of hard-won knowledge, channeled into quasi-instinctual reactions to the outer world. So-called primitive peoples have none of

the devil-may-care attitude when confronted with the reality of their environment. Above all, they have no desire to dominate it. Admittedly, the vernacular's unforgivable weakness is constancy. Unlike the apparel arts or pedigreed architecture, it follows no fads and fashions but evolves only imperceptibly in time. As a rule, it is tailored to human dimensions and human needs, without frills, without the hysterics of the designer. Once a life style has been established and habit has begotten a habitation, change for change's sake is shunned.[4]

It is difficult to resist the spell of Rudofsky's photographs of luminous cubic houses spilling down a hillside in Siros, of bosomy Apulian trulli, of tomblike Galician granaries, of a Dogon Big House symbolizing a procreating man. They leave us with an urge to travel, to search out what often are the last traces of a way of life being eroded by the seemingly inevitable progress of our industrial culture. But if the photographs force us to question that progress, they also leave us wondering about the possibility and, more important, about the desirability of such a return to the archaic, even if we are reminded that "archaic" here means not so much temporally prior as closer to the *archē*, the timeless origin: that is, more essential.

Would I want to spend the rest of my life in such an "old-world" community? I could probably afford it. But I would miss too much, always remain an outsider, and, more important, I would miss my own context. I have grown too accustomed to the comforts of modern life, too mobile, both literally and spiritually, to be able to recover such "serenity"; I have seen too much not to supplement Rudofsky's moving images with other equally moving but sadder images of squalor and starvation. To be sure, I would like to visit the magical places Rudofsky places on our coffee table. But this does not mean that I would gladly exchange what I now have for what I at times dream of and even escape to, no more than periodic visits to Disneyland or trips to the Alaskan wilderness mean that we would like to live in such an environment. The attraction of the vanishing traces of old-world cultures is inseparable from their location on the periphery of our life.

And yet Rudofsky is right to question why, "to stave off physical and mental deterioration," we should periodically escape to surroundings that we experience as figures of a vanishing but more original mode of dwelling. The Austrian Rudofsky found his figure of paradise above all in white-washed Thera, the southernmost of the Cyclades, whose supposed "*primitivity*" he had celebrated already as a young man in his doctoral dissertation: "*perfection* as expressed in a marvellous unity of past and present, whch imparts to the stranger a sensation of timelessness."[5] Houses, half-tunneled into the soft volcanic rock, with walls of lava blocks and often covered by a barrel vault of a primitive concrete made of "the local pumice stone and pozzolana, a volcanic ash that, mixed with lime, yields an exceedingly firm hydraulic cement,"[6] seemed to belong to the landscape just as much as the vineyards and fig trees, the menacing crater and wine-dark Aegean; each subtly different, adjusting itself to its curious site in its own way, its soft contour, which Rudofsky likens to a loaf of bread, unhampered by the need to obey the dictates of level and plumb line, ruler and compass, and yet bound to its neighbor by the subtle rule of this special soil and sky. And not only here does the *genius loci*[7] speak in seemingly timeless images of perfection: the same can be said of countless "old-world" villages and towns, which preserve context without sacrificing individuality and without being conscious of either. In the case of Thera an "agitated topography," re-presented by the "dancing rhythms of the steps,"[8] and the Mediterranean sun with its sharp shadows saw to that. New means of communication have brought such sights closer to us even though they are part of forces that must exile such sites to the periphery of our world, endowing them with an aura of unreality. Such magical, seemingly timeless habitations appear to fall out of historical time. They belong with narratives that begin with the "Once upon a time," that time when there was no time, that introduces the Brothers Grimm's fairy tales.[9] Seen against the background of such a town, everyday activities present themselves as timeless paradigms, especially in the medium of photography: a woman climbing steps and another occupied with the perpetual whitewashing of walls, roofs, and pavements are figures of the enduringly human that have no place in the world of television antennas and cars. The attack on space manifested by the revolutions in transportation and communication threatens to destroy such humanity, as does the desire for an ever higher standard of living, for ever more gadgets, ever new thrills.

Few tasks facing the architect are more difficult than the introduction of modern buildings into such an almost ageless context. Rudofsky gives the example of government-sponsored new housing that, following the earthquake of 1956 that devastated Thera, was to provide for the homeless. Even the Housing Department's Ministry of Public Works recognized that it would not do to rely on the clichés of the then-triumphant international style. Designers were asked to respect the island's strong vernacular. "Nevertheless, in the course of planning, designing, and decision making, the traditional houses' languid lines were resolutely straightened out, their wayward curves stiffened into half-circles, the dimensions of rooms, doors, and windows standardized, and the foundations laid out perfectly parallel in homage to the Right Angle."[10] Gone were the subtle individuality and freely molded forms of the old houses. No doubt, the designers recognized the strength of the local building tradition, but their attempt to develop a modern language that would fit into this context failed. Although clearly indebted to the pregiven vocabulary, streamlined and disciplined, the new houses lacked a soul. An obvious measure of the modern designers' failure was the islanders' refusal to appropriate what the government so thoughtfully had furnished. They continued to prefer the old ways of building and dwelling.

Essentially the same story repeated itself in countless villages, towns, and cities, where such natural catastrophes as earthquakes and fires—but more often such human-made catastrophes as war or resolute modernization—made rebuilding necessary. Again and again a desire to honor the *genius loci* led historical sensitivity into an unfortunate alliance with modern design to produce buildings that borrow certain aspects of the vernacular, say the general shape of a house, especially the established roof form, without preserving the former's life.[11] I am thinking of postwar rebuilding in such deeply scarred cities as Ulm or Nuremberg; but also of such unfortunate compromises with the past as New Haven's city hall (fig. 101). Too often attempts to preserve something of the strength of the old urban context end up with mechanical or theatrical gestures that underscore their own emptiness.

Rudofsky calls his celebration of the "old-world" vernacular "frankly polemic."[12] It is indeed impossible to miss the intended contrast between "the serenity of the architecture in so-called underdeveloped countries" and "the architectural blight in industrial countries," which is blamed on "architectural design"—what Rudofsky calls "pedigreed architecture"—or on technological thinking, what Ruskin already called the "prevalent

101 | City Hall, New Haven. Photo by author.

feeling of modern times, which desires to produce the largest results at the least cost"[13] and lets us treat nature as no more than a source of materials to be used and used up. The vernacular celebrated by Rudofsky, by contrast, is nonconfrontational and ecology minded without having to mind ecology. Pedigreed architecture and engineering are both made to appear as products of a fall into sin that, like the first fall, means inevitably also a fall out of the natural realm. Primitive architecture figures paradise, although Rudofsky draws the leit-motiv of his essay not from Genesis but from Seneca's letter to Lucilius: "Life is the gift of the immortal gods, living well is the gift of philosophy. Was it philosophy that erected all the towering tenements, so dangerous to the persons who dwell in them? Believe me, that was a happy age, before the days of architects, before the days of builders."[14] To up-to-date architecture Rudofsky opposes archaic building, where the very modern dream of timeless dwelling colors his presentation of the assembled material.

2

Despite its pronounced antimodernism, Rudofsky's dream of an architecture without ar-chitects was shared by some of the founders of the modern movement. Little separates his juxtaposition of vernacular and pedigreed architecture from Adolf Loos's description of the effect of the introduction of an architect-designed villa into an Austrian lakeside village:

Everything breathes beauty and peace.

What's this then? A false note disturbs this peace. Like an unnecessary screech: among the peasants' houses, which were not made by them but by god, there is a villa. The work of a good architect, or a bad one? I don't know. I only know that peace, rest, and beauty have fled.

Architecture and Building

Before god there are neither good nor bad architects. . . . In towns, in the realms of Beelzebub, there may be fine distinctions, as there are even in kinds of crime. And I therefore ask: why is it that every architect, whether he is good or bad, harms the lakeside?[15]

The atheist Loos does not hesitate to invoke God and Beelzebub to present the contrast between the villa and buildings that were not so much built by peasants as created by nature, using their building only as her medium. Themselves products of nature, such buildings cannot but fit into the natural context. This fit gives them a look of natural necessity. Whatever an architect designs inevitably breaks such harmony. With his work the city invades the countryside, and in keeping with a tradition that has Cain build the first city, Loos assigns the urban realm to the devil. No matter how successful, architects belong to that realm.

Why must every architect, whether good or bad, harm the lakeside? Precisely because she would be more than a mere builder: an artist. As an art, architecture has always already fallen out of the quasi-natural order of building. The architect takes her task to be more exalted than the construction of a merely serviceable structure; she wants to create something beautiful, fashion an aesthetic object. As pointed out earlier, aesthetics has long taught that such objects should be appreciated as self-sufficient wholes. To be appreciated as such wholes they must either distance themselves from their context—that is, stand out as figures on the ground provided by the landscape—or incorporate it; they must either turn their back to their setting, like so many modern works of architecture that appear to just happen to be in this particular place (Loos's unnecessary screech), or engage that context, confront it as recalcitrant material to be appropriated, transformed, and integrated into the artist's composition. Either approach is difficult to reconcile with contextualism. Pedigreed architecture inevitably tears the landscape, and such tearing scars. As peasant dwellings all over the world can teach us, building need not be such a violation.

Loos accuses the architect of having no culture, where "culture" names "the harmony between the inner and the outer man which alone guarantees sensible thinking and acting."[16] Loos's idealized peasant by contrast has culture precisely because he has not yet fallen out of the natural order, which narrowly circumscribes his possibilities. Because he allows his creativity to be ruled by natural wants and instincts always already bound by a particular site and climate, whatever he creates, be it a tool, a field path, or a house, has the look of inevitability. Not yet do human beings oppose themselves to the situation into which they have been cast. Instead of confrontation there is harmony. The devil wants confrontation, God harmony.

Where Loos differs from Rudofsky is in his conviction that the paradise of peasant culture lies behind us, that any attempt now to return to it would betray the possibilities of a genuinely human existence opened up by science and technology. It would be irresponsibility to squander their potential for liberation. But if we cannot and should not attempt to return to what Loos describes as the innocent but less than fully human paradise of peasant culture, need we give up hope for a modern analogue? Here it is important to keep in mind that it is not old-world architecture as such that preserves context: the scattered older houses that have survived in many modern cities look quite out of context. It is not the modern context shaped by technology that our building ought to honor? Loos's critique of architecture opens up the possibility of a truly modern contextual approach to building, no longer regional but international. Paradise can be regained on the basis of technology. "Technological culture" is not the oxymoron it appears to be for Rudofsky. No more than the peasant harms the lakeside "does the engineer, who builds a railway to the lake or ploughs deep furrows in its bright surface."[17] Bound by considerations of efficiency, the engineer has to be attuned to his or her materials and the laws of nature. All ornament, indeed all aesthetic extravagance, is ruled out. Modern bridges and harbors, with their mazes of docks and cranes, are thus beautiful in rather the same way as the work of the peasant builder. They communicate a similar attunement to the natural order, a similar harmony between inner and outer. A well-built car or plane cannot help but be beautiful. Or think of the beauty of silos or industrial architecture. The engineer is the peasant's modern counterpart.

Such sentiments were characteristic of early modernism. Le Corbusier was only one architect to extol the engineer:

Not in pursuit of an architectural idea, but simply guided by the results of calculation (derived from the principles which govern our universe) and the conception of a LIVING ORGANISM, the ENGINEERS *of today make use of the primary elements and, by coordinating them in accordance with the rules, provoke in us architectural emotions and thus make the work of man ring in unison with universal order.*

Thus we have the American grain elevators and factories, magnificent FIRST-FRUITS of the new age. THE AMERICAN ENGINEERS OVERWHELM WITH THEIR CALCULATIONS OUR EXPIRING ARCHITECTURE.[18] (fig. 102)

102 | Vertical Assembly Building, John F. Kennedy Space Center, Cape Canaveral, Florida. Photo by author.

"Inspired by the law of Economy and governed by mathematical calculation," the engineer puts us into accord with universal law. "He achieves harmony."[19] But as the strain placed on the environment by technology demonstrates, to be in accord with universal law does not yet mean to be in tune with what we usually understand by "nature." Nuclear devastation is in accord with universal law; so are acid rain, oil spills, and asphalt deserts. Universal law is quite indifferent to human needs. Rudofsky's warning of the progressive deformation of landscape by technological progress cannot be dismissed. It calls into question the substitution of a modern, industrial contextualism for a primitive, agrarian one.

Not that his idealization of "old-world" rural life does not raise equally serious questions: when Loos likens his peasant builders to animals, he renders his own idealization of peasant life problematic. As the *animal rationale,* the thinking animal, the human being is also the always already displaced animal, who, if he is to create a home for himself, may not leave the world alone. Descriptions of old-world peasants as natural builders are misleading. We may think of the incandescent buildings of Thera as belonging to this island on the Aegean, as we think of the Parthenon as belonging to its rock, but that landscape to which they now appear to belong is a landscape shaped and transformed by human labor, including building. All building has its origin in a confrontation of nature that is never free of violence. As the essentially displaced animal, the human being has always already lost paradise. Thera never was paradise, even if we moderns may read it as a figure of paradise. There is no paradise to be recovered. Certainly such recovery is not accomplished by timid attempts to return to some archaic vernacular; and yet attempts to return human life to a more intimate relationship to nature remain appealing. Even Le Corbusier had once been convinced by yet another Austrian, the backward-looking Camillo Sitte, of the desirability of such a return: "Sitte's arguments were skillful, his theories seemed correct; they were based on the past. In fact, they were the past—and the miniature past, the sentimental past, the rather insignificant flower on the roadside. This was not the past of apogees; it was the past of compromises. Sitte's eloquence went well with this touching renaissance of the 'home,' which in a paradox worthy of the cottage, was defined grotesquely to divert architecture from its proper task ('regionalism')."[20]

Ronchamp lets us wonder to what extent Le Corbusier finally freed himself from the "sentimental" past (see figs. 72, 95). But the young Le Corbusier wanted something altogether different: to all regionalism he opposed an essentially universal architecture of confrontation. Instead of celebrating submission to pregiven contexts, Le Corbusier celebrated the violence inherent in all building, which has only been underscored by the new means technology has placed at the builder's disposal. What moves Le Corbusier is not so much the apparent timelessness of old-world culture as the intoxicating pace of modern life: "Cars, cars, speed, speed! One is carried away, seized by enthusiasm, by joy. Not by enthusiasm at seeing the shiny bodywork glistening in the light of the headlamps. But enthusiasm over the joy of power. The frank, ingenuous enjoyment of being at the center of power, of energy. We share in this power. We are part of this society whose dawn is breaking."[21] Timid contextualism cannot be reconciled with such joy at the dawn of a brave new world, which welcomes the force that tears apart slowly grown land- and townscapes. "Its energy is like a torrent swollen by storms: a destructive fury. The town is breaking in pieces, the town cannot last, the town is no good any longer. The town is too old. The torrent has no bed."[22] Le Corbusier understands architecture as an "assault upon nature." It looks not backward, anxious to preserve inherited contexts, but forward to the creation of unheard-of new contexts in which old-world architecture will look sadly out of place, a relic left over from our darker past.

By now technology has demonstrated its destructive potential in a way that invites us to see in Le Corbusier's dawn the twilight of the old day. We don't even need to think of atomic war and ecological crisis. Suppose reason were to triumph over such irrationality and technological thinking were to find solutions for all the problems produced by a still underdeveloped technology: would that assault upon nature celebrated by Le Corbusier leave us a truly humane environment? Why does the thought of all landscape transformed into technoscape, of the triumph of asphalt and vinyl siding, frighten us?

As already pointed out, Le Corbusier was much too much of an artist himself to accept the reduction of the architect to the engineer. While he gave us the programmatic slogan, "The house is a machine for living in," in the same place he also insisted on what separates the architect from the mere engineer: architecture is an art, and for the genuine artist there is "no longer a question of customary use nor of tradition, nor of constructional methods, nor of adaptation to utilitarian needs. It is a question of pure invention, so personal that it may be called the work of one man."[23] Corbusier understands the Parthenon as such an invention: "Passion, generosity and magnanimity are so many virtues written into the geometry of the handling of the contour,—volumes disposed in precise relationships. Phidias, Phidias the great sculptor, made the Parthenon." Architecture is art and "art is poetry: the emotion of the senses, the joy of the mind as it measures and appreciates, the recognition of an axial principle which touches the depth of our being."[24] Such an understanding of the architect as artist has to place him or her in opposition to just those forces of custom, tradition, and utilitarian needs to which Rudofsky would submit building. But this is of course to be expected: as much as any modern architect Le Corbusier is associated with "pedigreed architecture." Such architecture is confrontational by its very nature as art. It inevitably speaks with a loud voice. But need it therefore also be that unnecessary screech condemned by Loos?

3

As we have seen, Heidegger's description of a Black Forest farmhouse endows it with many of the same values Rudofsky discovers in "nonpedigreed" architecture. But Heidegger has also provided an interpretation of the architectural type that has provided much "pedigreed" architecture with its authorizing paradigm, the Greek temple (fig. 103):

A building, a Greek temple, portrays nothing. It simply stands there in the middle of the rock-cleft valley. The building encloses the figure of the god, and in this concealment lets it stand out into the holy precinct through the open portico. By means of the temple, the god is present in the temple. This presence of the god is itself an extension and delimitation of the precinct as a holy precinct. The temple and its precinct, however, do not fade away into the indefinite. It is the temple work that first fits together and at the same time gathers around itself the unity of those paths and relations in which birth and death,

Temple of Hera II, so-called Temple of Poseidon,
Paestum. Credit: Alinari/Art Resource, N.Y.

103

disaster and blessing, victory and disgrace, endurance and decline acquire the shape of destiny for human being. The all-governing expanse of this open relational context is the world of this historical people. Only from and in this expanse does the nation first return to itself for the fulfillment of its vocation.[25]

Transporting human beings into the presence of a god, the temple lets them experience a particular place as holy, thus providing their life with a focus. So understood, architecture, as opposed to mere building, has an essentially public function: its task is to help gather scattered individuals into a genuine community by presenting the powers that preside over its life. Architecture is a presentation of the divinities.

The generality of Heidegger's description raises questions: Which temple is he speaking about? The temple work is said to first open up the world of the Greek people. But how can this be? Does the building of any particular temple not presuppose the Greek world? Perhaps we should say rather that each temple re-presents and lights up this world in its own unique way by transporting those who visit it into the presence of a divinity, be it Zeus or Athena, Aphrodite or Apollo.

If it is difficult to take literally Heidegger's claim that it is the temple that first opens up the Greek world, it is equally difficult to take literally his moving description of how the temple first makes visible the environment: "Standing there, the building rests on the rocky ground. This resting of the work draws up out of the rock the mystery of the rock's clumsy, yet spontaneous support. Standing there, the building holds its ground against the storm raging above it and so first makes the storm itself manifest in its violence. The luster and gleam of the stone, though itself apparently glowing only by the grace of the sun, yet first brings to light the light of the day, the breadth of the sky, the darkness of the night. The temple's firm towering makes visible the invisible space of the air."[26] But were earth, sea, and sky, trees, grass, and animals not part of the temple's pregiven context? How can Heidegger claim the temple presents this context for the first time, that it is only the temple that brings to light the light that allowed the temple's builders, too, to see? Hyperbole here appears to approach nonsense.

But we have to take seriously Heidegger's claim that the temple—and we can generalize to every genuine work of architecture—renders visible the landscape that provides its setting, as it illuminates the historical world to which it belongs, providing it with a unique focus. What grants the temple such power of illumination? Heidegger speaks of the temple's "firm towering" and "steadfastness." Standing there, the temple "holds its ground." We say of someone who refuses to yield to an enemy that she holds her ground. Would Heidegger then have us liken the temple's relationship to its setting as a kind of war? Yes, although he would no doubt insist that "war" here translates the Greek *polemos,* which he understands with Heraclitus as *eris* and translates as *Auseinandersetzung* or "confrontation." *Auseinandersetzen* means primarily to set apart so that what is thus set apart is rendered visible in its own proper being. As an assertive presencing of stone ordered by spirit, the temple sets itself apart from the earth that supports it, establishes itself as a figure on the ground of the pregiven landscape. Setting itself apart from its context, the temple brackets that context in a manner that must be understood exclusively and inclusively. As a seemingly self-sufficient presence the temple draws our attention, pushing its setting at a distance. Thus distanced, the setting is, so to speak, put in a frame. Framed, it is re-presented. The temple thus lets us look again not just at itself, at its form and materials, but at its site. By confronting its context instead of quietly submitting to it, the work of architecture becomes a light that illuminates its surroundings, including other buildings.

The temple work is said by Heidegger not only to set forth the earth, that upon and in which "historical man grounds his dwelling in the world," but to open up that world, where "world" names "not the mere collection of the countable or uncountable, familiar and unfamiliar things that are just there," but the most encompassing context which gives meaning to all our actions and thoughts.[27] In *Being and Time* Heidegger shows how the world is opened up or revealed precisely when our usual ways of dealing with persons or things break down in some way, by fissures in some usually taken for granted context: a chair that has lost its leg becomes *conspicuous* in its now useless presence. Or suppose you are doing a jigsaw puzzle; a particular, strangely shaped piece cannot be found, but just its absence renders the other pieces *obtrusive* in their current uselessness. Or take a window that should have been washed long ago and now *obstinately* refuses to be overlooked. Conspicuousness (*Auffälligkeit*), obtrusiveness (*Aufdringlichkeit*) and obstinacy (*Aufsässigkeit*) constitute disturbances in the usually smooth texture of everyday life, which—precisely because it allows us to take things more or less for granted—lets us only half see them.[28] Familiarity veils. Fissures in that texture help lift that veil, endowing things with a new presence (fig. 104). It is to such presence that Michael Benedikt would recall architecture: "There are valued times in almost everyone's experience when the world is perceived afresh: perhaps after a rain as the sun glistens on the streets and windows catch a departing cloud, or, alone, when one sees again the roundness of an apple."[29]

Although Heidegger is not concerned with architecture when he discusses conspicuousness, obtrusiveness, and obstinacy in *Being and Time* but is concerned to show how

104 | Deserted house, San Juan, Puerto Rico. Photo by author.

within everyday life the world is lit up by disturbances in our usual ways of dealing with persons or things, the relevance of that discussion to his later interpretation of the world-establishing power of architecture should be apparent. Insofar as it is also a work of art, the work of architecture is precisely a building that because it effects such disturbances renders itself conspicuous and therefore present, communicating a particular way of standing in the world, a particular ethos. We may want to say that what renders the work of architecture conspicuous is its beauty, but if so we should keep in mind the traditional insistence on the uselessness of the beautiful. Ornament and beautiful proportions constitute breaks in the context ruled by utility. As a useless and for this reason conspicuous insertion into a particular setting, the work of architecture renders that setting obtrusive. Thus every work of architecture places other buildings in the light of the world it has opened up. And works of architecture are obstinate. The German *aufsässig* is perhaps better translated as "rebellious." Works of architecture refuse to fit into the pregiven context without speaking up. They stand up to that context and hold their ground. In that sense works of architecture may be considered rebellious buildings.

From this perspective Rudofsky's "frankly polemic" celebration of "old-world" building may seem an attack on the very essence of architecture. But here it is important to distinguish the standpoint of the author, who is modern precisely in his discontent with the modern world, and that of those who built and dwelled in the structures he illustrates. His praise of nonconfrontational building contrasts strikingly with his own self-consciously confrontational style. In the context of our modern world his images and descriptions have somewhat the same function as Heidegger's description of the Black Forest farmhouse: they are meant to provoke, to make us uneasy about our all-too-comfortable way of life. Rudofsky's invocation of the timeless vernacular of old-world building rebukes our vernacular, with its concern to be up to date, subject to the latest fad or fashion.

What would an architecture look like that attempted to heed Rudofsky's lessons? Would Luis Barragán have met with his approval? or Venturi? or the architectural experiments of his fellow Austrian, Hundertwasser? Whatever the answer, this much is clear: any such attempt should result in a bulding that would confront and stand up to the modern context, calling us to a different way of life, a different ethos. As a contemporary version of old-world building it would be not another such building but a work of architecture.

4

The contrast between contextualist vernacular building and confrontational architecture is part of the history of building, which may be likened to an evolving ellipse with these two foci. Like all art, architecture in this special sense refuses to submit to the context of the established and accepted; it departs from and confronts building. Its very point is to let us take leave from the everyday, if only to return us to it, now with eyes more open, with greater awareness of what everyday routines inevitably obscure. What Heidegger says of the Greek temple, that it lets the god be present, has its analogue in the presence of God in every church or in the presence of shared values in civic monuments. Architecture calls us out of the everyday to another place, one a bit closer to the ideal. A piece of utopia lives in all architecture. This utopian aspect has to bring architecture into conflict with what would seem to be the very point of building, which is to help make us comfortable in our world, where expectations of what comfort requires can be expected to change with changing conditions. Architecture is, however, also building. This returns us to the tension that rules what Rudofsky calls pedigreed and I called genuine architecture: like all building, architecture too should make us comfortable, while, like all art, it should make us uncomfortable, fill us with dreams of a better world, of genuine community.

But this way of putting the matter presupposes an overly reductive understanding of the requirements of dwelling. To feel at home in the world we not only require shelter but need to illuminate that world with myths, be they of gods or God, or of shared rights and virtues. If it is to meet the requirements of dwelling, building has to assume a mythopoeic—and that means inevitably also a public and political—function. This is to say that vernacular building requires the illumination provided by architecture, where architecture can be either conservative or revolutionary: that is, serve the old or present new gods.

Is architecture still able to meet this function? What do we today have to learn from a Greek temple or a medieval cathedral? No longer do such works have the power to assign us our place in their world; we visit them rather as we visit museums, expecting knowledgeable guides, preferably with a Ph.D. in art history. As Heidegger points out, even "when for instance, we visit the temple in Paestum at its own site or the Bamberg cathedral in its own square—the world of the work that stands there has perished."[30] And not only has the world of these works perished; our world no longer appears to want such world-establishing work. No longer do we look to art, let alone architecture, to gather individuals once more into genuine community. The ethical function that art once had today has been claimed by reason.

Unfortunately reason has proved unequal to the assumed task. We live in the ruins of the inherited value system. To support this claim—I shall return to it in my conclusion—I would have to show that, notwithstanding the efforts of philosophers from Plato to Kant and indeed right down to the present, pure reason has shown itself incapable of discovering the true ends of human actions. Such discovery requires the aid of myth. And even if our understanding of reality makes it difficult to take myth seriously, even if it may have become hard to separate the mythmaker from the fool, the mythopoeic function of art remains indispensable.

The need for art, and especially for architecture, remains. What kind of architecture? Temple and cathedral lie behind us. Not only has the kind of community their building presupposed and reaffirmed been lost, but few of us would wish it to return, for it is incompatible with one of our own ruling myths: the myth of the value of personal freedom. That myth has freed art, too, from its former servitude to religion and state. But if art has thus gained a new freedom, the price of such emancipation has been its peripheral placement in a world ruled by the economic imperative.

Where does that leave building? Outside of art, it would seem, which has become "a private concern of the artist."[31] Where does that leave architecture? The following chapters address that question.

The Publicness of Architecture

19

1

Inquiries into the origin and essence of building have tended to focus on the house. But can such a focus do justice to the public character of architecture and thus to the distinction between building and architecture? The history and histories of architecture argue otherwise. Nikolaus Pevsner's *An Outline of European Architecture*,[1] from which I drew the distinction between architecture and building, is quite representative. A glance at the "List of Text Figures" speaks for itself: as one should expect, all illustrations are of what Rudofsky called pedigreed architecture. Of the fifty-seven figures preceding an illustration of Michelozzo's Palazzo Medici in Florence (begun in 1444), all are of ecclesiastic architecture, except for Diocletian's Palace in Split, a Pompeian basilica, and the Palace of the Flavian Emperors in Rome in the introductory chapter; Charlemagne's palace in Ingelheim (early ninth century); Harlech Castle (chiefly 1286–1290); and Cothay Manor (late fifteenth century). And churches continue to dominate well into the eighteenth century, only to disappear altogether thereafter: the last church illustrated is Jacques-Germain Soufflot's Ste.-Geneviève (begun in 1755), secularized and transformed by the French Revolution into the Panthéon. No new architectural type emerges to take the place of the church. The plates complement but do not change this picture. The history of European architecture is told here as a history of "pedigreed architecture," and in Christian Europe this means above all the history of church architecture.

That this is indeed the standard account is confirmed when we leaf through Christian Norberg-Schulz's *Meaning in Western Architecture*.[2] A more inclusive work than Pevsner's history, its first chapter is on Egyptian architecture and speaks of temples and mortuaries. The dread of death and a sense of the sacred here intersect, where sacred architecture also means public, communal architecture. And sacred, communal architecture dominates the following chapters. To be sure, things change a bit when we turn to Rome: illustrated are not only temples but triumphal arches, city gates, and imperial villas, as well as apartment houses and a house in Pompeii. Still, architecture here means mainly public building, and much of that, although by no means all, still has an obvious connection to the sacred. The next three chapters, on early Christian architecture, Romanesque architecture, and Gothic architecture, deal almost exclusively with churches. Only some illustrations of the Palazzo Pubblico and streets in Siena and one of the Vladislav Hall in the castle in Prague (1482,

1502) indicate the beginning of a turn to the secular. Things change as we come to the chapter on Renaissance architecture: while church architecture still dominates, the palazzo asserts itself as a significant genre. With the turn to Mannerism, villas and palazzos begin to dominate, although in the chapter on Baroque architecture churches once more predominate. Emphasis changes radically in the chapters on the Enlightenment and then on modern architecture: only two illustrations show churches, one Schinkel's painting of an imagined Gothic cathedral (1813), the other Le Corbusier's Notre-Dame du Haut in Ronchamp. Housing, and now not just or even primarily apartment houses but private homes, together with office buildings, factories, theaters, and museums, begins to occupy the best architects. There is a proliferation of building tasks, of which not one can claim the significance that once belonged to the church.

Books like Marvin Trachtenberg and Isabelle Hyman's *Architecture, from Prehistory to Post-Modernism: The Western Tradition* or Spiro Kostof's *A History of Architecture: Setting and Rituals* broaden the picture considerably but don't really change it.[3] That this should be the case, even in the latter, is a bit surprising, given the author's stated premise that "*all* buildings of the past, regardless of size or status or consequence should ideally be deemed worthy of study"—Kostof rightly points out that "modest structures in the periphery of monuments are not simply of intrinsic value; they are also essential to the interpretation of the monuments themselves. Slave cabins, outhouses, herb gardens, and water vats complete the meaning of the plantation house."[4] But to grant such dependence of monuments on peripheral architecture hardly challenges the usefulness of Pevsner's distinction between architecture and building. To be sure, such a challenge is in the air; it might even be called "politically correct." Many of us have, as Kostof points out, become increasingly attracted to the aesthetic charms of an "architecture without architects." And no doubt, "Its appeal proves how unwarranted it is to claim that even the humblest of structures is untouched by aesthetic concern or devoid of aesthetic appeal" (pp. 14–15). But, as I attempted to show in chapter 2, as long as our attention remains focused on "aesthetic appeal" we will not be able to do justice to what architecture has been and meant. Nor do we do justice to architecture when we view it as "a medium of cultural expression" (p. 19)—just about everything a culture produces can be understood to express it in some way or other. Architecture, I have suggested, not only expresses but intends to express cultural values and concerns. It does not just communicate, it is intended to communicate. Kostof himself points to what warrants the distinction between building and architecture when he continues: "To be sure, this is an innocent sort of visual order. There is no conscious theory behind it, no intellectualized system of form. But it demonstrates that delight is an elusive thing that may apply as readily to the random and unstudied as it does to the calculated designs of the professional" (pp. 14–15). What has generally been considered architecture is not innocent.

Kostof, however, resists the pointer he here provides. He appeals rather for

a more inclusive definition of architecture and, consequently, a more democratic view of architectural history. The aim is to put aside the invidious distinctions between architecture and building, architecture and engineering, architecture and speculative development; to treat buildings with equal curiosity whether they are religious in intent, monumental, utilitarian, or residential; to discriminate carefully among styles or conventions of forms without discriminating against any of them; and to have genuine respect for the architectural achievement of cultures regardless of origin and their racial and theological identities. (pp. 15–16)

It is telling that, despite such admirable and timely open-mindedness, in the present book at least Kostof finds it difficult to live up to the ideal he proclaims: only in the first five chapters, which bring us to the Greek temple, is nonpedigreed architecture prominently represented. After that public architecture, especially temples and churches, predominates. The urbanization of Europe, leading first to the Renaissance and then to the transformation of the architectural environment by industry, brings the expected, accelerating shift away from sacred architecture. And despite the book's title, despite illuminating forays into the Near and Far East and into the Americas before Columbus, and despite the first chapters, this remains very much a history of Western architecture. Focused on a relatively small number of outstanding works of architecture from a very small number of European countries, this is definitely not a history of building.

2

As this brief survey suggests, the history of Western architecture justifies both Pevsner's distinction between building and architecture and his choice of Lincoln Cathedral as a paradigm: until the Renaissance—and indeed, especially in Catholic countries, well into the eighteenth century—this history has been pretty much a history of sacred architecture, in which sacred also meant communal. One-sided emphasis on the house, which we meet with so often in speculations about the essence or origin of building, must therefore be questioned. The history of building should not be equated with the history of architecture but includes it. And while most buildings have of course been quite ordinary houses, these have not figured prominently in histories of architecture. And rightly so: not only has the history of building turned around two poles—one marked by the house, the other by the temple or church; one comparatively private, the other comparatively public; one comparatively profane, the other comparatively sacred—but the latter has traditionally been privileged, as witnessed by the expenditure of labor and wealth.[5] The history of architecture has been anything but democratic. Attempts to ground architectural practice by locating the origin of building in the primitive hut fail to do justice to sacred architecture, as architectural theorizing came to recognize: the church building, as we have seen, gained its legitimacy as a representation not of the first house but of real and imagined structures that were thought to have had God as their real author, including especially the Heavenly City and the temple Solomon is said to have built in Jerusalem.

It is therefore significant that architectural theory has turned not around one but two paradigms. It is an ellipse that has one center in the house, tied to the family more than to the individual, the other center in the church or temple; it is significant also that in the eighteenth century the former came to displace the latter. Still, we must not forget that while the idea of the original house has haunted architectural theory, so has that of a sacred structure of divine origin. While the former addresses itself more to the need for physical control, the latter addresses itself more to the need for spiritual control. It is possible to relate these two foci as ground and figure. What is discussed as architecture in histories of architecture is first of all architecture that presents itself as a figure on the ground of more or less anonymous building, and we may not forget that this figure-ground relationship is repeated by individual buildings, including even the most modest houses. Consider, for example, the history of portals and main doors, whose public, re-presentational function invites architectural treatment and calls for ornament.

Works of architecture re-present buildings. One could put the matter this way: architecture re-presents and by so doing illuminates the vernacular of building. Churches thus represent and re-present houses. To return to the Thomistic definition of the church as the house (the Latin *domus*, "house," becomes the German *Dom*, "cathedral") in which the community joins in celebration of the sacrament, this house not only is called "church" but signifies the Church, that is to say an ideal communal dwelling. Just about every medieval city provides striking illustrations, and so does many a New England village: the New England meeting house preserves the idea of the church as a special house, a house in which the community joins in sacred celebration, even if no elaborate attempt is made to articulate the spiritual significance of the building.

The ethical function of architecture is inevitably also a public function. Sacred and public architecture provides the community with a center or centers. Individuals gain their sense of place in a history, in a community, by relating their dwelling to that center. But simply placing an ambitious work of architecture on a ground of buildings does not necessarily provide these buildings with a center—this is one lesson taught by Brueghel's Tower of Babel, which turns a cold shoulder to the surrounding city. It is not difficult to come up with modern analogues. Most obvious perhaps is the analogy with the official architecture of totalitarian states, which self-consciously employed architecture to help forge a new community. I have already mentioned the disturbing affinity between Heidegger's failed attempt to appropriate the greatness of our culture's Greek beginning for the German present and Nazi architecture, which boasted of having achieved "a harmonious correlation between Hellenic serenity and the austere simplicity of modern functional architecture"[6] (see fig. 116). It is a recipe found irresistible not just in totalitarian states, such as Hitler's Germany, Mussolini's Italy, or Stalin's Russia. Particularly close to the Babylonian paradigm was the proposed scheme for the Palace of the Soviets, which was to be taller than the Eiffel Tower and the Empire State Building, an extravagant scheme haunted by the constructivist ghost of Vladimir Tatlin's (by then no longer welcome, because much too modernist) Monument to the Third International, its interlocking, upward spiraling helices intended to symbolize the upward spiraling progress of the Marxist dialectic.[7] But we need not move that far afield to step into the shadow of Babel's tower: not long ago I visited Houston—with its ensemble of tall buildings reaching skyward from the flat Texan plain, it made as powerful an impression as any architecture I have seen, but an impression that disturbed me. These splendid skyscrapers by some of our most distinguished architects created a sense of nonplace. No city I know appears quite as close to the Wonderful City of Oz. Very different was my impression of Minneapolis, from which I had just come. Most important here is not which town has the stronger architecture—what do we mean by "stronger"?—but the way that the architecture relates to the ground provided by the existing buildings and by the land,

and to some ideal vision of the city of the future. This is connected to the problem of the relationship of the language of architecture to the vernacular. Venturi got hold of something important when he wanted to recall architecture to the vernacular. His pointer deserves to be taken up and given more thoughtful development.

3

I pointed out that the history of building has revolved around two poles, the first marked by more or less private building—not just by the house but also by such functional sheds as factories, stores, lobster sheds, barns, places to store grain, and the like—the second, privileged over the first, by public architecture serving a quite evident ethical and thus also a communal function—first of all by the temple but also by such public buildings as palaces, city halls and city gates, fountains, and theaters. For much of the history of Western architecture the church has thus represented the leading architectural task, although city hall (just think of the city halls of Florence, Siena, Antwerp, or Augsburg) and palace (think of the Escorial and Versailles, as well as their offspring) at times laid claim to comparable or even greater significance. Still, despite such challenges, the church could claim preeminence until the Enlightenment put an end to its privilege. Not that it yielded that privilege to some other building task: the very idea of *the* leading building task became increasingly questionable. And perhaps this is as it should be. Given the shape of the modern world, does it still make sense to privilege one building task over all the others? Is there still and should there be an architectural type capable of establishing or reestablishing a communal world as the Greek temple on Heidegger's interpretation was able to do?

That for many centuries the church had that function is obvious. What allowed it to play that part? Let me return once more to the traditional understanding of the church as a place where a multitude joins in celebration of the sacrament. Thus joined, the members of the community leave both home and work behind. Ruskin had suggested that we are at leisure when in church and that just because it served leisure the church remained a fit task for the architect. But much of our leisure time we spend of course at home; talk of leisure fails to capture the communal significance of attending a service, and it fails to do so in a way that is quite analogous to the way talk of aesthetic pleasure fails to do justice to what I have called the ethical function of art. I would like to suggest the following analogy: just as the church presents itself as a figure on the ground of ordinary buildings, so the time of religious festivals—think of celebrating Easter or Christmas—presents itself as a figure on the ground of ordinary time. Such celebrations recall us to and interpret the significance of the limiting experiences of human life, the mysteries of death, birth, marriage, rebirth. Repeating some paradigmatic event, they recall us to what matters in life, re-present what matters. In this sense festivals cast a light on everyday experience. They illuminate it. The same, I have suggested, goes for works of architecture: they cast a light on and illuminate more ordinary buildings. In the case of the Christian church such illumination gains its special significance from a master narrative that is taken to be authoritative. That narrative invites an interpretation of the significance of every human life by referring it to the life of Christ. Life thus gains its measure as Christ's birth, death, and resurrection are granted paradigmatic significance. The church recalls human beings to that paradigm. What happens, however, when this text and the paradigm it has offered lose their authority for the whole society? What can we put in the place that with the death of God has become empty? But perhaps this is the wrong question. Should we not rather ask: does it still make sense to demand of architecture that it create works that help establish and interpret the world in such a way that human beings are once again gathered in what I have called, questionably no doubt, genuine community?

To say that the church has lost much of its former significance in the modern world is obviously not to deny that many churches continue to get built. But what function do they have in the life of the community as a whole? Churches today cater only to subcommunities; no longer do they have the power to establish the ethos of the entire community to which we belong. Even for most persons who consider themselves and indeed are genuinely religious, religion no longer has the power to illuminate the whole; it is in fact only a small part of their lives. This peripheral significance of the religious expresses itself in the peripheral placement of churches in the urban fabric. Church architecture as a whole has become peripheral in the twentieth century. There are of course some outstanding modern churches; Ronchamp usually gets first mention, although I would be quick to add Alvar Aalto's Imatra Church or Gottfried Böhm's church in Neviges. But what is their significance to the society to which they belong?

The disintegration of the old value system—and such disintegration is necessarily also a disintegration of what was once genuine community—finds expression in the proliferation of leading building tasks. Nikolaus Pevsner's *History of Building Types* can serve as an example.[8] Some building types are excluded, churches especially, for having been covered too well already; schools and dwellings are also left out. What then are the building types Pevsner covers? Here is his table of contents:

1. National monuments and monuments to genius
2. Government buildings from the late twelfth to the late seventeenth centuries
3. Government buildings from the eighteenth century: Houses of parliament
4. Government buildings from the eighteenth century: Ministries and public offices
5. Government buildings from the eighteenth century: Town halls and law courts
6. Theatres
7. Libraries
8. Museums
9. Hospitals
10. Prisons
11. Hotels
12. Exchanges and banks
13. Warehouses and office buildings
14. Railway stations
15. Market halls, conservatories, and exhibition buildings
16. Shops, stores and department stores
17. Factories

Is any one of these building types capable of assuming the role once played by the church? That is to say, does the type allow architecture to speak of human beings in a way that touches the whole of life and helps build a community?

4

In his *Verlust der Mitte* (the title given to the English translation, *Art in Crisis,* fails to capture the meaning of the German, which suggests that the crisis of modern art has its origin in a loss of society's spiritual center), Hans Sedlmayr asserts that, since the end of the eighteenth century, only six or seven artistic tasks have come to claim anything like the significance that once belonged to the church. Excluding most of the architectural types appearing on Pevsner's list, Sedlmayr mentions only "landscape garden, architectural monument, museum, theater, exhibition, factory."[9] We may quarrel with that list, wondering, for example, whether the house should not have been included—for a number of modern architects, most notably Frank Lloyd Wright, it would seem to have been *the* leading artistic task. But leaving such questions aside, at least for the time being, I would like to take a closer look at Sedlmayr's idea of the "leading artistic task," which, like Gropius, he takes to mean pretty much "leading architectural task."

Sedlmayr offers the following fourfold characterization: Artistic tasks may be called leading:

1. *because the form-giving fantasy likes to return especially to them;*
2. *because the attitude here gains its greatest security and often a clearly defined type evolves;*
3. *especially because from them emanates, if only in a limited realm, something like the power to form a style, because other tasks adjust and subordinate themselves to them;*
4. *because consciously or unconsciously they appear with a claim to occupy the place of the great sacred architecture of the past and to form a center of their own.*[10]

Here, too, sacred architecture provides the model for all architecture, which in turn presupposes that any adequate concept of dwelling has to make room for the dimension of the sacred. Having elided, or at least obscured, this dimension, modernity faces the task of reoccupying the place occupied for so many centuries by temple or church, the architectural representative of the community's spiritual center.

While we must grant Sedlmayr that modern architecture cannot appeal to a similar center, it is not at all clear that this calls for a reoccupation of the place once occupied by temple and church. Given all the decenterings that have shaped modern life, we arguably might better abandon the idea of leading artistic tasks, especially the idea of leading architectural tasks, freighted as this idea is with expectations connected with the traditional understanding of the church as the leading architectural type.

Sedlmayr presupposes that our dwelling requires a spiritual center; also that such a center cannot be freely laid down but must be experienced as in some sense given, as in this sense transcending the individual's freedom; also that such a center must join a community. Something of the sort does indeed seem necessary: any center that we know to derive its authority only from our own free will has to strike us as arbitrary. Meanings must be discovered; they cannot be willed without self-deception. If perhaps not a center, at least some authority must be recognized, if there is to be responsible decision—this is the point of Heidegger's talk of divinities, even if his words raise barriers to easy appropriation. Without such authority it is difficult to see why one should decide on one course of action rather than another; without something like a higher measure we become the plaything of what Plato calls "our passionate and fitful temper."[11] We all need to cast ahead of ourselves shared dreams or thoughts of an ideal existence, measure our present dwelling by some ideal dwelling, and these projections must seem arbitrary unless experienced as responding to what our only obscurely glimpsed essence demands. The distinction between building and architecture answers to the need for such projections.

As I have described it, the very point of architecture is to let us take leave from the everyday, but only to return us to it, now with eyes more open and a greater awareness of what matters. What Heidegger says of the Greek temple, that it lets the god be present, has its analogue in the presence of God in every church, or in the presence of shared values in civic monuments—think of the Capitol (fig. 105), of the Washington, Jefferson, and Lincoln memorials, or of Civil War monuments (see fig 113). Architecture has an ethical function in that it calls us out of the everyday, recalls us to the values presiding over our lives as members of a society; it beckons us toward a better life, a bit closer to the ideal. One task of architecture is to preserve at least a piece of utopia, and inevitably such a piece leaves and should leave a sting, awaken utopian longings, fill us with dreams of another and better world.

105 | Capitol, Washington, D.C. Photo by author.

Grave and Monument

20

1

Insistence on the publicness of architecture has to collide with that privatization of art we have come to take pretty much for granted. Loos's already-cited distinction between the work of art, which satisfies no need and is "a private concern of the artist," and the house, which does and is responsible to everyone, speaks to that collision. "The work of art wants to tear human beings out of their comfortable adjustment to the world. The house serves to make us comfortable. The work of art is revolutionary. The house conservative. The work of art points out to humanity new paths and thinks of the future. The house thinks of the present."[1] Although the private concern of the artist and responsible to no one, the work of art is said to look forward to a transformed humanity, thus acquiring a public significance after all. The artist on this view is a prophet without authority. Untimely in Nietzsche's sense, because it challenges its time, the modern work of art has to appear irresponsible and ambiguous because it would serve a future whose contours remain uncertain.

What role then does Loos leave to an architecture that insists on being more than just building? His paradigm is a simple grave: "When we find in the forest a mound, six feet long and three feet wide, raised by a shovel to form a pyramid, we turn serious and something in us says: here someone lies buried. *That is architecture*."[2] Hardly distinguished as an aesthetic object, this modest mound may seem to lack what we would ordinarily consider the aesthetic interest to qualify it as a work of art, that is, as a work of architecture. But more important to Loos is its ethical function: the confrontation with death prevents us from going on with the usual business of life and carries us to another place, a place that lies, usually well submerged, within the self.

"Ethical function" is given here primarily a private significance. Loos's grave is not what we would usually consider an architectural monument; it does not serve to honor some illustrious personage. As if to remind us that death levels the hierarchies and distinctions that in the world separate individuals, the person beneath Loos's modest forest mound is left unnamed. What matters is not who lies buried, but that a human being lies buried here. The grave gestures thus toward the solidarity of mortals, even as it shatters such solidarity by facing each individual with his or her own mortality, with the fact that, as Heidegger insisted, in the most fundamental sense no human being can die for another. Bringing us home to our selves, Loos's forest grave at the same time lets us feel homeless in the everyday with all its familiar cares and concerns, bids us attend to the essential: our one death-bound life. Genuine art, as Loos understands it, recalls us to what Heidegger calls authenticity: it invites us to take leave from what we usually call reality, but only to free us and to return us to our true selves.

2

Loos's forest grave hardly deserves to be called a work of architecture: graves become architecture only when re-presented by some structure. Such public re-presentation, Loos suggests, remains as the only legitimate architectural task: "Only a very small part of architecture belongs to art: the sepulchre and the monument. Everything else, everything that serves a purpose, it to be excluded from the realm of art."[3] As so often, Loos is speaking in hyperboles. Still, the history of architecture does argue for a profound link between architecture and death. For many of us the history of architecture begins thus with the pyramids, with monumental tombs. And when we look to prehistory, the history of architecture almost reduces to a history of tombs. Howard Colvin can thus start his *Architecture and the After-Life* with the observation: "Architecture in western Europe begins with tombs. The earliest surviving structures that we can recognize as architecture were funerary monuments."[4] Thousands of neolithic tombs survive, enormous stones raised, as Jacob raised the stone that had served him for a pillow, into a vertical position and covered with horizontal slabs, sheltering the dead, sheltering also the living from the dead—and one function of funerary architecture would appear to have been from the very beginning the need to help mark the boundary separating the realm of the living from the realm of the dead, to ensure that the dead would confer blessing rather than curse on the living. With the distinction between the living and the dead, Hegel suggests, "the spiritual begins to separate itself from what lacks spirit. The concrete, individual spirit here begins to assert itself," as the dead are protected from the terror of time. (It thus seems only fitting to Hegel that Herodotus thought that the builders of the pyramids were the first ones to believe in the soul's immortality.)[5]

The effort required to move, say, stones of more than forty tons demonstrates that the building of such monumental tombs was communal work.[6] No doubt, conspicuous monuments to the dead have always been thought to serve not only the needs of the dead—"with the nomadic chieftain, horses, servants, even wives were all entombed to serve his needs on the eternal steppes"[7]—but much more those of the living, especially those in power. Such monuments provided them with occasions to represent their dominion over a particular region, to legitimate such dominion by honoring its founding heroes, to help preserve it by promising that what the past had established would not fall victim to the ravages of time.[8] Grave monuments also serve to call the community to the powers presiding over it, to its divinities. Thus "when at Newgrange we find that the entrance is so arranged that at the winter solstice the rising sun shines through a specially formed aperture, down to the entrance passage and into the burial chamber at the heart of the mound, it is clear that we are looking at more than just a burial place"[9] (see fig 71). An effort is made to open the dark realm of death to the light of the life-renewing, ever-returning sun. The monument thus expresses a conviction that the darkness of death will not have the last word, that life will triumph over death.

Proper burial was thought necessary to allow the dead to journey to whatever life awaited them in and beyond the tomb. As Eliade observes, like the rites following birth or like rites of marriage, rites of death in primitive societies were rites of passage, special, to be sure, in that the survivors could at best preside over part of the deceased person's journey, who had to undergo further ordeals until he could take his proper place in the realm of the dead.[10] But proper burial was not only a last service the living owed the dead; it was also thought necessary to prevent the dead from hurting the living. The Romans thus thought that "if burial was denied, the ghost of the dead would roam the earth in perpetual distress, and might do untold harm to the living. Even if safely conducted to the nether world, it could still exercise an influence over the living that might just as likely be malevolent as benevolent. It was, therefore, imperative to treat the dead with due respect and, above all, to give them proper burial."[11] Today we no longer believe in ghosts who, distressed by our neglect, might harm us. In keeping with our efforts to push death and the dead out of our lives, our cities allow the dead only a peripheral importance. What Colvin says of Great Britain also holds of this country: the triumph of the cemetery in its nineteenth-century form "has been relatively short-lived. Death is no longer an event to be celebrated by major ceremonial, the grave no longer a place to be marked by substantial architectural or sculptural monuments. Indeed many nineteenth-century British cemeteries lie neglected, vandalised and overgrown. Only the village churchyard can still, in sympathetic hands, retain something of a romantic melancholy so perfectly captured by Gray's *Elegy*."[12] In the Catholic south, Colvin notes, things have remained different. On the little island of Vieques off Puerto Rico the cemetery thus remains the most striking communal monument (fig. 106).

What if any price do we moderns pay for our neglect of the dead? Our own life points to the answer: our past has made us the persons we now are. To deny a part of our past inevitably means to deny part of ourselves. And the past that we have to affirm to affirm ourselves does not begin with our birth; it includes our parents, our ancestors, the society or societies that helped form us. We may, to be sure, insist that this past is, just like our biological makeup, a given that we must appropriate and shape as a sculptor kneads clay into an aesthetic whole. But as and indeed much more than the properties of clay limit the sculptor's possibilities, our attempts to shape our lives are limited by the past, for while the sculptor is separate from his or her material, we are what we have become. To deny one's past is to trade a concrete for an abstract self. The authority of the past is anchored in our own being. To be sure, just as our past does not determine who we are to be, it does not furnish us with measures beyond challenge. The past speaks with many voices, presents us with heroes and villains, with models that invite repetition and warning examples of what should never happen again. Past actions should be repeated only when found worthy of repetition, and such a judgment of worth requires an ideal that cannot simply be read off the past but necessitates an interpretation of the past. This does not deny that our past circumscribes even our future possibilities. Rupture with the past means inevitably also a

Cemetery, Vieques, Puerto Rico. Photo by author.

rupture within the self, a rupture that will visit the individual in much the same way as ghosts of the badly buried were supposed to have visited the living.

What holds for the individual also holds for the community, more especially for the city, as Robert Jan van Pelt shows with his discussion of ancient Athens as an urban paradigm. "The citizens' present, future and past acts made up the city's public realm. This translated into a threefold public time, which comprised the time of the living, the time of the city and the time of the dead." The time of the dead was present to the living in the necropolis, usually located just outside the city proper. In ancient Athens it was thus located "in front of the western and most important entrance to the city."[13] Similarly, "when one approached a Roman city one of the first things one noticed was the tombs of its citizens."[14]

With the rise of Christian Europe burial increasingly took place in or near the church.[15] Only in the wake of the Reformation did burial gradually return to cemeteries outside the city proper: "At Geneva one of the first acts of the newly established Protestant republic in 1536 was to close all the parochial cemeteries within its walls and to convert the extensive graveyard of a plague hospital on the south-western outskirts into a general cemetery for the city."[16] But only the Enlightenment, mostly for reasons of health, put an end to burial in churches. In 1804 Napoleon thus required every city "to establish a cemetery at a distance of at least 35–40 metres from its boundaries."[17] For the British Isles comparable legislation was passed only half a century later. "It was a characteristic feature of the new European cemeteries that they owed their existence to secular rather than to ecclesiastical initiative and were under the control of municipalities or boards rather than of the local clergy. Many of them catered for religious denominations of all kinds and the officiating clergy came and went with the undertakers."[18] As burial becomes less of a communal, more of a familial, and finally a private affair that leaves the bereaved pretty much alone, having to bury his or her grief within him- or herself, the grave monument loses much of its significance. How many of us still live close enough to the graves of our parents or ancestors to take care of their graves, sink a trowel into the earth that now holds them, plant different flowers as the seasons change, remembering them and our own past as we tend their graves, drawing strength from the dead? Most cemeteries today are ill kept and many urban cemeteries have acquired reputations as dangerous places, not really recommended for commemorative meditation.

What have we lost? What strength can we draw from the dead? In what sense does a healthy urban fabric need to give room to the dead? Van Pelt discusses the Athenian necropolis as "the moral and the pragmatic foundation of the public realm."[19] Here the citizen is reminded not just of his forebears but of the generations who have gone before him, of the heroes who worked and passed laws, fought and died to make possible the city to which he owes himself, a city he must love if he is to love himself. Thus Pericles admonished those gathered to bury the dead of the first year of the Peloponnesian War to draw strength from these deaths:

For this offering of their lives made in common by them all they each of them individually received that renown that never grows old, and for a sepulchre, not so much that in which their bones have been deposited, but that noblest of shrines in which their glory is laid up to be eternally remembered upon every occasion on which deed or story fall for its commemoration. For heroes have the whole earth for their tomb; and in lands far from their own, where the column with its epitaph declares it, there is enshrined in every breast a record unwritten with no table to preserve it, except that of the heart. These take as your model, and judging happiness to be the fruit of freedom and freedom of valour, never decline the dangers of war.[20]

With its epitaph, the column honoring the dead invites the living not only to remember the fallen hero but to confront the ever-present possibility of their own death, attending in the face of that possibility to who they are and measuring what gives significance to their lives by what gave significance to the fallen hero's life; not just to remember him but to remember him as an example, to repeat his willingness to subordinate his own death-bound life to the life of the city. Ready to die, the hero overcomes his natural selfishness and thus triumphs over death.

Socrates teaches essentially the same lesson in the *Crito*, in which he describes the personified laws of Athens admonishing him to affirm himself as just a part of the far more significant ongoing order of the city. Since the laws allowed his parents to marry and watched over his rearing and education, how can Socrates deny that he is their child and slave, as his parents were before him? The country is said to be worthier and more sacred than parents and ancestors. Justice thus commands him to submit to the unjust judgment of his fellow Athenians.[21] Love of country is shown to be inseparable from the rightly understood love of self. Only such love can found the citizens' morality.

Just as the history of architecture is for the most part a history of buildings that owed their existence to an elite, so histories of funerary architecture "have been concerned with the privileged dead: for only the rich and the powerful could normally afford to be buried in tombs that were architectural monuments,"[22] taking effective steps that the name of the deceased and his achievements would not be forgotten. But if personal pride—the pride of someone in the position to take steps to ensure that after his death his name would not be forgotten or the pride of those who by glorifying the deceased glorified themselves—no doubt helped build countless funerary monuments, it should not let us forget the power of the old belief that by honoring the dead with proper rites and a monument the living help ensure that the dead will prove a source of blessing. Every grave bears witness not only to human mortality but also to the historicity of life. The care that tends the grave builds tradition and thus community. "Just as agriculture fixes nomadic wandering by tieing it to firmly established property, so it is graves, monuments, and service to the dead that first unite human beings, and provide even those who otherwise have no abode, no definite property, with a place where they come together, with holy places that they defend and refuse to surrender."[23] Especially the care that preserves a hero's memory preserves the community and shapes its presiding values.

Sophocles thus describes how the sacred hidden tomb of the blind exile Oedipus became a source of blessing for Attica.[24] Proud Oedipus may seem an unlikely hero and it seems only fitting that the site of his death should not have been honored with a public monument: why should a community thus honor an exile who, though he solved the sphinx's riddle, stumbled into transgression, short-tempered though thinking himself wise? Unable to escape the dark oracle, unable to master a dire fate, unwittingly Oedipus killed his father, married his mother, and, once forced to recognize his blindness, blinded himself; he wandered through Greece, only to meet after a violent life with a uniquely gentle death in the grove of the Erinyes, the dread daughters of earth and darkness, appearing now, however, as the beneficent, peace-granting Eumenides ("the gracious ones"). By allowing only one person—not faithful Antigone but Theseus, the king of Athens—to witness this mysterious end, Sophocles underscores the political significance of this private death. Oedipus charges Theseus with guarding its secret, charges him also with passing it on to his successors so that its mystery would be preserved and thus, as the oracle had foretold, bless Athens:

Son of Aegeus, I will unfold that which shall be a treasure for this thy city, such as age can never mar. Anon, unaided, and with no hand to guide me, I will show the way to the place where I must die. But that place reveal thou never unto mortal man,—tell not where it is hidden, nor in what region it lies; that so it may ever make for thee a defence, better than many shields, better than the succouring spears of neighbours.

But, for mysteries that speech may not profane, thou shalt mark them for thyself, when thou comest to that place alone: since neither to any of these people can I utter them, nor to mine children, dear though they are. No, guard them thou alone; and when thou art coming to the end of life, disclose them to thy heir alone; let him teach his heir, and so thenceforth.[25]

How are we to understand the blessing emanating from this exile's invisible grave, emanating still from Sophocles' tragedy? What communal ethos is established by preserving the mystery of this death? Earlier I spoke of death as the shipwreck of pride. To preserve the mystery of Oedipus's death means to fortify oneself against undue pride, and was it not pride that was to lead to the downfall of Athens? "Full many States lightly enter on offence, e'en though their neighbour lives aright. For the gods are slow, though they are sure, in visitation, when men scorn godliness, and turn to frenzy."[26] We think of Alcibiades. Pride scorns godliness and poses the deepest threat to the social fabric. Godliness cannot mean following the dictates of the gods, for as Oedipus learned, the gods do not tell humans clearly what they are to do. As Heraclitus says, "The lord whose oracle is in Delphi neither speaks out nor conceals, but gives a sign."[27] A later commentator explains, "Never thus does divine knowledge reach human beings as a distinct word, but always only as a pointing; never therefore does it give him clear knowledge, but it only releases premonition, insecurity, fear, shuddering—dread."[28] Every human being stands between the never clear messages of the divine and common sense. For this reason every human being should remain open to the uncertain call of the divine, even if obedience to that call forces her to challenge her community; but, as the example of Socrates shows, no human being can be so confident of being in the right as to turn in pride against his community. To preserve the mystery of the death of Oedipus means thus also to preserve the piety that preserves cities and nations.

It also means to repeat a humanity that extended hospitality to the stranger, the human being, a humanity that Oedipus's native Thebes, that his brother-in-law and sons had refused him, a humanity Athens itself betrayed in the Peloponnesian War, especially when, insisting that might makes right, it mercilessly massacred the unfortunate Melians. Finally, this preservation means to guard the mysterious boundary separating the realm of the living from the realm of the dead and thus to protect the living from the dead so that they may go on living. Thus the chorus concludes the play by exhorting the living to cease lamentation.

There is a sense in which the invisible tomb of Oedipus and Theseus's guardian-ship of its secret, both repeated and celebrated by Sophocles, provide us with an understanding of the ethical function of every tomb and funerary rite. They all call us beyond pride, call on us also to acknowledge the inscrutability of the divine and warn us not to be too confident in how we have interpreted its call; they warn us especially not to obscure that call by putting in its place some human artifact. Thus they warn against idolatry, though, as we shall see, by their very nature monuments threaten to become golden calves.

Calling us beyond pride, commemoration of the dead strengthens an ethos that bids us take our place in the ongoing realm of the living. Just as funerary monuments mark the threshold that separates the realm of the living and the realm of the dead, allowing the living to keep their distance from the dead sufficiently to discover in them a source of strength, so funeral rites mark the threshold that separates the time of the living from the time of the dead, marking the threshold in such a way as to bound it, limiting the time allotted to mourning to return the grieving to life. And so Theseus sends Antigone and Ismene back to ancient Thebes; and Pericles concludes his funeral oration with the words, "And now that you have brought to a close your lamentations for your relatives, you may depart."[29] Every gravestone, every tomb, every monument keeps present the mystery of death that is inseparable from life. As boundary markers, they confer blessings on us precisely when we respect that boundary.

4

Christianity offered a radically new interpretation of the old belief that the dead have the power to bestow blessings on the living. Christ's death on the cross, shameful to the unbelieving pagan, for the faithful carried the promise of bodily resurrection, signified the victory of eternal life over death. Every church is a monument to the dead Christ (fig. 107). As such it is also a monument to the victory of life over death, a victory that finds architectural expression in choir arches built in the image of Roman triumphal arches. This triumph is purchased by Christ's sacrifice: cross after cross keeps present the blessing of his death-defying death.

With its belief in the resurrection of the body, Christianity brought a changed understanding of the significance of burial and tomb. The practice of cremation, common in antiquity, was abandoned.[30] While the Greeks and Romans thought the bodies of the dead, however much in need of proper burial, a source of pollution, Christians found in the bodies of martyrs a source of spiritual strength. "To possess the body of a saint was to have a monopoly of his good offices in this world and the next; to possess even a fragment of his mortal remains was to acquire a share in his spiritual capital. In theory, Christians worshipped only one God (triune though he might be), but in practice martyred saints

Hans Leinberger, crucifix, St. Martin, Landshut.

107 | Photo by author.

provided a substitute for the innumerable local divinities of Antiquity."[31] Having themselves conquered death, everything associated with them, but especially the presence of their mortal remains, served to sanctify a place. In such sacred places it was good to be buried. From them flowed blessings that served human dwelling by comforting sinners fearful of the end.

Along with such fears and hopes went a changed attitude toward the tomb. To be sure, pride—the pride of a wealthy individual or family, of a monastery or a city, of a bishop or a king—continued to build many of the most splendid sepulchres. As always, in glorifying the deceased the living represented and celebrated themselves and their power. But while very much at work, such all-too-worldly pride was too much an expression of vanity to be readily accepted—what was supposed to matter to the Christian was, after all, not so much to be remembered on this earth by future generations but to live forever with God. Fortunately for art and architecture, pride mingled readily with faith in the efficacy of prayers and masses to shorten the poor soul's progress through purgatory; thus while "the pagan tomb was designed to keep alive a man's memory on earth, the purpose of the Christian one was to secure him a place in the queue for Heaven on the Day of Judgment. For this the prayers of the faithful and, above all, proximity to the body or the relics of a saint were important."[32] But such prayers and masses also served the living by helping to confirm their membership in the ongoing community of the faithful, a community over which death was thought to have no power.

I touched on this meaning of the church as a tomb of saints in my earlier discussion of Johann Michael Fischer's Augustinian priory church at Diessen (see fig. 100).[33] What can such architecture still mean to us? To be sure, light and dark, verticals and horizontals, ellipses and circles continue to speak, but what does such a church still have to tell us? Already the enlightened contemporaries of the builders of Diessen were no longer able to understand themselves as members of the City of God and thus to find their lives' measure and at the same time banish the terror of death. Nor did the world-denying lives of saints seem exemplary. Far more relevant seemed the virtuous heroes of democratic Athens and republican Rome, heroes very much of this world. Churches like Diessen belong to a past that lies behind us; remembered mostly by historians, its saints no longer receive the pious care that alone lets the living enjoy the blessings of the dead. Gone is the world that built this church and that it helped build, destroyed by a reason that replaced the community of faith with its own universal community; that banished, along with the promise of heaven, the fear of purgatory and hell; that could find only superstition in the cult of saints and ridiculed burial practices that counted on the power of their intercession and found edification in the exhibition of their jewel-encrusted bones.

The very triumph over death celebrated by Christian architecture in the image of the cross had to seem illusory to the Enlightenment. Schopenhauer's critique of Gothic architecture for pretending that the vertical could triumph over the horizontal, a pretense supported by and supporting in turn faith in what Schopenhauer considered the self-contradictory idea of eternal life, applies equally to a church like Diessen. Christian verticality is charged with refusing to take seriously enough human mortality. Here lies one key to the Enlightenment's return to classical architecture, which promised an answer to the pretense of Christian architecture, to its false verticality. The Greek temple's balancing of vertical and horizontal, of load and support, seemed to call on human beings to find meaning not in some impossible beyond but here on earth, obedient only to nature and to reason. Much more is thus at stake in the shift from late Baroque to neo-classicism than just a change of taste: at issue is the opposition between an ethos that seeks meaning beyond and another that seeks it within this world.

The disintegration of the church paradigm is a precondition of the passion with which the leading architects of the Enlightenment embraced the monument. Colvin is right to link such passion to the Enlightenment's neo-classical ideals. Revolting against what they experienced as the capricious architecture of the Rococo, architects rediscovered the beauties of perennial Platonism and sought relief in the stern, timeless beauty of elementary geometric forms. The fact that "the best-known mausolea of Antiquity were pyramidal (Caius Cestius) or cylindrical (Caecilia Metella) or in the form of a small rectangular temple or a circular tempietto"[34] offered further legitimacy. The theorists of neo-classicism left no doubt about the ethical significance of their choice of style. Rococo capriciousness was associated with moral lassitude and a lack of honesty. The ancients were to help the moderns fulfill the promise of fifth-century Athens and republican Rome.

Loss of faith in an afterlife did not put an end to thoughts of a good death, such as the heroic sacrifice of one's life for what is felt to be more important, especially one's country. Quite the opposite: modernity has continued to hold on to the conviction that only what is worth dying for has the power to make life worth living, to the thought that only what transcends the individual's death-bound life can give it meaning. But human beings transcend themselves, transcend their mortality, above all in their reason, which opens up the infinite realm of the spirit, and with it thoughts of a progress toward a humanity no longer burdened by superstition and by the chains that for so long have enslaved it. Such secular self-transcendence, too, is reconfirmed by martyrs, heroes whose self-sacrifice testifies to the selflessness of which human beings are capable even without the false promise of divine rewards. The soldier's death especially gained a new ethical significance. The dead of Thermopylae and Marathon are among the paradigmatic martyrs the Enlightenment held up for emulation. Their death gains significance from the worthiness of the way of life they defended, which the Enlightenment understood as a figure of what it hoped for itself: a rebirth of democratic Athens in the modern age. As the boundary of life, death continues to offer the living ciphers of a personal self-transcendence that alone can justify our existence. Threatening to undercut all meanings, death yet hints at meanings strong enough to meet its annihilating challenge. The architecture of death helps keep such ciphers present among the living.

In how they represented death in the built environment, too, the ancients were thought to have pointed the way for the moderns. In good Enlightenment fashion Laurenz Hirschfeld thus described how "all the towns, all the public places, even the main streets of Greece, were crowded with superb monuments erected to do honour to merit. . . . Tombs were not hidden like ours, but exposed along the main roads to the view of passers by. Numerous places of public promenade were embellished with statues of the wisest and most valiant citizens. A number of buildings were even erected with the sole purpose of housing such honourable monuments."[35] Hirschfeld was preaching to the converted. The monument could claim to best serve the ethical function of architecture for a humanity come of age.

Consider the monuments in Washington. If the United States has something like a national cathedral, is it not these monuments, placed on the Mall as on a gigantic town green, which represent the democratic ethos of the country in the image of Egypt, Athens, and Rome? Of these the Washington Monument is most difficult to justify. Confidently Robert Mills's enormous obelisk establishes a new center, as such a fitting tribute to "the father of his country," but its austere simplicity only asserts; it does not attempt to interpret the significance of the newly established order. This task is left to the Jefferson and Lincoln Memorials, which quite appropriately invoke the heritage of Rome and Athens. Maya Lin's Vietnam Memorial (fig. 108) adds a crypt to this church, re-presenting it in a way that questions all national monuments, questions also the later addition of a flagpole and Frederick Hart's sculptural group of *Three Fighting Men,* which was intended to soften that challenge. The rules-and-information package that was sent to all who competed in the design competition specified that the monument should "honor the service and memory of the war's dead, its missing, and its veterans—not the war itself. This monument should be conciliatory, transcending the tragedy of war."[36] But how could honoring those who fought and died in this war transcend its tragedy? By honoring sacrifice no matter how questionable the cause? With some justice Charles Krauthammer suggested that the monument gave neither context nor meaning to those who had suffered and died in Vietnam, while another critic, Tom Carhart, himself a Vietnam veteran, called it "a black gash of sorrow."[37] And so

108 | Maya Lin, Vietnam Memorial, Washington, D.C. Photo by author.

it is. In Vincent Scully's words, Maya Lin was "able to find a visual equivalent of the sense of sorrow, the fundamental sorrow which is the basic fact of war."[38] By preserving such sorrow, the Vietnam Memorial calls the living to a community beyond the national and ideological divisions that monuments too often honor.

5

I have likened the monuments on Washington's Mall to a cathedral. The simile is not at all arbitrary: the Enlightenment's transformation of Christian churches into monuments has symptomatic significance. Consider above all Quatremère de Quincy's transformation of Soufflot's Ste.-Geneviève, begun only some thirty years after Diessen in an already classicizing Baroque style, into the Panthéon, a hall of fame commemorating the nation's "grands hommes," in 1791. Not only were all Christian symbols removed, but de Quincy also "did away with the two towers . . . at the east end designed by Soufflot, and had the windows in the wall built up in order that all the light might come from above in the true manner of the antique," decisions that strengthened the contrast of building and sky, reduced what remained of Baroque verticality, lightness, and movement in Soufflot's design, and bound the building more firmly to the earth—all thought to make the building more "antique."[39] This monument presents itself quite literally as a secularized Christian church, in which culture replaces God, its heroes Christian saints.

The idea for such a national hall of fame had its most obvious precursors in socially advanced England, first of all in Westminster Abbey, where England honored not only her political leaders but also her artists—its poet's corner dates back to the 1730s—and in St. Paul's, which honors her military heroes. In both the hall of fame by now has gotten much the better of the church. We should also not forget William Kent's Temple of British Worthies in the park at Stowe (1733), where "princes and statesmen stand side by side with scientists [Bacon, Newton], the philosopher [Locke], the architect [Inigo Jones] and the poets [Shakespeare, Milton, and Pope, the last still alive at the time], and on the same level"[40]—now, however, not in a church but in a landscape setting. An essentially religious aura still surrounds all such monuments, which seeks to celebrate the time-transcending greatness of the human spirit as a source of continuing meaning. Monuments recall us to the values that have presided over our community by keeping alive the memory of those who were willing to subordinate their personal welfare and even survival to these values. Remembering them, we reaffirm our membership in our community; this remembrance becomes at the same time the resolve to ensure that community will endure.

It was the Parisian Panthéon that King Ludwig of Bavaria sought to answer with his Walhalla (fig. 109), which "as the greatest temple of its kind erected since the ancient world, . . . has some claim to be regarded as the climax of the whole Neo-classical movement."[41] It was in 1807, in French-occupied Berlin, a year after he had visited Paris, where work was just beginning on the most ambitious ensemble of monuments the world had yet seen—the trio of the Madeleine, the Colonne Vendôme, and the Arc de Triomphe, all glorifying the new Caesar and his victorious armies—that Ludwig conceived of this "Pantheon of Germans," an edifying temple that would help build a sense of national identity. But it was only following Napoleon's defeat at Leipzig that Ludwig announced a competition for his Walhalla and buildings intended to transform Munich into a worthy royal capital.

Although easily convinced to call his German hall of fame not Pantheon but Walhalla, Ludwig resisted those who wondered whether German heroes would best be honored with a Greek temple. For instance, the king's favorite painter, Peter von Cornelius, asked pointedly: "Are we not being inconsistent when we try to glorify our nation by the erection of a great building whilst ignoring the great and splendidly original German style of architecture?"[42] Why should a building rising above the Danube, so that, in the king's own words, "the German might depart from it more German and better than when he arrived,"[43] be built in the image of the Parthenon? Ludwig was not to be shaken in his conviction, shared by his architect Leo von Klenze, who in 1817 wrote then–Crown Prince Ludwig: "Just as Palladio became great and immortal through an inspired adaptation of Roman architecture to the exigencies of his own time and country, I shall attempt to do likewise with the works of the Greeks; that is the only way to be anything more than a pale plagiarist."[44] By then it had become a commonplace that the Greeks had carried architecture to a perfection that we moderns could only hope to emulate, and it hardly could have surprised the educated that Ludwig should have insisted on a repetition of the Greek style, convinced that it was better to have a "worthy imitation of all that was great in antiquity, than a less beautiful original creation."[45] But the extraordinary hold of Greece, and more especially Greek architecture, on the Enlightenment has to be placed also in the context of the attempt to put something more in keeping with the demand of reason and nature in place of the inherited old order, which was now associated with tyranny and superstition. The adoption of a classical vocabulary is thus more than the arbitrary choice of a past paradigm. It has its ground in what is felt to be essential and thus has a critical function.

In this respect there is a certain similarity between the American and the German situation, although just as it is easier to defend the American adoption of a classical vocabulary—Jeffersonian classicism and the principles stated in the Declaration of Independence belong together—so that vocabulary blended much more readily into the American architectural vernacular. If Americans could with some justice understand themselves in the image of democratic Athenians and republican Romans, in Germany democracy and republican government remained a dream, a dream that for some of the best became also a dream of America.

Certainly Germany, too, had experienced if not a revolution, then a profound break with its past and had fought its own war of liberation. Napoleon had put an end to the moribund old Germany when he abolished what had become a caricature of the Holy Roman Empire, razing what by then was a political ruin, unwittingly doing more to establish German nationalism than any German could have done. But hopes for a democratic Germany were dashed by the Congress of Vienna, which left the nationalism awakened by the struggle against Napoleon in search of its own identity. No hero had emerged worthy of being celebrated with a monument as "the father of his country." Prussia, to be sure, could point back to Frederick the Great, and already in 1796 the Berlin Academy of Fine Arts did indeed announce a competition to honor the great king with a monument— Friedrich Gilly's extraordinary, if unsuccessful, design was to inspire architects for many

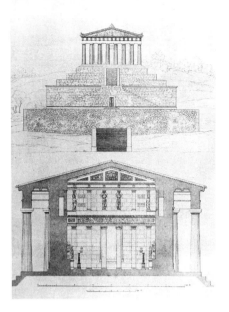

years to come—but this was before Napoleon's entrance into Berlin only a few years later. More important, Frederick the Great at that time hardly was a hero to all Germans. Such heroes did appear when following the Franco-Prussian War Bismarck founded a new Germany and had the Prussian king Wilhelm crowned emperor. The hundredth birthday of this "father of the Fatherland" led to a veritable "monument boom,"[46] which honored both emperor and Iron Chancellor with mostly heavy and heavy-handed monuments, built in a groping medievalizing, archaic style that celebrated the presumably self-legitimating power of the Second Empire. But in 1807 Ludwig could only scan the German past, looking not for one hero but for heroes worthy of inclusion in his Greek Walhalla, and he was thinking more of thinkers and poets, composers and painters than of military leaders or statesmen: if Germany was to recover Greek glory following its liberation from Napoleon, celebrated in the Walhalla's pediments as a repetition of the defeat of Augustus's legions in the Teutoburger Wald, such recovery was thought of primarily in cultural, not in political or military, terms. As if to amend for this all-too-humanistic monument, Ludwig decided to celebrate the Wars of Liberation against Napoleon with a second and now unambiguously martial and heroic monument, the Befreiungshalle in Kelheim (1842–1863; fig. 110). A much more original adaptation of the classical vocabulary than the Walhalla, what renders it problematic, and problematic in an exemplary fashion, is hinted at by Watkin and Mellinghoff's description: "The building became a sculptural object, proud and bare like a petrified ancient tumulus monument, uncluttered with windows. Its naked cylindrical volume is dominated by a

Grave and Monument

ring of eighteen great buttresses on which stand female figures, twenty feet high, representing the German provinces, carved by Johann Halbig. Above them is a continuous Doric colonnade of fifty-four marble columns."[47] The history of neo-classicism is shadowed by a petrified, sublime classicism that seeks to banish the terror of death with naked monuments, which do not so much signify immortality as substitute for it.

By its very essence, the sublime represents an assault on human dwelling. It is not at all surprising that, appropriating Klenze's appropriation of the Greek for their own ends, Hitler and his architects should have chosen a sublime and austerely classical vocabulary: "That a movement which in the political sphere represents the strongest reaction to all the dark aspects of German individualism and particularism, German 'formlessness' and German negation of the community, in the artistic sphere too should choose a formal language determined by its character of discipline and rule, adherence to norms, simple purposiveness, and objective clarity is founded in a more profound spiritual necessity."[48] Once again German architects were to achieve a more truly German architecture by turning their back on what was strongest in their own architectural tradition. This classicism, too, was not supposed to be a slavish copying of the Greek paradigm. And it did indeed live up to this demand, moving the Greek paradigm in the direction of a sublimely rigid, archaic architecture of death, a translation quite in keeping with Hitler's promise to liberate the individual from the burden of his or her individuality, which means also from the fear of death, as it is in keeping generally with the appeal of totalitarianism.

6

It should perhaps be expected that as reason triumphed over the old faith, death, its terror no longer checked by hope for eternal life, should have come to preoccupy the living as never before. Just when the Cartesian promise that reason would render human beings the masters and possessors of nature proved to have been much more than one philosopher's idle boast, death asserted itself ever more insistently as the one power reason could not master, a *mysterium tremendum et fascinans* that casts its dark but also seductive shadow over the optimistic beginning of the modern world. The central importance given to funerary architecture thus helps define the artistic culture of the Enlightenment. So Colvin observes, "For the first time in European history funerary art and architecture ceased to be concerned exclusively with funerary occasions and infiltrated both the stage and the garden."[49] More sweepingly Sedlmayr claims that the monument came to draw all building tasks into its orbit: "Most welcome are those whose form is most readily assimilated to that of the monument, tasks, therefore, where the window can be dispensed with or reduced to a minimum. Thus museums and libraries were then planned in lapidary-simple cubic form, which receive their light, quite impractically, only from above, and the prison with its deeply moving atmosphere of a timelessness becomes a favorite theme (*Fidelio!*). This triad, monument—prison—museum, illustrates the character of the time like nothing else."[50] Even houses and churches came to be conceived in the image of monuments.

Representative of this turn to the monument is Boullée, who "gave up his career as a government architect in order to devote himself to writing and to drawing visionary schemes for vast public buildings, many of which were funerary monuments and necropolises for which no commission was ever likely to be forthcoming." Colvin gives a Loosian reason for such preoccupation: no architectural task is as likely to allow the architect to avoid the compromise that considerations of economy and utility usually make necessary as the monument.[51] This helps explain why, more perhaps than the history of any other building type, the history of the monument has to make room for never-executed, utopian designs, from designs by Ledoux, Boullée, and Gilly down to the monuments Wilhelm Kreis designed for Hitler. But we must keep in mind that more important than concerns to protect the purity of their art were the designers' dreams of a sacred architecture beyond the church, a sacred architecture for the modern age. The megalomaniacal, inhuman scale of so many of these designs—their sublime, time-defying, archaic, or "Egyptian" quality— answers to modern individualism and its dread of death, which is always also a dread of individual life, answers the dread of individual dying by glorifying death in the service of some abstract collective, be it humanity or the nation, that dwarfs the individual with its importance.

An often-cited example of the architectural sublime is Boullée's design for a monument to Newton (ca. 1785), the paradigmatic modern genius, who was to be honored with an immense globe, its interior a representation of the starry sky—a revision of the Christian understanding of the cathedral as a representation of the cosmos (figs. 111 and 112). Pevsner also points out that "the perfection of the sphere is the most complete contrast to the arbitrariness and flippancy of the Rococo, just as the enormous scale is an answer to the *petitesse* of the Rococo. These are the answers of a Classicist, but the starry sky, the awesomeness of the night are the answer of a Romantic, and the Boullée-Ledoux generation was in fact both, radically Classical and radically Romantic,"[52] which is just to say that neo-classicism was a profoundly romantic classicism, a classicism marked by the tension between finite and infinite, between clear geometric figures and their ominous ground—Ledoux's and Boullée's designs belong with David's *Andromache Grieving over the Dead Hector* or the *Oath of the Horatii*.[53]

The sublime has often been discussed in terms of such tension, and Boullée explicitly invokes the sublime in his discussion of his monument to Newton: "Sublime spirit! Vast and profound genius! Divine being! Newton! Accept the homage of my poor talents! Ah! If I dare to make it public, it is only because I am convinced that in this work of which I shall speak I surpassed myself. O Newton! You, by the extent of your vision and the sublimity of your genius, have determined the shape of the world: I have conceived the idea of enveloping you within your discovery. I shall envelope you within yourself."[54] The architect opposes his little self to Newton's vast genius. But from that modern hero issues a light that allows Boullée to transcend himself and reach up to the infinity of human reason, reaching so high that the artist may dare to envelop Newton's genius with an immense sphere, symbol of the comprehended cosmos: as Newton's genius embraced the universe, so Boullée's sphere, age-old symbol of perfection, encloses the starry sky within. A monument to Newton, the monument is not only that: it is also a monument to human reason, which, awakened by Newton's genius, recognizes itself capable of comprehending and thus of enfolding the vast universe. Here lies the key to the healing power of the sublime: what at first presents itself as a threatening abyss, the terror of endless time and infinite space threatening to

Étienne-Louis Boullée, Newton Cenotaph, section at day. Source: Jean-Marie Pérouse de Montclos, *Étienne-Louis Boullée (1728–1799). De l'architecture classique à l'architecture révolutionnaire* (Paris: Arts et Métiers Graphiques, 1969).

111

Étienne-Louis Boullée, Newton Cenotaph, section at night. Source: Jean-Marie Pérouse de Montclos, *Étienne-Louis Boullée (1728–1799). De l'architecture classique à l'architecture révolutionnaire* (Paris: Arts et Métiers Graphiques, 1969).

112

reduce to insignificance the limited life span given to each human being, becomes a source of delight once the human being recognizes that as a being of reason he or she transcends him- or herself as a being of nature. If Boullée's monument can help found a community, this cannot be national but must be the community of all beings who recognize that they belong to reason: a community so vast that it leaps over all that separates France and England, leaps also over all the little communities that normally provide human beings with sufficient shelter to not be crushed by their mortality.

One aspect of Boullée's design undercuts this reading: vast as Boullée's sphere is meant to be, the magic of the starry sky within is unmasked as merely a remarkable piece of theater by the silence of the empty paper background. Boullée's dome is in fact a representation much more of the firmament of ancient cosmology, of the closed world of the ancients, than of the infinite universe of the moderns. The sphere encloses only an artistic representation of the night sky and invites thoughts that Newton, too, might have replaced nature with an artifact, might have taken the measure only of a human representation of nature—thoughts that return us to the *mysterium tremendum et fascinans* of the infinite and thus to the mystery of death, which is the other side of the absorbing mystery of our individuality.

It is striking in the brief quote above how often Boullée uses the word "I." There is indeed a close relationship between the experience of the sublime and a preoccupation with self, as Burke had already noted when he linked the pleasure we take in the sublime to the passions that belong to self-preservation, as opposed to the pleasure we take in the beautiful, which he links to the passions that let us seek the community of our fellow human beings, especially to sexual desire.[55] The sublime leaves the observer alone, even as he or she recognizes him- or herself to be a member of a human community that remains of necessity altogether abstract.

7

As we have seen, from the very beginning neo-classicism looked beyond the classical vocabulary of Roman and Greek architecture to more archaic, less beautiful perhaps, but more sublime "Egyptian" paradigms. Thus in his design for a monument to Frederick the Great, Friedrich Gilly raised his "sanctuary," another re-presentation of the Parthenon, on a much more archaic-looking, massive substructure that was to shelter the sarcophagus of the king. Like the massive triumphal gate that was to offer entry to the sacred precinct, it not only recalls designs by Ledoux and Boullée but has an archaic, vaguely Egyptian look, reinforced by the surrounding obelisks. In a related way Klenze, responsive to Ludwig's wishes, raised his Parthenon, the Walhalla, on an archaic architecture of terraces and steps that holds a crypt in which busts of still-living heroes had to await their death to be transported into the temple above.[56] A classical architecture of fame thus rises from the base provided by an archaic architecture of death, somewhat in the way the Washington, Jefferson, and Lincoln memorials now rise above Maya Lin's Vietnam Memorial.

When considering such aesthetic preferences we should not lose sight of the temporal horizon, of the way this horizon shifted with the rise of secular individualism: high-minded rectitude, the cult of reason, love of geometry, and the dread of time belong together (see chapter 15). It is not surprising that following the model provided by Roman funerary monuments, so many monuments of the time should have turned to ancient Egypt. The seemingly ageless pyramids especially offer themselves as paradigmatic works of architecture, at least if, with Vitruvius, we demand of building above all durability. Such a demand has to turn against the organic. It is impossible to build durable structures with living matter; even if founded in the requirements of life, building has to embrace what excludes life: dead, inorganic matter and geometric forms.[57] Durability is best represented by a resolute denial of every organic trace. Insistently every pyramid communicates such a denial. The Egyptian pyramids thus present themselves as perfect houses for the dead. As such they have provided funerary architecture with perhaps its most obvious model.

An especially moving example of this genre is the pyramidal monument of undressed granite raised to the Confederate dead in Richmond's parklike Hollywood Cemetery in 1869 (fig. 113), a worthy precursor of Maya Lin's Vietnam Memorial. The message of this pile of rough stones is underscored by the modest, almost identical grave markers in the surrounding cemetery. Visiting the monument in its leafy setting brought to my mind Trakl's lament for the dead of a different war:

Und leise tönen im Rohr die dunkeln Flöten des Herbstes.
O stolzere Trauer! ihr ehernen Altäre,
Die heiße Flamme des Geistes nährt heute ein gewaltiger Schmerz,
Die ungebornen Enkel.

And gently sound in the reeds the dark flutes of autumn.
O prouder sorrow! You iron altars,
Today a powerful sorrow feeds the spirit's hot flame,
The unborn descendants.[58]

Trakl addresses to the iron altars his lament over the unborn descendants. Can iron or stone, can a pyramid alleviate such sorrow? Crushed by the horror of World War I, Trakl committed suicide. And what meaning can we give to so many sacrifices to a questionable cause? It is far easier to build memorials to the dead of what is felt to be a just war, especially when it ended in victory. Preserving their memory is at the same time a reaffirmation of the ongoing community they helped preserve, a celebration not just of life but of a particular way of life. The other side of the preoccupation with death is concern with a secular self-transcendence, with possibilities of projecting individual life unto the horizon not of God's eternal city but of advancing humanity. So understood the future can give meaning to personal sacrifice and challenge the grave's terror. Yet what if the war was lost and its cause unjust? And what monument can give meaning to the victims of the Holocaust? But by awakening us to a humanity deeper than regional or national allegiance, just such monuments that call into question and force us to struggle with the meaning of the death they commemorate bless the living.

8

There are funerary monuments that assault us with their scale and death-defying stony geometry in a way that would silence all questions of the value of the sacrifice they honor, as if to be thus honored were already sufficient justification. Every faith finds reconfirmation in its martyrs. That individuals found the strength to sacrifice themselves for some person or cause helps give these the appearance of something worth dying for and exhorts the living to follow the martyrs' example. And especially when a regime's legitimacy is open to question, monuments to its martyrs can be used to silence critics. Napoleon thus decreed in 1806 that the unfinished church of the Madeleine should be transformed into a peripteral temple, "un monument à la Grande Armée, pourtant sur le frontispice: L'Empereur Napoléon aux Soldats de la Grande Armée."[59] Together with the Colonne Vendôme and the Arc de Triomphe it was to be part of a trio of monuments glorifying the new Caesar and his victorious armies. Later Hitler and Speer were to dream of a much more gigantic triumphal arch, an arch so large that its opening would have had room for its Napoleonic precursor. On it were to appear, carved in granite, the names of the 1,800,000 dead of World War I, whose death in an indefensible cause the rhetoric of this arch transforms into a heroic sacrifice that calls on the living to follow their example.[60] Inside this huge arch and completely dwarfed by it Speer wanted to place an example of classical architecture, as if to proclaim the victory of a prehistoric disregard of the value of individual life over Greek humanism. The triumph of the sublime over the beautiful could not be more explicit. In architecture the sublime is always a temptation.

The Representation of Life

21

1

The previous chapter explored the claim that sepulchre and monument remain as the only legitimate tasks for an architecture that takes itself seriously as art, where "art," as Loos here understands it, has not only an aesthetic but also an ethical function: "The work of art points out to humanity new paths and thinks of the future."[1] And monuments, too, even as they recall the past, think of the future. But what sort of future? Given a firmly established way of life, this question receives a ready answer: in such cases monuments help to confirm some already-established shared ethos. But what if the common sense needed to support such a shared ethos has eroded, when the heroes have been knocked off their pedestals? —sometimes literally, as in post–World War II Germany or much more recently in Russia, more often just figuratively. To be sure, Loos's simple forest grave continues to speak, but in a private and all but mute way that threatens to render the very thought of re-presenting it with some architecturally ambitious monument inappropriate, almost obscene. Such a grave fails to provide the orientation necessary to allow human beings to dwell in Heidegger's sense. Recall his interpretation of dwelling as a "staying within the fourfold": a simple grave may well open us to earth and sky, and also to our own mortality, but where are Heidegger's "divinities," those messengers of the godhead, understood by him as the fundamental measure of human being? What sense can we, living as we do in the ruins of a building that has lost its foundation (see fig. 99), make of such fundamental measures? The nineteenth century still sought to find such a measure in history, as the weakening authority of Jerusalem meant greater authority for Greece. Thinking especially of the latter, Heidegger, in *Being and Time* at least, could still invoke a loyalty that is "at the same time the only possible way of revering the sole authority which a free existing can have—of revering the repeatable possibilities of existence."[2] Unfortunately history speaks with increasingly many voices: to draw a measure from it means inevitably to have granted some of these possibilities a special authority, means, in Heidegger's words, to have chosen one's "hero."[3] Such a choice makes it easy to defend the ethical significance of monuments, but what makes the decision more than arbitrary? The greater our historical knowledge, the more difficult it becomes to accept the authority of supposed heroes, or, more generally, to discover in history our measure.

That holds also for architects wondering in what style they should build. That postmodern historicism lacks the show of conviction communicated by its nineteenth-

Jean Louis Charles Garnier, Paris Opéra. Detail of façade. Credit: Rapelye/Art Resource, N.Y.

114

century precursor should not surprise us: critical reflection has made us disenchanted modernists too reflective, too aware of the arbitrariness of conventions, to leave us content with pastiches of the past. Increasingly we experience such historicizing as mere theater. Theatricality was indeed one of the cardinal sins with which modernists had charged nineteenth-century culture, especially its architecture, decked out with quilting made up of fragments drawn from the great styles of the past. And how can theatricality be defended? Theatrical behavior suggests superficial role-playing—"Don't be so theatrical"—a dishonest concealment of reality, more especially of our own selves, behind masks and disguises. Authenticity would seem to preclude theatricality. And is this not true of buildings as well as of persons? Think of the "honesty" of a grain elevator. How theatrical in comparison is the Paris Opéra (1861–1875; fig. 114), which not only established its architect, Charles Garnier, as the best-known architect in France but deserves to be considered the paradigmatic work of architecture in the second half of the nineteenth century, flagship of the approach to architecture associated with the École des Beaux-Arts.[4] That this paradigm should be a theater, more specifically an opera house, is hardly an accident.

Like so many buildings of the time, the Opéra hides its quite up-to-date structural frame of iron beneath a splendid neo-Baroque skin. This extravagant architecture not only functions as a theater but also theatrically re-presents a theater: it puts on an act.

Garnier accompanied his masterpiece with *Le Théâtre,* a treatise in which he laid down the principles of theater architecture as he had come to understand them, both as a practicing architect and as a thoughtful observer of the leading theaters of Europe. In a manner recalling Laugier, Garnier begins with an attempt to found his architectural practice in the state of nature. Rather like Burke, he takes the desires for affection and self-preservation to the basic; but right after them, he claims, "the most natural, the most instinctive, is without doubt, the theatrical sentiment." Human being is being with others; as such, according to Garnier, it is essentially theatrical. Wherever two or three people gather, there is theater, at least in principle. "All that happens in the world is in sum only theater and representation."[5] Garnier sees all the world as a stage, life as a sequence of dramatic, tragic, or comic scenes. "To see or to make oneself be seen, to understand and to make oneself be understood, that is the fated circle of humanity; to be actor or spectator, that is the condition of human life" (p. 2).

A critic of Garnier may well want to insist on the difference between genuinely being oneself and putting on an act. Garnier could have replied with a question: is it possible to be really oneself before other persons? Insisting on the essentially social character of human beings, Garnier leaves no room for Heideggerian authenticity: we all put on acts, adopt poses, cast ourselves in certain roles, and observe others doing the same. And because we are all actors and spectators, we take pleasure in the theater, which may be understood as a concentrated re-presentation of life that raises its natural theatricality to a higher power and thus makes it conspicuous. Precisely because the theater draws its paradigms from the theater of life, it delights, interests, and instructs; as an idealizing re-presentation of life the theater inevitably has an ethical function and can thus become "the school of the people" and "the glory of humanity" (p. 4).

On this understanding of the significance of the theater Garnier bases his claim that, given the spiritual situation of our age, church and theater must be considered its two leading building types. Both are linked by Garnier to leisure and placed in opposition to work, "that necessity of life." Both are theatrical in a broader sense in that we go to them to watch spectacles: to the church to witness the spectacle of the divine, to the theater to be moved by the human spectacle (p. 8). Both, although perhaps not visited by all, exist for all. While with many romantics Garnier continues to give the church its traditional place of honor, it is the pleasure human beings take in spectacles that really matters: "The ancient saying still is, and will never cease to be timely: *panem et circenses;* food for the body and food for the spirit, that is the word of the human species, the immortal word; it will survive revolutions, monarchies, and republics, just as love and all original passions will survive all governments" (p. 8). The equation of the theater with Roman spectacles is telling—and troubling—as is the equation of both with food for the spirit: as if the spirit knew no other food than what is offered in the arena.

Spectacles demand proper settings. Theatrical spectacles demand stage and auditorium; Garnier insists on a sharp separation between the two, corresponding to a sharp separation between actor and spectator, so very different from the theater of life, in which the roles constantly blur and change. Like Wagner and Nietzsche, Garnier finds his professed model in antiquity, notes the decline of theatrical culture in the Middle Ages, and welcomes its resurgence in the following centuries, which led to the evolution of the theater as a firmly established architectural type in the seventeenth century, especially in Italy. It is indeed above all the Baroque theater that informs Garnier's understanding of what a theater should be, as it has informed theater architecture ever since.[6]

From Garnier's understanding of the theater as one of only two leading building types follows the insistence that it be given a splendid appearance. With pride he cites his own Opéra: those who enter it are overwhelmed; they cannot help but feel uplifted. The sumptuous elegance that now surrounds them, so different from their everyday environment, shapes their thoughts, their character, even the way they speak and their bearing. Garnier suggests that by entering his Opéra the spectator becomes part of a reality transfigured in the image of a Veronese canvas. He did not forget that, before the spectators sit down in their seats and the performance begins, they are also actors, as they are during intermissions and again after the final curtain falls. His Opéra forces each spectator, too, to play a role, even if he or she is usually quite willing to collude with such coercion. Role-playing is part of what makes theatergoing a festive event. Such acting, too, needs a proper stage—this, especially, is what demands the Opéra's splendid staircase (fig. 115) and festive foyer.

Such transformation invites further examination: does Garnier want us to lose ourselves to the spectacle he has prepared for us? What Nietzsche wrote, not about Garnier's Opéra but about Wagner's Bayreuth Festival, comes to mind:

115 | Jean Louis Charles Garnier, Paris Opéra. Grand staircase. Credit: Giraudon/Art Resource, N.Y.

One leaves oneself at home when one goes to Bayreuth, one renounces the right to one's own tongue and choice, to one's own taste, even to one's own courage, as one possesses it within one's own four walls against God and the world. Nobody brings the finest sense of his art with him to the theater, least of all the artist who works for the theater—lacking is solitude; all that is perfect tolerates no witnesses. . . . In the theater one becomes folk, herd, woman, pharisee, voting cattle, patron, idiot—Wagnerian: even the most personal conscience succumbs there to the leveling magic of the large number; the neighbor reigns; one becomes neighbor.[7]

Theater here means magic and seduction; absorbed in its spectacles we surrender ourselves. Countless modernists followed Nietzsche in this understanding of the essential inauthenticity of the theater. Michael Fried speaks for them when he claims that "theater and theatricality are at war today, not simply with modernist painting (or modernist painting and sculpture), but with art as such—and to the extent that the different arts can be described as modernist, with modernist sensibility as such."[8] Modernism has indeed laid claim to an honesty that has to place it "at war" with the theater. Such a war is demanded, for example, by Heideggerian authenticity.

But can we today still idealize authenticity? Do we still believe in the possibility of really being oneself? What would that mean? When we try to seize our own self, do we not always discover only more masks, poses, roles? Is Garnier not right to refuse the opposition of authenticity and theatricality? His Opéra, at any rate, can teach us disillusioned modernists how easy it is to delight in such festive theatricality. Was Pevsner not right to call the Opéra "glorious"?[9] Does life itself not demand theater, as Garnier insists? And must not architecture, if it is to serve life, also embrace the theater? Today Garnier's own naively confident description of his doubly theatrical masterpiece may well fill us with a certain nostalgia: at least one side of us would like to be able to embrace the theater so wholeheartedly. We would-be postmodernists cannot simply dismiss the assertion of the theater as a—perhaps even *the*—leading architectural task.

3

In chapter 19 I discussed Hans Sedlmayr's list of the six or seven architectural tasks that since the Enlightenment have claimed something like the significance that once belonged to the church. Among these the theater deserves a special place: not only does it join architect, painter, and sculptor once more in a genuine *Gesamtkunstwerk,* but the nineteenth century's rhetoric placed the theater quite explicitly in the position once occupied by the church. Garnier's Opéra is only the high point of a series that includes Schinkel's Berlin Schauspielhaus (1818–1821); Dresden's first opera house (1834–1841), which was almost immediately destroyed by fire, and its successor (1871–1878)—both by Gottfried Semper, who designed the latter as a somewhat scaled-down version of the magnificent Festival Theater he had designed for King Ludwig II of Bavaria; also Otto Brückwald's Festspielhaus in Bayreuth (1872–1876) and Semper's Burgtheater in Vienna (1871–1878).

Bound up with the elevation of the theater into a leading architectural task is a new understanding of the significance of drama, more especially of opera, which Wagner was not alone in endowing with a religious significance, although this "genius of mid-century"[10] looks back not to the Christian church but to the Greek theater. Not that Wagner thinks we moderns can or should attempt to recover the art of the ancient Greeks. Our task is

> to widen the garb of religion, *in which alone it was a communal Hellenic art[,] . . . to widen this garb of the specifically* Hellenic religion *to the bond of the religion of the future—that of* universality—*in order to form for ourselves even now a just conception of the art work of the future. Yet, unfortunate as we are, it is precisely the power to close this bond, this* religion of the future, *that we lack, for after all, no matter how many of us feel this urge to the art work of the future, we are* singular *and* individual. *An art work is religion brought to life; religions, however, are created, not by the artist, but by the folk.*[11]

Théophile Gautier's celebration of the Paris Opéra, and indeed any opera house, as "une sorte de cathédrale mondaine de la civilisation" is in the same spirit.[12]

Wagner conceived the artwork of the future as the creation of the folk, fully aware that modernity with its emphasis on the individual must render such folkish talk anachronistic or utopian. Certainly his own operatic art could not claim to present us with the hoped-for art; it offered no more than theatrical metaphors of the artwork of the future. The product of his unique genius, it appealed not to the folk but to the bourgeoisie of Wilhelminian Germany, who found in Bayreuth edifying entertainment. Despite Wagner's hopes, his *Festspiele* were in the end no more than aesthetic interludes in the real business of life, mere theater, lacking the strength to restore that sense of genuine community that is inseparable from every genuinely religious festival.

No one has written more eloquently of the hopes associated with Bayreuth than Nietzsche in the last of his *Untimely Meditations: Richard Wagner in Bayreuth*. Only a short time later Nietzsche was of course to turn against Wagner and what he had come to recognize as a merely aesthetic theater, but here he presents himself to us as a convert, or as someone who has been seduced. All who participate in the Bayreuth Festival, we learn, are rendered untimely by such participation, that is, lose their place in the modern age—dare we say, using today's jargon, become "postmodern"? There is of course an obvious rejoinder: yes, they do indeed lose their place in the modern age, but, as all aesthetes do, at the cost of reality, which they forsake for aesthetic illusion. The young Nietzsche would have rejected that suggestion: he is convinced of the ethical significance of Wagner's work. Wagner is celebrated as the new Aeschylus and Nietzsche praises the *Ring of the Nibelungs* as "the most moral music" that he knows: "e.g., where Brünnhilde is awakened by Siegfried; here he [Wagner] reaches up to a height and holiness of mood that lets one think of the snowy peaks of the Alps."[13] The experience is one of the sublime and the sacred. And the vocabulary of the sacred keeps returning in his essay, which is not surprising to the reader of *The Birth of Tragedy:* both works present us with case studies of the attempt to reoccupy the place left vacant with the death of God.

That the author of "The Artwork of the Future" should have felt flattered and welcomed this attempt to attribute a genuinely ethical and religious significance to his work is to be expected. To support such an attribution Nietzsche had to reject any merely aesthetic understanding of Wagner's music drama:

For us Bayreuth means the morning consecration on the day of battle. One could not do us a greater injustice than if one were to think that what mattered to us were art alone: as if art could be a healing opiate with which to put away all that is miserable in our world. We see in the tragic image of Bayreuth rather the battle of the select few with everything that confronts them as seemingly insuperable necessity, with power, law, tradition, contract, and all the organization of things. These few cannot live a more beautiful life than when, battling for justice and love, they ready themselves for death and sacrifice.[14]

What is experienced as the stale old order is here the enemy. Wagner's work hallows our dissatisfaction with the modern world. At the same time it presents us with ideal images of a more natural, simpler existence. "The individual is to be consecrated to something suprapersonal—this is what tragedy wants: he shall unlearn the terrifying anxiety that death and time bring. For even in the smallest moment, in the shortest atom of his life, he can meet with something holy, which outweighs all battle and all need—this is what it means to possess a tragic sense."[15] What Nietzsche expected from Wagner's *Gesamtkunstwerk* is clear enough: the establishment of an ethos that would overcome the spirit of revenge, that ill will against time, in which he later was to locate the deepest source of our self-alienation. This is the same role he had ascribed in *The Birth of Tragedy* to Attic tragedy. Tragedy reveals to us mortals our lot: ever striving to master life, we are yet at the mercy of higher powers, fate and the gods if you will, powers we cannot control and that yet preside over the meaning of human existence. We are limited also in our autonomy by a fate we have not chosen, which is ours only because we were born into a particular family, a particular historical context. Tragedy may be understood as a celebratory re-presentation of paradigmatic stories of heroic suffering. Re-presenting such stories it reestablishes the communal ethos and its affirmation of life. I would like to underscore that tragedy is intended to help us unlearn the spirit of revenge. Those who cannot banish the terror of time and death will of necessity become selfish, as they seek to hang on to their own being in the face of that terror. Tragedy re-presents the human condition in its subjection to time, but it also re-presents those moments when human beings are touched by something holy, which more than outweighs time's terror.

That Nietzsche read into Wagner his own hopes for a renewal of Europe is evident. These hopes were easier to maintain as long as Bayreuth had not yet become a reality, when he could visit Wagner in the Swiss Tribschen, this "distant island of the blessed," as he later was to call it.[16] As Wagner became more and more preoccupied with the realities of Bayreuth, Nietzsche became more and more aware of how he himself had substituted for the real Wagner an ideal image of his own construction. Bayreuth opened Nietzsche's eyes, not only to who Wagner really was but also to the role that illusion, self-deception, and wishful thinking had played in his own understanding of Wagner. At the same time he became aware of the extent to which Wagner's theater depended on illusion and wishful thinking.

Beginning with this disillusionment we find Nietzsche becoming increasingly suspicious of illusion. The artwork of the future that was to return to art its ethical function settled for the appearance of such a return. Wagner's theater turned out to be escapist after all, an anaesthetic and an opiate. Nietzsche thus came to understand not just Wagner's theater but theater in general as profoundly dishonest. For when he condemned Wagner and Bayreuth, at issue was much more: he saw a culture that, having lost its faith, sought refuge in bad faith. "Bad faith" is so labeled because it is accompanied not only by a recognition of the distance that separates the content of such faith from reality but by a desire to preserve such distance, a desire that denies the theater its critical potential and renders it aesthetic—"culinary," as Brecht put it.[17]

That the theatrical spirit represented by both Wagner and Garnier helped shape the spiritual situation of the entire age is witnessed by its architecture: consider once more Garnier's Opéra, itself a theatrical re-presentation of a Baroque theater. Or consider the worldwide triumph of the architecture of the École des Beaux Arts, which at the World's Columbian Exhibition in Chicago in 1893 captured American with its theatrical Baroque classicism. All this is theater, a theater that repeated itself in city after city. In Vienna it was the age of Hans Makart, whose theatrical paintings belong with the Ringstrasse, and it is no accident that the leading architect associated with the Ringstrasse, Gottfried Semper, was also to be the architect of the Festspielhaus that Wagner and his patron King Ludwig II of Bavaria had planned for Munich.[18] A revealing caricature of the nineteenth century's architectural theater is provided by the castles Ludwig had built for himself—Linderhof, Herrenchiemsee, Neuschwanstein—with their representations of stage sets for scenes from Wagner's operas. By re-presenting this theater yet once more, translating it into an amusement park, Walt Disney later revealed its escapist appeal.

That despite his ambition to recover something of the ethical significance of Greek theater Wagner in fact aestheticized the existing theater is shown by the way he wanted spectators to lose themselves to the theatrical event; to become absorbed in the stage happening, oblivious to the musicians actually performing on their instruments, now hidden in the sunk orchestra pit; oblivious to their neighbors, all but invisible in the darkened auditorium. Not the folk, but the half-mad king, weary of a world that had reduced his kingship to little more than a theatrical performance and dreaming of other worlds, of bygone splendor, alone in the darkness, lost to himself, lost in the spectacles unfolding on stage, was the ideal spectator of Wagner's theater, a spectator eager to trade reality for fantasy and with sufficient funds to realize at least fragments of that fantasy in architecture.

The real meaning of Wagner's theater was revealed to Nietzsche by the opening of Bayreuth in 1876. Everyone was there, wanting to see and be seen: Kaiser Wilhelm, the emperor of Brazil, King Ludwig. As Garnier would have expected, the interest of many visitors centered more on those celebrities than on the events on the stage. Quite appropriately, Nietzsche must have thought, the spectacle unmasked itself in its pretensions: at one point when Walhalla was to appear the stage mechanism failed. Instead of the glorious abode of the gods all one could see was a gaping void and before it a stage manager, with rolled-up sleeves, desperately trying to correct whatever went wrong. This may be too good an anecdote to be true. To Nietzsche, at any rate, the visit was a shattering experience: what had been put in the place of the sacred and holy unmasked itself as no more than human contrivance, human construction. Soon he could not stand it any more; he sought refuge in Klingenbrunn, a small village in the Bavarian Forest, and began work on *Human, All Too Human*.

4

The vehemence of Nietzsche's rejection of Wagner and the theater needs to be understood against the background of the hopes that in *The Birth of Tragedy* had led him to hail Wagner's music drama as a repetition of Greek tragedy and Greek tragedy as an essentially sacred celebration. Again, such hopes were only the other side of his profound rejection of the Enlightenment's conviction that reason can teach us how to achieve the good life by mastering reality and ourselves. Reason itself, Nietzsche thought, had undermined such conviction; he was thinking especially of Kant, whose *Critique of Pure Reason* had demonstrated that reason is unable to give us understanding of the things themselves, and of Schopenhauer, who had insisted that Kant's confidence that pure practical reason could at least provide our life with a measure was mistaken. Today many would point to Heidegger and Derrida. But if reason has indeed undermined trust in reason, which supported the ethos that the Enlightenment had put in the place of the old faith, all that remains would seem to be either a return to some preceding ethos or the establishment of a new one. The self-destruction of the rationalist tradition that had supported modernism calls for a new construction to put in place of what had been destroyed.

Where then are we to find the blueprint for such a construction? To Nietzsche the answer seemed obvious: if modernity is the problem, a premodern world must point the way to the hoped-for postmodern world. Where we seek this premodern world will depend on where we locate the origin of the modern. If with Nietzsche we locate the origin in Socrates' trust in reason, his turn to the tragic age of the Greeks has a certain inevitability. A repetition of Attic tragedy was to overcome the nihilistic tendencies inherent in modernity. But when writing *The Birth of Tragedy* Nietzsche thought that such a repetition was already being realized. In Richard Wagner he believed to have found the genius who would once again fashion not a mere imitation of Greek tragedy but an equivalent work that would do for our world what Aeschylus did for the ancient Greeks. Had not Wagner's music drama demonstrated the possibility of a modern renewal of the ethical function of Greek tragedy? Such an understanding of tragedy gives it a function not unlike that of the mass: instead of joining in the celebration of the sacrament, the community joins in the celebration of a tragic festival.

Greek tragedy was performed in outdoor theaters, each nestled into some hillside. This then gives powerful support to the suggestion that when we look for a building type to put in the place once occupied by the church we would do well to look to the theater, but to the theater considered in the image of the Greek theater, which served the self-representation of the body politic with celebrations of heroic manhood.[19] The theater here envisioned must distance itself from the modern theater, which instead of joining individuals in a communal celebration invites theatergoers to remain passive and to surrender themselves to the performance, transporting them into another world rather like a framed picture; the similarity finds its architectural expression in proscenium arch and stage curtain, which help isolate the "aesthetic island" of the theatrical event from reality.[20] The extent to which Wagner's theater sought the aesthetic becomes clear when we compare it with its Greek precursor, invoked by Wagner when he insisted that every spectator should have an unobstructed view of the whole stage. However, what links Wagner's theater to its Baroque precursor is more significant than such classicizing innovations. That he should have moved his performances inside is easy enough to understand.[21] But more important than coping with the weather is the fact that moving indoors allows for a much more effective establishment of aesthetic distance by increasing the traditional separation of auditorium and stage, spectator and actor. Along with this goes the pictorialization of the stage, in which lighting has a special significance. One function of that pictorialization is the progressive de-emphasis on the element of social self-representation that had always been an important part of going to the theater: such self-representation retreats into the time preceding and following the performance and the intermissions.

Nietzsche might have said that in Bayreuth, too, the theater of the Baroque, more especially Baroque opera, had triumphed over Greek tragedy, indeed had done so more completely than in Garnier's Opéra, which demonstrates greater awareness of what already with the Greeks had been a primary function of the theater—not just to let the audience lose itself to the staged spectacle but to allow the polis to represent itself: *repraesentatio maiestatis.*[22] But if social self-representation has always been inseparable from the festal quality of a visit to the theater, this conflicts with an understanding of the theatrical performance as a special kind of aesthetic object. The Baroque's progressive pictorialization of the theater, which had its telos in the transformation of the performance into a moving picture, prepared for Wagner's more resolute aestheticizing of the theater—and not just Wagner's, but our own.

No modern art form has remained so profoundly indebted to the Baroque as the theater, and more especially opera.

On hearing the word "theater," most people will automatically conjure up an architectural structure with certain definite characteristics: a closed building, horseshoe-shaped, with several levels of boxes rising vertically and rows of seats in the ground floor area called the orchestra. These arrangements for the spectator force a raised platform in front of which on the ground level is an enclosed area, the orchestra pit, reserved for musicians. Above and at the front of the stage rises a fixed architectural frame, the proscenium. On a deep stage behind the proscenium the players play and constantly changing usually painted scenery is displayed.

This understanding of what a theater is, is such an integral part of our heritage that few people realize it was developed only in the course of the seventeenth and eighteenth centuries in Europe.[23]

The history of the theater, however, invites us to question the way the stage is thus placed under the hegemony of perspectival painting. That Théophile Gautier should have pointed to the circus as a point of departure for a renewal of the theater[24] points to the price paid by the pictorialization of the theater—later Hans Poelzig was to convert a circus into Berlin's Grosses Schauspielhaus (1918–1919). We should keep in mind that no more than Greek theater or Shakespeare's theater were the theatrical performances that were part of religious festivals and processions in the Middle Ages and still in the Baroque dependent on elaborate stages or stage sets: "In the case of the mystery plays, the different locales where the events occurred were suggested by separate structures, variously called places or houses or mansions, built of temporary materials, with the town-folk shifting from one to another as the sequence evolved. Instead of the sets moving, the audience moved. No longer confined to one place as a self-contained representation of a mythic past, the spectacle merged with the real world and became a dynamic, continuous enactment of a miraculous present—like the Mass itself."[25] This conception of the theater never quite disappeared. Thus it was such an understanding of the possible significance of theater that led Eduard Devrient to hold up the Passion Play of Oberammergau as a model for the future,[26] and essentially the same conception led to the institution of the Salzburger Festspiele as a kind of anti-Bayreuth: the cathedral square was rediscovered as a more fitting space for the staging of Hugo von Hoffmannsthal's version of *Everyman* than any theater.

But such attempts to free the theater from the hegemony of painting only underscore its power. Since the Renaissance, beginning in Italy, we meet with ever more elaborate attempts to apply the newly gained mastery of perspective to the theater. Paintd scenery came to be considered essential. First came rag-covered painted frames; demands for rapid changes of scenery lead to the introduction of three-sided canvas-covered prisms, the so-called *periacti,* which soon were to give way to movable wings. Architecture responded to these changes: Giovanni Battista Aleotti's Accademia degli Intrepidi in Ferrara thus established the familiar type of the Baroque theater, an establishment that brought with it up-to-then unimagined possibilities of creating illusionary spaces, an art of which different members of the Bibiena family were the acknowledged masters.[27]

Already in the Baroque period the theater asserted itself as an art form to rival the church. Its appeal was such that even church architecture came under its sway, unable to resist the possibilities theatrical illusionism had opened up (see fig. 100). Here we must ask whether this turn to the theater does not also represent a turn to superficiality, a charge that has been leveled against such works as Bernini's Cornaro Chapel or the Asam brothers' Rohr (see fig. 85). Works such as these invite us to apply Maritain's claim—that Renaissance art placed the observer "on the floor of a theater," that with it "the lie installed itself in painting"[28]— also to church architecture, to oppose Baroque theatricality to medieval piety. But to do so is to forget that participation in a religious festival denies the stance of an aesthetic observer. No matter how illusionistic the frescoes, how theatrical the high altar, there is a sense in which what Irving Lavin says of mystery plays still holds of any genuine church service: instead of passively watching a moving picture, the faithful participate in a communal action. If the celebration of the mass is also a theatrical performance, "theatrical" here may not be thought in terms of a theater subjected to the hegemony of Albertian perspective and the radical separation of spectator and actor. To be sure, quite self-consciously the Baroque church built its high altars in the image of an illusionistic stage, a stage for the celebration of the mass; but such celebration demands participation. This sacred theater allows for no sharp boundary separating spectator and actor, reality and theatrical illusion. And if theater is to furnish more than aesthetic experiences, if it is to reclaim the ethical function of the Greek, the medieval, and to a considerable degree still the Baroque theater, would it not have to be a theater of this type?

If this is granted, the illusionistic theater of the Baroque and the associated building type would seem to be a liability. This lends interest to attempts to develop alternatives, such as Ledoux's theater in Besançon (1778–1784), which "has semicircular, graded amphi-theatrical seating[;] Ledoux calls this explicitly 'the progressive form which makes humanity equal.' Besançon also had a sunk orchestra, the first, it seems, to try out this Wagnerian feature."[29] But despite their invocations of the Greek theater, such innovations did not really challenge the Baroque pictorialization of the stage. Key here is the relationship between stage and auditorium, between actor and spectator, the extent to which the stage is to be experienced as a different, framed, illusory world. The most obvious way to challenge that separation is to project the stage into the auditorium, a challenge that culminates in the twentieth century's theaters-in-the-round, first realized in Gropius's design of a Total-Theater for Erwin Piscator.[30]

5

The hopes the young Nietzsche had invested in Wagner, hopes for a post-Christian but nevertheless once again religious art, for a return of art to myth, have remained. Such hopes helped to define especially the culture of the years preceding World War I with its wide-spread talk of a new beginning (art nouveau), a new youth (Jugendstil); these hopes, still fed by Wagnerian ambitions, focused on the theater, even as there was increasing conviction that if it deserved to be thus singled out, it had to be rescued from the merely aesthetic, had to be brought back to reality, into the community, to bridge the gulf that had opened up between art and life and thus recapture something of the significance of a religious festival. Quite in the spirit of Nietzsche, the young Peter Behrens thus conceived "the theater, as architecture and as cultural institution, as the apogee of that new, earnestly sought culture."[31] Theatrical performances were to be both "Festivals of Life and of Art," as Behrens titled a booklet published in 1900. As the subtitle explained, such festivals were to provide human-ity with its "highest cultural symbol."[32] In Richard Dehmel's *Lebensmesse* he found the ap-propriate work, appropriate precisely because it claimed to be more than just art: a mass but not centered on the dead Christ; a mass of life, of eros. As Behrens wrote Dehmel: "we ourselves shall build art a temple, in which holiness shall reign."[33] Behrens could not have been clearer about his intention to return art to the sacred: "Dehmel's *Lebensmesse,* through its liturgical quality, is a work which appears peculiarly predestined for presentation in such á new Bühnenstil. Since the poet wrote with this intuition, the work actually inaugurates the new style. If drama has derived from religious cults, then I see a great sign for the evolving theater style in the fact that again poets live who can give us and our times the forms for a Cult of Life. We will build the house from its foundation. Dehmel's *Lebensmesse* is a cornerstone, most solemnly formed."[34]

Although, like so many of the nineteenth and twentieth century's most interesting designs, Behrens's theater was never built, his design and commentary give us a clear idea of what he intended: the centralized plan was to counteract the separation of spectators and actors, or rather of the congregation and "the priests of the word, of the beautiful gesture, and of the dance."[35] The seating resembled that of the Greek theater: each participant had clear, easy, and direct contact with the broad and shallow simple stage. "A small orchestra was to be centered in front of the stage and between the two broad ranks of low marble steps which allowed passage between the stage and a processional area on the cross-axis. This processional area would serve both the movements of the actors and the arrival and departure of the congregation."[36] The baroque pictorialization of the stage was eliminated. Behrens thus rejected Wagner's theater with its "plastic painting, painted architecture, illustrative music and similar devices which contrive to counterfeit nature or art in an anti-stylistic mixture."[37]

But Behrens's theater—this church to the cult of the beautiful life, intended to overcome the conception of the stage as an "aesthetic island," framed by the proscenium arch, protected by the orchestra pit—was itself just such an island, as was the beautiful life it meant to serve. And such an island was the artist's colony in Darmstadt that gave rise to this vision of the theater as the highest *Kultursymbol*. It was condemned to be no more than just such a symbol by its unwillingness to descend into the reality of the modern world, a world shaped by science and technology. "These sciences have their material triumphs, it was acknowledged, but against this positivistic intellectual world one must assert the 'unhistorical' and the 'super-historical.' History and art, and with them life, must be pulled away from the materialist grasp of positivism. New triumphs, it was hoped, would be achieved through this freedom from Wissenschaft. The hubris of the positivist was matched by that of the poet."[38] Anderson here puts his finger on what renders all attempts to recast the world based on a refusal of the reality of the modern world versions of the aesthetic. But what might such an attempt look like were it to actually confront that reality?

6

If, as I have suggested, the opposition between building and architecture is essential to the latter as it has traditionally been understood, then architecture will have a future only if the place once occupied by temple and church can in some sense be reoccupied. It is not difficult to see why the theater should have been given this place: does the theater not have its origin in religious rites? And has it not dreamed again and again of recovering its origin in the sacred? And both religious action and theatrical performance draw festal figures on the ground of the everyday.

But is it not a futile and misguided undertaking to reoccupy the place once held by temple and church? Were not the nineteenth century's attempts to endow the theater with a quasi-religious significance born of an unwillingness to accept modernity's nonhierarchical, secular, democratic ethos, which lets us be suspicious of all attempts to speak of "the leading building task"? Kaufmann appears to be right in suggesting that ever since the French Revolution "any type of building has been considered worthy of an architect's abilities."[39] Why insist on the two foci of my ellipse? And why turn to the theater?

An answer is hinted at by Garnier in his brief introductory remark to his book on the theater, which places the need for affection even before that for self-preservation. Affection alone, however, cannot forge a lasting bond. This requires the mediation provided by a shared way of life, requires entry into a language game—a game understood with Wittgenstein as a "whole, consisting of language and the actions into which it is woven."[40] To enter into such a game is rather like learning to play a certain part: it presupposes opportunities to see others in the same role. To repeat Garnier's dictum: "to be actor or spectator, that is the condition of human life." But if playing such a part is to be experienced as more than a meaningless routine that has little to do with who we really are, it must be supported by dreams and ideals that put us in touch with what most deeply moves us—with the gods, the Greeks might have said; with the claims of reason and nature, the Enlightenment insisted; with the subconscious, we might say—at any rate, with a power that, while obscured by the routines of the everyday, still needs to be recalled from time to time if our lives are not to become superficial and hollow. Religious festivals have served such a function. So has theater. From the very beginning architecture has thus been theatrical in the sense of providing a setting that invites idealizing re-presentations of everyday life. But do we still need art, more especially the theater, for such re-presentations? Related to that question is another: do we still know how to celebrate communal festivals that help to illuminate everyday life? The latter is the more fundamental question. Bound up with it is yet another: do we still need architecture, as opposed to mere building?

Dreams of Utopia

22

1

Dreams of a better life are inseparable from the good life, which also entails dreams of a better home. But human beings are social animals. Given the communal character of our dwelling, an oneiric city must thus take its place beside Bachelard's oneiric house. With good reason the Bible thus places our dwelling in between the tree of life and the crystal cube of the City of God, between paradise—a bounded garden located in a past from which we are cut off by the Fall, a place where nature was in tune with human needs, where peace reigned and the lion lay down with the lamb, where food was plentiful and sex untroubled by shame—and the perfectly ordered Heavenly City illuminated by the glory of God, a city to which is admitted nothing unclean but only those whose names are written in the Lamb's book of life. The garden vision of paradise is thus complemented by the geometric, urban vision of paradise not just regained but raised to a higher level, an oneiric city onto which human beings projected their hopes for a better dwelling on this earth: "And I saw the holy city, new Jerusalem, coming down out of heaven from God, prepared as a bride for her husband" (Rev. 21.2, RSV). Having the glory of God, "its radiance" is said to be "like a most rare jewel, like a jasper, clear as crystal" (21.11). "The city was pure gold, clear as glass" (21.18), sheltered by a high wall, its foundations "adorned with every jewel" (21.19): jasper, sapphire, agate, emerald, onyx, carnelian, chrysolite, beryl, topaz, chrysopase, jacinth, and amethyst, each of its twelve "gates made of a single pearl," its street "pure gold, transparent as glass" (21.21), a city where God himself will be with his people; and "he will wipe away every tear from their eyes, and death shall be no more, neither shall there be mourning nor crying nor pain any more, for the former things have passed away" (21.4).

For many centuries the descriptions of the City of God found in the book of Revelation provided dreams for a better future an authoritative focus. Their very sketchiness invited imaginative elaborations, utopian projections of an ideal architecture whose very ideality precluded the opposition of the two poles of my ellipse, the distinction between building and architecture—"And I saw no temple in the city, for its temple is the Lord God the Almighty and the Lamb" (21.22)—just as it precluded a distinction between profane and sacred time: eternally the mass is celebrated in the Heavenly City, of which the earthly celebration is but an earthly representation.[1] But if this crystal utopia has to collapse my ellipse into a circle that has its center in God, the built church only represents this ideal city here on earth; as such a representation it preserves the distance that separates a life lived in between heaven and earth from the eternal life promised to the faithful, a distance figured in turn by the distance that separates ordinary dwellings from the church.

The very distance of the ideal from the everyday invites attempts to abolish such distance, attempts not just to measure existing conditions by the ideal in order to improve them but to realize this ideal here on earth. And did the very idea of a Heavenly Jerusalem not suggest a direction for such attempts? For while, as I pointed out in chapter 7, every chapel, church, and cathedral was considered a figure of the Heavenly Jerusalem, that ideal city appeared to be more closely figured by the terrestrial Jerusalem, a city that, as Isaiah had foretold, at the end of time was to be transformed into its heavenly original. The distance between figure and figured, earth and heaven, would then be abolished. And since the revelation to John claims to show God's servants "what must soon take place" (1.1), again and again this transformation presented itself as a possibility that would soon become reality here on earth, in the individual's own lifetime, a vision of heaven on earth, inviting especially those dissatisfied with their lives to do their best to ensure that the hoped-for event would actually take place. The thought of such a transformation of earth into heaven—a thought that tended to mingle with thoughts of abundant shelter and food, an abolition of the privilege of wealth as of self-centeredness, and also a return to that easy sexuality, unburdened by original sin, that Adam and Eve must have enjoyed in paradise—has haunted Christianity from its beginning to the present day. Taken together, these ideas have become powerful if often destructive agents of change whenever conditions make it impossible for the impoverished and disadvantaged, for the frustrated and displaced, to consider the world they lived in as in any way like a home. Countless people thus have been driven by millennial expectations to attempt to establish the blessed city in this life, here on earth, by revolutionary action, only to have their endeavor to realize the promise of the crystal cube, this perfect geometric solid, transform the earth into a version of hell.

In *The Pursuit of the Millennium* Norman Cohn chronicles "the process by which traditional beliefs about a future golden age, or messianic kingdom become, in certain situations of mass disorientation and anxiety, the ideologies of popular movements of a peculiarly anarchic kind."[2] He tells of the joyful anticipation with which Tertullian reports that in Judea a walled city had been seen in the sky for forty days, "a sure sign that the Heavenly Jerusalem was about to descend. It was the same vision which . . . was to hypnotize the masses of the People's Crusades as they toiled towards Jerusalem, some nine centuries later" (p. 9). Not quite the same, as anxious awaiting of the Heavenly City's descent would give way to thoughts of seizing a sword, smiting the infidels, and liberating holy Jerusalem, which thus liberated would reward the toils of the faithful with those pleasures and riches life had denied them and that the fabled East was thought to hold. "No wonder that—as contemporaries noted—in the minds of the simple folk the idea of the earthly Jerusalem became so confused with and transfused by that of the Heavenly Jerusalem that the Palestinian city seemed itself a miraculous realm, abounding both in spiritual and in material blessings" (p. 45). This idea fired the imagination of the hordes of poor people, who, hearing charismatic preachers like Peter the Hermit call for a crusade, seized this promise of an escape from poverty and the plague, famine and oppressive lords, and sought to recapture

Jerusalem from the infidel, hoping to find there the good life denied to them at home. "And no wonder that when the masses of the poor set off on their long pilgrimage the children cried out at every town and castle: 'Is that Jerusalem?'—while high in the heavens there was seen a mysterious city with vast multitudes hurrying towards it" (p. 45).

The same vision later inspired the discontented artisans and poor people who in 1534 streamed to Münster to establish there the New Jerusalem, abolishing private property and, invoking the power of genuine community, instituting free love. Faced with a hostile world that soon laid siege to the city, this New Jerusalem became an armed camp, where, led by their king Jan Bockelson, who "explained that pomp and luxury were permissible for him because he was wholly dead to the world and the flesh" (p. 298), the starving faithful awaited Christ's imminent return and the time when they would all be dukes. They clung in the end to the hope that God would raise their beleaguered city with golden chains into heaven, only to be slaughtered when the besiegers finally stormed Münster, an end Cohn invites us to read as a figure of the end of the Third Reich, which was fed on a "similar quasi-religious salvationism":

This salvationism, too, is of a peculiar kind, in that the salvation promised is terrestrial and collective. The Heavenly City is to appear on this earth; and its joys are to crown not the peregrinations of individual souls, but the epic exploits of a "chosen people." And such a revolutionary movement is of a peculiar kind, in that its aims and promises are boundless. A social struggle is imagined as uniquely important, different in kind from all other struggles known to history, a cataclysm from which the world is to emerge totally transformed and redeemed. But this, again, is the very thing that in our time has most clearly characterized the two great totalitarian movements, Communist and Nazi, especially in their early, revolutionary stages. (p. 308)

2

Just as millenarianism and its promise of an earthly paradise have shadowed twentieth-century politics, so utopian hopes of actually constructing some secularized version of the New Jerusalem here on earth have been very much part of the spirit presiding over the evolution of twentieth-century architecture, often merging with attempts to build some secularized version of the Gothic cathedral. While both millennial and utopian expectations address dissatisfactions with existing conditions, both also threaten to leap over the human condition.

To show that especially in its beginning much modern architecture figured utopia, one could examine the origins of the Bauhaus. It is not an accident that the four-page pamphlet that Gropius published in 1919 to state its aim and program had for its frontispiece a woodcut by Lyonel Feininger, which translates a Gothic cathedral into Cubist-inspired crystalline forms, creating thus an image of a reconciliation of modernity and medieval spirituality, a vision the artist developed almost into a formula in many of his paintings. This choice of frontispiece implies a critique of the architecture of the day, as does the term *Bauhaus,* which, in the spirit of William Morris, van de Velde, and Hoffmann,[3] promises a renewal of the craft tradition of medieval mason's lodges rather than a continuation of the academies of the eighteenth and nineteenth centuries and of the kind of training they offered. Apprentices, journeymen, and masters were to be joined in a working community radically different from that of teachers and students.

We should no forget here the special aura with which romanticism had endowed the ethos thought to have governed medieval lodges, an ethos of which Free Masonry preserves distant traces: the commitment to work toward a more harmonious world to be established in the image of the Heavenly Jerusalem. The light and crystalline order of the new architecture figure a utopian dwelling, just as order and light of the Gothic cathedral figured the City in Heaven.[4] Gropius shared this understanding of architecture as an expression anticipating our deepest interests and insisted that this ethical function be returned to it:

What is architecture? The crystalline expression of man's noblest sentiments, his ardour, his humanity, his faith, his religion! That is what it once was! But who living in our age that is cursed with practicality still comprehends its all-embracing, soul-giving nature? We walk through our streets and cities and do not howl with shame at such deserts of ugliness! Let us be quite clear: these grey, hollow, spiritless mock-ups in which we live and work will be shameful evidence for posterity of the spiritual descent into hell of our generation, which forgot that great, unique art: architecture.[5]

In his own way Gropius, too, thus insists on the ethical function of the arts: they all are to serve the requirements of genuine dwelling, and to do so they must subordinate themselves to architecture as to the master art that most completely serves the requirements of dwelling. Gropius's appointment as head of the Bauhaus gave him an opportunity to work toward the realization of such dreams.

The Bauhaus program's very first sentence announces the dream that inspired it:

The ultimate aim of all visual arts is the complete building! To embellish buildings was once the noblest function of the fine arts; they were the indispensable components of great architecture. Today the arts exist in isolation, from which they can be rescued only through the conscious, cooperative efforts of all craftsmen. Architects, painters, and sculptors must recognize anew and learn to grasp the composite character of a building both as an entity and in its separate parts. Only then will their work be imbued with the architectonic spirit which it has lost as "salon art."[6]

Gropius's call for "the complete building" may simply seem to demand of architecture what aestheticians have long demanded of all genuine art. But Gropius was too much of a builder to accept the separation of art from life on which the aesthetic approach insists, a separation that, as I showed in part 1 of this book, finds expression in the decorated sheds of the nineteenth and twentieth centuries. The call for the complete building was a declaration of war on the decorated shed. But if that separation was to be overcome, art had to be rescued from its self-imposed isolation, had to be brought back to earth and returned to everyday life, just as the artist had to be brought back into the community. Given such demands, the unavoidable entanglement of architecture with the problems of living and dwelling that denies it the aesthetic completeness possible in the other arts becomes an asset that allows architecture to lead these arts out of their isolation from each other and from life to a different and more profound completeness. The complete building addresses itself to the entire human being, not only to the aesthetic observer. While it promises something like the completeness associated with the aesthetic object, it does so without taking its leave from life. Instead of offering us an escape into aesthetic experience, it means to transform the environment in which we work and live into a work of art and thus rescue it from contingency.

Gropius too was moved by that old dream of a reconciliation of art and reality that has haunted romantics from Friedrich Schiller to Ernst Bloch, Herbert Marcuse, and Norman O. Brown and in which we can recognize a secularization of dreams of the descent of the City of God down to earth. Inseparable from such dreams are thoughts of a radical transformation of existing conditions. In an address to the students of the Bauhaus Gropius gave clear expression to his revolutionary hopes, fed by a sense that the old world had died in the trenches of Verdun:

We find ourselves in a colossal catastrophe of world history, in a transformation of the whole of life and the whole of inner man. This is perhaps fortunate for the artistic man, provided he is strong enough to bear the consequences, for what we need is the courage to accept inner experience, then suddenly a new path will open for the artist. . . . No large spiritual organizations, but small, secret, self-contained societies, lodges. Conspiracies will form which will want to watch over and artistically shape a secret, a nucleus of belief, until from the individual groups a universally great, enduring, spiritual-religious idea will rise again, which finally must find its crystalline expression in a great Gesamtkunstwerk. And this great total work of art, this cathedral of the future, will then shine with its abundance of light into the smallest objects of everyday life.[7]

If the other side of the completeness of aesthetic experiences is the isolation of the aesthetic observer, if the aesthetic approach is part of a splintering of life and community into more or less autonomous spheres and individuals, the ideal of the complete building has its counterpart in the ideal of a completely integrated dwelling, a dwelling that leaves behind the fragmentation of atomic individuals and returns them to the community. The complete building would thus erase the boundaries between aesthetic, ethical, and technological considerations. The architect is asked not just to build but to edify. He or she is to shape the space and time of everyday experience in such a way that individuals are recalled from the dispersal into which they are led by the modern world to an order in which they can recognize their place and vocation. Given this conception of the task facing the architect, the glance back to the Gothic cathedral cannot surprise: as a representation of the City of God it has long provided an obvious example for an architecture that answers to the longing for building that will help us discover our place, our ethos. "Structures created by practical requirements and necessity do not satisfy the longing for a world of beauty built anew from the bottom up, for the rebirth of that spiritual unity which ascended to the miracle of the Gothic cathedrals."[8] Projecting this idealized past into the future Gropius dreams of an architecture that once again will be "the crystalline expression of man's noblest thoughts, his ardour, his humanity, his faith, his religion!"[9] But "faith" here means faith in reason and in the solidarity of a liberated humanity. The new cathedral envisioned by Gropius is very much a socialist cathedral. And it is a cathedral to be built on the basis of technology. The Gothic cathedral is replaced with the crystal palaces of modern architecture, which speaks of a confidence in the emancipatory power of the new technology. The architecture envisioned by Gropius answers to the longing for a new religion, a longing widespread at the time[10]—we met with it already in Heidegger, whom it made vulnerable to the quasi-religious appeal of National Socialism, whose "truth and greatness" he located in 1935 in "the encounter of planetarily determined technology and modern man."[11] The problem faced by us indeed remains how to integrate technology into a better dwelling instead of allowing our dwelling to be distorted and perhaps destroyed by the uncontrolled progress of technology. The possibility of such integration, a possibility of which both Ruskin and Loos had despaired, was eagerly pursued by Gropius as it must be by any committed modernist.

By claiming the Gothic cathedral as the precursor of his utopian architecture, Gropius claims for modern architecture, too, something like a religious significance. All religion is marked by its integrative power; every genuine religion has to embrace the whole, cannot survive, as Louis Dupré points out, "as a particular aspect of life."[12] This places religion in sharp opposition to that splintering of life that finds expression in a slogan like "art for art's sake" or "business is business." Art for art's sake and religion have to be enemies. It is thus hardly surprising that the dream of the complete building becomes the dream of the new cathedral.

But if the association of architecture and religion is readily suggested by the conception of the complete building, it also threatens to push this ideal architecture into a lost past or an uncertain future. It is difficult to reconcile the kind of integration demanded here with the centrifugal forces inseparable from modernity. Is the dream of the complete building more than a utopian anachronism? The social function of utopian thinking demands that it place itself in opposition to what is taken for granted, that like a plough it break the crust of the established and accepted to prepare for a new kind of dwelling. Gropius recognized the utopian character of his dream and knew that its realization could not be ensured by human willing and planning. As Heidegger was to insist, the kind of building that provides for genuine dwelling must itself grow from such a dwelling. The integrated life has to give birth to and cannot simply be generated by the architect's work. Gropius was thus willing to grant that we shall not see the realization of the complete building, that its realization depended on something like grace. Still, although convinced that the ideal of the complete building cannot be realized given the shape of our time, although prepared to admit that we shall not see buildings that are more than splinters, Gropius yet demands that this ideal of the complete building should give direction to architecture. Whatever steps can be taken that will integrate the arts and life should be taken. In the absence of faith the dream of a recovery of the architecture of faith becomes the dream of an artistic integration of life. And Gropius was too much of a realist, too insistent on building (and also on building his Bauhaus), not to allow reality to clip the wings of his dreams: that the members of the Bauhaus soon found it necessary to exchange the title "master" for the more established "professor" is not insignificant.

As Loos recognized so clearly,[13] the danger with all attempts to transform the built environment into a *Gesamtkunstwerk,* a complete or total work of art, is that they tend to make the architect into a kind of dictator who in designing an architectural environment imposes on others his or her vision of how they are to live. Implicit in the demand for the complete building are totalitarian tendencies, and we may well wonder whether architects like Paul Ludwig Troost and Albert Speer did not come closer to realizing the dream of a new cathedral than did the Bauhaus. Nazi architecture, too, did not hesitate to invoke the cathedral to challenge the building practices of the day:

for the first time since the early German cathedrals buildings are rising that are completely removed from the everyday: self-representation of the most primordial natural powers of an awakened, racially conscious people, incarnation of a faith become stone. In these buildings the Führer forms the image of the most noble traits of the German community. In them architecture becomes the educator of a new people. The artistic genius of the creator of the German worldview (Weltanschauung) gave them the style of that heroism which leads the decisive political battle against disintegration and decline to victory. The psychic greatness commemorated in stone will even in most distant ages illuminate the entire people with the heroic spirit of its founder. These buildings of faith, whose destiny it is to give visible expression to the experience of this worldview, stand before us, great and unique. They become a sacred precinct of our people. [14]

Just as there is a sense in which it is not so much individual architects who built the cathedrals but God, so there is a sense in which it is not so much architects like Troost and Speer who built the architecture of the Third Reich but Hitler, who was being celebrated as "the nation's highest and final good," the person in whom it finds its "perfection."[15] We have to grant the architect of the new Germany something like artistic genius, but it is the genius of a creator of kitsch, for what defines kitsch is, as Hermann Broch pointed out, precisely the reoccupation of the infinite by the finite. Kitsch always substitutes for the divine some golden calf, in this case Hitler for the Redeemer, the German nation for the City of God.[16]

Like Gropius, like so many others including Heidegger, Hitler dreamed that a radically renewed Germany might rise from the ashes of World War I. And the would-be architect Hitler, too, looked to a new architectural style to help found the new German reality. In a building like Troost's Haus der Kunst in Munich (fig. 116) the political form of life does indeed find its unmistakable expression in a style that rules the monumental architecture of the Third Reich. The paradigm of the Christian cathedral here gives way to the Greek temple, thought to provide the necessary classical counterweight to a tendency toward formlessness and individualizing self-destruction supposed to threaten especially the German.[17] This paradigm, however, is transposed into a lean monumentality that reduces the individual to insignificance, a transposition that helps to define what we can call "monumental kitsch."

Even more convincingly the National Socialist utopia found expression in its urban planning, beginning with the establishment, entrusted to Troost, of a processional route

Paul Ludwig Troost, Haus der Kunst, Munich.
Source: *Die Kunst im Dritten Reich,* July and
116 | August 1937.

in Munich, the city to which National Socialism traced its origin and in which the movement's first martyrs lay buried. The path was to lead from the now sacred Beer Hall, the route "marked with 240 pylons each honoring one of the 240 men who had died in the struggle against the German state and the enemies of the Volk between November 9, 1923, and January 30, 1933," to the Feldherrnhalle, where a monument was to be erected for the movement's "blood witnesses"; from there it would continue to the Königlicher Platz, which was transformed from a grassy square into a sea of granite slabs flanked with two "Temples of Honor," containing the martyrs' coffins and still-standing party buildings.[18] This raises Klenze's already rather dry classicism to a higher and now crushingly monumental level: "Here something new came into being whose deepest meaning is a political declaration." And indeed, so it did and so it was: the new square called for a uniformed humanity. Filled with soldiers declaring their loyalty to Hitler, the square declared a transformed ethos: "what mattered was not the change in material but the changed attitude, and this attitude also speaks to us in other buildings."[19] An inhuman scale, geometric order, and stony, clean surfaces promise to deliver us from the burden of time and individuality.

While van Pelt calls Munich a "corruption of the Athenian necropolis," he invites us to understand the Nazi Party rally grounds in Nuremberg as "a reinterpretation of the Athenian Agora in Volkish terms."[20] The example set in Munich was further monumentalized. But the utopian idea pursued by the Nazis found its final and most complete expression in the planned transformation of Berlin into Germania, with its projected avenue joining that triumphal arch whose opening would have had room for the Arc de Triomphe and a gigantic domed hall where for a thousand years a hundred thousand were to join in thanksgiving and praise of the founder of a rejuvenated world.[21] Plans for the new capital continued to occupy Hitler and his architects almost to the end. As late as 1944 architects were invited to enter a competition concerning the "total reconstruction" of bombed Berlin. Goebbels and Speer's master plan envisioned a garden city of ten million people. Plans were to have been completed by the end of 1944.[22]

4

One breathes healthier air when one turns from such not so much utopian as millennial dreams to the increasingly down-to-earth concerns of the Bauhaus (fig. 117). Not solely pragmatic considerations soon forced it to leave behind its romantic beginning, as especially the challenge of van Doesburg helped direct it toward a much more resolute embrace of technology. However, a building like the Faguswerk in Alfeld or a text like Gropius's 1910 "Program for the Founding of a General Housing-Construction Company Following Artistically Uniform Principles,"[23] which was to help along the industrialization of building, suggests that the founder of the Bauhaus had long held the conviction that allowed him to now write: "The entire architecture of the 'arts and crafts' of the last generation . . . is with very few exceptions a lie. In all of these one can recognize the false and spastic effort 'to make Art.' They actually stand in the way of the pure joy in the art of 'building.' Today's architect has forfeited the right to exist. . . . The engineer on the other hand, unhampered by esthetics and historical inhibitions, has arrived at clear and organic forms. He seems to be slowly taking over the heritage of the architect, who evolved from the crafts."[24]

One master who welcomed this turn and its pragmatic sobriety was the painter Oskar Schlemmer. Schlemmer sympathized with the romanticism that helped establish the Bauhaus: "The Staatliches Bauhaus, founded after the catastrophe of the war, in the chaos of the revolution and in the era of the flowering of an emotion-laden, explosive art, be-

117 | Walter Gropius, Bauhaus, Dessau. Credit: Bildarchiv Foto Marburg/Art Resource.

comes the rallying-point of all those who, with the belief in the future and with sky-storming enthusiasm, wish to build the 'cathedral of socialism.' The triumphs of industry and technology before the war and the orgies in the name of destruction during it, called to life that impassioned romanticism that was a flaming protest against materialism and the mechanization of art and life."[25] But new values had surfaced in the meantime. Schlemmer, too, thought himself on the threshold of a new faith: "Reversal of values, changes in point of view, name, and concept result in the other view, the next faith. Dada, court jester in this kingdom, plays ball with paradoxes and makes the atmosphere free and easy. Americanisms transferred to Europe, the new wedged into the old world, death to the past, to moonlight, and to the soul, thus the present time strides along with the gestures of a conqueror." The new gods are reason and science, their servant the engineer. "Mathematics, structure, and mechanization are the elements and power and money are the dictators of these modern phenomena of steel, concrete, glass, and electricity."[26] Finally the reasonable individual will assume responsibility for creation: consummation of the Enlightenment's promise. Schlemmer's new faith is a humanist one that presupposes the death of God. As Schlemmer understood this faith, it demanded a retreat from the ambitions associated with the word "cathedral."

Originally the Bauhaus was founded with visions of erecting the cathedral or the church of socialism, and the workshops were established in the manner of the cathedral building lodges ("Dombauhütten"). The idea has for the time being [1922] receded into the background and with it certain definite ideas of an artistic nature. Today we must think at best in terms of a house, perhaps even only think so, but in any case in terms of the house of the simplest kind. Perhaps, in face of the economic plight, it is our task to become pioneers of simplicity, that is, to find a simple form for all of life's necessities which at the same time is respectable and genuine.[27]

Pleading for a return to the house, or, even more modestly, for reflections on what might constitute the basic requirements of dwelling, Schlemmer opposes himself to what he himself considers the romantic aspirations that helped found the Bauhaus, rejecting them at least "for the time being."

One may well wonder at this "for the time being": does it not betray, despite what one may think all-too-justified misgivings, a hankering after the authoritative and authoritarian architecture of the past, from whose shadow architecture had to emerge to be up to the transformations wrought by science and technology and up to their promise of emancipation? The turn from the cathedral to the house might be understood as a return to what has to provide all architecture genuinely of this age with its point of departure: individual dwelling and building responsive to its requirements. Such a return would also have to reject my metaphor of an ellipse having its two foci in temple and house. Architecture has only one focus, but this focus should now be sought not with the temple but with the house, or more precisely with houses; not with God, nor with a reified community, but with individual human beings. What answers to the latter is not an urban structure, organized and dominated by architectural monuments, but a collection of houses, organized and held together by a support system shaped and organized by our need to live and work as members of a community. Lewis Mumford thus praises William Morris for achieving, at least symbolically, a genuine revolution when he recognized that while "the factory was the nucleus of the paleotechnic community, the house was to become the nucleus of the bio-technic age,"[28] the age that had succeeded in making technology fully subservient to the requirements of human life.

"Believe me," William Morris wrote, "if you want art to begin at home, as it must, we must clear our houses of troublesome superfluities that are forever in our way; conventional comforts that are not real comforts, and do but make work for servants and doctors; if you want the golden rule that will fit every-body, this is it: have nothing in your house that you do not know to be useful or believe to be beautiful." This clearing away of historic debris, this stripping to the skin, was the first essential mark of the new architecture, as it was, in effect, for the new life and cosmic relations that was introduced by the systematic sciences. In building: the open window, the blank wall, the unlittered floor: nothing for show and nothing that cannot be shown.[29]

With good reason Mumford celebrates Frank Lloyd Wright as the prophet of the biotechnic economy of the future. As in all great architecture, buried within Wright's houses is a piece of utopia, communicated by the way they "effect a synthesis of nature, the machine, and human activities and purposes."[30] Mumford points out that such emphasis on the house fails to address the problem of communal integration—it is telling that in 1932 Wright published *The Disappearing City*, an ideal version of the kind of decentralized urban development that in the intervening years has swallowed so much of the landscape. But the ever more apparent problem of communal cohesiveness, reflected equally in suburban sprawl and in the often ruinous state of the core of our cities, forces us to question Wright's utopia with its garden-tilling families on plots of at least one acre. It returns us to the question of how to reoccupy the place of temple and cathedral, a question that should not be divorced from another: is such talk not part of an inheritance that architecture and architectural theory must shed if it is to address the real problems? This is the burden from which Mumford attempted to free architecture: "Heretofore architectural monuments had alone been the center of appreciation and the accepted source of style: the Pantheon, the Maison Carrée, the palace of Diocletian at Spalato, the cathedral of Strasbourg, St. Mark's in Venice. These monumental buildings, crystallizations of a whole social order, were mis-takenly seized as starting points of architectural design. In the middle of the nineteenth century this error had been carried so far that little cottages cowered behind massive Greek pediments, and the student of architecture began his apprenticeship with a study of the decorative elements of classic monumental forms."[31]

Mumford's biotechnic utopia is not so very distant from the dreams of such socially conscious Bauhaus masters as Schlemmer. But that such a scaling back of the ambition that found expression in the image of a modern cathedral and the call for an intimate alliance between art and technology should have met with spirited opposition from some of the Bauhaus masters was to be expected. It is not surprising either that among the opponents should have been Feininger, the artist who created the image on the cover of the first Bauhaus program. "With absolute conviction I reject the slogan 'Art and Technology—

A new Unity'—this misinterpretation of art is, however, a symptom of our times. And the demand for linking it with technology is absurd from every point of view. A genuine technologist will quite correctly refuse to enter into artistic questions; and on the other hand, the greatest technical perfection can never replace the divine spark of art."[32] As I showed in chapter 15, we have to grant both claims. But I also suggested that though technology must keep its distance from art and cannot replace art, this does not mean that art cannot turn to technology and re-present its essence by celebrating new materials and new construction techniques. And if it is irresponsible to present a vision of future community that refuses to take account of technology's liberating promise, then any version of the cathedral of the future will have not just to exhibit mastery of what Schlemmer called the "modern phenomena of steel, concrete, glass, and electricity," but to speak of that promise by their artistic re-presentation.

5

The suggestion that National Socialism's political program for architecture and Gropius's dream of a New Cathedral have their roots in the same cultural situation—a situation shaped by the experience of World War I and its destruction of a fabric that, threadbare as it may have been, still had furnished many with a sense of shelter; shaped also by the resulting openness to everything that seemed to promise some shelter to replace what had been lost; shaped by a renewed receptivity to all sorts of utopian visions—may seem difficult to reconcile with the evident hostility with which Nazis and proto-Nazis met the Bauhaus and its efforts almost from its beginning, hostility that forced it to migrate from Weimar to Dessau, then to Berlin, only to be dissolved in 1933. No doubt, the Nazis considered the Bauhaus a symbol of the powers it considered its enemies: a rootless internationalism, communism, foreign interests. And it was indeed a stronghold of a reason and a humanity that refused to betray themselves by wrapping themselves in the German flag.

Still, there is a sense in which it was the accident of Hitler's personal architectural convictions that prevented the vision of the New Cathedral from becoming contaminated by an association with National Socialist ideology. Hitler fancied himself an architect and had strong opinions about architecture, stronger than, say, his feelings about music; these opinions gave birth to the popular bombast of Troost and Speer and prevented an understanding between National Socialism and modern architecture. Gropius and Mies, like so many architects who want to build, even when the money needed to support such building is of questionable origin, were not altogether impervious to Nazi blandishments and, given a more supportive leadership, might easily have followed Heidegger's lead.[33] Finally it was Hitler himself who saved them from the Nazis. Charles Jencks calls our attention to Gropius's disappointing if not altogether surprising letter to Goebbels, expressing his hope to place the new architecture at the service of the then–newly established National Socialist state: "Can Germany afford to throw overboard the new architecture and its spiritual leaders, when there is nothing to replace them . . . ? But above all I myself see this new style as the way in which our country can finally achieve a valid union of the two great spiritual heritages of the classical and the Gothic. Schinkel sought this union, but in vain. Shall Germany deny itself this great opportunity?"[34] Mies van der Rohe's willingness to sign a patriotic appeal issued by the Nazi architect Schulze-Naumburg is a similar embarrassment, as is his acceptance of the commission to design the Reichsbank.[35] And while we would like to see modern art and architecture in unshakable opposition to totalitarianism, we should not be too surprised by such willingness to collaborate, which, Jencks suggests, was more the rule than the exception. I would only question that what we have here—in the case of Gropius, for example—is merely an all-too-human opportunism willing to sacrifice principle to expediency. It would be comforting if it were so. But I find it hard to overlook the similarity between the program presented by National Socialism, which also insisted on an overcoming of disintegration and fragmentation, which also wanted to subordinate the individual to the collectivity, and the ideas that found expression in the manifestoes of some of the leading modern architects.

One senses the affinity that links the utopian wing of modern architecture to totalitarianism in texts like Bruno Taut's "A Programme for Architecture" (1918): "Art— that is one single thing when it exists! Today there is no art. The various disrupted tendencies can find their way back to a single unity only under the wings of architecture, so that every individual discipline will play its part in building. Then there will be no frontiers between the applied arts and painting and sculpture. Everything will be one thing: architecture."[36] So far this sounds very much like Gropius. But Taut continues: "The direct carrier of the spiritual forces, moulder of the sensibilities of the general public, which today are slumbering and tomorrow will awake, is architecture. But this revolution, . . . this architecture, will not come of themselves. Both must be willed—today's architect must prepare the way for tomorrow's buildings. They must receive public assistance to make it possible."[37] Taut also sees the task of integration as one that denies autonomy to the separate arts. Architecture is seen as the master art that draws the others out of their isolation. But the desire for integration goes further: the individual and all that expresses and reenforces individuality are seen as forces that stand in the way of the required integration. Taut is a revolutionary who sees in the individualism of bourgeois society the enemy. He is only being consistent when he demands the abolition of the distinction between private and public architecture. Quite explicitly he thus demands the collapse of my ellipse, with its two foci, into a circle. The architect is asked to think big, to imagine large-scale housing projects in which theater and music would find their place—invited to dream of megastructures that would collapse the distinction between public and private, sacred and profane. The architects of the Russian revolution were such dreamers; another such dreamer was Frank Lloyd Wright's student Paolo Soleri: no longer is the architect content with the model provided by the Gothic cathedral. After all, in the medieval city it was still possible to distinguish between private and public. The house is not integrated into the church, although it relates to and is illuminated by it. Just such integration was demanded by Taut. In this respect his paradigm would appear to be not so much the medieval city as the Heavenly Jerusalem, which found its closest realization on earth in the monastery that similarly attempted to integrate the important human functions, if at the price of an elision or distortion of sexuality.

The affinity of certain tendencies of modern architecture to totalitarianism is instructive. For one, it teaches us not to expect too much from the architect. The answer to the question of dwelling should never be entrusted to one person, no matter what his or her genius. And replacing the architect of genius with some collectivity, as Bruno Taut wanted to do, does not really help. We should no more sacrifice the individual to the collectivity than to a leader or artist of genius. The rights of the individual must be recognized alongside and in their inevitable tension with the rights of the community. And that is to say also that the rights of building must be recognized alongside and in their inevitable tension with the rights of architecture. Once more the image of the ellipse with a private and a public focus provides a useful starting place.

23

1

Too committed are we to our own individual selves, to freedom, to spaces that invite endless exploration, not to distrust those who with Sedlmayr mourn "the loss of the center"; we are too suspicious of all building that would strongly place or root us to dream of some healing, consoling utopia. Many of us feel too strongly placed by our life-world; we long not for reoccupations of some lost center but for decentering, disorienting heterotopias,[1] for spaces that like Piranesi's *Carceri* (fig. 118) invite endless exploration. We dream of journeys of discovery no longer burdened by the nostalgia for home, journeys into the wildernesses beyond and within. Is Dante's Ulysses not more likely to be our hero than Homer's? "The traveler must realize that the sought-for adventure, to be total, must be limitless, that therefore the voyage must be prolonged indefinitely, and that *one cannot return from it*."[2] Such distrust of all centers and supposedly firm boundaries delights in ruins, welcomes the deconstruction of the Towers of Babel raised by architects and philosophers claiming arrogantly to provide for a supposedly genuine dwelling. It welcomes what has come to be called "deconstruction," itself an architectural metaphor, which is of course not just a metaphor but an intellectual movement, or perhaps fashion, that, while it may have peaked, has had a decisive impact on all the humanities—especially on philosophy, whose traditional reliance on architectural metaphors of construction it calls into question—and has had an impact even on architecture: the Museum of Modern Art's exhibition "Deconstructivist Architecture" (1988) spoke thus of "the emergence of a new sensibility" fascinated by possibilities of contaminating, disrupting, violating, and subverting architecture. That the marriage of architectural construction and wordy deconstruction should not have been an easy one but instead a relationship of continuing confrontation, in which one partner inevitably calls the other into question, is to be expected: Mark Wigley is right to call architecture the Achilles' heel of deconstruction,[3] a place where deconstruction exhibits its vulnerability with unusual clarity, as is demonstrated by Derrida's collaboration with Bernard Tschumi and Peter Eisenman—a collaboration that threatens to reduce deconstructive discourse to no more than a curiously cerebral kind of decoration.

Clearly it should be more than that: the very term "deconstruction" invites us to confront and question the architectural metaphors that have figured decisively in the discourse of religion and philosophy, invites us to think of God and the philosopher in the image of the architect. All three are conceived as builders, each in the image of the other two, where figure and figured reverse places and intertwine in ways that in the end have to call into question the very idea of well-founded building that grants possibilities of genuine dwelling. We have grown suspicious of all sorts of "edification," especially of the "architecture" raised by philosophers. Appealing to Nietzsche, Sarah Kofman thus opposed to the system-building philosopher-spiders that suck the blood out of life—*die Philosophen spinnen!*—the new philosophers who reveal the poison hidden in all such buildings and thus promise to return us to life.[4] To speak here with Kofman of poison is to invite an appropriation of Nietzsche as the physician of a culture all too ready to seek refuge in lifeless architecture of all sorts, all too eager to imprison itself in architecture. Is Nietzsche that physician? Important here is no so much whether Kofman's appropriation does justice to Nietzsche's many-voiced texts—whether they offer better support for deconstructive readings than, say, for Heidegger's very different appropriation or for Alfred Bäumler's National Socialist interpretation—but what is at issue. That deconstruction should have chosen Nietzsche for its hero is no accident: Nietzsche does call into question any version of what I have called the ethical function of architecture and he does so in a way that communicates a postmodern care for the anarchic self that has to be suspicious of all attempts to bind creativity and freedom to some supposed *archē* or essence or place. Nietzsche would seem to dream of something very different, as is suggested by the following two quotes, both ambiguous pointers toward an architecture for tomorrow. The first invites us to think of architecture in the image of the labyrinth: "If we willed and dared an architecture according to the kind of souls we possess (for that we are too cowardly!) the labyrinth would have to be our model!"[5] The second invites us to think of the city of the future in the image of Venice: "Together one hundred deep solitudes form the city of Venice—this is its magic. An image for the human beings of the future."[6]

Giambattista Piranesi, Prison (*Carceri*). Credit: Beinecke Rare Book and Manuscript Library, Yale University.

118

2

The myth of the labyrinth holds a special place in the thinking of Nietzsche, who likened himself to Dionysus, Cosima Wagner to Ariadne, Wagner himself to the Minotaur, theatrical Bayreuth to the labyrinth.[7] But Nietzsche gives a new twist to an old tradition when he writes that if we only had the courage, we moderns would model our buildings on the labyrinth. For himself Nietzsche claims the required courage.[8] In *Ecce Homo* he thus speaks of the fascinated curiosity that draws him to the labyrinth, a curiosity linked to what Nietzsche considers his vocation: "There are cases where what is needed is an Ariadne's thread leading into the labyrinth. He who has the task to bring on the great war, the war against the virtuous (the good and virtuous, Zarathustra calls them, also 'most men,' also 'beginning of the end') has to be willing to buy some experiences at almost any price; the price could even be the danger of losing oneself."[9] Why should there be a need to return to the labyrinth? Are labyrinths not structures that we dread to enter, structures that were built precisely to make us lose our way? Yet the way we are drawn to the labyrinths artfully constructed by poets, painters, and landscape architects suggests that something in us delights in just such disorienting spaces.

Labyrinth and center belong together, and we should keep in mind the profoundly ambiguous symbolism of the center: God is called the center of creation, but at the earth's center lurks the devil, and at the center of the labyrinth dwells the Minotaur. The way to the true center leads therefore through a dark and dangerous labyrinth, which conceals its own deadly center. Traditionally the labyrinth thus describes a condition the hero has to enter and pass through if he is to gain access to the true center, step into the true light; his quest demands of him the courage to forsake the seeming security of the everyday for a realm where every sound threatens danger, where the ear matters rather than the eye. Christian thinkers thus thought our world a labyrinth. The title of a work like John Amos Comenius's *Labyrinth of the World and the Paradise of the Heart* (1663) speaks for itself: the Fall lets us wander in a labyrinth, longing for paradise, this bounded space that allowed human beings to dwell near the center. Hence the tendency recurs to think of architecture as a repetition of our lost home, as a reestablishment of the center, of the architect as a godlike creator. But human building lacks the strength to recover what has been lost, even when the work produced is a church: by proudly signing their names in large labyrinths set into the floor of the nave, the builders of the cathedrals at Chartres, Reims, and Amiens invite us to interpret their work as a repetition of the work of their ancestor Daedalus,[10] thus calling their own pride into question and reminding the faithful that what human art here has so splendidly fashioned is also but a labyrinth, through which they have to pass on their way to salvation. This life is not so much a dwelling as a journeying. And so Comenius does not look to human ingenuity to show us a way out of the labyrinth: corrupt nature cannot be mended by Worldly Wisdom; home is sought not without, in this labyrinthine world, but within, in the heart.

Just this claim, that human effort, that reason should lack the strength to show us a way out of the labyrinth, is at odds with modern confidence in the power of reason to build human beings a house and to defeat the power of the labyrinth. Descartes thus offers his newfound method as the thread of Ariadne. It is worth noting that, true to his stance between Counter-Reformation and modernity, he casts himself in the role of Theseus: the method is a gift and in thanksgiving Descartes vows a pilgrimage to that Christian Ariadne, the Virgin of Loreto.

Such manifestations of piety are difficult to reconcile with our image of Descartes as a founding hero of the modern age, who descended into the labyrinth of doubt and, guided only by reason, gained the needed orientation. A century later Johann Christoph Gottsched thus tells his readers that philosophy, in his case the rationalism of Christian Wolff, allowed him to "see order and truth in the world, which before had seemed to him like a labyrinth or a dream."[11] Not divine grace but reason provided the Enlightenment with the thread of Ariadne that allowed it to replace the Baroque labyrinth with that perfect cosmos revealed or rather constructed by a philosopher like Leibniz.

If Descartes presents himself as a philosophical Theseus,[12] able to lead us out of the labyrinth of appearance and opinion, the philosopher's self-presentation did not go unchallenged. Father Bourdin, the author of the seventh set of objections to the *Meditations,* speaks for a tradition that had to suspect behind the philosopher's confidence the sin of pride, when he invokes not Theseus but Icarus: "Other methods indeed of constructing houses lay very stable foundations, e.g. of squared stones, brick, rough rock, and countless similar substances, reposing on which the walls mount upwards. But your method proceeds quite otherwise and, in its attempt to get something, not out of something but out of nothing, it tears down, digs up, and cuts away every scrap of the old foundations. It changes its attitude completely but, lest in its flight, it should seem to have no wings to propel it, like Icarus it assumes new ones and fixes them on with wax" (2:329). Descartes ridicules the good father, who, by fusing the architectural metaphor that introduces the *Meditations* (1:144) with the Icarus image, is said to have attributed wings to architecture. Reaffirming the architectural metaphor—"Everywhere in my writings I made it clear that my procedure was like that of Architects planning houses" (2:325)—he claims a religious significance for his work by insisting that the chapel he has built rests on firm foundations. Father Bourdin calls that procedure into question, warning of the dreadful "spectres that lurk in these underground excavations," of "that subterranean gloom" into which Descartes descends to look for his foundation (2:327, 328). As he understands it Descartes's path leads not out of but back into the labyrinth, that is to say, away from God, leads toward nothingness and death, letting him fall, like Icarus, into the deadly abyss.

Is Descartes Theseus? Or is he Icarus? Or perhaps Daedalus—in which case the fact that this archetypal architect's main work was the labyrinth invites reflection and places not just architecture but the modern world that Descartes helped build in a questionable light. To be sure, the successes of our science and our worldwide technological culture seem to validate Descartes's confidence in our ability to understand reality and to assert ourselves as its master. But while Hegel, the greatest of all philosophical architects, could still say that it is with Descartes that "the education, the thinking of our age begins," that "here, we can say, we are at home and like the sailor, after long journeying about the raging sea, call 'land,' "[13] we have lost such confidence. Nietzsche especially is invoked as a kind of antipode to Descartes, a thinker supposed to have refuted Descartes's claim to have found Ariadne's thread and now showing us the way back into the labyrinth that is our world.

3

Such invocation of Nietzsche, however, calls itself into question. Someone who wants to enter the labyrinth, a desire that invites challenge, must think of him- or herself outside. The claim that "if we willed and dared an architecture according to the kind of souls we possess (for that we are too cowardly!) the labyrinth would have to be our model" suggests tension between our souls and the world we have to live in. The problem for Nietzsche is not that our modern world is too labyrinthine, but that it seems to exclude the labyrinth, not that Descartes's building today lies in ruins, but that, while it would perhaps be better if it had collapsed, it nevertheless still stands. Nietzsche, too, recognizes that there is an important sense in which we moderns have indeed left the labyrinth; he presupposes that Descartes, even if unable to provide the edifice of science with the firm foundation he had sought, was nevertheless able to raise it in a way that allowed it to endure and enabled others to continue the work he had begun.

Nietzsche's early fragment *On Truth and Lie in an Extramoral Sense* has become popular with postmodernists eager to deconstruct versions of Descartes's chapel. But only a careless reading of this text will overlook how close Nietzsche here remains to other philosophical builders, to Kant and especially to Schopenhauer. That we ourselves have constituted the world of science is no reason to question "the eternal consistency, omnipresence, and infallibility of the laws of nature."[14] Quite the opposite: the turn to the subject allowed a thinker like Kant to conclude that, in Nietzsche's words, "so far as we can penetrate here—from the telescopic heights to the microscopic depths—everything is secure, complete, infinite, regular, and without any gaps. Science will be able to dig successfully in this shaft forever, and all the things that are discovered will harmonize with and not contradict each other."[15] Nietzsche advances no considerations to dispute such confidence. Readers of this text who focus on the many ways in which Nietzsche here emphasizes "the artistic process of metaphor formation" should keep in mind his insistence that this process, with which every sensation is said to begin, also is said to presuppose Kant's pure intuitions, time and space, and therefore "relationships of succession and number." "The only way in which the possibility of subsequently constructing a new conceptual edifice from metaphors themselves can be explained is by the firm persistence of these original forms. That is to say, this conceptual edifice is an imitation of temporal, spatial, and numerical relationships in the domain of metaphor."[16] Every explanation of metaphor formation is here said to presuppose a world of objects in Kant's sense, a world supported by pure intuitions that bear a striking resemblance to Cartesian clear and distinct ideas.

What lets Nietzsche dream of the labyrinth is precisely that he experiences this all too well established Cartesian, Kantian world-building as stifling, as a prison. The young Nietzsche is here close to Dostoevsky's man from the underground, who also emphasizes human creativity and sees such creativity threatened by an all too successful science. What Nietzsche finds problematic about the modern world is that it is too well built, too much like a cosmos that assigns us our place, imprisoning creativity and imagination. What makes Descartes such a problematic thinker then is not his failure but precisely his undeniable success. The understanding of reality bound up with our science and technology threatens to bury imagination and creativity.

Nietzsche likens the conceptual edifice raised by science to a Roman columbarium. Exchanging honey for ashes, science is the graveyard of perception. Reason's burial work begins as soon as there is speech.

Just as the Romans and Etruscans cut up the heavens with rigid mathematical lines and confined a god within each of the spaces thereby delimited, as within a templum, *so every people has a mathematically divided conceptual heaven above themselves and henceforth thinks that truth demands that each conceptual god be sought only within his own* sphere. *Here one may certainly admire man as a mighty genius of construction, who succeeds in piling up an infinitely complicated dome of concepts upon an unstable foundation, and, as it were, on running water. Of course, in order to be supported by such a foundation, his construction must be like one constructed of spider's webs; delicate enough to be carried along by the waves, strong enough not to be blown apart by every wind.*[17]

Nietzsche is quite aware of that power of self-transcendence that raises the enduring edifice of science, a power inseparable from rationality. The question is, at what cost?—and Descartes already hinted at the cost when he excluded final causes from science. There are no values, no ends, no center to be discovered in this nature. The building raised by science is built with mute matter. No longer do stones speak. No longer do we experience nature as a book in which we can read. Here we have a first clue to the meaning of Nietzsche's pronouncement in *Human, All Too Human*: "Stone is more stone than it used to be."[18] But just this loss of the center, this silence casts the individual back onto his or her own freedom. This is how Tafuri understands Piranesi's *Campo Marzio*: "It is almost too facile to read into this the anticipation of what would become the impotency of the signified in the Victorian age. The 'loss of the center' is undergone and sublimated by Piranesi, accepted without disguising its negativity. The 'negative' now becomes the *egoism* and the *silence* of form."[19]

4

The problem with science then is not that it is unable to raise a lasting structure, but that it is unable to build an edifice in which we can actually live. The distance that separates the world of science from the life world helps to define the spiritual situation of our time. Something of that distance is suggested by Nietzsche's description of the scientist as someone who "builds his hut right next to the tower of science so that he will be able to work on it and to find shelter for himself beneath those bulwarks which presently exist. And he requires shelter, for there are frightful powers which continuously break in upon him, powers which oppose scientific 'truth' with completely different kinds of 'truths' which bear on their shields the most varied sorts of emblems."[20] Once more there comes to mind Brueghel's image of the Tower of Babel, which stands for our prideful attempt to rely on reason to establish that center denied to us by our condition.

There is tention between reason and imagination: while the former insists on rule and order, the latter is anarchic in its very essence, challenging what science would have us accept as reality by opposing to it the realms of myth and art. The imagination refuses the ideal of truth as a correspondence between our discourse and the things. And yet it too knows something like truth: Nietzsche speaks of a "creative correspondence" to a "present intuition." The imagination knows its own responsibility, a responsibility that presupposes freedom from the tyranny of reason. And even though reason would marginalize the imagination, its drive toward metaphors "is not truly vanquished and scarcely subdued by the fact that a regular and rigid new world is constructed as its prison from its own ephemeral products, the concepts."[21] "Prison" is a misleading translation of *Zwingburg,* which refers to a tyrant's strong castle, a structure that, like Brueghel's Tower of Babel, looms over the surrounding landscape. Those it dominates do not live in it, even if they are bound by the rule it represents. Similarly we are dominated by but cannot live in the house of reason. What we consider proper discourse, to be sure, is discourse obedient to the rule of the tyrant in the castle. But to really live we must keep ourselves open to the anarchic realm of perception, imagination, and affect, for here is the source of all meaning and value. We need the enchantment of myth, as developed in *The Birth of Tragedy.*

The metaphor of a "columbarium of concepts" suggests an affinity between the work of reason and death. Concepts are the ashes of live intuitions. The pursuit of truth leads beyond time and thus beyond life. But if the pursuit of truth seeks to translate life out of time, such translation cannot finally succeed. As Sartre knew, the project to elevate the human subject into God turns out to be the pursuit of a contradiction, whose seductive promise we bear within ourselves. The attempt to defeat the essential insecurity of human existence by subjecting life to the rule of reason threatens to transform such life, even before death, into a living death. What endows the castle of reason with its suffocating authority is our own overly great preoccupation with our finitude and temporality, our attempt to secure what finally cannot be secured. Thus it is we who allow the tyrant to rule and distort our lives, and that rule will be broken not by reasoning more carefully but by a different pathos, by an overcoming of what Zarathustra calls "the spirit of revenge": "the will's ill will against time and its 'it was.' "[22] The problem Nietzsche would have us face is a problem not so much of epistemology but of ethics. And it is precisely because our attempts to secure our existence have so effectively left the Baroque labyrinth behind that Nietzsche dreams of it, seeking "an Ariadne's thread leading into the labyrinth," where the path into the labyrinth is a path into the darkness we bear within ourselves, as well as a journey toward death. Precisely because we are so firmly placed by our culture, we dream of chaos and letting go, "dream of effortless rolling downward—the modern festival mood."[23]

5

That we thus dream of chaos and letting go, of buildings in the image of the labyrinth, is hardly a sign of spiritual health. Indeed Nietzsche considers it rather a symptom of decadence, as becomes clear when we look at his pronouncement about "an architecture according to the kind of souls we possess" in its context: in a manner that recalls Hegel's *Vorlesungen über die Ästhetik,* although without Hegel's valorization of the progress of reason, Nietzsche here suggests that everything Greek has become strange to us moderns. "The Greek is very foreign to us—. . . how simple the Greeks were to themselves in their own understanding. How much we surpass them in understanding human beings! But how labyrinthine our souls and our conceptions of souls are, compared to theirs. If we willed and dared an architecture according to the kind of souls we possess (for that we are too cowardly!) the labyrinth would have to be our model! Our own music, the music that really speaks to us, already hints at it. (For it is in music that people let themselves go, because they think no one could see them *beneath* their music.)"[24] A labyrinthine music figures the labyrinthine architecture of which we dream, so different from all Greek temples.

While Nietzsche here contrasts the modern and the Greek, he also draws a contrast within the decadent modern. Our dreams of a labyrinthine architecture contrast with what we actually take to be beauty in architecture: "What is the beauty of a building today? The same as the beautiful face of a woman lacking spirit: something masklike."[25] In both cases a formal beauty no longer has anything to tell us, is mute. What is here called into question is precisely the kind of beauty on which aesthetics has so often insisted: a self-sufficient but mute plenitude. As I showed in earlier chapters, for architecture this means a formal beauty that no longer stands in an essential relationship to the building that is the bearer of such beauty: the beauty of the work of architecture comes to be thought of as something extra, mere decoration, in its superficiality rather like a mask or decal, easily peeled off. Nietzsche's longing for the labyrinth belongs with his resistance to all decorated sheds.

The statement about the masklike beauty of modern architecture occurs in the section of *Human, All Too Human* entitled "Stone is more stone than it used to be." Stone used to be more than just stone: it also had a meaning. Stone spoke and helped architecture to speak. As postmodern architecture rediscovered, buildings once had something of the quality of texts, as did nature. Today we stand before both without understanding. "On the whole we no longer understand architecture, at least not in the way we understand music." We no longer understand the symbolism of architectural forms. "On a Greek or Christian building everything originally had a meaning, gesturing toward a higher order of things: this mood of an inexhaustible significance surrounded the building like a magical veil." Beauty here remained linked with but subordinate to meaning. Beauty entered the system only on the side, without detracting in any essential way from "the basic mood of the uncanny sublime that belonged to what was consecrated by the proximity of the gods and magic; beauty at most mitigated the terror—but this terror was everywhere the presupposition."[26] Architecture, so understood, lets us participate in a *mysterium tremendum et fascinans;* Nietzsche, too, speaks of the proximity of the gods. But our modern world knows nothing of gods, and if we still experience such a *mysterium* then it is within rather than without. And it is music rather than architecture that speaks to us of this realm, where Nietzsche links "Night and Music": "Only in the night and the half-night of dark forests and caves could the ear, the organ of fear, really develop itself, where it did develop, according to the way of life of the fearful. . . . In the light there is less need for the ear."[27] Music belongs with the fearful darkness of the labyrinth.

Our failure to understand architecture as we still understand music is of a piece with our inability to read in the book of nature and our eagerness to descend into the labyrinth of the self. And just as the labyrinth belongs with Mannerism and Baroque, so, Nietzsche suggests, does modern music.

> *The spirit of the Counter-Reformation is the spirit of modern music. . . . And even now one might ask: and if our newer music were able to move stones, would it join these into an antique architecture? I very much doubt it. For what reigns in music, the affect, the pleasure in heightened, far-extended moods, wanting to become alive at any cost, the quick change of sentiment, the sharp contrast between light and shade, the juxtaposition of ecstasy and the naive—all this reigned in the visual arts once before and created new laws of style:—but it was neither in antiquity nor in the Renaissance.*[28]

The stony hardness of our architecture and of our world lets us long for life, even at the price of architectural order. The de-constructive enterprise is born of such longing.

To dream of an architecture in the image of the labyrinth means therefore also to dream of an architecture in the image of music, which for Nietzsche means to dream of Venice: "When I look for another word for music, I always find only the word Venice."[29] This brings us back to the second remark that introduced this chapter: "Together one hundred deep solitudes form the city of Venice—this is its magic. An image for the human beings of the future." Heidegger cites this remark in a letter to Jaspers, who, pleading for dialogue, had charged Heidegger with monological thinking; and Heidegger agrees with what his old friend Jaspers had said about the need for dialogue, but only to add—a characteristic addition very much in keeping with Heidegger's understanding of authenticity— that "much, however, would have been gained if monologues were allowed to remain what they are. It almost seems to me that they are not as yet [genuine monologues]. For that they are not as yet strong enough," and he goes on to remind Jaspers of what Nietzsche had said about Venice.[30] Jaspers would have us resist the seductive magic of Nietzsche's Venice, which exchanges community for "one hundred profound solitudes," the lonely crowd.

Tafuri cites the same remark in *The Sphere and the Labyrinth,* where it introduces a discussion of New York, this "allegory of the Venice of modern times," a prophecy of the city of the future: "the city as a *system of solitudes,* as a place wherein the loss of identity is made an institution, wherein the maximum formalism of its structures gives rise to a code of behavior dominated by 'vanity' and 'comedy.' From such a viewpoint, New York is already the 'new Venice.' The fragments of the future contained in the Serenissima of Nietzsche have already exploded into the metropolis of total indifference and therefore of the anguished consumption of multiplied signs."[31]

To be sure, most of us are still assigned roles that grant us place, identity, and a measure of security. However, increasingly we experience such roles as arbitrary and readily exchanged for others, experience ourselves as actors who assume this or that mask but see no essential relationship between themselves and these masks. Yet, Nietzsche observes, "Every time the human being begins to discover to what extent he plays a role and to what extent he is able to be an actor, he becomes an actor. . . . With this a new flora and fauna of human beings arise which cannot grow in more solid, more limited ages[;] . . . with this appear every time the most interesting and most excitingly crazy ages of history, in which the 'actors' and all kinds of actors are the real rulers." Architects cannot flourish in such ages. "The power to build now weakens; the courage to make plans extending to the distant future is discouraged; there begins to be a lack of those with organizational genius—who still dares to undertake works where one would have to reckon with millennia for their completion? That basic faith becomes extinct, which would allow someone to reckon in this fashion, to promise, to anticipate the future in the plan, to offer it as a sacrifice to his plan, the faith namely that the human being has value only in as much as he is *a stone in a great building:* for this he has to be first of all firm, must be stone, . . . especially not—actor."[32]

Nietzsche here suggests that our life gains worth only when we can understand ourselves as parts of a more encompassing structure. And to banish the terrors of the labyrinth, he, too, dreams of builders, including statesmen, who require material hard as stone, a dream Hitler sought to realize: "What from now on cannot be built is a society in the old sense of the word; to build this building everything is lacking, first of all the material. *We, all of us, are no material for a society:* this is a truth whose time has come. It does not seem to matter to me that . . . our esteemed socialists believe, hope, dream, especially scream and write just about the opposite; by now one reads their slogan 'free society' on every table and wall. Free society? Yeah! Yeah! But you know of course, gentlemen, out of what that is built? out of wooden iron! Out of the famous wooden iron! And not even wooden."[33] But if we cannot build "a society in the old sense of the word," if indeed, as Loos knew, such a society could never be built but had to grow, why can we not fashion a new society, we who "must live in 'an artificial world that has lost its coordination and has splintered into many parts which, because of their lack of interconnection, lacerate man and create extreme anarchy.'"[34] If disintegration and chaos threaten the modern metropolis, why not counter chaos with an artificial constructed order? This is what, according to Francesco Dal Co, the avid Nietzsche reader Mies tried to do: "Mies counters Guardini's 'world without center' with rigid demands for order, as though interpreting Guardini's thought, designing his own rigorous, Schinkelesque volumetric compositions to encompass ascetically shaped spaces."[35]

Very similar words might have described Speer's ambitions. So understood the architect's building mirrors the totalitarian state, it too being an artificially constructed order. Nietzsche helps us understand why liberal democracy should have totalitarianism for its shadow,[36] and why the modern metropolis should have called forth an austere architecture. In both cases "the power to build" presupposes a will to power.[37] "The most powerful have always inspired the architects; the architect was always under the suggestion of power. In the building pride, the triumph over gravity, the will to power become visible; architecture is a kind of power-persuasion in forms, at times persuading, even flattering, at others merely commanding. The highest feeling of power and security finds expression in what possesses a great style. Power that no longer requires proof."[38] Such dreams of an architecture of the hardest stone (fig. 119), figuring a similarly constructed society, an architecture that can dispense with proof, that simply overpowers, betray a will to power that cannot forgive itself

Paul Ludwig Troost, Haus der Kunst, Munich.
Source: *Die Kunst im Dritten Reich,* July and
119 | August 1937.

its essential lack of power. But all creation, all building, will finally be experienced as arbitrary when not based on a "creative correspondence" to a "present intuition," a response to an intuition that, like Platonic recollection, lies beyond and yet grounds communication. For those who know nothing of such responsibility, creative intuition has to become anarchic freedom and the burden of such freedom will lead to a longing for a stony architecture strong enough to crush freedom.

Building, too, demands responsibility. But responsibility requires openness to a reality that binds freedom and thus makes it positive. No longer able to appeal to God or to reason. Nietzsche is left with *Homo natura* as the terrifying *ewige Grundtext,* the eternal basic text that we must free from later misinterpretation so that it will once again provide our texts, our interpretations of who we are and should be, with a measure.[39] Like those who appealed to the book of nature, Nietzsche here posits a text that also provides a ground, leaving us to wonder whether rigorous questioning will not show this fusion of text and ground to be but another wooden iron, the supposed *Grund* to be but another *Abgrund,* an abyss. But if those who insist on the rule of reason will be left with just such an *Abgrund,* that rule should not go unchallenged. Such challenge does not issue from reason but responds to an intuition that life has worth only to those who experience themselves as parts of a larger ongoing whole; but it is an intuition that refuses to think, let alone want to establish that whole as a stony edifice constructed of human beings who are themselves hard as stone.[40]

Conclusion:
The Shape of Modernity and the Future of Architecture

1

In chapter 18 I remarked on the disturbing generality of Heidegger's often-cited evocation of a Greek temple: which temple does he have in mind? Earlier in "The Origin of the Work of Art" he had mentioned the temple at Paestum (fig. 120): are we to think then of the ancient Poseidonia and of its most famous temple, once thought to have been built in honor of the sea god?[1] But Heidegger knows why he chooses to speak in general terms of "a Greek temple": the indefinite article gestures toward the essential. And if his description refers to any particular temple, this temple is found not so much in Greece or southern Italy as in the spiritual landscape of Hegel's *Lectures on Aesthetics,* which discuss architecture as humanity's first attempt to give external reality to the divine.

Architecture is in fact the first pioneer on the highway toward the adequate realization of the Godhead. In this service it is put to severe labour with objective nature, that it may disengage it by its effort from the confused growth of finitude and the distortion of contingency. By this means it levels a space for the God, informs His external environment, and builds Him his temple, as a fit place for the concentration of Spirit, and its direction to the absolute objects of intelligent life. It raises an enclosure for the congregation of those assembled, as a defense against the threatening of the tempest, against rain, the hurricane, and savage animals. It in short reveals the will thus to assemble, and although under an external relation, yet in agreement with the principles of art.[2]

Much of this is taken up by Heidegger, but nothing in Hegel's text answers to Heidegger's insistence that "the Work lets the earth be an earth."[3] Hegel develops a much more oppositional understanding of the relationship of architecture to nature: the temple's builders impose a spiritual, and that means for Hegel a truly human, order on a recalcitrant material. In the face of an initially indifferent environment human beings assert and celebrate their humanity when they level the ground, break the stone, raise walls and columns: thus they defend themselves against nature, not only or even primarily against physical threats—such defense is the task of more modest building—but against nature's disturbing contingency. This struggle relies on and exhibits the power of the universal. Hegel thus assigns the Greek temple its place in his story of the spirit's progress, a progress that seeks complete domination of the earth and wants to break down whatever walls separate persons, races, and regions;

120

and the more the human spirit comes into its own, the more decisively it has to devalue the sensible and leave behind not just architecture, this "first pioneer on the highway toward the adequate realization of the Godhead," but all art. Science and technology mean a far more complete mastery of the earth than art could ever provide.[4]

Heidegger's description of a Greek temple has to be understood as a rewriting of Hegel that, by understanding art as a presentation of the earth, challenges the way Hegel opposes spirit and earth and thus his understanding of the spirit's progress. This challenge also calls into question Hegel's pronouncements on the future of art, even as these pronouncements in turn call into question Heidegger's understanding of architecture and art—calling into question as well this book's understanding of architecture's ethical function, which owes much to Heidegger.

When Hegel speaks of art "on the side of its highest vocation," he is thinking of such art not just as in some way serving an already established ethos but as an autonomous mode of pursuing truth; this means he is conceiving it in opposition to what I have called the aesthetic approach. "Fine art," according to Hegel, "is not art in the true sense of the term until it is also thus free, and its *highest* function is only then satisfied when it has established itself in a sphere which it shares with religion and philosophy, becoming thereby merely one mode and form through which the *Divine,* the profoundest interests of mankind, and spiritual truths of widest range, are brought home to consciousness and expressed."[5] Why should this "highest function" be denied to art today? I have already hinted at the answer: is it not reason that should reveal to us our profoundest interests and what truly matters? But if so, we can grant art an ethical significance only in the comparatively trivial sense in which it is placed in the service of an ethos already established by reason.

Something like that could also have been said by Nietzsche, who in *The Birth of Tragedy* blames the death of tragedy—and tragedy here provides the paradigm of an ethical art work—on the Socratic spirit, which Nietzsche caricatures, or at any rate characterizes by its naive trust in reason to guide us to the good life. But is such trust really naive? Is it not rather, as Hegel thought, inseparable from humanity's homecoming? Nietzsche to be sure would have had little patience with talk of a spiritual homecoming. But he could have agreed. Given such a trust in reason—to him naive, to Hegel justified—a claim such as Heidegger's, that art first establishes the truth that matters, must be rejected as hopelessly confused: confused about art and confused about truth. After the Enlightenment has done its work art can furnish no more than occasions for aesthetic enjoyment, offering something like a vacation from the serious business of life, unless for pedagogical reasons we find it useful to wrap independently established moral maxims in an artistic dress. But such a subjection of art to some preestablished morality only underscores that "the fair days of Greek art, as also the golden time of the later middle ages, are over,"[6] never to be recovered.

Hegel would not want to speak of blame in this connection, no more than we would want to blame the adult for having lost the innocence of childhood. Such "loss" is simply the price of growing up. We have "passed beyond the point at which art is the highest mode under which the absolute is brought home to human consciousness. The type peculiar to art-production and its products fails any longer to satisfy man's highest need. We are beyond the stage of reverence for works of art as divine and objects deserving our worship. The impression they produce is one of a more reflective kind, and the emotions which they arouse require a higher test and a further verification. Thought and reflection have taken their flight above fine art."[7]

2

Any attempt to use "The Origin of the Work of Art," and more especially its description of a Greek temple, as a pointer to help direct architecture today, will have to contend with its epilogue, where Heidegger makes explicit the challenge posed by Hegel and cites these famous propositions from the *Lectures on Aesthetics*:

Art no longer counts for us as the highest manner in which truth obtains existence for itself.

One may well hope that art will continue to advance and perfect itself, but its form has ceased to be the highest need of the spirit.

In all these relationships art is and remains for us, on the side of its highest vocation, something past.[8]

To be sure, we can still "visit the temple in Paestum at its own site or the Bamberg Cathedral on its own square," but "the world of the work that stands there has perished" (pp. 40–41; fig. 121). We still appreciate their beauty, experience it perhaps all the more keenly precisely because the divinities such beauty once served no longer claim us. But while we continue to appreciate temple and church both as aesthetic objects and as historic monuments, they

121

are no longer the works they once were: "As bygone works they stand over against us in the realm of tradition and conservation. Henceforth they remain merely such objects. Their standing before us is still indeed a consequence of, but no longer the same as their former self-subsistence" (p. 41).

Not only have they lost "their highest vocation," but Heidegger has difficulty naming world-establishing work that could take their place. There is an obvious objection: does not Heidegger himself precede his discussion of the Greek temple with descriptions of two much more recent works, Van Gogh's painting of a pair of peasant shoes and Conrad Ferdinand Meyer's poem "Roman Fountain," both created long after Hegel lectured on aesthetics? But do they represent art "on the side of its highest vocation" or do they remain bound to that aesthetic approach Heidegger links to the dying of art?—a dying, he suggests, that "occurs so slowly that it takes a few centuries" (p. 79). In this connection the choice of a poem by C. F. Meyer, a poet often linked to aestheticism, is significant. Heidegger acknowledges that these examples do not refute Hegel; he insists "The judgment that Hegel passes in these statements cannot be evaded by pointing out that since Hegel's lectures in aesthetics were given for the last time during the winter of 1828–29 at the University of Berlin, we have seen the rise of many new art works and art movements. Hegel never meant to deny this possibility. But the question remains: is art still an essential and necessary way in which that truth happens which is decisive for our historical existence, or is art no longer of that character? If, however, it is such no longer then there remains the question why this is so" (p. 80). If Heidegger could point to works that show that art remains "an essential and necessary way in which that truth happens which is decisive for our historical existence," Hegel would stand refuted, but Heidegger claims no such refutation. And is Hegel not right when he claims that the modern world no longer has room for art, and especially architecture, "on the side of its highest vocation"?

Consider once more the proposed understanding of works of architecture as public figures on the ground of comparatively private buildings, where temple and church provide the obvious paradigms, but paradigms that have lost their authority and belong to the past; the question then becomes whether to reoccupy the place once occupied by sacred architecture, and if so how. But despite building types that may have claimed a comparable significance—for example, city hall in the Renaissance; palace in the Baroque; monument, theater, and museum in the nineteenth century—today the very thought of architecture as an expression of "the profoundest interests of mankind, and spiritual truths of widest range" appears at odds with the spirit of the age, as does the attribution of an ethical function to architecture. Some version of the aesthetic approach, which would have us understand works of architecture, with Pevsner and Venturi, as decorated sheds in the broadest sense, seems more in keeping with the way we think about art and architecture. But as Heidegger knows, this aesthetic approach has to mean the death of architecture in Hegel's highest sense. Thus, while "The Origin of the Work of Art" challenges Hegel's aesthetics and its metaphysical presuppositions, it is not just rhetoric when Heidegger continues: "The truth of Hegel's judgment has not yet been decided; for behind this verdict there stands Western thought since the Greeks, which thought corresponds to a truth of beings that has already happened. Decision upon the judgment will be made, when it is made, from and about this truth of what is. Until then the judgment remains in force" (p. 80). The world we live in argues for Hegel: we, too, tend to connect art in its highest sense with the past.

3

What matters here is not Hegel. At stake is our own understanding not just of art but of our own place in the world. Consider the extent to which Hegel's pronouncements continue to be supported by our common sense: do we not consider museums the most proper depositories for what once was art "on the side of its highest vocation"? Stepping into such a "temple of art," or for that matter a concert hall, we enter an aesthetic church, a sublime and rather chilly necropolis where one is silent or speaks in hushed tones. And isn't the same true when we visit a great work of architecture, say Parthenon or Pantheon, Amiens cathedral or St. Peter's in Rome? Our attitude is shaped in part by a still almost religious reverence and respect, but also by a sense that what truly matters lies elsewhere. Such works need preserving precisely because they are in danger of losing their place in our world and therefore need to be protected and given a special place, often at great expense.

If the claim that Hegel's thesis about the death of art is supported by our common sense is to be more than a superficial assertion, it must be possible to show that both are supported by similar considerations. Three assumptions deserve to be singled out:

1. Art eludes our conceptual grasp. That art surpasses reason, that there is something mysterious about all genuine art, has become a platitude often expressed in the claim that a work of art cannot finally be explained or in the related truism that we cannot give a recipe that will ensure the production of masterpieces. The elusiveness of art is taken for granted by anyone who insists that art requires inspiration or genius.

2. There still is widespread conviction that art in its highest sense gives us unique insight into what matters. This suggests that there is a sense in which works of art can legitimately be said to be true or false, a sense in which beauty and truth cannot finally be disentangled. Far more questionable than the first, this claim is challenged by those who insist that the point of art is primarily to provide a special kind of pleasurable experience, that is, by all committed to what I have called the aesthetic approach. That approach tends to make art into high-class entertainment, though we should not be too quick to insist that this demeans art. To be sure, many of us, especially many artists, expect more from art than just entertainment, no matter how rarefied, expect somehow to be edified or enlightened. Decisions to build museums, theaters, and concert halls in the image of temples reflect such expectations. Measured by them, much modern art is all too often found disappointingly empty, at times fun, often annoying, too frequently boring. Like Hegel, we demand more of art, demand that it grant insight into what is and what matters. But the more we insist on such insight, the more difficult we will find it not to agree with Hegel's claim that art in its highest sense belongs to the past. What then is it about the modern world that on Hegel's view denies art "on the side of its highest vocation" a future? This leads me to the third presupposition, which concerns not art, but truth.

3. Only what can be comprehended and expressed in clear thoughts and propositions deserves to be called real. Truth is linked here to conceptual transparency, an understanding that found its classical expression in Cartesian method and that triumphed in modern science and technology.

It should be evident that these three assumptions do not form a coherent set, that we can hold on to any two but not to all three. Hegel appears to do so only by claiming that truth has come into its own only in the modern period. On this view it is nothing other than the inevitable progress of the human spirit that has to leave art "on the side of its highest vocation" behind.

4

Hegel's understanding of art and more especially of the place of architecture within the other arts is bound up with his understanding of history. History, Hegel insists, is not just a sequence of events without rhyme or reason, as Schopenhauer thought, but must be understood, despite all setbacks and defeats, as a fundamentally irreversible process, leading to an ever-increasing freedom: history is the progress of freedom. As such it is also the progressive emancipation of humanity from its initial enslavement to nature, that is, the progress of technology. That this progress has to bring with it increasing mobility requires no comment. But is Hegel right? In its general outline I find it difficult to dispute his understanding of progress. Despite continuing nationalistic and religious betrayals of the hopes of the Enlightenment, predictions of the eventual triumph of these hopes receive support from the progressive expansion of European culture into a world culture less and less willing to grant authority to such "natural" givens as distinctions of gender or race, nationality or religion.

Such a view of history is in keeping with the traditional understanding of the human being as the *animal rationale*. Hegel, too, understands the human being as a citizen of two worlds, entangled by his body in matter but also able to transcend such entanglement, lifted by reason to a realm of thought and freedom, which places him in opposition to nature and fills him with the desire to subject it to the hegemony of the spirit. In something as simple as a child throwing stones into the water and enjoying the expanding rings, Hegel finds evidence of this drive to appropriate the natural given by transforming it in the image of the human spirit. History is the progress of such appropriation, where art and architecture are part of the effort to make the natural and sensible our own, to rob it of its character of being a mute, alien other and thus to transform it into a dwelling place fit for human beings. To carve a statue, to build a pyramid is to humanize nature, to breathe spirit into matter. There is thus a sense in which, like the Bible, Hegel places humanity between a garden—or rather a wilderness, which is nature—and an ideal city, that truly human environment whose full realization remains a task. Art, too, brings about an incarnation of the spirit in the sensible; its goal, too, is the humanization of the sensible, where humanization means spiritualization—an understanding of art that forces us to ask whether science and technology do not allow for far more effective mastery and must in the end leave art behind, whether the building of that ideal city is not primarily the task of thinkers, politicians, and engineers.

By forcing the history of art into this scheme, Hegel is able to distinguish three types of art, which also name historic phases: (1) the symbolic, in which matter still predominates, as spirit struggles to find adequate expression in the sensible but remains imprisoned in matter; (2) the classical, which finds spirit and matter in perfect balance; and (3) the romantic, in which spirit predominates over matter. The progress of art is seen accordingly as leading from oriental art, which Hegel understands as primarily symbolic; to classical art, which remains for Hegel, too, the unsurpassed apex of art; and finally to romantic art, by which he understands the art of the Christian and the modern period. These three types are associated with particular arts: architecture is associated especially with the symbolic type; sculpture especially with the classical; and painting, music, and poetry especially with the romantic.

I shall return to the obvious violence that this linear reading of the history of art does to art's actual history, especially to non-Western art. But let us begin with a closer look at Hegel's understanding of the symbolic mode, which holds the key to his understanding of architecture, this first spiritualization of matter. The material of architecture "is matter itself as an external object, a heavy mass that is subject to mechanical laws; and its forms persist as the forms of inorganic Nature coordinated with the relations of the abstract understanding such as symmetry and so forth."[9] Straight lines, rectangles, symmetry, and arithmetic and geometric proportions here have decisive importance. The very abstractness of this vocabulary prevents architecture from doing justice to the concreteness of the Idea as manifest in the human spirit. In its abstract spirituality architecture almost demands that the spiritual be given a more concrete, a more fully human expression: another art, sculpture, is thus required to make the god truly present. The Greek temple, on Hegel's interpretation, has thus already subordinated architecture to sculpture. In the sculpted image of the god he finds the perfect reconciliation of spirit and body. Greek religion remains tied to art, on this view, as Christian religion never can be, because the latter has recognized that the spiritual dwells not in nature but within the individual. Such inwardness prevents Christian art from linking the sacred as intimately to the visible as does the Greek. The spirit refuses full incarnation. The incarnated God must die, so that humanity can advance "from God as such to the devotion of the *community,* that is to God as He is alive and present in the subjective consciousness."[10]

Here lies the key to the transition from classical to romantic art, which already foreshadows the loss of art's highest vocation. Greek art, according to Hegel, cannot be surpassed as art: its defect, if we can speak here of a defect at all, is one that attaches to all art, indeed to the entire sensible dimension. Modern inwardness with its emphasis on reflection, its recognition of the divinity of reason, knows that thought alone can finally do justice to what most deeply matters. "The reflective culture of our life of to-day makes it inevitable, both relatively to our volitional power and our judgment, that we adhere strictly to general points of view, and regulate particular matters in consonance with them, so that universal forms, laws, duties, rights, and maxims hold valid as the determining basis of our life."[11] This is why thought and reflection have to overtake the fine arts. That our approach to what remains of art in its former high sense should have become increasingly cerebral is therefore to be expected. The term "concept art," which would reduce works of art to occasions for reflection, signals the death of art "from the side of its highest vocation." It has its architectural counterpart in "concept architecture": think of Peter Eisenman's architectural appropriation of deconstruction.

If we accept some such understanding of the essence of art and architecture and of their history, we also have to accept that modern art has lost its ethical function, except in the derivative sense in which it may serve an independently established ethos. Any attempt to reclaim that function will then have to be criticized as retrogressive or dismissed as simply anachronistic, as it fails to take seriously enough the shape of modernity. Architecture in its highest sense will then have to be considered a thing of the past, and while many may mourn this, such mourning would have to be considered as pointless as wishing to be returned to that wonder which was ours when we were still children. Hegel himself was aware of the loss, too close to Winckelmann and to his former roommate, the poet Hölderlin, not to be saddened by it, but those who deplore this death of art are consoled by the recognition of its necessity.

This claim of necessity invites consideration of Hegel's logocentric, Eurocentric bias. That his description of the development of art is far too one-dimensional and linear requires no comment. It was indeed not derived from a careful examination of the then-available evidence, but represented an at times willful fitting of such evidence into a scheme derived from Hegel's reasoned determination of art and its place in the history of the spirit. We could thus point to the inadequacy of Hegel's account, especially to non-European cultures, and hope to refute him.

But such a refutation, justified though it would be in many respects, could hardly be decisive. Nor of course would name-calling—although the charge of "logocentrism" does point to what is essential: if we grant Hegel the central importance he places on the logos, on spirit and freedom, we grant him the substance of his case. And if human freedom demands that the individual liberate him- or herself from the accidents of what happens to be the case, also of what he or she may happen to be, then our real home should not be sought by looking to nature, toward a particular region or *genius loci;* rather it must be a spiritual home, to which the sensible, and that means also art and especially architecture, cannot do justice. From this point of view, our physical dwellings should have a look of mobility, replaceability. Such "logocentrism" has to bring with it an insistence on the inessential nature of what now come to be considered the accidents of location, birth, gender, race. Does the attempt to assign an ethical function to art, and especially to architecture, not represent a cultural regression? Is it not reason alone that in the end should determine our ethos? Hegel's philosophy is born of the confidence that humanity has finally come of age, that human beings have finally begun to assert themselves as the masters of nature, including their own nature. On this interpretation architecture is no longer very important, and the loss of architecture in its highest sense cannot really be considered a loss at all but needs to be understood as one more sign that humanity is finally coming of age.

And yet, even affirming the legitimacy of reason's emancipatory promise, acknowledging the very real mastery of nature that reason has brought us, and reiterating that it would be irresponsible to turn our backs on the Enlightenment, our own nature and the world we live in, still so distant from the projected ideal, force us to recognize that Hegel has exaggerated the power of the human spirit and has lost sight of the whole human being. Hegel's faith that reality and our reason are finally commensurable is itself blind to reality, blind especially to our own reality. Here lies the significance of Heidegger's understanding of art as a presentation of the earth. With Heidegger I want to insist on the rift between spirit and nature, word and reality. To be sure, we must grant Descartes that there is a sense in which we can be said to understand reality precisely to the extent that we can model it, can know how to reproduce it. But is it not sufficient to contemplate some concrete natural object, say a rock or a tree, to recognize that there is another sense in which we can be said to understand reality precisely when we recognize the inadequacy of all our attempts to describe it, recognize that reality will finally always transcend and elude our grasp? All that is fully comprehended is a product of our own spirit and as such lacks reality: take the definition of a circle, which provides us with a rule for its construction. But this ideal circle, figured only by whatever circle we may actually draw, lacks reality. To the claim that we understand reality to the extent that we can produce it, we have to add that precisely to that extent we lose reality. To an understanding of reality that makes our ability to grasp it clearly and distinctly its measure, we need to oppose another that recognizes that something is experienced as real precisely when we know that we cannot finally understand it. Reality transcends our understanding. Art recalls us to this transcendence. Heidegger's "earth" gestures toward this dimension, as does Nietzsche's "Dionysian."

An analogous point must be made with respect to what Hegel has to say about our "reflective culture" and our adherence "strictly to general points of view." A look at our political and social reality suffices to render such pronouncements at best a declaration of an ideal too weakly rooted in our affective life to be experienced as binding and therefore unable to establish genuine community.

In Hegel's philosophy, and to modernity, the ineliminable transcendence of reality announces itself first as the concrete, sensuous, arbitrary, and contingent, including the arbitrariness of desires. The place that as a matter of fact I occupy to reason has to appear as a place that I just happen to occupy. The sex that as a matter of fact determines who I am to reason appears as a contingent fact that does not touch my essence. This goes for all my physical characteristics, also for my desires, also for my particular background. Reason lets me see the factual as the merely contingent; it lets me see the world *sub specie possibilitatis,* from the vantage point of possibility. But if my biological and historical makeup are all understood as merely contingent facts, who is this "I"? When I take away all my supposedly accidental, contingent properties, what remains? In the end, as Kierkegaard saw, such a self would have to become itself empty and abstract, a mere ghost of a self, unclaimed and indifferent to the world. Such a self would have no use for architecture.

At this point the need for a fuller self-affirmation—which means also the need for architecture and its ethical function—reappears. More immediately and more fully than any other art, architecture, as Hegel recognized, re-presents the essential strife between spirit and matter, mirroring the essential strife within the human being as the *animal rationale.* The modern world, to the extent that it is ruled by the Cartesian project to render the human being the master and possessor of nature, would be rid of such strife, not recognizing that values, even as they are acknowledged, endorsed, and pruned by the *ratio,* claim us only as long as they yet retain their roots in the earth. Architecture is needed to recall the human being to the whole self: to the *animal* and to the *ratio*, to nature and spirit.

By now it should have become clear that what is at stake when Heidegger returns in the epilogue to "The Origin of the Work of Art" to Hegel's thesis of the death of art is not just art or architecture, but our future.

5

Problems of building are inevitably also problems of dwelling. Such problems cannot be solved by abstract theorizing. What such theorizing at most can hope to do is call attention to questionable assumptions, to different possibilities—perhaps recall us to dimensions of our being that we ourselves must recognize to matter if a philosopher's words are to matter. That is why the reader of Heidegger's "Origin of the Work of Art" should not forget its epilogue: it helps to forestall any reading that would invest that essay with an authority that does not belong to it, inviting us to become more questioning. And so I invoked it and Hegel in this conclusion to call into question my own ascription of an ethical function to architecture and the related privileging of architecture over building, in order to ask once more: is architecture "on the side of its highest vocation" not a thing of the past, something that belongs into a museum, as does Heidegger's temple, as does his Black Forest farmhouse? This question is shadowed today by the Nazis' authoritarian appropriation of both temple and farmhouse.

But if this shadow should make us tread more warily, it should not prevent us from attempting to take a few steps, should not prevent us from confronting the problem with which Heidegger was wrestling in "The Origin of the Work of Art." That problem was given a provocative formulation by the church architect Rudolf Schwarz in a lecture delivered the evening before Heidegger spoke at the same conference on "Building Dwelling Thinking": "Many of you who like to travel and to look at works of art will not like to hear me say this: that unfortunately you do not really understand these works. But that is a fact. If you really want to understand a Baroque cathedral, you have to reenact it spiritually so to speak. Here all those beautiful books and words are of little help. You have to join in the great celebration of the community before the eternal, so that you carry yourself into this work and in this manner understand it, not only with your all too clever eye, but with body and soul."[12] To understand a Baroque church with our "clever eye," as an aesthetic object, is not really to understand it, for a church building is rather like a score that requires to be performed "with body and soul," requires the festal celebration of the mass that the church building serves, requires, that is, participation in the communal festival the building serves, participation that reaffirms the individual's membership in a community and his or her allegiance to its presiding values. But let me continue with the cited passage: "It does not help at all to draw pretty houses. There are modern architects who are especially clever at that sort of thing; they take away whole walls and then they replace them with display windows, and the front lawn is brought right into the living room and other such pretty things. All this is good and well, but such tricks will never lead us to a house. Rather to an often highly admirable aesthetic construction of a houselike character."[13] The shift from church to house is significant, just as is Heidegger's shift from temple to farmhouse, reminding us once more of the distance that separates us moderns from temple and church. But do we even understand what a house is? This, too, would require knowing how to use it, that is to say, knowing how to dwell. When Schwarz suggests that many "houses" designed by modern architects are better called "aesthetic constructions of a houselike character," this formulation inverts the priority of building acknowledged by an understanding of the work of architecture as a decorated shed in a way that invites comparison with what Venturi has to say about "ducks": a "duck" could be defined as an aesthetic object of a shedlike character.

But if this does not get us a genuine house, how do we get one? Schwarz's answer seems even more old-fashioned than the example of a Black Forest farmhouse Heidegger was to offer the same audience the following morning. "I am terribly sorry to have to say this, but you only get a house by marrying and by devoting yourself unconditionally to that great law. That may well be much more demanding than designing a house with wonderfully large windows. But I don't think we can arrive at a house in any other way. And this should be the first step towards establishing a decent house, then a village, then a city."[14] Such emphasis on marriage must have seemed embarrassingly narrow-minded and old-fashioned even when the lecture was given. And if we generalize and take Schwarz to mean that only proper dwelling gets us a real house, this leaves us with what seems an empty platitude. But Schwarz's main points deserve to be taken seriously. Above all, we should not expect too much from architects: whether what they build turns out to be a real house, a real school, a real monument, a real church will depend on how their work is appropriated. This they cannot control. All they can hope to furnish is a suitable framework. To do so they must of couse attempt to anticipate such appropriation, help shape it, but they cannot and should not try to dictate what form dwelling should take.

Problems of dwelling are above all not architectural but ethical problems. Such problems, however, pose problems for the architect, whose very art they threaten. Schwarz, too, ties this threat to the increasing inability or unwillingness of individuals to commit themselves to something larger than their own mortal selves. To existing as an individual Schwarz opposes existing as a part; as a Christian builder of churches, he dreams of a family-centered Christian socialism.[15] Most of us lack the faith that is a presupposition of such dreams. Nevertheless, we must acknowledge that to live a meaningful life, to dwell in this sense, we must recognize ourselves as parts of a larger ongoing community. Such community in turn depends on certain shared values; and the inevitably precarious and changing authority of such humanly established values must be supported by our evolving and often warring desires and affects, as mediated and structured by society and reason. This revision of Heidegger's understanding of dwelling calls for an architecture responsive to our essential incompleteness, our need for others, for genuine, concrete community; it must be responsive also to a reason that demands the universal. Such architecture would present inevitably precarious interpretations of our ethos, of our place in a larger order.

Schwarz raises the obvious question: "Of course there will be those clever people, who ask: are we today still capable of this? I don't know whether we are capable of this, but the architect has to make this demand. If there is and if there is supposed to be real architecture, then one has to go this bitter road. I can't help it."[16] Why is the road to what is here called "real architecture" so bitter? It is bitter, first of all, because it goes against our desire to place ourselves at the center; bitter also because we have to recognize how difficult it is, no matter what our intentions, to read the contours of the order in which we are to stand, which is to grant us a sense of place and which architecture is to help reveal. How easy it is here to deceive oneself, to worship some golden calf or other. But I am convinced that Schwarz is right to insist that the order architecture in its highest sense should help establish must have its measure in and be an interpretation of an order that is glimpsed rather than created—in this sense a transcendent order. That was recognized by those medieval builders who built their churches as an imitation of the cosmos. It was recognized in a very different and today perhaps more instructive way by the theorists of the primitive hut, who recognized that we moderns have no other authority to appeal to than reason *and* nature. But if here alone we can find the origin of the authority of all orders we might establish, that origin does not provide anything like a stable ground but is present only in precarious interpretations. To this ever-elusive origin our dreams of ideal dwelling have to return. Again and again, as we saw, architecture has thus been understood as a revealing representation of an ideal building, corresponding to some dream of essential dwelling: a groping representation, if you wish, of an ideal of essential humanity.

There is an obvious objection, an objection that can use arguments I have stated in this book: does such emphasis on the community not shortchange the individual? Is Schwarz's understanding of architecture not uncomfortably close to that of the Nazis, who, responding to a widespread fear of freedom and disorientation, quite self-consciously enlisted architecture in authoritarian world-building and similarly celebrated communal order at the expense of the individual and his rights and responsibilities? Must we not insist on these? The answer to such a charge of authoritarianism is not difficult to give: interpretations of ideal dwelling must acknowledge that they are finally no more than precarious conjectures. My metaphor of an ellipse with both a private and a public focus is another such conjecture, which depends for whatever authority it may have on the reader's appropriation. To insist that such a conjecture provides firm ground is to erect a golden calf, putting a human creation in the place of the transcendent and thus the never quite comprehended and shifting ground of all our valuations. Worship of such a golden calf may banish feelings of uncertainty and insecurity, but at the cost of personal responsibility, of the ability to respond to what more deeply claims us. As Speer proved, works of architecture, too, can claim the authority of the golden calf. What is needed today is something else: an architecture that without surrendering its ethical function knows that it lacks authority and cannot and should not provide more than precarious conjectures about an ideal dwelling.

Such conjectures should recognize both poles of my ellipse, recognize not only the community but also the individual, as well as the inevitable tensions between the two, just as they should recognize the inevitable tension between spirit and nature. Building that serves genuine dwelling must preserve and re-present these tensions: the tension between private and public, festal places and places of work, temple and house, nature and city. Using a traditional language we can say: genuine dwelling requires an affirmation of ourselves as fallen, given that the traditional understanding of the Fall still provides an illuminating metaphor for the human condition.

Why did Adam fall? A suggestive answer is found in Augustine's *City of God:* "we cannot believe that Adam was deceived and supposed the devil's word to be the truth, and therefore transgressed God's law, but that he, by the drawing of kindred, yielded to the woman, the husband to the wife, the one human being to the only other human being. . . .The man could not bear to be severed from his companion, even though it involved a partnership in sin."[17] This hints at the possibility of a Promethean reading of the fall. Adam, Augustine tells us, sinned with his eyes open. He did this not to claim a godlike position for himself, but because he knew it was more important for him to be with Eve than with God. He would rather know Eve, working and facing an inevitable death together with her, than to be in paradise without her. I would like to suggest that such a leave-taking from God for the sake of a genuinely human community is the foundation of any genuinely human dwelling. It is this leave-taking, this fall, this expulsion into insecurity and uncertainty, that alone lets us develop into responsible individuals. Every human being has to repeat it for him- or herself. But human beings are not self-sufficient: having lost their place in paradise, they have to find their place in a genuinely human order; they have to know and join themselves to one another.

I have used the language of the Fall story, but this should not obscure the fact that the pattern to which I am here pointing could have been expressed using very different languages: for example, that of Plato, or that of Nietzsche. In no way is it tied to belief in God. Only when this is kept in mind can the Fall retain its significance for us all, teach us that just by virtue of having become individuals, human beings have always already been sent forth into insecurity and uncertainty. And even if they cannot and should not try to force their way back into some dreamed-of paradise, they can and must keep themselves open to the always-mediated claim of a reason and a reality that they have not created, keep themselves open especially to the claims of the other, to the claims of the community, to the claims of coming generations.

There is a continuing need for the creation of festal places on the ground of everyday dwellings, places where individuals come together and affirm themselves as members of the community, as they join in public reenactments of the essential: celebrations of those central aspects of our life that maintain and give meaning to existence. The highest function of architecture remains what it has always been: to invite such festivals.

Only if we can return to such an architecture will we have refuted Hegel's claim that the future leaves no room for architecture "on the side of its highest vocation." No more than Heidegger or Schwarz can I predict that this will happen. But it seems to me important that we do our best to ensure that it will. We need architecture for our mental health, and in a much more profound sense than Ruskin thought.

What contours to give to the idea of such an architecture is the problem with which I have been struggling in the last part of this book. Consider once more the suggestion that works of architecture be understood as public figures on the ground of comparatively private buildings, where temple and church provide paradigms that have lost their authority. How are we to reoccupy the place once held by sacred architecture? I have looked

122 | Volker Giencke, Red Stage, Graz, Austria.
Credit: Volker Giencke.

123 | Volker Giencke, Red Stage, Graz, Austria. View
from back. Credit: Volker Giencke.

at monument and theater as possible candidates. The list can no doubt be increased—thus there could have been a whole chapter on the museum. More in tune with the world we live in would have been a chapter on shopping malls. The landscape park seems to me to hold great promise, precisely because it is not as exclusively oriented toward the past as are museum and monument. This is not to deny that the re-presentation of our communal inheritance is a necessary condition of genuine dwelling, which gains its significance as a creative repetition of that inheritance. But if such repetition is not to be blind, if it is indeed to be creative, it may not allow the inherited to obscure the promise of the future. For this reason there should have been a chapter on the school as a building task that allows the community to give architectural expression to its commitment to coming generations. But perhaps today it is not so much buildings to which we should look in search of architecture, but to the potentially festal quality of public spaces, of squares, streets, and parks, which invites re-presentation by modest, often ephemeral structures. Volker Giencke's Red Stage in Graz invites emulation[18] (figs. 122 and 123).

If each of these building tasks holds some promise, not one of them nor all together can take the place of temple and church. One reason for this is what Loos recognized as the modern privatization of the sacred, a privatization that denies art communal authority and lends support to the thesis that architecture is and should remain for us, from the side of its highest vocation, something past. With good reason we have learned to be suspicious of all architecture that confidently embraces architecture's traditional ethical function. Any architect who today wants to address that function has to be aware that he does so without authority, that he is a bit like the fool who says what he thinks needs to be said but can only hope that others will listen. For this reason we may want to entertain suggestions that the architectural folly be included in any list of building types that promise to address our need for architecture. This is not the place to write a history of such follies, in which the follies that animated eighteenth-century parks—including not only artificial ruins, memorials, and hermitages but pleasure pavilions of various kinds, such as Chinese pagodas, Moorish kiosks, and rustic chalets—would deserve extensive treatments. Such a history might well conclude with some modern follies, such as the unusually successful folly adjoining the Canadian Centre for Architecture or recent designs by Steven Holl.[19] The latter's utopian project for the Porta Vittoria sector on the periphery of Milan, including a Dario Fo pavilion, a Primal Soup Kitchen, and a Hotel for Unhappy Lovers, suggests possibilities of introducing into the context of the modern city theatrical and festal spaces, punctuated by works of architecture that, lacking authority and responsible to no one, are gently revolutionary and let us dream of utopia.

Notes

1 Introduction: Postmodern Prelude

1. Alberto Pérez-Gómez, *Architecture and the Crisis of Modern Science* (Cambridge: MIT Press, 1983), pp. 3, 4, 6.

2. Spiro Kostof, *A History of Architecture: Settings and Rituals* (New York and Oxford: Oxford University Press, 1985), pp. 558, 559. See Pérez-Gómez, *Architecture and Modern Science*, pp. 17–39.

3. Sigfried Giedion, *Space, Time and Architecture,* 5th ed. (Cambridge: Harvard University Press, 1974), p. xxxii.

4. Ibid., p. xxxiii.

5. I agree with Beatriz Colomina that architecture, as distinct from mere building, is interpretive and critical. But to thus assign to architecture a hermeneutic and critical function should not lead us to forget that architecture must also be understood as building. We should resist her interpretation of Ariadne as the true architect of the labyrinth because she interpreted it with her famous thread; see "Introduction: On Architecture, Production and Representation," in *Architectureproduction,* ed. Beatriz Colomina (New York: Princeton Architectural Press, 1988), p. 7. And we should also resist those who, in the spirit of deconstruction, would confuse architecture with verbal architecture. Despite all his architectural metaphors, Kant was not an architect. That this platitude even needs stating points to widespread confusion in architectural theory.

6. See Martin Heidegger, "Brief über den Humanismus," in *Wegmarken,* vol. 9 of *Gesamtausgabe* (Frankfurt: Klostermann, 1976), pp. 353–357. Heidegger here appeals to Heraclitus, fragment 119: *Ēthos anthrōpōi daimōn,* "Man's character is his daimon"; G. S. Kirk and J. E. Raven, *The Presocratic Philosophers* (Cambridge: Cambridge University Press, 1962), p. 213.

7. Nikolaus Pevsner, *An Outline of European Architecture* (Harmondsworth: Penguin, 1958), p. 23.

8. Ibid.

9. With J. Fergusson we might call such a bicycle shed "structurally ornamental though wholly without ornament." See Bruce Allsop, *The Study of Architectural History* (New York: Praeger, 1970), p. 64.

10. Robert Venturi, Denise Scott Brown, and Steven Izenour, *Learning from Las Vegas: The Forgotten Symbolism of Architectural Form,* rev. ed. (Cambridge: MIT Press, 1977), p. 87.

11. Giedion, *Space, Time, and Architecture,* p. xxxii.

12. "Postmodernism: Definition and Debate," *AIA Journal,* vol. 27, no. 5 (May 1983), pp. 238–247, 286–301. See Karsten Harries, "Modernity's Bad Conscience," *AA Files,* no. 10 (Autumn 1985), pp. 53–60.

13. "Postmodernism: Definition and Debate," p. 239.

14. See Hans Blumenberg, *The Legitimacy of the Modern Age,* trans. Robert M. Wallace (Cambridge: MIT Press, 1983).

15. "Postmodernism: Definition and Debate," p. 239.

16. Ibid., p. 244.

17. Vincent Scully, introduction to *Complexity and Contradiction in Architecture,* by Robert Venturi, 2nd ed. (New York: Museum of Modern Art, 1977), p. 10.

18. Venturi, *Complexity and Contradiction in Architecture,* p. 17.

19. On the interesting, see Søren Kierkegaard, "The Rotation Method," in *Either/Or,* trans. Walter Lowrie, D. F. Swenson, and L. M. Swenson (Garden City, N.Y.: Doubleday, 1959), 1:279–296, and Karsten Harries, *The Meaning of Modern Art* (Evanston, Ill.: Northwestern University Press, 1968), pp. 54–60.

20. See Anthony Vidler, "Behind the Mask," as yet unpublished contribution to the conference "Abbau—Neubau—Überbau: Nietzsche and an Architecture of Our Minds," sponsored by the Getty Center for the History of Art and the Humanities, Weimar, October 11–13, 1994, which reverses Nietzsche's evaluation of the supposedly "decadent 'feminine' values of ornament and mask."

21. Jean-François Lyotard, "An Answer to the Question, What Is the Postmodern?" in *The Postmodern Explained: Correspondence, 1982–1985,* trans. ed. Julian Pefanis and Morgan Thomas, trans. Don Berry (Minneapolis: University of Minnesota Press, 1993), pp. 1–16.

22. John Pastier, "First Monument of a Loosely Defined Style," *AIA Journal,* vol. 72, no. 5, (May 1983), p. 236.

23. Heinrich Wölfflin, *Principles of Art History: The Problem of the Development of Style in Later Art,* trans. M. D. Hottinger (New York: Dover, n.d.), p. 229.

24. Ada Louise Huxtable, "After Modern Architecture," *New York Review of Books,* vol. 30, no. 19 (December 8, 1983), p. 34.

25. Christian Norberg-Schulz, *Intentions in Architecture* (Cambridge: MIT Press, 1965), p. 219.

26. Arthur Drexler, *Transformations in Modern Architecture* (New York: Museum of Modern Art, 1979), p. 17.

27. Ludwig Wittgenstein, *Philosophical Investigations,* trans. G. E. M. Anscombe (New York: Macmillan, 1953) par. 123.

28. Cf. Rudolf Schwarz, *Vom Bau der Kirche,* 2nd ed. (Heidelberg: Lambert Schneider, 1947), p. 143.

29. Roger Scruton, *The Aesthetics of Architecture* (Princeton: Princeton University Press, 1979), p. 4.

2 The Aesthetic Approach

1. Bruce Glaser, "Questions to Stella and Judd," interview ed. Lucy R. Lippard, in *Minimal Art: A Critical Anthology,* ed. Gregory Battcock (New York: Dutton, 1968), pp. 157–158.

2. See Karsten Harries, *The Broken Frame: Three Lectures* (Washington, D.C.: Catholic University of America Press, 1989).

3. Erwin Panofsky, *Meaning in the Visual Arts* (Garden City, N.Y.: Doubleday, 1955), p. 11.

4. Matila Ghyka, *The Geometry of Art and Life* (New York: Dover, 1977), p. 10.

5. Panofsky, *Meaning in the Visual Arts,* p. 10.

6. Alexander Gottlieb Baumgarten, *Reflections on Poetry,* trans. Karl Aschenbrenner and William B. Holther (Berkeley: University of California Press, 1954).

7. Alexander Gottlieb Baumgarten, *Metaphysica* (Halle: Hemmerden, 1779), par. 452.

8. Baumgarten, *Reflections on Poetry,* par. 68.

9. See Aristotle, *Poetics* 7, where the beautiful object is understood as "a whole, made up of parts" (1451a2). As an example of such an ordered whole, a well-constructed tragedy will have "beginning, middle, and end."

10. Baumgarten, *Metaphysica,* pars. 73, 74.

11. Just as the metaphysician discovers in God the origin and organizing center or *focus perfectionis* of all that is, so the aesthetician discovers the artwork's origin and organizing center or *focus perfectionis* in its theme. See Baumgarten, *Metaphysica,* par. 94.

12. In my book *The Bavarian Rococo Church: Between Faith and Aestheticism* (New Haven: Yale University Press, 1983), I traced just one manifestation of this turn to the aesthetic. I was pleased to discover that in *Absorption and Theatricality: Painting and Beholder in the Age of Diderot* (Berkeley: University of California Press, 1980), Michael Fried had noted a parallel evolution in French painting of the period. In their different ways, both books locate in the eighteenth century the threshold that separates the modern, aesthetic approach to art from an older approach that placed art in the service of religious or political concerns. See also Karsten Harries, "Authenticity and Theatricality: Second Thoughts on the Bavarian Rococo Church," *Stanford Literature Review,* vol. 5 (Spring–Fall 1988), pp. 179–195.

13. Such a critique is implied by the Third Moment's explanation of the beautiful: "*Beauty* is the form of the *purposiveness* of an object, so far as this is perceived in it *without any representation of a purpose*" (Immanuel Kant, *Critique of Judgment,* trans. J. H. Bernard [New York: Haffner, 1951], p. 73). Baumgarten's understanding of beauty as perceived perfection, where perfection is thought in terms of an organizing theme, implies that beauty involves representation of a purpose. Kant disputes that beauty can, as Baumgarten would have it, "actually be resolved into the concept of perfection." What at first may seem to be just a squabble between philosophers reveals its significance once we recognize that what is at issue is a shift in taste from patterns of subordination and an emphasis on hierarchical organization to a preference for patterns of coordination and the juxtaposition of contrasting elements, a preference that can be traced

in all the arts of the period. Presence now replaces unity as the key to aesthetic success. See Kant, *Critique of Judgment,* par. 15, pp. 62–65. For an account of the shift from the architectural system of the Renaissance to the architectural system, in many ways already modern, that evolved in the Age of Reason, see Emil Kaufmann, *Architecture in the Age of Reason: Baroque and Post-Baroque in England, Italy, and France* (New York: Dover, 1968).

14. Paul Weiss, *Nine Basic Arts* (Carbondale: Southern Illinois University Press, 1961), p. 5.

15. Arthur Schopenhauer, *The World as Will and Representation,* trans. E. F. J. Payne (New York: Dover, 1969), 1:178.

16. Michael Fried, "Art and Objecthood," in *Minimal Art: A Critical Anthology,* pp. 145, 147.

17. For a fuller account of the aesthetic approach, see Harries, *The Broken Frame.*

18. Kant, *Critique of Judgment,* par. 51, p. 166.

19. Alexander Tzonis and Liane Lefaivre, *Classical Architecture: The Poetics of Order* (Cambridge: MIT Press, 1986), p. 9.

20. Ibid., p. 243.

21. Paul Valéry, *The Art of Poetry,* trans. Denise Folliot (New York: Vintage, 1961), p. 192.

22. Tzonis and Lefaivre, *Classical Architecture,* p. 276.

23. Ibid., pp. 9, 35, 117, 152–153.

24. Weiss, *Nine Basic Arts,* p. 68.

25. Ibid., p. 84.

26. As Anthony Vidler points out, Ledoux "clearly understood the 'experimental' nature of these designs. He called the House and Workshop of the Coopers 'an experiment, to awaken with boldness of thought and execution' the 'apathetic sleep of architects and reformers'" (*Claude-Nicolas Ledoux: Architecture and Social Reform at the End of the Ancien Régime* [Cambridge: MIT Press, 1990], p. 316).

3 The Promise of Decoration

1. John Ruskin, *The Seven Lamps of Architecture* (New York: Noonday, 1974), p. 15. This work is hereafter cited parenthetically in the text.

2. Vitruvius, *The Ten Books of Architecture,* trans. Morris Hickey Morgan (New York: Dover, 1960), book 1, chap. 3, p. 17.

3. Martin Heidegger, *Sein und Zeit,* 7th ed. (Tübingen: Niemeyer, 1953), p. 410.

4. Adolf Loos, "Ornament und Verbrechen," in *Trotzdem: 1900–1930* (Innsbruck: Brenner, 1931), pp. 79–92; translated as "Ornament and Crime," in *Programs and Manifestoes on 20th-Century Architecture,* ed. Ulrich Conrads, trans. Michael Bullock (Cambridge: MIT Press, 1975), pp. 19–24. For a discussion of the context of the original lecture, first delivered in 1910 (not 1908, as commonly thought), see Burkhardt Rukschcio, "Ornament und Mythos," in *Ornament und Askese,* ed. Alfred Pfabigan (Vienna: Brandstätter, 1985), pp. 57–68. Rukschcio shows that Loos's critique was directed above all against Josef Hoffmann, and in the originally delivered lecture with a directness that left nothing to interpretation. See also Joseph Rykwert, "Adolf Loos: The New Vision," in *The Necessity of Artifice* (New York: Rizzoli, 1982), pp. 67–73.

5. See Karsten Harries, *The Bavarian Rococo Church: Between Faith and Aestheticism* (New Haven: Yale University Press, 1983), pp. 196–219.

6. See Carl E. Schorske, *Fin-de-Siècle Vienna: Politics and Culture* (New York: Vintage, 1981), especially pp. 24–115, "The Ringstrasse, Its Critics, and the Birth of Urban Modernism."

7. See for example Le Corbusier, *Towards a New Architecture,* trans. Frederick Etchells (New York: Praeger, 1960), p. 27: "Architecture has nothing to do with the various 'styles.' The styles of Louis XIV, XV, XVI or Gothic, are to architecture what a feather is on a woman's head; it is something pretty, though not always, and never anything more." The distinction between style and ornament, on the one hand, and architecture, on the other, parallels that drawn already by John Locke between feminine ornamented speech and masculine straight talk. See *An Essay Concerning Human Understanding,* ed. Peter H. Nidditch (Oxford: Clarendon Press, 1975), p. 508. On feminine ornament vs. masculine building, see Peter Haiko and Mara Reissberger, "Ornamentlosigkeit als neuer Zwang," in *Ornament und Askese,* pp. 110–119, and Jacques Le Rider, "Modernismus/Feminismus—Modernität/Virilität: Otto Weininger und die asketische Moderne," in ibid., pp. 242–260. Also see Anthony Vidler, "Behind the Mask," unpublished contribution to the conference "Abbau—Neubau—Überbau: Nietzsche and an Architecture of Our Minds," sponsored by the Getty Center for the History of Art and the Humanities, Weimar, October 11–13, 1994, and

Beatriz Colomina, *Privacy and Publicity: Modern Architecture as Mass Media* (Cambridge: MIT Press, 1994), pp. 36–37.

8. Charles Garnier, *Le Nouvel Opéra de Paris,* quoted in David van Zanten, "Architectural Composition at the École des Beaux-Arts from Charles Percier to Charles Garnier," in *The Architecture of the École des Beaux-Arts,* ed. Arthur Drexler (New York: Museum of Modern Art, 1977), p. 279.

9. Loos, "Ornament and Crime," p. 20.

10. Adolf Loos, "Ladies' Fashion," in *Spoken into the Void: Collected Essays, 1897–1900,* trans. Jane O. Newman and John H. Smith (Cambridge: MIT Press, 1982), p. 102.

11. Loos, "Ornament and Crime," p. 20.

12. Ibid., p. 21.

13. See Roman Sandgruber, "Wiener Alltag um 1900," in *Ornament und Askese,* p. 43.

14. Arthur Drexler, "Engineer's Architecture and Its Consequences," in *Architecture of the École des Beaux-Arts,* p. 51. For a comparison of Loos and the Shakers see Rukschcio, "Ornament und Mythos," p. 63.

15. Loos, "Ornament und erziehung," in *Trotzdem,* p. 205.

16. For a discussion of Loos's America experience see Benedetto Gravagnuolo, *Adolf Loos: Theory and Works,* trans. C. H. Evans (New York: Rizzoli, 1982), pp. 42–51.

17. Loos, "The Luxury Vehicle," in *Spoken into the Void,* p. 39.

18. Ibid., p. 40.

19. Loos, "Plumbers," in *Spoken into the Void,* pp. 45–46.

20. Named after Dr. Daniel Gottlieb Schreber, who in the middle of the nineteenth century called for such workers' gardens as an antidote to the ills of the modern city. Cf. Loos, "Der tag der siedler" and "Die moderne siedlung" (in *Trotzdem,* pp. 186–189, 211–240).

21. Loos, "Der tag der siedler," p. 186.

22. I cannot agree with Gravagnuolo that "the myth of a happy return to an uncontaminated and regenerative Nature remains profoundly alien to Loos' thought" (*Adolf Loos,* p. 50). The death of God gives both nature and art a special significance. Consider in this connection Loos's late Khuner house on the slopes of the Semmering (pp. 204–205).

23. Hence Loos's vehement critique of Werkbund and Wiener Werkstätte. See Massimo Cacciari, *Architecture and Nihilism: On the Philosophy of Modern Architecture,* trans. Stephen Sartraelli (New Haven: Yale University Press, 1993), p. 111.

24. Loos, "Vorwort," in *Trotzdem,* p. 3.

25. Loos, "Der schönste innenraum, der schönste palast, . . . ," in *Trotzdem,* p. 59; "Heimatkunst," in *Trotzdem,* pp. 138, 137. Such admiration calls into question this claim by Cacciari: "The wall is form, calculated space-time—it is 'abstract.' It would be absurd, 'Wagnerian,' to attempt to reconcile it with this interior, this lived experience, with the space of the multiplicity of languages that make up life. Therefore, the bourgeois, philistine concept of the home—the concept of a totality of dwelling, of a reciprocal transparence between interior and exterior—on which every Stilarchitektur has been based up to this point, is intrinsically, logically false" (*Architecture and Nihilism,* p. 107). Logic here has been overburdened: not logic but the progress of culture has overtaken such architecture. Today it would be irresponsible to try to resurrect it.

26. For an excellent discussion of the privatization of art that helped define Loos's aesthetic stance, see Carl E. Schorske, "Abschied von der Öffentlichkeit: Kulturkritik und Modernismus in der Wiener Architektur," in *Ornament und Askese,* pp. 47–56.

27. Loos, "Ornament und erziehung," p. 206.

28. Ibid., p. 205.

29. Loos, "Architektur," in *Trotzdem,* p. 110. The Romans were the moderns of antiquity. There is a sense in which Loos may be said to have continued that struggle of Rome against Athens that in the eighteenth century had pitted Lodoli and Piranesi against Laugier. See John Wilton-Ely, *Piranesi as Architect and Designer* (New York: Pierpont Morgan Library; New Haven: Yale University Press, 1993), pp. 35–62. Also see Joseph Rykwert, "Lodoli on Function and Representation," in *The Necessity of Artifice,* p. 121.

30. Loos, "Architektur," pp. 110–111.

31. Loos, "Ornament und erziehung," p. 202.

32. Ibid., p. 204.

33. Ibid.

34. Ibid., p. 202.

35. See Gottfried Semper, *Der Stil in den technischen und tektonischen Künsten, oder praktische*

Aesthetik (Frankfurt: Verlag für Kunst und Wissenschaft, 1860), 1:217.

36. Loos, "The Principle of Cladding," in *Spoken into the Void*, p. 67. See Colomina, *Privacy and Publicity*, pp. 264–265.

37. Loos, "The Principle of Cladding," p. 66.

38. Ibid., p. 67. From here the step to decorative use of sculptures by Kolbe and Lehmbruck by Mies van der Rohe, to Le Corbusier's use of work by Jacques Lipchitz, Léger, and himself is not so very large. See Joseph Rykwert, "Ornament Is No Crime," in *The Necessity of Artifice*, p. 94.

39. Loos, "Potemkin City," in *Spoken into the Void*, p. 95.

40. Ibid.

41. Adolf Hitler, *Mein Kampf*, trans. Ralph Mannheim (Boston: Houghton Mifflin, 1943), p. 19, cited in Schorske, *Fin-de-Siècle Vienna*, p. 46.

42. Loos, "Ornament und erziehung," p. 204. The influence of Otto Weininger's *Geschlecht und Charakter* is evident. See Jacques Le Rider, "Modernismus/Feminismus—Modernität/Virilität," pp. 242–260.

43. Loos, "Ornament and Crime," p. 19.

44. See Werner Hofmann, "Das Fleisch Erkennen," in *Ornament und Askese*, pp. 120–129.

45. Loos, "Ladies' Fashion," p. 99.

46. Ibid. Cf. Francesco Dal Co, "Dwelling and the 'Places' of Modernity," in *Figures of Architecture and Thought: German Architecture Culture 1880–1920,* trans. Stephen Sartarelli (New York: Rizzoli, 1990), pp. 46–47.

47. Loos, "Ladies' Fashion," p. 100. See Angela Völker, "Kleiderkunst und Reformmode im Wien der Jahrhundertwende," in *Ornament und Askese*, pp. 142–155.

48. Loos, "Ladies' Fashion," p. 103.

49. Charles Garnier, *Le Théâtre*, quoted in van Zanten, "Architectural Composition," p. 278.

50. Loos, "Ladies' Fashion," p. 102.

51. Loos, "The Luxury Vehicle," p. 40.

52. Loos, "Ornament and Crime," p. 24.

53. Immanuel Kant, *Kritik der Urteilskraft*, A 50. See Karsten Harries, "Laubwerk auf Tapeten," in *Idealismus mit Folgen: Die Epochenschwelle um 1800 in Kunst und Geisteswissenschaften*, ed. Hans-Jürgen

Gawoll and Christoph Jamme (Munich: Fink Verlag, 1994), pp. 87–96.

54. See Harries, *Bavarian Rococo Church*, pp. 196–199.

55. Clement Greenberg, "Recentness of Sculpture," quoted in Michael Fried, "Art and Objecthood," in *Minimal Art: A Critical Anthology*, ed. Gregory Battcock (New York: Dutton, 1968), p. 124; Kant, *Kritik der Urteilkraft*, A 177.

56. Kant, *Kritik der Urteilkraft*, A 49; *Critique of Judgment*, trans. J. H. Bernard (New York: Hafner, 1951), par. 16, p. 66.

57. August Endell, "Formenschönheit und dekorative Kunst," cited in Peg Weiss, *Kandinsky in Munich: The Formative Jugendstil Years* (Princeton: Princeton University Press, 1979), p. 34.

58. August Endell, "Möglichkeit und Ziele," cited in ibid., p. 39.

59. Ibid., p. 43.

60. See Emil Kaufmann, *Architecture in the Age of Reason: Baroque and Post-Baroque in England, Italy, and France* (New York: Dover, 1968), pp. 141–180. Anthony Vidler, while remaining "convinced by Kaufmann's formal insights, as he sensed a Ledoux whose approach anticipated the elementarism of a later period" (*Claude-Nicolas Ledoux: Architecture and Social Reform at the End of the Ancien Régime* [Cambridge: MIT Press, 1990], p. xv), has pointed out the many ways in which Ledoux nevertheless remains a characteristic representative of the cultural situation in prerevolutionary France. The conjunction of a geometric elementarism and a concern that architecture speak, a concern for *architecture parlante*, offers a key to the epochal threshold marked by the French revolution.

61. See Karsten Harries, "The Broken Frame," in *The Broken Frame: Three Lectures* (Washington, D.C.: Catholic University of America Press, 1989), pp. 64–89.

62. Loos, "Ornament and Crime," p. 22.

63. Cf. Loos, "Ornament und erziehung," p. 202: "Form or ornament is the result of the unconscious collective work of the members of an entire culture. Everything else is art. Art is the genius's own will."

64. This distinction between decoration and ornament invites comparison with that proposed by Oleg Grabar in *The Mediation of Ornament*, The A. W. Mellon Lectures in the Fine Arts 1989, Bol-

lingen Series XXXV, 38 (Princeton: Princeton University Press, 1992), p. 5: "Ornament, as an initial definition, is differentiated from decoration in the sense that decoration is anything, even whole mosaic or sculpted programs, applied to an object or to a building, whereas ornament is that aspect of decoration which appears not to have another purpose but to enhance its carrier." Applied decoration is here contrasted with ornament that enhances its carrier. How is such enhancement to be understood? I agree with Grabar that something is clearly wrong with the following definition: "In the *Encyclopedia of the Arts,* a standard statement of generally accepted verities, ornament 'refers to motifs and themes used . . . without being essential to structure and serviceability . . . [but] for the purpose of embellishment' " (p. 25). While Grabar agrees that ornament "brings beauty to whatever it adorns," he recognizes that such beauty may not be thought of as a merely external embellishment: to ornament something is to "complete it," to "make it perfect": in this sense ornament is "independent from but essential to the expression of that action or of the reality" (p. 26). Grabar's analysis of the mediating function of ornament leads him, too, to conclude that ornament finally has what I would call an ethical function (cf. p. 236).

4 The Promise of Ornament

1. John Ruskin, *The Seven Lamps of Architecture* (New York: Noonday, 1974), p. 7.

2. Adolf Loos, "Ornament and Crime," in *Programs and Manifestoes on 20th-Century Architecture,* ed. Ulrich Conrads, trans. Michael Bullock (Cambridge: MIT Press, 1975), p. 24.

3. Adolf Loos, "Architektur," in *Trotzdem: 1900–1930* (Innsbruck: Brenner, 1931), p. 107.

4. Ernst Bloch, *Das Prinzip Hoffnung,* 3 vols. (Frankfurt: Suhrkamp, 1980).

5. See Karsten Harries, "The Ethical Significance of Modern Art," *Design for Arts in Education,* vol. 89, no. 6 (July/August, 1988), pp. 2–12.

6. Loos, "Ornament and Crime," p. 24.

7. It has become fashionable to understand Loos as the architect who has recognized and accepted nihilism as the condition of the modern metropolis and has done so without nostalgia. See, e.g., Massimo Cacciari, *Architecture and Nihilism: On the Philosophy of Modern Architecture,* trans. Stephen Sartarelli (New Haven: Yale University Press, 1993):

"In philosophical terms, the problem that presents itself in Loos is that of the possibility and meaning of dwelling in the age of Nietzschean nihilism fulfilled" (p. 199). Cacciari offers a fuller description:

The Cafe Nihilismus and the Nihilismus house on the Michaelerplatz ("der neue Raum") are necessarily situated in the Nihilismus city, the Metropolis where all the social circles of Gemeinschaft have been shattered. City and style, as community organism or the nostalgia for such, are synonymous. . . . But the place of the synthesis between art and handicraft, the real place of "applied art" and "musical drama," the place of communal resolution of conflict, is the city, not the Metropolis. In the Metropolis these past relations can only appear as ornament. . . . Ornament hides the true metropolitan relations, it falsifies. (p. 112)

See also Benedetto Gravagnuolo, *Adolf Loos: Theory and Works,* trans. C. H. Evans (New York: Rizzoli, 1982), e.g., p. 56: "The houses 'without ornament' mirror the nihilism of the metropolis which—for Loos—is not tragic in itself but only appears so to those who are constantly trying to do away with it"; and Gevork Hartoonian, *Ontology of Construction: On Nihilism of Technology in Theories of Modern Architecture* (Cambridge: Cambridge University Press, 1994). All these interpretations are indebted to Manfredo Tafuri and Aldo Rossi and shadowed by Benjamin's bleak understanding of history as "one single catastrophe which keeps piling wreckage upon wreckage" (Walter Benjamin, "Theses on the Philosophy of History," in *Illuminations,* trans. Harry Zohn [New York: Schocken, 1968], p. 257). See Cacciari, *Architecture and Nihilism,* pp. 143–149. But while I find such an approach to Loos's theory and architecture often illuminating, I question the unexamined construal of the metropolis as a destiny that must be accepted or that must lead either to an unjustifiable nostalgia for a supposedly better past or to an equally unjustifiable hope for a better future. Like Heidegger's *Ge-Stell,* the metropolis, so understood, invites by its very nature a barren, radical negation. I also question the understanding of Loos as a nihilist. "Nihilism" and "metropolis" are catchwords that block understanding, blind us to the countless little meanings available to us despite all the horrors of history. Cf. Karsten Harries, "Questioning the Question of the Worth of Life," *Journal of Philosophy,* vol. 88, no. 11 (November 1991), pp. 684–690.

8. See chapter 24.

9. Hermann Broch, "Hofmannsthal und seine Zeit," in *Gesammelte Werke: Essays* (Zurich: Rhein,

1955), 1:43. See Karsten Harries, "Decoration, Death, and Devil," in *Hermann Broch: Literature, Philosophy, Politics,* ed. Stephen D. Dowden (Columbia, S.C.: Camden House, 1988), pp. 277–298. Also Paul Michael Lützeler, "Herman Broch als Kritiker des Wien der Jahrhundertwende," in *Ornament und Askese,* ed. Alfred Pfabigan (Vienna: Brandstätter, 1985), pp. 178–190.

10. Broch, "Der Zerfall der Werte," in *Erkennen und Handeln: Essays* (Zurich: Rhein, 1955), 2:7–8. The essay appeared originally as a set of discourses inserted into the third part of Broch's trilogy, *Die Schlafwandler* (1928–1931), set in 1918.

11. Loos, to be sure, would have rejected the very idea of wanting to create a modern architectural style. In one sense there was no need to create such a style: it had already evolved, reflecting our modern way of life. But this was not a style that sought to heal the rift separating art and technology. Quite the opposite: that rift helped to define the style. For an individual or a group of individuals to attempt to create a style seemed to Loos wrongheaded. No easy road leads from Loos to the Bauhaus.

12. Hundertwasser, "Mould Manifesto against Rationalism in Architecture," in *Programs and Manifestoes,* pp. 157, 160.

13. Georg Lukács, *Aesthetik* (Neuwied and Berlin: Luchterhand, 1963), 1:453–454.

14. See Karsten Harries, "Modernity's Bad Conscience," *AA Files,* no. 10 (Autumn 1985), pp. 53–60.

15. Broch, "Hofmannsthal," p. 44.

16. Georg Lukács, *Die Zerstörung der Vernunft* (Neuwied and Berlin: Luchterhand, 1954), p. 176.

17. Friedrich Nietzsche, *Nachgelassene Fragmente, Frühjahr–Sommer 1888,* in *Sämtliche Werke: Kritische Studienausgabe,* ed. Giorgio Colli and Mazzino Montinari (Munich: Deutscher Taschenbuch Verlag; Berlin: de Gruyter, 1980), 13:500. This edition will hereafter be abbreviated as CM. *The Will to Power,* trans. Walter Kaufmann and R.J. Hollingdale (New York: Vintage, 1968), book 3, par. 822, p. 435.

18. Broch, "Hofmannsthal," p. 44.

19. Georg Lukács, "Es geht um den Realismus," in *Werke* (Neuwied and Berlin: Luchterhand, 1970), 4:328.

20. Friedrich Nietzsche, "Der Fall Wagner, 7," CM 6:27; "The Case of Wagner, 7" in *Basic Writings of Nietzsche,* trans. Walter Kaufmann (New York: Modern Library, 1968), p. 626.

21. Broch, "Der Zerfall der Werte," p. 9.

22. Owen Jones, *The Grammar of Ornament* (London: Studio Editions, 1986), pp. 82, 154, 155.

23. Ibid., pp. 1, 67.

24. Ibid., pp. 77–78.

25. Alexander Tzonis and Liane Lefaivre, *Classical Architecture: The Poetics of Order* (Cambridge: MIT Press, 1986), pp. 107–108.

26. Broch, "Der Zerfall der Werte," p. 10.

27. Ibid., p. 11.

28. Ibid.

29. Hans Sedlmayr, *Verlust der Mitte* (Frankfurt: Ullstein, 1959), p. 73.

30. Ibid., p. 74.

31. Bloch, *Das Prinzip Hoffnung,* p. 448.

32. Michael Müller, *Die Verdrängung des Ornaments: Zum Verhältnis von Architektur und Lebenspraxis* (Frankfurt: Suhrkamp, 1977), p. 5.

33. Oswald Spengler, *Der Untergang des Abendlandes* (Munich: Beck, 1923), 1:254.

34. Friedrich Nietzsche, *Ecce Homo,* "Warum ich so gute Bücher schreibe," 4, CM 6:304.

35. Emil Staiger, *Die Kunst der Interpretation* (Munich: Deutscher Taschenbuch Verlag, 1971), pp. 11–12.

36. See Hubert Langauer, "Metaphern der Macht: Ornament und Askese bei Hofmannsthal," in *Ornament und Askese,* p. 193.

37. See Karsten Harries, "Heidegger and the Problem of Style in Interpretation," *Irish Philosophical Journal,* vol. 6 (1989), pp. 250–274.

38. Arnold Hauser, *The Philosophy of Art History* (Cleveland: Meridian Books, 1963), p. 210.

39. Ernst H. Gombrich, *Art and Illusion* (Princeton: Princeton University Press, 1969), p. 20.

40. Such talk of the world-establishing power of style suggests an answer to a question that must pose itself to the attentive reader of Heidegger's often-cited description of a Greek temple in "The Origin of the Work of Art"; that is, how are we to think the temple's world establishing power? I would like to suggest that every work of architecture strong enough to establish or reestablish a

shared ethos does so by virtue of its specific style—I refer the reader to my analysis of the style of the Bavarian Rococo church in *The Bavarian Rococo Church: Between Faith and Aestheticism* (New Haven: Yale University Press, 1983). Such a suggestion should not seem surprising if we keep in mind Heidegger's claim that it is mood that discloses our being-in-the-world as a whole. Style communicates mood. Only by virtue of a shared style can a work of architecture establish a common world.

41. Lukács, "Es geht um den Realismus," p. 317.

42. Broch, "Der Zerfall der Werte," p. 42.

43. Ibid., p. 19.

5   The Decorated Shed

1. See Bruce Allsop, *The Study of Architectural History* (New York: Praeger, 1970), pp. 63–68, which discusses J. Fergusson's *History of Architecture* (1865) and Banister Fletcher's *History of Architecture on the Comparative Method* (1896).

2. Robert Venturi, Denise Scott Brown, and Steven Izenour, *Learning from Las Vegas: The Forgotten Symbolism of Architectural Form,* rev. ed. (Cambridge: MIT Press, 1977), p. 87.

3. Ibid., p. 7.

4. Joseph Rykwert, *The First Moderns: The Architects of the Eighteenth Century* (Cambridge: MIT Press, 1980), p. 390.

5. See Yvan Christ and Ionel Schein, *L'Oeuvre et les rêves de Claude-Nicolas Ledoux* (Paris: Chêne, 1971), and Anthony Vidler, *Claude-Nicolas Ledoux: Architecture and Social Reform at the End of the Ancien Régime* (Cambridge: MIT Press, 1990).

6. Emil Kaufmann, *Architecture in the Age of Reason: Baroque and Post-Baroque in England, Italy, and France* (New York: Dover, 1968), p. 165. Cf. Vidler, *Ledoux,* pp. 316–322.

7. Kaufmann, *Architecture in thr Age of Reason,* p. 163.

8. Vidler calls attention to Ledoux's transformation of the then-current understanding of the rhetorical function of character: Ledoux had "given the idea of characterization a determining role in the formation of his aesthetic, less in Blondel's terms as a proper framing for the decorative program, than as a totalizing force that controlled the internal form and the external expression of a building" (*Ledoux,* p. 145).

9. Immanuel Kant, *Kritik der Urteilskraft,* A 163.

10. Ibid., A 52–60.

11. For brevity's sake, I shall use "Venturi" in the text when I should be writing "the authors of *Learning from Las Vegas.*" That work is hereafter cited parenthetically in the text.

12. Owen Jones, *The Grammar of Ornament* (London: Studio Editions, 1986), p. 67: "The Moors ever regarded what we hold to be the first principle in architecture—to decorate construction, never to construct decoration." See also proposition 5 of his "General Principles": "Construction should be decorated. Decoration should never be purposely constructed" (p. 5). Jones's "first principle in architecture" invites comparison with Loos's "principle of cladding."

13. Ibid., p. 33.

14. J. Fergusson, *History of the Modern Styles of Architecture,* 3rd ed. (London, 1891), p. 5, cited in Allsop, *Study of Architectural History,* p. 64.

15. Marcel Duchamp, "Painting . . . at the Service of the Mind," in *Theories of Modern Art: A Source Book by Artists and Critics,* comp. Herschel B. Chipp (Berkeley: University of California Press, 1969), pp. 393–394. See also Karsten Harries, "The Painter and the Word," *Bennington Review,* no. 13 (June 1982), pp. 19–25.

16. If Duchamp's turn to "'literary' painting" invites comparison with Venturi's turn to an "architecture of communication," it also brings to mind Eisenman's various attempts to introduce elements into his architecture that, precisely because they do not fulfill any obvious function, because they are in an important sense redundant, invite the attentive observer to understand them as riddles to be thought about and deciphered, as pointers to an esoteric spiritual meaning or markers rendered intelligible only by philosophical speculation—in Houses I and II by the speculative grammar of Noam Chomsky, in later work by Derrida's practice of deconstruction. I am grateful to Stuart Lathers for pursuing with me the issue of "marking" in architecture and for working out in some detail the similarity between Eisenman's use of "markers" and the use made of a similar practice by such Baroque architects as Borromini and Johann Michael Fischer—with the difference that the deep geometric structure buried in their churches, "marked," e.g., by their cornices, possesses a symbolic significance bound up with a Christian worldview, while Eisenman gestures toward a world that has replaced God with nothing. That

such architecture, too, invites understanding as a decorated shed, even if decoration has now become hermetic and cerebral, requires no comment.

17. Something like this is indeed admitted by Denise Scott Brown in her preface to the revised edition of *Learning from Las Vegas*. What we should learn from Las Vegas, she tells us, "is not to place neon signs on the Champs Elysees or a blinking '2 + 2 = 4' on the roof of the Mathematics Building, but rather to reassess the role of symbolism in architecture, and, in the process, to learn a new receptivity to the tastes and values of other people and a new modesty in our designs and in our perception of our role as architects in society. Architecture for the last quarter of our century should be socially less coercive and aesthetically more vital than the striving and bombastic buildings of our recent past. We architects can learn this from Rome and Las Vegas and from looking around us wherever we happen to be" (p. xvii).

18. Ibid., p. 53. The quote is from August Heckscher, *The Public Happiness* (New York: Atheneum, 1962), p. 289.

19. Ibid., p. 50.

6 The Language Problem

1. Heinrich Klotz, *The History of Postmodern Architecture* (Cambridge: MIT Press, 1988), p. 5.

2. Klotz provides a convenient overview. See ibid., pp. 3–5.

3. Manfredo Tafuri, *Theories and History of Architecture,* trans. Giorgio Verrecchia (New York: Harper and Row, 1980), p. 174.

4. See Martin Heidegger, *Sein und Zeit,* 7th ed. (Tübingen: Niemeyer, 1953), pp. 80–81.

5. Roger Scruton, *The Aesthetics of Architecture* (Princeton: Princeton University Press, 1979), p. 159.

6. Ibid.

7. Ibid., p. 161.

8. Alexander Tzonis and Liane Lefaivre, *Classical Architecture: The Poetics of Order* (Cambridge: MIT Press, 1986), pp. 6, 245.

9. Wolfgang T. Otto, *Der Raumsatz: Neue Gestaltungsprobleme der Architektur* (Stuttgart: Deutsche Verlags-Anstalt, 1959), pp. 25, 26.

10. Ibid., p. 26.

11. Scruton, *Aesthetics of Architecture,* p. 162.

12. Ibid., p. 163.

13. Ibid., p. 164.

14. See ibid., pp. 174–177.

15. Tzonis and Lefaivre, *Classical Architecture,* pp. 26–27, 90, 101, 163.

16. Scruton, *Aesthetics of Architecture,* p. 165.

17. Charles Morris, *Foundations of the Theory of Signs* (Chicago: University of Chicago Press, 1938). For some implications of that theory for architecture, see Christian Norberg-Schulz, *Intentions in Architecture* (Cambridge: MIT Press, 1965), pp. 56–66.

18. Umberto Eco, "Function and Sign: Semiotics of Architecture," *Via,* vol. 2 (1973), pp. 135–136.

19. David Macaulay, *Motel of the Mysteries* (Boston: Houghton Mifflin, 1979).

20. To show this was one point of my book on the Bavarian Rococo church, although I felt no need to use Eco's vocabulary. See *The Bavarian Rococo Church: Between Faith and Aestheticism* (New Haven: Yale University Press, 1983), especially pp. 176–195.

21. Eco, "Semiotics of Architecture," p. 151.

22. Ibid., p. 136.

23. Ibid., p. 131.

7 Representation and Symbol

1. See Charles Jencks, *The Language of Post-Modern Architecture* (New York: Rizzoli, 1977), p. 54. There also see the expected before and after images.

2. Ibid., p. 9, once again with the familiar before and after images.

3. Christian Norberg-Schulz, *Intentions in Architecture* (Cambridge: MIT Press, 1965), p. 126.

4. Louis Dupré, *The Other Dimension* (Garden City, N.Y.: Doubleday, 1972), p. 1.

5. Hans Sedlmayr, *Die Entstehung der Kathedrale* (Zurich: Atlantis, 1950), and Otto von Simson, *The Gothic Cathedral: Origins of Gothic Architecture and the Medieval Concept of Order,* 2nd ed. (New York: Harper and Row, 1964).

6. Thomas Aquinas, *Summa theologiae,* III, 83, 3 ad 2m. Hegel, too, considers the house the basic type that governs church architecture: the church is a house large enough to allow the community to assemble within, but more important is the intent

to lift the individual above the finite. See Georg Wilhelm Friedrich Hegel, *Vorlesungen über die Aesthetik,* in *Jubiläumsausgabe,* ed. Hermann Glockner (Stuttgart: Fromann, 1937), 13:335.

7. See Rudolf Schwarz, *Vom Bau der Kirche,* 2nd ed. (Heidelberg: Lambert Schneider, 1947), p. 141.

8. See Abbot Suger, *On the Abbey Church of St. Denis and Its Art Treasures,* ed., trans., and annotated by Erwin Panofsky (Princeton: Princeton University Press, 1979), p. 52: "We have thought it proper to place on record the description of the ornaments of the church by which the Hand of God, during our administration, has adorned His church, His Chosen Bride."

9. von Simson, *Gothic Cathedral,* p. 8.

10. Günter Bandmann, *Mittelalterliche Kunst als Bedeutungsträger* (Berlin: Mann, 1951), p. 89.

11. von Simson, *Gothic Cathedral,* pp. 21–58.

12. Ibid., p. 13.

13. Walter Gropius, "Programme of the Staatliches Bauhaus in Weimar," in *Programs and Manifestoes on 20th-Century Architecture,* ed. Ulrich Conrads, trans. Michael Bullock (Cambridge: MIT Press, 1975), p. 49.

14. von Simson, *Gothic Cathedral,* p. 13.

15. See Friedrich Ohly, *Schriften zur mittelalterlichen Bedeutungsforschung* (Darmstadt: Wissenschaftliche Buchgesellschaft, 1977).

16. Hans Jantzen, *Ottonische Kunst* (Hamburg: Rowohlt, 1959), pp. 72, 75. For an account of the significance of the Reichenau, see also John Beckwith, *Early Medieval Art* (New York: Praeger, 1964), pp. 96–98, 118–120, 126–127; and Wolfgang Schöne, *Über das Licht in der Malerei* (Berlin: Mann, 1983), pp. 22–26.

17. Panofsky, introduction to *On the Abbey Church of St. Denis,* by Abbot Suger, p. 15.

18. Suger, *On the Abbey Church of St. Denis,* pp. 65–67.

19. Ibid., pp. 47–49.

20. On the "spiritual perspective" of medieval art and architecture, see Friedrich Ohly, "Vom geistigen Sinn des Wortes im Mittelalter," in *Schriften zur mittelalterlichen Bedeutungsforschung,* p. 15.

21. Schöne, *Über das Licht in der Malerei,* pp. 37–42.

22. von Simson, *Gothic Cathedral,* pp. 121–122.

23. Ibid., p. 37.

24. See Hans Blumenberg, *Die Genesis der kopernikanischen Welt* (Frankfurt: Suhrkamp, 1975).

25. Joseph Rykwert, *On Adam's House in Paradise: The Idea of the Primitive Hut in Architectural History* (New York: Museum of Modern Art, 1972), pp. 121–140.

26. Ibid., p. 12.

27. Marc-Antoine Laugier, *An Essay on Architecture,* trans. Wolfgang and Anni Herrmann (Los Angeles: Hennessey and Ingalls, 1977), p. 11. This work is hereafter cited parenthetically in the text.

28. Rykwert, *On Adam's House in Paradise,* p. 192.

29. For a charming account of the origins and variety of human habitations, see Eugène Viollet-le-Duc, *The Habitations of Man in All Ages,* trans. Benjamin Bucknall (1876; reprint, New York: Arno, 1977).

30. Johann Wolfgang von Goethe, "Von deutscher Baukunst," in *Schriften zur Kunst I,* vol. 33 of *Goethes Sämtliche Werke, Jubiläums-Ausgabe* (Stuttgart and Berlin: Cotta, n.d.), p. 6.

31. Christian Norberg-Schulz, *Intentions in Architecture* (Cambridge: MIT Press, 1965), p. 125.

32. See Gottfried Semper, *Der Stil in den technischen und tektonischen Künsten, oder praktische Aesthetik,* (Frankfurt: Verlag für Kunst und Wissenschaft, 1860), 1:217.

33. See e.g., Hans Jacob Wörner, *Architektur des Frühklassizismus in Süddeutschland* (Munich and Zurich: Schnell und Steiner, 1979).

34. Wolfgang Herrmann, "Semper's Position on the Primitive Hut," in *Gottfried Semper: In Search of Architecture* (Cambridge: MIT Press, 1989), p. 166.

8   Representation and Re-Presentation

1. Francesco Milizia, *Memorie degli architetti antichi e moderni,* 3rd ed. (Parma, 1781), 1:xi–xii; cited in Joseph Rykwert, *On Adam's House in Paradise: The Idea of the Primitive Hut in Architectural History* (New York: Museum of Modern Art, 1972), p. 67.

2. Johann Wolfgang von Goethe, "Baukunst" (fragment, 1795), in *Gesamtausgabe,* ed. Wolfgang Freiherr von Löhneysen (Stuttgart: Cotta, 1961), 16:670.

3. Ibid., p. 671. See Hermann Bauer, *Rocaille: Zur Herkunft und zum Wesen eines Ornament-Motivs* (Berlin: de Gruyter, 1962), p. 71.

4. Friedrich Wilhelm Joseph von Schelling, *Philosophie der Kunst,* vol. 5 of *Sämtliche Werke* (Stuttgart and Augsburg: Cotta, 1859), par. 107, p. 578. See Bauer, *Rocaille,* p. 71. Cf. Demetri Porphyrios, "Classicism Is Not a Style," in *Classicism Is Not a Style,* ed. Demetri Porphyrios (London: Architectural Design and Academy Editions, 1982), p. 57: according to Porphyrios the task of architecture "is to lift itself above the contingencies of building, by commemorating those very contingencies from which it sprung in the first place." Commemoration—i.e., remembrance—and representation belong together.

5. Bauer, *Rocaille,* p. 72.

6. Georg Wilhelm Friedrich Hegel, *Vorlesungen über die Aesthetik,* in *Jubiläumsausgabe,* ed. Hermann Glockner (Stuttgart: Fromann, 1937), 13:309.

7. Ibid., p. 311.

8. Ibid., p. 314.

9. Cf. the discussion of "perfection" in chapter 2, pp. 21–23.

10. Hegel, *Vorlesungen über die Aesthetik,* 13:315. Cf. Aristotle's insistence that a successful tragedy possess beginning, middle, and end, defined as follows: "A beginning is that which is not itself necessarily after anything else, and which has naturally something else after it; an end is that which is naturally after something itself, either as its necessary or usual consequent, and with nothing else after it; and a middle, that which is by nature after one thing and has also another after it" (*Poetics* 7, 1450b21–33); trans. I. Bywater, in *The Complete Works of Aristotle,* rev. Oxford ed., ed. Jonathan Barnes, vol. 2 (Princeton: Princeton University Press, 1984).

11. Francesco Conte Algarotti, "Saggio sopra l'architettura" (1756), in *Opere* (Leghorn, 1764), 2:162; cited by Emil Kaufmann, *Architecture in the Age of Reason: Baroque and Post-Baroque in England, Italy, and France* (New York: Dover, 1968), p. 96.

12. Algarotti, "Saggio," p. 65; cited in Kaufmann, *Architecture in the Age of Reason,* p. 97.

13. Cf. Joseph Rykwert, "Lodoli on Function and Representation," in *The Necessity of Artifice* (New York: Rizzoli, 1982), p. 121: "Yet the little building [Lodoli's San Francesco della Vigna in Venice], miserable as it is—Memmo's apologies are perfectly justified—suggests that he was after something more ambitious: the invention of new ornamental forms based on the nature of materials to use the cant modern phrase, but more accurately (and according to the terminology favored by Lodoli himself) to display the energies inherent in them by a translation into a geometrical analogue."

14. Martin Heidegger, "The Origin of the Work of Art," in *Poetry, Language, Thought,* trans. Albert Hofstadter (New York: Harper and Row, 1971), p. 46.

15. Edward Bullough, Psychical Distance as a Factor in Art and an Esthetic Principle," in *A Modern Book of Esthetics: An Anthology,* ed. Melvin Rader (New York: Holt, 1952), p. 404.

16. See Karsten Harries, *The Meaning of Modern Art* (Evanston, Ill.: Northwestern University Press, 1968), pp. 131–143, 159.

17. Cf. Martin Heidegger, *Feldweg-Gespräche* (1944/45), in *Gesamtausgabe* (Frankfurt: Klostermann, 1995), 77:47–48. Heidegger here discusses decoration (*Zier und Schmuck*) that, without calling too much attention to itself, allows the decorated to "show forth more beautifully," perhaps even to show itself for the first time.

18. This link of ornament to frame invites comparison with Christopher Alexander et al.'s discussion of "Frames as Thickened Edges" and of "Ornament" in *A Pattern Language: Towns, Buildings, Construction* (New York: Oxford University Press, 1977), pars. 225, 249: "The main purpose of ornament in the environment—in buildings, rooms, and public spaces—is to make the world more whole by knitting it together" as does the decoration of a carpet "in which each part is simultaneously figure and boundary and in which the design acts as boundary and figure at several different levels simultaneously" (p. 1148). Such decoration illustrates that authors' claim that "a thing is whole only when it is itself entire and also joined to its outside to form a larger entity. But this can only happen when the boundary between the two is so thick, so fleshy, so ambiguous, that the two are not sharply separated, but can function either as separate entities or as one larger whole which has no inner cleavage in it" (p. 1148). But if ornament often functions to bind the ornamented into a larger whole (see pp. 56–59 above), such binding is inseparable from its representational function, as the authors of *Pattern Language* half-recognize when they admonish the architect: "Search around the building, and find those edges and transitions which need emphasis or extra binding energy" (p. 1151). The portal of a church is ornamented, not so much because it is a seam but "because this seam—the boundary of

the entrance to the church—is so important, symbolically, to the people who worship there" (p. 1150).

19. Marc-Antoine Laugier, *An Essay on Architecture,* trans. Wolfgang and Anni Herrmann (Los Angeles: Hennessey and Ingalls, 1977), p. 14.

20. See the first chapter of John Summerson, *Heavenly Mansions* (New York: Norton, 1963).

21. Arthur Drexler, "Engineer's Architecture and Its Consequences," in *The Architecture of the École des Beaux-Arts,* ed. Arthur Drexler (New York: Museum of Modern Art, 1977), pp. 48–49.

22. Ibid., p. 49.

23. Owen Jones, *The Grammar of Ornament* (London: Studio Editions, 1986), pp. 70–71.

24. Ibid., p. 71.

25. Ibid., p. 34.

26. On Nilson see Karsten Harries, "The Broken Frame," in *The Broken Frame: Three Lectures* (Washington, D.C.: Catholic University of America Press, 1989), pp. 64–89.

27. Bauer, *Rocaille,* p. 40. See also Karsten Harries, *The Bavarian Rococo Church: Between Faith and Aestheticism* (New Haven: Yale University Press, 1983), pp. 26, 212–214.

28. "Semantics and Poetry," in *Princeton Encyclopedia of Poetry and Poetics,* enlarged ed., ed. Alex Preminger, Frank J. Warnke, and O. B. Hardison (Princeton: Princeton University Press, 1974), p. 758.

29. Ibid., p. 759.

30. William Carlos Williams, "Queen Anne's Lace," in *The Complete Collected Poems, 1906–1938* (Norfolk, Conn.: New Directions, 1938), pp. 86–87.

31. See Karsten Harries, "Metaphor and Transcendence" and "The Many Uses of Metaphor," in *On Metaphor,* ed. Sheldon Sacks (Chicago: University of Chicago Press, 1978), pp. 71–88, 165–172.

32. See Christian Norberg-Schulz, *Intentions in Architecture* (Cambridge: MIT Press, 1965), p. 63.

33. Manfredo Tafuri, *Theories and History of Architecture,* trans. Giorgio Verrecchia (New York: Harper and Row, 1980), p. 174.

34. Norberg-Schulz, *Intentions in Architecture,* p. 123.

35. Cf. Hegel, *Vorlesungen über die Aesthetik,* 13:295.

36. See Friedrich Ohly, "Vom geistigen Sinn des Wortes im Mittelalter," in *Schriften zur mittelalterlichen Bedeutungsforschung* (Darmstadt: Wissenschaftliche Buchgesellschaft, 1977), pp. 1–31.

37. Alanus de Insulis, "Rhythmus alter, quo graphice natura hominis fluxa et caduca depingitur," in *Patrologia Latina,* ed. Jacques-Paul Migne (Paris: Migne, 1855), 210:579.

38. Cf. Christian Norberg-Schulz, *The Concept of Dwelling: On the Way to Figurative Architecture* (New York: Rizzoli, 1985), p. 133.

9 Tales of the Origin of Building

1. Wallace Stevens, "Notes Toward a Supreme Fiction," in *The Palm at the End of the Mind,* ed. Holly Stevens (New York: Vintage, 1972), p. 210.

2. Leszek Kolakowski, *The Presence of Myth* (Chicago: University of Chicago Press, 1989).

3. Joseph Rykwert, *On Adam's House in Paradise: The Idea of the Primitive Hut in Architectural History* (New York: Museum of Modern Art, 1972), p. 13.

4. Vitruvius, *The Ten Books of Architecture,* trans. Morris Hicky Morgan (New York: Dover, 1960), book 2, chap. 1, 1, p. 38.

5. Gottfried Semper, "The Basic Elements of Architecture," in *Gottfried Semper: In Search of Architecture,* by Wolfgang Herrmann (Cambridge: MIT Press, 1989), p. 198. In Vitruvian fashion Semper considered the hearth the soul of the house. It provided the key to his other elements of architecture: a mound to support the fire, roof and enclosure to protect it and those gathered around. A Caribbean hut he saw at the Great Exposition in the Crystal Palace in London in 1851 provided a paradigm: here "all elements of ancient architecture appear in the most unadulterated form: the hearth at the center, the mound surrounded by a framework of poles as terrace, the roof carried by columns, and the mats as space enclosure or wall" (*Der Stil in den technischen und tektonischen Künsten, oder praktische Aesthetik* [Munich: Bruckmann, 1863], 2:276; quoted in Wolfgang Herrmann, "Semper's Position on the Primitive Hut," in *Gottfried Semper,* p. 169).

6. Frank Lloyd Wright, *The Natural House* (New York: New American Library, 1970), p. 32. Cf. Christopher Alexander et al., *A Pattern Language:*

Towns, Buildings, Construction (New York: Oxford University Press, 1977), no. 181, pp. 838–843: "The Fire."

7. Vitruvius, Ten Books of Architecture, book 2, chap. 1, 3, p. 39.

8. In this connection Nold Egenter claims that the by now well-studied nests of the higher apes allow us to say that "the original built-hut actually exists and, by implication, the first master-builders, too." Nold Egenter, The Present Relevance of the Primitive in Architecture, vol. 1 of Architectural Anthropology (Lausanne: Structura Mundi, 1992), p. 133.

9. See Rykwert, On Adam's House in Paradise, chap. 7, "A House for the Soul," pp. 183–192.

10. Ibid., p. 190.

11. Ibid., p. 185.

12. Ibid., p. 186.

13. Georg Wilhelm Friedrich Hegel, Vorlesungen über die Aesthetik, in Jubiläumsausgabe, ed. Hermann Glockner (Stuttgart: Fromann, 1937), 13:276.

14. Ibid., p. 277. See Herodotus, The Persian Wars, book 1, chap. 181.

15. Paul Weiss, Nine Basic Arts (Carbondale: Southern Illinois University Press, 1961), p. 69.

16. Christian Norberg-Schulz, Intentions in Architecture (Cambridge: MIT Press, 1965), p. 111. See also pp. 112–114.

17. Egenter, Present Relevance of the Primitive, p. 153.

18. Seneca is quoted in Bernard Rudofsky, The Prodigious Builders: Notes towards a Natural History of Architecture with Special Regard to Those Species That Are Traditionally Neglected or Downright Ignored (New York: Harcourt Brace Jovanovich, 1977), p. 9.

19. Norberg-Schulz, Intentions in Architecture, pp. 114–118.

20. This use of "typology" may seem confusing to readers familiar with Aldo Rossi's understanding of "typology" as "the study of types of elements that cannot be further reduced, elements of a city as well as of an architecture. The question of mono-centric cities or of buildings that are or are not centralized, for example, is specifically typological" (The Architecture of the City [Cambridge: MIT Press, 1984], p. 41). "Type" here names what we can call a formal schema. Rossi bases his own understanding of "type" on the definition given by Quatremère de Quincy in his Dictionnaire historique

d'architecture (see also p. 182 nn. 11, 12). Supported by work by Giulio Carlo Argan, Alan Colquhoun, Rafael Moneo, and Anthony Vidler, this understanding of "type" and "typology" has by now come to be almost taken for granted.

21. Nikolaus Pevsner, A History of Building Types (Princeton: Princeton University Press, 1976).

22. Ibid., p. 9.

23. Hannes Meyer, "Building," in Programs and Manifestoes on 20th-Century Architecture, ed. Ulrich Conrads, trans. Michael Bullock (Cambridge: MIT Press, 1975), p. 119.

24. Sigfried Giedion, Space, Time and Architecture, 5th ed. (Cambridge, Mass.: Harvard University Press, 1974), p. 25.

25. Ibid.

26. Walter Gropius, The New Architecture and the Bauhaus, trans. P. Morton Shand (Cambridge: MIT Press, 1965), p. 33.

27. Judith and Bernard Raab, Good Shelter: A Guide to Mobile, Modular, and Prefabricated Houses, Including Domes (New York: Quadrangle, 1975), p. 25. This work is hereafter cited parenthetically in the text.

28. Adolf Loos, "The Poor Little Rich Man," in Spoken Into the Void: Collected Essays, 1897–1900, trans. Jane O. Newman and John H. Smith (Cambridge: MIT Press, 1982), p. 127.

29. Raab and Raab, Good Shelter, p. 41.

30. Norberg-Schulz, Intentions in Architecture, p. 118.

31. Ibid., p. 119.

32. Le Corbusier, Towards a New Architecture, trans. Frederick Etchells (New York: Praeger, 1960), pp. 65–66.

33. In his perspective view of the House of the Agricultural Guards, Ledoux thus presents the house as mediating between cosmic order and rustic shelter. See Anthony Vidler, Claude-Nicolas Ledoux: Architecture and Social Reform at the End of the Ancien Régime (Cambridge: MIT Press, 1990), p. 314: "The sphere, which rests lightly on the ground, supported by buttresses that serve as bridges to the main entrances, is triangulated between, on the left, a rude shed of branches and leaves—the traditional shelter of shepherds—and, on the far horizon, the rising sun, whose rays bathe the scene in bucolic spendor. The original 'type' of the rural hut is here mediated through the 'type'

or origin of nature into a symbolic form of universal guardianship."

10   Building and Dwelling

1. Joseph Rykwert, *On Adam's House in Paradise: The Idea of the Primitive Hut in Architectural History* (New York: Museum of Modern Art, 1972).

2. Martin Heidegger, "Bauen Wohnen Denken," first published in *Darmstädter Gespräch Mensch und Raum* (Darmstadt: Neue Darmstädter Verlagsanstalt, 1952), pp. 72–84. Translated by Alfred Hofstadter as "Building Dwelling Thinking," in *Poetry, Language, Thought* (New York: Harper and Row, 1971), pp. 145–161; quoted passage, p. 160. I have substituted "sky" for "heaven" as a translation of *Himmel,* and "place" for "location" as a translation of *Ort.* This work is hereafter cited parenthetically in the text.

3. See Francesco Dal Co, "Dwelling and the 'Places' of Modernity," *Figures of Architecture and Thought: German Architecture Culture,* in *1880– 1920,* trans. Stephen Sartarelli (New York: Rizzoli, 1990), pp. 13–81. Like so many analysts of the metropolitan condition, Dal Co sees "no harmony" in modern urban dwelling; he observes, "If dwelling is nothing but the unresolved manifestation of the lacerations of living and hence an experience given to regret, then it is up to modern man to know this condition to its fullest extent, to the essence of metropolitan homelessness" (p. 42). But while modernity and harmonious dwelling are impossible to reconcile, I cannot quite agree with Dal Co when he claims that for Heidegger, too, dwelling

is not the harmonious expression of the relationship to the preexistent place; and that every organicist conception that embraces the nostalgia for a virtuous and mythic "prehistory" of dwelling is, in essence, based on a regret for the lost blood-tie between the land and the refuge. The belief that the refuge is continuity with the given place; that the home is a completion of the natural landscape; that the extension of man's hand from it, as it attempts to seize "usables," is the continuation of a fraternal relationship with nature, the "kinship" that endures in the communality of the search for nourishment—all of these beliefs are to be found in Spengler as well as in Tönnies, and also to a lesser extent in Sombart. Heidegger's considerations turn this thinking upside down: without dwelling there can be no place; it is construction that evokes the place and transforms the space. (p. 38)

To be sure, in *Being and Time* Heidegger, very much in the spirit of his place and time, makes

homelessness constitutive of the human condition. But soon he was forced to recognize the onesidedness of such an understanding. Although essentially homeless, we yet dream and need to dream of home. From the earliest publications of the aspiring theologian to the very end there is thus a great deal of nostalgia in Heidegger's writings. Titles like "Schöpferische Landschaft: Warum bleiben wir in der Provinz?" "Vom Geheimnis des Glockenturms," and "Sprache und Heimat" speak for themselves. One could perhaps say that Heidegger makes such nostalgia constitutive of authentic modern dwelling: we moderns need to confront our homelessness. Heidegger's Black Forest farmhouse thus conjures up a home that is indeed "the harmonious expression of the relationship to the preexistent place." Its description is meant to challenge us "to build out of dwelling," where "dwelling" names not something first made possible by human building but rather "the manner in which mortals are on the earth" ("Building Dwelling Thinking," pp. 161, 148), a dwelling that, precisely because constituted by the loss of home, needs to be illuminated by figures of home.

4. This characterization is called into question by, even as it calls into question, Heidegger's insistence on the essential homelessness of human beings in *Being and Time.* To be sure, there already Heidegger had pointed out that first of all and most of the time we feel at home in the world; and in *The Genesis of Heidegger's "Being and Time"* (Berkeley: University of California Press, 1993), Theodore Kisiel calls our attention to the way Heidegger, in his lecture course "Basic Concepts of Aristotelian Philosophy" (1924), "still seems to accept pleasure as the background disposition of being-in-the-world" (p. 296). The "lightness of being" is said to "belong to joy" (p. 295). But *Being and Time* links authentic existence to a recognition of our essential homelessness in the world. Any thoughtful appropriation of Heidegger needs to confront this apparent tension in his thought. See Martin Heidegger, *Sein und Zeit,* 7th ed. (Tüingen: Niemeyer, 1953), pp. 188–190, 276–278; trans. John Macquarrie and Edward Robinson, *Being and Time* (New York: Harper and Row, 1962), pp. 232–235, 320–323.

5. Cf. Dal Co's rather different interpretation of this passage in "Dwelling and the 'Places' of Modernity," pp. 37–38.

6. See Enrique Larrañaga, "Towards an Architectural Theory of Dwelling in Hispanic America" (master's thesis, Yale University, 1983), pp. 177–219.

7. Mircea Eliade, *Cosmos and History: The Myth of the Eternal Return,* trans. Willard R. Trask (New York: Harper Torchbooks, 1959), pp. 76–77.

8. Dal Co, *Figures of Architecture,* p. 39.

9. Martin Heidegger, "The Origin of the Work of Art," in *Poetry, Language, Thought,* p. 47.

10. Ibid., p. 49.

11. Martin Heidegger, ". . . Poetically Man Dwells . . .," in *Poetry, Language, Thought,* p. 223.

12. Ibid., p. 225.

13. It is instructive to read Heidegger's essay in the context in which it was first delivered. See *Darmstädter Gespräch.*

14. Martin Heidegger, "Die Gefahr," in *Bremer und Freiburger Vorträge, 1949,* vol. 79 of *Gesamtausgabe,* (Frankfurt am Main: Klostermann, 1994), pp. 46–67.

15. Walter Gropius, *The New Architecture and the Bauhaus,* trans. P. Morton Shand (Cambridge: MIT Press, 1965), p. 33.

16. René Descartes, *Discourse on Method* 6, in *The Philosophical Works,* trans. Elizabeth S. Haldane and G. R. T. Ross (New York: Dover, 1955), 1:119.

17. Heidegger, "Die Gefahr," p. 47. For a fuller discussion of this "neglect of things" see Karsten Harries, "Philosophy, Politics, Technology," in *Martin Heidegger: Politics, Art, and Technology,* ed. Karsten Harries and Christoph Jamme (New York: Holmes and Meier, 1994), pp. 225–242.

18. See especially Heidegger's postscript to "The Origin of the Work of Art," pp. 79–81. Cf. Gropius, *New Architecture and the Bauhaus,* p. 90: "Thus our informing conception of the basic unity of all design in relation to life was in diametrical opposition to that of 'art for art's sake,' and the even more dangerous philosophy it sprang from: business as an end in itself."

19. Heidegger, "Die Gefahr," p. 46.

20. Martin Heidegger, "Die Überwindung der Metaphysik," in *Vorträge und Aufsätze* (Pfullingen: Neske, 1954), p. 97.

21. Heidegger, "Die Gefahr," p. 56.

22. Robert Jan van Pelt, "Apocalyptic Abjection," in Robert Jan van Pelt and Carroll William Westfall, *Architectural Principles in the Age of Historicism* (New Haven: Yale University Press, 1991), pp. 317–381.

23. Martin Heidegger, "Das Ge-Stell," in *Bremer und Freiburger Vorträge,* p. 27. For a fuller discussion of the statement and the outrage it provoked, see Harries, "Philosophy, Politics, Technology," pp. 233–234, 244 n. 35.

24. van Pelt, "Apocalyptic Abjection," p. 335.

25. Heidegger, "Building Dwelling Thinking," p. 161.

11 Space and Place

1. Robert Frost, "Mending Wall," in *The Poetry of Robert Frost,* ed. Edward Connery Latham (New York: Holt, Rinehart, and Winston, 1969), p. 34.

2. Joseph Addison, *Spectator,* no. 412 (23 June 1712); reprinted in Joseph Addison and Richard Steele, *Selected Essays from "The Tatler," "The Spectator," and "The Guardian,"* ed. Daniel McDonald (Indianapolis: Bobbs-Merrill, 1973), pp. 464–465.

3. See Nicholas of Cusa, *On Learned Ignorance,* trans. Jasper Hopkins (Minneapolis: Banning, 1981), book 2, chap. 12, p. 117. Also Karsten Harries, "The Infinite Sphere: Comments on the History of a Metaphor," *Journal of the History of Philosophy,* vol. 13, no 1. (January 1975), pp. 5–15.

4. Friedrich Nietzsche, *Nachgelassene Fragmente, Herbst 1885–Herbst 1886,* in *Sämtliche Werke: Kritische Studienausgabe,* ed. Giorgio Colli and Mazzino Montinari (Munich: Deutscher Taschenbuch Verlag; Berlin: de Gruyter, 1980), 12:127. *The Will to Power,* trans. Walter Kaufmann and R. J. Hollingdale (New York: Vintage, 1968), preface, p. 8

5. Arthur Schopenhauer, *The World as Will and Representation,* trans. E. F. J. Payne (New York: Dover, 1969), 2:3.

6. Ivan Turgenev, *Fathers and Sons,* trans. Constance Garnett (New York: Modern Library, 1950), pp. 148–149.

12 The Voices of Space

1. That architecture must base itself on such antecedently given meanings was a commonplace in the eighteenth century. Cf. Anthony Vidler, *Claude-Nicolas Ledoux: Architecture and Social Reform at the End of the Ancien Régime* (Cambridge: MIT Press, 1990), p. 146:

"The character of monuments," wrote Ledoux, "like their nature, supports the propagation and purification of morals." In this sense, Ledoux was echoing Rousseau's nostalgia for an original moral language, where social signs were

presumably transparent to the things they signified, before, as Rousseau wrote, "art had fashioned our manners and taught our passions to speak an affected language." In such a time, "our morals were rustic but natural, and the difference between actions announced at first sight the differences among characters." Such a utopia of characters, transparent to their appearance, where representation simply announced what it stood for without artifice, was joined by Ledoux with the idea that in this first Golden Age language was in the first instance gestural, figural, and an immediate visual expression of the passions; "one speaks," Rousseau had put it, "better to the eyes than to the ears."

And am I not similarly echoing Rousseauian nostalgia when I invoke a natural language of space? That the hope for a transparent, prelinguistic "speaking," a hope that resonates in the title of this chapter, is indeed utopian must be admitted. But the discourse of the eyes is not reducible to that of the ears: even though every supposed state of nature can be shown to be a historically conditioned construct, such constructs are part of our unending attempts to defeat arbitrariness by grounding (or criticizing) the established and accepted. And here "reason" and "nature," even if never "pure," remain as the only still available authorities.

2. Cf. Christian Norberg-Schulz, *The Concept of Dwelling: On the Way to Figurative Architecture* (New York: Rizzoli, 1985), especially pp. 111–125.

3. See Rudolf Schwarz, *Vom Bau der Kirche,* 2nd ed. (Heidelberg: Lambert Schneider, 1947), pp. 32, 84. Also see Kent C. Bloomer and Charles W. Moore, with a contribution by Robert J. Yudell, *Body, Memory, and Architecture* (New Haven: Yale University Press, 1977), especially p. 1; J. J. Gibson, *The Ecological Approach to Visual Perception* (Boston: Houghton Mifflin, 1979), especially pp. 127–143; Maurice Merleau-Ponty, *The Primacy of Perception,* trans. James M. Edie (Evanston, Ill.: Northwestern University Press, 1973).

4. Frank Lloyd Wright, *The Organic House* (New York: New American Library, 1954), p. 15.

5. Ibid., p. 16.

6. Ibid.

7. Heinrich von Kleist, "Empfindungen vor Friedrichs Seelandschaft," in *Sämtliche Werke* (Stuttgart: Phaidon, n.d.), p. 836.

8. Wolfgang Stechow, *Dutch Landscape Painting of the Seventeenth Century* (Ithaca: Cornell University Press, 1981), p. 47.

9. Norberg-Schulz, *Concept of Dwelling,* p. 37.

10. Cf. Georg Wilhelm Friedrich Hegel, *Vorlesungen über die Aesthetik,* in *Jubiläumsausgabe,* ed. Hermann Glockner (Stuttgart: Fromann, 1937), 13:276.

11. See Schwarz, *Vom Bau der Kirche,* p. 21.

12. Martin Heidegger, *Sein und Zeit,* 7th ed. (Tübingen: Niemeyer, 1953), pp. 197–198.

13. Arthur Schopenhauer, *The World as Will and Represenation,* trans. E. F. J. Payne (New York: Dover, 1966), 2:411.

14. Ibid., p. 417.

15. Ibid., pp. 417–418.

16. Piet Mondrian, "Statement, ca. 1943," in *Theories of Modern Art: A Source Book by Artists and Critics,* comp. Herschel B. Chipp (Berkeley: University of California Press, 1969), p. 362.

17. Carl Lamb, *Die Wies* (Munich: Süddeutscher Verlag, 1964), p. 88.

18. Ibid., p. 89.

19. Quoted in ibid.

20. Ibid., p. 90.

21. That this is not at all an idiosyncratic preference is suggested by Christopher Alexander et al. in *A Pattern Language: Towns, Building, Construction* (New York: Oxford University Press, 1977), no. 138, pp. 656–659: "Sleeping to the East."

22. Mircea Eliade, *The Sacred and the Profane: The Nature of Religion,* trans. Willard R. Trask (New York: Harcourt, Brace, and World, 1959), pp. 37–41.

23. See Schwarz, *Vom Bau der Kirche,* p. 21.

24. Ibid., p. 34.

25. Søren Kierkegaard, *Either/Or,* trans. Walter Lowrie, D. F. Swenson, and L. M. Swenson (Garden City, N.Y.: Doubleday Anchor, 1959), 1:135–228.

26. See John Hix, *The Glass House* (Cambridge: MIT Press, 1974).

27. Paul Scheerbart, "Glass Architecture," in *Programs and Manifestoes on 20th-Century Architecture,* ed. Ulrich Conrads, trans. Michael Bullock (Cambridge: MIT Press, 1975), p. 32.

28. Cf. Alexander et al., *A Pattern Language,* no. 203, pp. 927–929: "Child Caves."

29. Sigfried Giedion, *The Eternal Present: The Beginnings of Art* (New York: Pantheon, 1962), p. 525.

30. In the seventeenth century the city of Augsburg thus developed a master plan focused on three very costly fountains that punctuate the city's old axis. Today they continue to gather this city into a coherent whole.

31. Mircea Eliade, *Cosmos and History: The Myth of the Eternal Return,* trans. Willard R. Trask (New York: Harper Torchbooks, 1959), pp. 17, 18.

13 Learning from Two Invisible Houses

1. Gaston Bachelard, *The Poetics of Space,* trans. Maria Jolas (Boston: Beacon, 1958), p. 15. This work is hereafter cited parenthetically in the text.

2. Cf. however chapter 10 n. 3, above.

3. Carl Gustav Jung, *Symbole der Wandlung: Analyse des Vorspiels zu einer Schizophrenie* (Zurich: Rascher, 1952), p. 260.

4. See Karl Joel, *Seele und Welt, Versuch einer organischen Auffassung* (Jena: Diederichs, 1912), p. 83.

5. Frank Lloyd Wright, *The Natural House* (New York: New American Library, 1970), p. 16. This work is hereafter cited parenthetically in the text.

6. Martin Heidegger, *Sein und Zeit,* 7th ed. (Tübingen: Niemeyer, 1953), p. 391; *Being and Time,* trans. John Macquarrie and Edward Robinson (New York: Harper and Row, 1962), p. 443.

7. William Hubbard, *Complicity and Conviction: Steps toward an Architecture of Convention* (Cambridge: MIT Press, 1981).

8. See Harold Bloom, *The Anxiety of Influence* (New York: Oxford, 1973).

9. Heidegger, *Sein und Zeit,* p. 385.

10. Hubbard, *Complicity and Conviction* p. 155.

11. Ibid., p. 153.

12. Ibid., p. 158.

13. Bachelard, *Poetics of Space,* p. 61. Cf. Le Corbusier, *Towards a New Architecture,* trans. Frederick Etchells (New York: Praeger, 1960), p. 244:

Everybody, quite rightly, dreams of sheltering himself in a sure and permanent home of his own. This dream, because it is impossible in the existing state of things, is deemed incapable of realization and so provokes an actual state of sentimental hysteria: to build one's own house is very much like making one's will. . . . When the time does arrive for building this house, it is not the mason's nor the craftman's moment, but that moment in which every man makes one poem, at any rate in his life. And so, in our towns and their outskirts, we have had during the last forty years not so much houses as poems, poems of an Indian summer, for a house is the crowning of a career . . . at that very moment when a man is sufficiently old and worn by life to be prey of rheumatism and death . . . and of crazy ideas.

To the house as poem Le Corbusier opposes the house as machine, an opposition closely linked to the aesthetic approach and subject to the same critique. Significant here is the Schopenhauerian link of poetry to death. Le Corbusier, to be sure, knew that that this is not a necessary link: poetry can serve life, and he experienced Phidias a just such a poet. Seeing the Parthenon "we are riveted by our senses; we are ravished in our minds; we touch the axis of harmony. No question of religious dogma enters in; no symbolical description; there is nothing but pure forms in precise relationships" (p. 204).

14 Building, Dwelling, and Time

1. See, e.g., Paul Weiss, *Nine Basic Arts* (Carbondale: Southern Illinois University Press, 1961), pp. 67–68.

2. Gotthold Ephraim Lessing, *Laocoon: An Essay upon the Limits of Painting and Poetry,* trans. Ellen Frothingham (New York: Noonday, 1961).

3. Ibid., p. 91.

4. Ibid., p. 17.

5. Geoffrey Scott, *The Architecture of Humanism: A Study in the History of Taste* (New York: Norton, 1974), p. 160.

6. Ibid., p. 159.

7. Ibid.

8. See John White, *The Birth and Rebirth of Pictorial Space* (New York: Harper and Row, 1972), p. 116.

9. Michael Fried, "Art and Objecthood," in *Minimal Art: A Critical Anthology,* ed. Gregory Battcock (New York: Dutton, 1968), p. 145 n. 19.

10. Clement Greenberg, "Towards a Newer Laocoon," in *Pollock and After: The Critical Debate,* ed. Francis Frascina (New York: Harper and Row, 1985), p. 42.

11. ibid., p. 43.

12. Peter Eisenman, "The End of the Classical: The End of the Beginning, the End of the End," *Perspecta,* vol. 21 (1984), p. 54.

13. Robert Morris, quoted by Fried in "Art and Objecthood," p. 144.

14. Karsten Harries, *The Bavarian Rococo Church: Between Faith and Aestheticism* (New Haven: Yale University Press, 1983), p. 86. See Bernhard Rupprecht, *Die bayerische Rokoko-Kirche* (Kallmünz: Lassleben, 1959).

15. Heinrich Wölfflin, *Principles of Art History: The Problem of the Development of Style in Later Art,* trans. M. D. Hottinger (New York: Dover, n.d.), p. 63. This work is hereafter cited parenthetically in the text.

16. Robert Venturi, *Complexity and Contradiction in Architecture,* 2nd ed. (New York: Museum of Modern Art, 1977), especially the preface.

17. Martin Heidegger, "Building Dwelling Thinking," in *Poetry, Language, Thought,* trans. Albert Hofstadter (New York: Harper and Row, 1971), p. 157.

18. See Martin Heidegger, "Über das Wesen der Universität und des akademischen Studiums," summer semester 1919, in *Zur Bestimmung der Philosophie,* vol. 56/57 of *Gesamtausgabe* (Frankfurt: Klostermann, 1987), pp. 205–214.

19. Ibid., p. 206.

20. Heidegger, "Building Dwelling Thinking," p. 160.

21. Martin Heidegger, "Die Gefahr," *Bremer und Freiburger Vorträge, 1949,* vol. 79 of *Gesamtausgabe,* (Frankfurt: Klostermann, 1994), p. 56. See also pp. 160, 164–165, above.

22. Arthur Schopenhauer, *The World as Will and Representation,* trans. E. F. J. Payne (New York: Dover, 1969), 1:37.

23. Mircea Eliade, *Cosmos and History: The Myth of the Eternal Return,* trans. Willard R. Trask (New York: Harper Torchbooks, 1959), p. 151.

15   The Terror of Time and the Love of Geometry

1. Vitruvius, *The Ten Books of Architecture,* trans. Morris Hickey Morgan (Cambridge: Harvard University Press, 1926), book 2, chap. 1, 1, p. 38.

2. Plato, *Philebus* 51c–d, trans. Benjamin Jowett. Cf. Le Corbusier, *Towards a New Architecture,* trans. Frederick Etchells (New York: Praeger, 1960), p. 31: "Architecture is the masterly, correct and magnificent play of masses brought together in light. Our eyes are made to see forms in light; light and shade reveal these forms; cubes, cones, spheres, cylinders or pyramids are the great primary forms which light reveals to advantage; the image of these is distinct and tangible within us and without ambiguity. It is for that reason that these are beautiful forms, the most beautiful forms. Everybody is agreed to that, the child, the savage, and the metaphysician."

3. Theo van Doesburg, an unpublished manuscript quoted by Charles Jencks, in *Modern Movements in Architecture* (Garden City, N.Y.: Doubleday Anchor, 1973), pp. 32–33.

4. Le Corbusier and Ozenfant, "Purism," in *Modern Artists on Art,* ed. Robert L. Herbert (Englewood Cliffs, N.J.: Prentice Hall, 1964), p. 60.

5. Ibid.

6. Le Corbusier, *Towards a New Architecture,* p. 186.

7. Walter Pichler and Hans Hollein, "Absolute Architecture," in *Programs and Manifestoes on 20th-Century Architecture,* ed. Ulrich Conrads, trans. Michael Bullock (Cambridge: MIT Press, 1975), p. 181.

8. Ibid., pp. 181–182.

9. Ibid., p. 182.

10. Peter Collins, *Changing Ideals in Modern Architecture* (London: Faber and Faber, 1971), p. 24. See also Joseph Rykwert, "The Nefarious Influence on Modern Architecture of the Neo-Classical Architects Boullée and Durand," in *The Necessity of Artifice* (New York: Rizzoli, 1982), pp. 60–65.

11. Theo van Doesburg, "Towards a Plastic Architecture," in *Programs and Manifestoes,* p. 79.

12. Ibid.

13. Franz Schulze, *Mies van der Rohe: A Critical Biography* (Chicago: University of Chicago Press, 1985), p. 256.

14. Le Corbusier and Pierre Jeanneret, "Five Points towards a New Architecture," in *Programs and Manifestoes,* p. 99.

15. Sergio Villari, *J. N. L. Durand (1760–1834): Art and Science of Architecture,* trans. Eli Gottlieb (New York: Rizzoli, 1990), p. 24.

16. Emil Kaufmann, *Architecture in the Age of Reason: Baroque and Post-Baroque in England, Italy, and France,* (New York: Dover, 1968), p. 210. Cf. Villari, *Durand,* p. 35.

17. Vitruvius, *Ten Books of Architecture,* book 1, chap. 2, p. 16.

18. Le Corbusier, *Towards a New Architecture,* p. 100.

19. Ibid., p. 186.

20. Ibid., p. 61.

21. Friedrich Nietzsche, *Zarathustra,* in *The Portable Nietzsche,* trans. Walter Kaufman (New York: Penguin Books, 1976), p. 252.

22. Thomas Hobbes, *Leviathan,* ed. Michael Oakeshott (Oxford: Blackwell, 1955), p. 64.

23. Martin Heidegger, "Überwindung der Metaphysik," in *Vorträge und Aufsätze* (Pfullingen: Neske, 1954), pp. 95–96.

24. "ABC Demands the Dictatorship of the Machine," in *Programs and Manifestoes,* p. 115.

25. Ibid.

16 Mold and Ruins

1. Hundertwasser, "Mould Manifesto against Rationalism in Architecture," in *Programs and Manifestoes on 20th-Century Architecture,* ed. Ulrich Conrads, trans. Michael Bullock (Cambridge: MIT Press, 1975), p. 157. This work is hereafter cited parenthetically in the text.

2. Dora Wiebenson has pointed out that the early history of the landscape garden leads to France as much as to England. I wish that she had included a fuller account of that early history and given more space to the significance of ruins. See her *Picturesque Garden in France* (Princeton: Princeton University Press, 1978).

3. Franz Kafka, "Der Bau," in *Die Erzählungen* (Frankfurt: Fischer, 1961), pp. 378–418. The following discussion is indebted to Walter Biemel's interpretation of the story in *Philosophische Analysen zur Kunst der Gegenwart* (The Hague: Martinus Nijhoff, 1968), pp. 66–140.

4. Johann Wolfgang von Goethe, "Ruysdael als Dichter," in *Schriften zur Kunst III,* vol. 35 of *Sämtliche Werke, Jubiläums-Ausgabe* (Stuttgart and Berlin: Cotta, n.d.), p. 7.

5. Hans Sedlmayr, *Verlust der Mitte* (Frankfurt: Ullstein, 1959), p. 77.

6. Ibid., p. 77.

7. Michael Fried, "Art and Objecthood," in *Minimal Art: A Critical Anthology,* ed. Gregory Battcock (New York: Dutton, 1968), pp. 136, 145, 147.

8. Ibid., p. 125.

9. Arthur Schopenhauer, 1:203.

10. Giorgio de Chirico, "Mystery and Creation," in *Theories of Modern Art: A Source Book by Artists and Critics,* comp. Herschel B. Chipp (Berkeley: University of California Press, 1969), p. 402.

11. See Karsten Harries, "Light without Love," in *The Broken Frame: Three Lectures* (Washington, D.C.: Catholic University of America Press, 1989), pp. 1–32.

12. Robert Morris, "The Present Tense of Space," *Art in America,* January/February 1978, p. 70.

13. Ibid., p. 73.

14. Ibid., p. 76.

15. Frank Lloyd Wright, *The Living City* (New York: Horizon, 1963), pp. 23–24; cited in Joseph Rykwert, *On Adam's House in Paradise: The Idea of the Primitive Hut in Architectural History,* (New York: Museum of Modern Art, 1972), p. 17.

16. Ibid.

17. Wright, *The Living City,* p. 25; cited in Rykwert, *On Adam's House in Paradise,* p. 18.

18. See Charles Jencks, *Modern Movements in Architecture* (Garden City, N.Y.: Doubleday Anchor, 1973), p. 276.

19. Ibid., p. 273; citing Reyner Banham.

20. Ibid., pp. 272–280.

21. Ibid., p. 277.

22. Ibid., p. 291.

23. David Greene, quoted in ibid., p. 297.

17 Death, Love, and Building

1. See Charles Jencks, *Modern Movements in Architecture* (Garden City, N.Y.: Doubleday Anchor, 1973), p. 274.

2. Cf. Karsten Harries, "Comments on Four Papers, ACSA Annual Meeting, 1991," *Environmental and Architectural Phenomenology Newsletter,* vol. 2, no. 3 (Fall 1991), pp. 10–12.

3. Plato, *Philebus* 51c.

4. Norman O. Brown, *Life against Death: The Psychoanalytical Meaning of History* (Middletown Conn.: Wesleyan University Press, 1959), p. 109.

5. See Karsten Harries, *The Bavarian Rococo Church: Between Faith and Aestheticism* (New Haven: Yale University Press, 1983), pp. 156–157.

6. Gaston Bachelard, *The Poetics of Space,* trans. Maria Jolas (Boston: Beacon, 1969), p. 102. This work is hereafter cited parenthetically in the text.

7. See pp. 184–185 above.

8. Aristotle, *Poetics* 6, 1449b24–49, trans. I. Bywater, in *The Complete Works of Aristotle,* rev. Oxford ed., ed. Jonathan Barnes, vol. 2 (Princeton: Princeton University Press, 1984).

9. Aristotle, *Rhetoric* 2.5, 1382a21–28, trans. W. Rhys Roberts, in ibid.

10. Aristotle, *Rhetoric* 2.8, 1385b11–22, trans. ibid.

11. See the discussion of "situation," pp. 223–224 above.

12. Martin Heidegger, "Building Dwelling Thinking," in *Poetry, Language, Thought,* trans. Alfred Hofstadter (New York: Harper and Row, 1971), p. 160.

13. Rudolf Schwarz, *Vom Bau der Kirche,* 2nd ed. (Heidelberg: Lambert Schneider, 1947), p. 96.

14. For a fuller discussion see Harries, *Bavarian Rococo Church,* pp. 160–170.

15. Martin Heidegger, "The Origin of the Work of Art," in *Poetry, Language, Thought,* pp. 40–41.

18   Architecture and Building

1. Bernard Rudofsky, *Architecture without Architects: A Short Introduction to Non-Pedigreed Architecture* (Garden City, N.Y.: Doubleday, 1964), n.p.

2. Cf. Heinrich Tessenow, "Metropolis, Town, Village," trans. Christiane Crasemann Collins, in Francesco Dal Co, *Figures of Architecture and Thought: German Architecture Culture, 1880–1920* (New York: Rizzoli, 1990), p. 316: "The high regard held by the city dweller for what pertains to the village is primarily due to his need for a correspondingly strong, external counterbalance to the large city. And vice versa. For the true village dweller, the large city is more or less paradise; and for the city dweller the village is paradise. Those who live in small towns appraise village and metropolis very circumspectly and therefore, probably most accurately."

3. Rudofsky, *Architecture without Architects,* n.p.

4. Bernard Rudofsky, *The Prodigious Builders: Notes towards a Natural History of Architecture with Special Regard to Those Species That Are Traditionally Neglected or Downright Ignored* (New York: Harcourt Brace Jovanovich, 1977), p. 13.

5. Ibid., p. 238, citing his doctoral dissertation, *Eine primitive Betonbauweise auf den südlichen Kykladen* (Vienna, 1931).

6. Ibid.

7. Cf. Christian Norberg-Schulz, *Genius Loci: Towards a Phenomenology of Architecture* (New York: Rizzoli, 1979).

8. Rudofsky, *Prodigious Builders,* p. 242.

9. Cf. Mircea Eliade, *Cosmos and History: The Myth of the Eternal Return,* trans. Willard R. Trask (New York: Harper Torchbooks, 1959), p. 21.

10. Rudofsky, *Prodigious Builders,* p. 242.

11. Consider the many examples given by Albert Knoepfli in *Alstadt und Denkmalpflege: Ein Mahn- und Notizbuch* (Sigmaringen: Thorbecke, 1975).

12. Rudofsky, *Architecture without Architects,* n.p.

13. John Ruskin, *The Seven Lamps of Architecture* (New York: Noonday, 1974), p. 16.

14. Rudofsky, *Prodigious Builders,* p. 9.

15. Adolf Loos, "Architektur," in *Trotzdem: 1900–1930* (Innsbruck: Brenner, 1931), p. 93, trans. in Joseph Rykwert, *On Adam's House in Paradise: The Idea of the Primitive Hut in Architectural History* (New York: Museum of Modern Art, 1972), p. 27.

16. Ibid., p. 94; trans. in Rykwert, *On Adam's House in Paradise,* p. 27.

17. Ibid., p. 93; trans. in Rykwert, *On Adam's House in Paradise,* p. 27. In "The Luxury Vehicle" Loos, however, had praised the Englishman who, quite willing to take full advantage of all machines had to offer, nevertheless abhorred them.

18. Le Corbusier, *Towards a New Architecture,* trans. Frederick Etchells (New York: Praeger, 1960), p. 33.

19. Ibid., p. 7.

20. Le Corbusier, "Guiding Principles of Town Planning," in *Programs and Manifestoes on 20th-Century Architecture,* ed. Ulrich Conrads, trans. Michael Bullock (Cambridge: MIT Press, 1975), p. 91.

21. Ibid., p. 90.

22. Ibid.

23. Le Corbusier, *Towards a New Architecture,* pp. 10, 202.

24. Ibid., pp. 203, 205.

25. Martin Heidegger, "The Origin of the Work of Art," in *Poetry, Language, Thought,* trans. Albert Hofstadter (New York: Harper and Row, 1971), pp. 41–42.

26. Ibid., p. 42.

27. Ibid., pp. 46, 44.

28. Martin Heidegger, *Being and Time,* trans. John Macquarrie and Edward Robinson (New York: Harper and Row, 1962), pp. 102–107.

29. Michael Benedikt, *For an Architecture of Reality* (New York: Lumen Books, 1987), p. 2.

30. Heidegger, "Origin of the Work of Art," pp. 40–41.

31. Loos, "Architektur," p. 107. Cf. Michael Müller, *Die Verdrängung des Ornaments: Zum Verhältnis von Architektur und Lebenspraxis* (Frankfurt: Suhrkamp, 1977), pp. 244–245.

19   The Publicness of Architecture

1. Nikolaus Pevsner, *An Outline of European Architecture* (Harmondsworth: Penguin, 1958).

2. Christian Norberg-Schulz, *Meaning in Western Architecture* (New York: Rizzoli, 1980).

3. Marvin Trachtenberg and Isabelle Hyman, *Architecture, from Prehistory to Post-Modernism: The Western Tradition* (Englewood Cliffs, N.J.: Prentice Hall; New York: Abrams, 1986); Spiro Kostof, *A History of Architecture: Setting and Rituals* (New York: Oxford University Press, 1985).

4. Kostof, *History of Architecture,* pp. 8 (see also 12), 15. This work is hereafter cited parenthetically in the text.

5. In the medieval city the city's walls and gates were by far the most expensive building project undertaken by the community, a project that primarily belongs to what here is considered building rather than to architecture, although insofar as walls and especially city gates served the self-representation of the community they posed also an architectural task.

6. Kostof, *History of Architecture,* p. 719. The quotation is not identified.

7. See Charles Jencks, *Modern Movements in Architecture* (Garden City, N.Y.: Doubleday Anchor, 1973), p. 82.

8. Nikolaus Pevsner, *A History of Building Types* (Princeton: Princeton University Press, 1976).

9. Hans Sedlmayr, *Verlust der Mitte* (Berlin: Ullstein, 1959), p. 13.

10. Ibid.

11. Plato, *Republic* 10, 605a, trans. Benjamin Jowett.

20   Grave and Monument

1. Adolf Loos, "Architektur," in *Trotzdem, 1900–1930* (Innsbruck: Brenner, 1931), p. 107. Cf. Michael Müller, *Die Verdrängung des Ornaments: Zum Verhaltnis von Architektur und Lebenspraxis* (Frankfurt: Suhrkamp, 1977), pp. 244–245. See also p. 282 above.

2. Loos, "Architektur," pp. 109–110.

3. Ibid., p. 107.

4. Howard Colvin, *Architecture and the After-Life* (New Haven: Yale University Press, 1991), p. 1.

5. Georg Wilhelm Friedrich Hegel, *Vorlesungen über die Aesthetik, in Jubiläumsausgabe,* ed. Hermann Glockner (Stuttgart: Fromann, 1937), 13:291.

6. Colvin offers this example:

to mine, transport, and assemble the material for one of the largest Irish tombs it is necessary to envisage a force of 1,000 men working more or less full-time for at least eight years. This in turn implies a population (and consequently a death rate) quite out of proportion to the capacity provided. Although neighboring communities may sometimes have co-operated in building megalithic tombs, it is fairly certain that most of these earliest mausolea were (like those of subsequent ages) intended as the resting-places of an elite, and if so, they may well reflect not only that elite's ideas of the proper way to dispose of its dead, but also a desire to reinforce its power and prestige by the building of conspicuous monuments. (Architecture and the After-Life, p. 3)

7. Ibid., p. 15.

8. See Helmut Scharf, *Kleine Kunstgeschichte des deutschen Denkmals* (Darmstadt: Wissenschaftliche Buchgesellschaft, 1984), p. 20.

9. Colvin, *Architecture and the After-Life,* p. 7.

10. Mircea Eliade, *The Sacred and the Profane: The Nature of Religion,* trans. Willard R. Trask (New York: Harcourt, Brace, and World, 1959), p. 185.

11. Colvin, *Architecture and the After-Life,* p. 56.

12. Ibid., p. 374.

13. Robert Jan van Pelt, "Athenian Assurance," in Robert Jan van Pelt and Carroll William Westfall, *Architectural Principles in the Age of Historicism* (New Haven: Yale University Press, 1991), p. 183.

14. Colvin, *Architecture and the After-Life,* p. 57.

15. Colvin lets the history of the Christian cemetery begin in the second half of the thirteenth century, with the Campo Santo in Pisa; see ibid., p. 364.

16. Ibid., p. 367.

17. Ibid., p. 368.

18. Ibid., p. 368.

19. van Pelt, "Athenian Assurance," p. 187.

20. Thucydides, *The Peloponnesian War,* book 2, chap. 6; trans. Richard Crawley (New York: Modern Library, 1951), pp. 107–108.

21. Plato, *Crito* 12.

22. Colvin, *Architecture and the After-Life,* p. 364.

23. Hegel, *Vorlesungen über die Aesthetik,* 13:293.

24. Heinrich Weinstock, *Sophokles* (Berlin: Verlag die Runde, 1937), pp. 199–213.

25. Sophocles, *Oedipus at Colonus,* trans. R. C. Jebb, in *The Complete Greek Drama,* ed. Whitney J. Oates and Eugene O'Neill, Jr. (New York: Random House, 1938), 1:662.

26. Ibid., p. 662.

27. Heraclitus, fragment 247, in G. S. Kirk and J. E. Raven, *The Presocratic Philosophers* (Cambridge: Cambridge University Press, 1962), p. 211.

28. Weinstock, *Sophokles,* p. 190.

29. Thucydides, *The Peloponnesian War,* book 2, chap. 6; trans. Crawley, p. 109.

30. Colvin, *Architecture and the After-Life,* p. 101.

31. Ibid., p. 105.

32. Ibid., p. 123.

33. See pp. 264–267 above.

34. Colvin, *Architecture and the After-Life,* p. 333.

35. Quoted from Laurenz Hirschfeld, *Theorie der Gartenkunst* (Leipzig, 1779–1785) in David Watkin and Tilman Mellinghoff, *German Architecture and the Classical Ideal* (Cambridge: MIT Press, 1987), p. 157.

36. Nicholas Capasso, "Vietnam Veterans Memorial," in *The Critical Edge: Controversy in Recent American Architecture,* ed. Tod A. Marder (Cambridge: MIT Press, 1985), p. 189.

37. Quoted in ibid., pp. 191, 193.

38. Quoted in ibid., p. 194.

39. Emil Kaufmann, *Architecture in the Age of Reason: Baroque and Post-Baroque in England, Italy, and France* (New York: Dover, 1968), p. 139. See also Joseph Rykwert, *The First Moderns: The Architects of the Eighteenth Century* (Cambridge: MIT Press, 1980), especially pp. 458 n. 94, 498 n. 152.

40. Nikolaus Pevsner, *A History of Building Types* (Princeton: Princeton University Press, 1976), p. 12.

41. Watkin and Mellinghoff, *German Architecture,* p. 157.

42. Quoted in ibid., p. 159.

43. Quoted in ibid., p. 160.

44. Quoted in ibid., p. 142.

45. Quoted in ibid., p. 158.

46. Scharf, *Kleine Kunstgeschichte des deutsche Denkmals,* p. 220.

47. Watkin and Mellinghoff, *German Architecture,* p. 169.

48. Georg Weise, in *Zeitschrift für Deutschkunde* (1935), quoted in *Die Bildenden Künste im Dritten Reich,* ed. Erich Wulf (Hamburg: Rowohlt, 1966), p. 261.

49. Colvin, *Architecture and the After-Life,* p. 328.

50. Hans Sedlmayr, *Verlust der Mitte* (Berlin: Ullstein, 1959), p. 22.

51. Colvin, *Architecture and the After-Life,* p. 332.

52. Pevsner, *History of Building Types,* p. 13.

53. See Rudolf Zeitler, *Klassizismus und Utopia,* studies edited by the Institute of Art History (Uppsala: University of Uppsala, 1954). Cf. Anthony Vidler, *Claude-Nicolas Ledoux: Architecture and Social Reform at the End of the Ancien Régime* (Cambridge: MIT Press, 1990), especially pp. 146–147, and Karsten Harries, *The Meaning of Modern Art* (Evanston, Ill.: Northwestern University Press, 1968), pp. 34–35.

54. Quoted in Pevsner, *History of Building Types,* pp. 13–14.

55. Edmund Burke, *A Philosophical Enquiry into the Origin of Our Ideas of the Sublime and Beautiful,* ed. J. Boulton (New York: Columbia University Press, 1958), p. 51.

56. Watkin and Mellinghoff, *German Architecture,* p. 161.

57. See Ernst Bloch, *Das Prinzip Hoffnung* (Frankfurt: Suhrkamp, 1980), 2:844.

58. Georg Trakl, "Grodek," *Gesang des Abgeschiedenen: Gedichte* (Wiesbaden: Insel, 1955), p. 55; my translation.

59. Quoted in Pevsner, *History of Building Types,* p. 16.

60. For a thoughtful discussion see Robert Jan van Pelt, "Apocalyptic Abjection," in *Architectural Principles in the Age of Historiciam,* pp. 333–334.

21 The Representation of Life

1. Adolf Loos, "Architektur," in *Trotzdem, 1900–1930* (Innsbruck: Brenner, 1931), p. 107.

2. Martin Heidegger, *Being and Time,* trans. John Macquarrie and Edward Robinson (New York: Harper and Row, 1962), p. 443.

3. Ibid., p. 437.

4. See David van Zanten, "Architectural Composition at the École des Beaux-Arts from Charles Percier to Charles Garnier," in *The Architecture of the École des Beaux Arts,* ed. Arthur Drexler (New York: Museum of Modern Art, 1977), pp. 111–323.

5. Charles Garnier, *Théâtre* (Paris: Hachette, 1871), p. 1. This work is hereafter cited parenthetically in the text.

6. See Irving Lavin, "On the Unity of the Arts and the Early Baroque Opera House," *Perspecta,* vol. 26 (1990), pp. 1–20.

7. Friedrich Nietzsche, *Nietzsche Contra Wagner,* "Wo ich Einwände mache," in *Sämtliche Werke: Kritische Studienausgabe,* ed. Giorgio Colli and Mazzino Montinari (Munich: Deutscher Taschenbuch Verlag; Berlin: de Gruyter, 1980), 6:420. This edition will hereafter be abbreviated as CM. The passage is almost identical with one in *The Gay Science* (book 5, par. 368).

8. Michael Fried, "Art and Objecthood," in *Minimal Art: A Critical Anthology,* ed. Gregory Battcock (New York: Dutton, 1968), p. 139.

9. Nikolaus Pevsner, *A History of Building Types* (Princeton: Princeton University Press, 1976), p. 84.

10. Hans Sedlmayr, *Verlust der Mitte* (Berlin: Ullstein, 1959), 36.

11. Richard Wagner, "Das Kunstwerk der Zukunft," in *Source Readings in Music History: The Romantic Era,* selected and annotated by Oliver Strunk (New York: Norton, 1965), p. 140.

12. Pevsner, *History of Building Types,* p. 86.

13. Nietzsche, *Richard Wagner in Bayreuth,* in CM 1:438.

14. Ibid., p. 451.

15. Ibid., p. 453.

16. Nietzsche, *Ecce Homo,* in CM 6:323.

17. Bertolt Brecht, *Schriften zum Theater* (Berlin and Frankfurt: Suhrkamp, 1957), p. 13.

18. See Sophie Gobran, "The Munich Festival Theater Letters," *Perspecta* 26, pp. 47–68.

19. John Winkler, "Representing the Body Politic," *Perspecta,* vol. 26 (1990), pp. 215–228.

20. José Ortega y Gasset, "Meditations on the Frame," *Perspecta,* vol. 26 (1990), pp. 185–190.

21. That already the Roman knew the roofed theater, that the Roman odeum was indeed such a theater, is claimed by George Izenour in "The Ancient Roofed Theater," *Perspecta,* vol. 26 (1990), pp. 69–82.

22. See Stephen Orgel, *The Illusion of Power: Political Theater in the Renaissance* (Berkeley: University of California Press, 1965) and Eberhard Straub, *Repraesentatio Maiestatis oder churbayerische Freudenfeste,* Miscellenea Bavarica, vol. 14 (Munich: Neue Schriftenreihe des Staatsarchivs, 1969).

23. Lavin, "On the Unity of the Arts," p. 1. See also Edmund Stadler, "Die Raumgestaltung im barocken Theater," in *Die Kunstformen des Barockzeitalters,* ed. Rudolf Stamm (Bern: Francke, 1956), pp. 190–226.

24. Stadler, "Die Raumgestaltung im barocken Theater," p. 190.

25. Lavin, "On the Unity of the Arts," p. 6.

26. Stadler, "Die Raumgestaltung im barocken Theater," p. 191.

27. See Karsten Harries, "Theater and Reality," in *The Bavarian Rococo Church: Between Faith and Aestheticism* (New Haven: Yale University Press, 1983), pp. 150–155.

28. Jacques Maritain, *Art and Scholasticism, and the Frontiers of Poetry,* trans. Joseph W. Evans (New York: Scribner, 1962), p. 52.

29. Pevsner, *History of Building Types,* p. 82. See Yvan Christ and Ionel Schein, *L'Oeuvre et les rêves de Claude-Nicolas Ledoux* (Paris: Chêne, 1971), pp. 142–145. Cf. Anthony Vidler, *Claude-Nicolas Ledoux: Architecture and Social Reform at the End of the Ancien Régime* (Cambridge: MIT Press, 1990), pp. 162–186.

30. Pevsner, *History of Building Types,* pp. 87–88.

31. Stanford Anderson, "Peter Behrens's Highest Kultursymbol, the Theater," *Perspecta,* vol. 26 (1990), p. 106.

32. Ibid., p. 117.

33. Peter Behrens, letter of June 1900, cited in Anderson, "Peter Behrens's Highest Kultursymbol," p. 120.

34. Peter Behrens, "Die Lebensmesse von Richard Dehmel als festliches Spiel," *Die Rheinlande,* vol. 1 (January 1901), p. 40, cited in ibid., p. 124.

35. Behrens, "Lebensmesse," p. 29, cited in ibid., p. 123.

36. Ibid., p. 106.

37. Behrens, "Lebensmesse," p. 28, cited in ibid., p. 126 n. 46.

38. Ibid., p. 132.

39. Emil Kaufmann, *Architecture in the Age of Reason: Baroque and Post-Baroque in England, Italy, and France* (New York: Dover, 1968), p. 153.

40. Ludwig Wittgenstein, *Philosophical Investigations,* trans. G. E. M. Anscombe (New York: Macmillan, 1953), par. 7.

22   Dreams of Utopia

1. Cf. Lotte Brand Philip, *The Ghent Altarpiece and the Art of Jan van Eyck* (Princeton: Princeton University Press, 1971), p. 61.

2. Norman Cohn, *The Pursuit of the Millennium,* 2nd ed. (New York: Harper Torchbooks, 1961), p. v. This work is hereafter cited parenthetically in the text.

3. Peter Gorsen, "Josef Hoffman: Zur Modernität eines konservativen Baumeisters," in *Ornament und Askese,* ed. Alfred Pfabigan (Vienna: Brandstätter, 1985), p. 82.

4. See Ernst Bloch, *Das Prinzip Hoffnung* (Frankfurt: Suhrkamp, 1980), 2:819–872.

5. [Walter] Gropius, [Bruno] Taut, and [Adolf] Behne, "New Ideas on Architecture," in *Programs and Manifestoes in 20th-Century Architecture,* ed. Ulrich Conrads, trans. Michael Bullock (Cambridge: MIT Press, 1970), p. 46.

6. Walter Gropius, "Programme of the Staatliches Bauhaus in Weimar," in *Programs and Manifestoes,* p. 49. Also in Hans M. Wingler, *The Bauhaus,* trans. Wolfgang Jabs and Basil Gilbert (Cambridge: MIT Press, 1978), p. 31.

7. Quoted in Wingler, *Bauhaus,* p. 36.

8. Gropius, Taut, and Behne, "New Ideas on Architecture," p. 46.

9. Ibid.

10. Cf. Joseph Rykwert, "The Dark Side of the Bauhaus," in *The Necessity of Artifice* (New York: Rizzoli, 1982), pp. 44–49. "I hope that I will not risk paradox if I now accuse the Bauhaus masters—not of an excessive rationalism—but rather of not stating the religious, or quasi religious postulates for what they were doing; or at any rate of not stating them explicitly. Only Itten and Klee have a clean record in this respect: and they were the two Bauhaus masters who realized most clearly the danger of van Doesburg's excessive devotion to modernity; to interpreting every technological advance as a spiritual leap forward" (p. 49). I especially welcome Rykwert's discussion of the importance of Rudolf Steiner.

11. Martin Heidegger, *Einführung in die Metaphysik* (Tübingen: Niemeyer, 1953), p. 152.

12. Louis Dupré, *The Other Dimension* (New York: Doubleday, 1972), p. 1.

13. Adolf Loos, "The Poor Little Rich Man," in *Spoken into the Void: Collected Essays, 1897–1900,* trans. Jane O. Newman and John H. Smith (Cambridge: MIT Press, 1982), p. 127.

14. "Nationalsozialistische Baukunst" (1939); reprinted in *Die Bildenden Künste im Dritten Reich: Eine Dokumentation,* ed. Joseph Wulf (Hamburg: Rowohlt, 1966), pp. 255–256.

15. *Das Schwarze Korps* (6/19/1935), p. 12; reprinted in *Die Bildenden Künste im Dritten Reich,* p. 270.

16. See Hermann Broch, *Dichten und Erkennen: Essays* (Zürich: Rhein, 1955), 1:43, 295–350.

17. Georg Weise, in *Zeitschrift für Deutschkunde* (1935), pp. 407–408; reprinted in *Die Bildenden Künste im Dritten Reich,* p. 261.

18. Robert Jan van Pelt, "Apocalyptic Abjection," in Robert Jan van Pelt and Carroll William Westfall, *Architectural Principles in the Age of Historicism* (New Haven: Yale University Press, 1991), pp. 328–329.

19. Rolf Badenhausen, "Betrachtungen zum Bauwillen des deutschen Reiches," *Zeitschrift für Deutschkunde* (1933), pp. 222–223; reprinted in *Die Bildenden Künste im Dritten Reich,* p. 250.

20. van Pelt, "Apocalyptic Abjection," pp. 333, 335.

21. Ibid., p. 334.

22. "Plan zum Neuaufbau Berlins–150 Architekten entwerfen Europas neueste Stadt," *Donau-Zeitung,* Belgrad (January 9, 1944); reprinted in *Die Bildenden Künste im Dritten Reich,* p. 268.

23. Reprinted in Wingler, *Bauhaus,* p. 20.

24. "The Viability of the Bauhaus Idea," circular of February 3, 1922; reprinted in Wingler, *Bauhaus,* p. 52.

25. Oskar Schlemmer, "The Staatliche Bauhaus in Weimar," in Wingler, *Bauhaus,* p. 65.

26. Ibid., pp. 65–66.

27. Oskar Schlemmer, "On the Situation of the Workshops for Wood and Stone Sculpture," in ibid., p. 60.

28. See Lewis Mumford, *The Culture of Cities* (New York: Harcourt, Brace and Company, 1938), p. 406.

29. Ibid., p. 407.

30. Ibid., p. 408.

31. Ibid., p. 406.

32. Letter to Julia Feininger of August 1, 1923; reprinted in Wingler, *Bauhaus,* p. 69.

33. For an account of Mies van der Rohe's relationship to National Socialism, see Franz Schulze, *Mies van der Rohe: A Critical Biography* (Chicago: University of Chicago Press, 1985), pp. 185–188, 195–205, 216–217.

34. Cited in Charles Jencks, *Modern Movements in Architecture* (Garden City, N.Y.: Doubleday Anchor, 1973), p. 119.

35. Ibid., pp. 46–50, 113. Jencks is depending on Barbara Miller Lane, *Architecture and Politics in Germany, 1918–1945* (Cambridge: Harvard University Press, 1968).

36. Bruno Taut, "A Programme for Architecture," in *Programs and Manifestoes,* p. 41.

37. Ibid.

23 Lessons of the Labyrinth

1. See Manfredo Tafuri, " 'The Wicked Architect': G. B. Piranesi, Heterotopia, and the Voyage," in *The Sphere and the Labyrinth: Avant-Gardes and Architecture from Piranesi to the 1970s,* trans. Pellegrino d'Acierno and Robert Connolly (Cambridge: MIT Press, 1987), pp. 25–64. For "heterotopia" Tafuri refers the reader to Michel Foucault, *The Order of Things: An Archaeology of the Human Sciences* (New York: Pantheon, 1970), pp. xviii ff.

2. Tafuri, " 'The Wicked Architect,' " p. 41.

3. Mark Wigley, *The Architecture of Deconstruction: Derrida's Haunt,* (Cambridge: MIT Press, 1993), p. 220. In support of the claim that architecture is indeed the Achilles' heel of deconstruction I call attention to Michael Benedikt's engaging *Deconstructing the Kimbell: An Essay on Meaning and Architecture* (New York: Lumen, 1991), which can be read as a salutary deconstruction of deconstruction in architecture. The Achilles' heel of deconstruction here is Louis Kahn's museum.

4. See Sarah Kofman, *Nietzsche and Metaphor,* trans. Duncan Large (Stanford: Stanford University Press, 1993), especially chap. 4, "Metaphorical Architectures."

5. *Morgenröte,* III, 169; in Friedrich Nietzsche, *Sämtliche Werke: Kritische Studienausgabe,* ed. Giorgio Colli and Mazzino Montinari (Munich: Deutscher Taschenbuch Verlag; Berlin: de Gruyter, 1980) 3:152. This edition will hereafter be abbreviated as CM.

6. *Nachgelassene Fragmente, Frühjahr 1880,* in CM 9:38.

7. *Der Fall Wagner,* "Nachschrift," in CM 6:45.

8. Draft version of *Ecce Homo,* in CM 14:484.

9. CM 15:497.

10. Hans Jantzen, *Kunst der Gotik* (Hamburg: Rowohlt, 1957), p. 59.

11. Cited in Richard Benz, *Deutsches Barock: Kultur des 18. Jahrhunderts* (Stuttgart: Reclam, 1949), part 1, p. 315.

12. "Rule V," in *Philosophical Works of Descartes,* trans. Elizabeth S. Haldane and G. R. T. Ross (New York: Dover, 1955), 1:14. This edition will hereafter be cited parenthetically in the text.

13. Georg Wilhelm Friedrich Hegel, *Vorlesungen über die Geschichte der Philosophie,* in *Jubiläumsausgabe,* ed. Hermann Glockner (Stuttgart: Fromann, 1937), 19:328.

14. CM 1:885; trans. "On Truth and Lie in an Unmoral Sense," *Philosophy and Truth: Selections from Nietzsche's Notebooks of the Early 1870's,* trans. and ed. Daniel Breazeale (Atlantic Highlands, N.J.: Humanities Press, 1979), p. 87. This translation will hereafter be cited as Breazeale.

15. CM 1:885; trans. Breazeale, p. 87.

16. CM 1:886; trans. Breazeale, p. 88.

17. CM 1:882; trans. Breazeale, p. 85.

18. *Menschliches, Allzumenschliches,* I, 218; in CM 2:178.

19. Tafuri, " 'The Wicked Architect,' " p. 40.

20. CM: 1:886; trans. Breazeale, p. 88.

21. CM 1:885; trans. Breazeale, p. 89.

22. CM 4:180; trans. in *The Portable Nietzsche* trans. Walter Kaufmann, (New York: Penguin Books, 1976), p. 252.

23. *Morgenröte,* IV, 271; in CM 3:213.

24. *Morgenröte,* III, 169; in CM 3:152.

25. *Menschliches, Allzumenschliches,* I, 218; in CM 2:179. Quite in this spirit, which links Loos to Nietzsche, Beatriz Colomina thus links modernity to the question of the mask and understands Vienna as a city of masks. See her *Privacy and Publicity: Modern Architecture as Mass Media* (Cambridge and London: MIT Press, 1994), pp. 23, 26.

26. *Menschliches, Allzumenschliches,* I, 218; in CM 2:178–179.

27. *Morgenröte,* IV, 250; in CM 3:205.

28. *Menschliches, Allzumenschliches,* I, 219; in CM 2:179–180.

29. *Ecce Homo,* "Warum ich so klug bin," 7; in CM 6:291.

30. *Martin Heidegger, Karl Jaspers: Briefwechsel 1920–1963,* ed. Walter Biemel and Hans Faner, letter of August 6, 1949 (Frankfurt am Main: Klostermann and Piper, 1990), p. 177. See also Karsten Harries, "Shame, Guilt, Responsibility," in *Heidegger and Jaspers,* ed. Alan M. Olson (Philadelphia: Temple University Press, 1994), p. 60.

31. Tafuri, "The Ashes of Jefferson," in *The Sphere and the Labyrinth,* p. 290.

32. *Die fröhliche Wissenschaft,* V, 356; in CM 3:596–597.

33. *Die fröhliche Wissenschaft,* V, 356; in CM 3:597.

34. Francesco Dal Co, "Mies," in *Figures of Architecture and Thought: German Architecture Culture, 1880–1920* (New York: Rizzoli, 1990), p. 270; Dal Co is quoting Hans Urs von Balthasar, *Romano Guardini: Reform aus dem Ursprung* (Munich: Kösel, 1970).

35. Ibid., p. 271.

36. I am indebted to Michael Halberstam for his insight into this connection.

37. Franceso Dal Co, to be sure, as if to guard against such an interpretation, emphasizes the way "Mies's *operari* is dominated by the dimension of waiting. 'Solitude and waiting' are said to be two complementary aspects of Nietzsche's vision" ("Mies," p. 265). But if such remarks invite the reader to link Nietzsche's will to power and Heidegger's *Gelassenheit,* and to bring both to bear on the architecture of Mies, that link is inevitably shadowed by the National Socialist specter.

38. *Götzendämmerung,* "Streifzüge eines Unzeitgemässen," 11; in CM 6:118.

39. *Jenseits von Gut und Böse,* VII, 230; in CM 5:169.

40. This chapter originated as a contribution for the conference "Abbau—Neubau—Überbau: Nietzsche and an Architecture of Our Minds," sponsored by the Getty Center for the History of Art and the Humanities, Weimar, October 11–13, 1994.

24   Conclusion: The Shape of Modernity and the Future of Architecture

1. This, the third of Paestum's three temples, dating from the middle of the fifth century B.C., is now generally known as the Second Temple of Hera.

2. Georg Wilhelm Friedrich Hegel, *Vorlesungen über die Aesthetik,* in *Jubiläumsausgabe,* ed. Hermann Glockner (Stuttgart: Fromann, 1937), 12:125. Trans. F. P. B. Osmaston as "Selections from 'The Philosophy of Fine Arts,' " in *Philosophies of Art and Beauty,* ed. Albert Hofstadter and Richard Kuhns (Chicago: University of Chicago Press, 1976), p. 439. This translation will hereafter be cited as Osmaston.

3. Martin Heidegger, "The Origin of the Work of Art," in *Poetry, Language, Thought,* trans. Albert Hofstadter (New York: Harper and Row, 1971), p. 46.

4. See Karsten Harries, "Hegel on the Future of Art," *Review of Metaphysics,* vol. 27, no. 4 (1974), pp. 677–696.

5. Hegel, *Vorlesungen über die Aesthetik,* 12:27; trans. Osmaston, p. 388.

6. Ibid., p. 31; trans. Osmaston, 391.

7. Ibid., pp. 30–31; trans. Osmaston, p. 391.

8. Heidegger, "The Origin of the Work of Art," p. 80. This work is hereafter cited parenthetically in the text.

9. Hegel, *Vorlesungen über die Aesthetik,* 12:124; trans. Osmaston, p. 438.

10. Ibid., p. 124; trans. Osmaston, p. 438.

11. Ibid., p. 31; trans. Osmaston, p. 391.

12. Rudolf Schwarz, "Das Anliegen der Baukunst," *Darmstädter Gespräch Mensch und Raum* (Darmstadt: Neue Darmstädter Verlagsanstalt, 1952), p. 67.

13. Ibid.

14. Ibid.

15. Cf. Rudolf Schwarz, *Vom Bau der Kirche,* 2nd ed. (Heidelberg: Lambert Schneider, 1947), p. 21. Mies van der Rohe wrote the foreword for the English translation by Cynthia Harris, *The Church Incarnate: The Sacred Function of Christian Architecture* (Chicago: Regnery, 1958). See also Franz Schulze, *Mies van der Rohe: A Critical Biography* (Chicago: University of Chicago Press, 1985), p. 316. A link between Schwarz and Mies was their shared admiration for the work of Romano Guardini, who wrote the introduction to the German edition of *Vom Bau der Kirche.*

16. Schwarz, "Das Anliegen der Baukunst," p. 68.

17. St. Augustine, *The City of God,* trans. Marcus Dods (New York: Modern Library, 1950), p. 459.

18. I am grateful to Eeva Pelkonen for introducing me to Volker Giencke's work. Her *Achtung Architektur!* (Cambridge: MIT Press, 1996) calls our attention to the significance of the contribution made by recent Austrian architects and makes a strong case for the central importance of peripheral architecture.

19. See the brochure that accompanied the exhibition, Emilio Ambasz and Steve Holl, *Architecture* (New York: Museum of Modern Art, 1989), and Steve Holl, *Within the City: Phenomena of Relations,* special issue of *Design Quarterly,* vol. 139 (1989).

Index